Photograph by Bill McGinn

ALSO BY BERNARD CLAYTON, JR.

The Breads of France
The Complete Book of Breads

The Complete Book

of

PASTRY

Sweet and Savory

Bernard Clayton, Jr.

ILLUSTRATIONS BY TOM STOERRLE

SIMON AND SCHUSTER • NEW YORK

Copyright © 1981 by Bernard Clayton, Jr.
All rights reserved
including the right of reproduction
in whole or in part in any form
Published by Simon and Schuster
A Division of Gulf & Western Corporation
Simon & Schuster Building
Rockefeller Center
1230 Avenue of the Americas
New York, New York 10020
SIMON AND SCHUSTER and colophon
are trademarks of Simon & Schuster
Manufactured in the United States of America

Library of Congress Cataloging in Publication Data

Clayton, Bernard.
    The complete book of pastry, sweet and savory.

    Includes index.
    1. Pastry.   2. Desserts.   3. Cookery,
International.   I. Title.
TX773.C53   641.8'65   80-28626
ISBN 0-671-24276-8

With Thanks . . .

My personal expression of thanks for help and encouragement in researching and writing this book has already gone to many people and groups throughout the United States and Europe. In the text of the book I have mentioned others who have been especially helpful and considerate. In addition, I would like to thank the people named below for their assistance and many kindnesses.

Pastry chefs Anker Hansen and Henry Anderson, of the Hotel d'Angleterre, Copenhagen.

Chef Harry Archondakis, Dionysus Zonar's, Athens, Greece.

Ann Bramson, New York City, Simon & Schuster senior editor, who has with zest and skill shepherded my manuscript to its final destination—into your hands and, I hope, your kitchen.

Madame Madeline Phillips, L'Epi d'Or, Boulangerie/Pâtisserie, Monaco.

Pierre Poilane, Paris, *premier boulanger/pâtissier* and an old friend.

Martha and the late G. Walter LaBorie, Menton, France, my sister and her husband, who have helped me immensely in planning travels through Europe in search of the best of food.

Joan Raines, New York City, my literary agent as well as a superb cook and critic.

Patricia Read, New York City, a highly respected editor and a friend, who with wit, wisdom and understanding has been of great help in putting together this book as she helped with *The Complete Book of Breads* and *The Breads of France*.

Chef Hermann G. Rusch, the Greenbrier Hotel, White Sulphur Springs, West Virginia.

Dr. and Mrs. Iur Mario Schädler, Berne, Switzerland.

Sylvia Vaughn Thompson, a fellow author from Malibu, California, with whom I discussed all manner of entrée pies on a canal boat floating through the heart of France.

Hanspeter Widmer, Confiserie Tschirren, Berne, Switzerland.

Above my desk in my studio kitchen are cookbooks to which I turn again and again to confirm a judgment, to check an obscure ingredient, to spell a name and on and on. How did the dish look to other eyes? How did it taste on another tongue?

I may not always have agreed with these writings, but they have stood staunchly on the shelf, in good times and bad, always ready to help.

Here is a list of well-thumbed volumes and their authors, who have written many other helpful books that may be favorites of yours.

James Beard	*The James Beard Cookbook* (Dell)
	The Theory and Practice of Good Cooking (Knopf)
	Delights and Prejudices (Simon & Schuster)
Karen Berg	*Danish Home Baking* (Host & Sons, Copenhagen)
Jane Carson	*Colonial Virginia Cookery* (Colonial Williamsburg, University Press of Virginia)
Samuel Chamberlain	*British Bouquet* and *Bouquet de France* (Gourmet Books)
Julia Child	*From Julia Child's Kitchen* (Knopf)
	Julia Child and Company (Knopf)
	Mastering the Art of French Cooking, I and II (Knopf)
Craig Claiborne	*The New York Times Cookbook* (Times Books)
	The New York Times Menu Cookbook (Harper & Row)
	The New York Times Cook Book (Harper & Row)
Betty Crocker	*Pie and Pastry Cookbook* (Bantam Books)
Dominique D'Ermo	*The Modern Pastry Chef's Guide to Professional Baking* (Harper & Row)
Margit Stoll Dutton	*The German Pastry Cookbook* (Chilton Books)
Gaston Lenôtre	*Lenôtre's Desserts and Pastries* (Barron's)
Dione Lucas and Marion Gorman	*The Dione Lucas Book of French Cooking* (Little, Brown)
Elaine Lumbra	*The Hoosier Cookbook* (Indiana University Press)
Samuel A. Maltz	*Bakery Technology and Engineering* (Avi Publishing)
Paula Peck	*The Art of Fine Baking* (Simon & Schuster)
Irma S. Rombauer and Marion Rombauer Becker	*The Joy of Cooking* (Bobbs-Merrill)
William J. Sultan	*Practical Baking* (Avi Publishing)

And these superb reference volumes:

> *Larousse Gastronomique* (Crown)
> Foods of the World series (Time-Life Books)
> *The Cook's Catalogue* (Harper & Row)

Also, the collection of cookbooks of the Lilly Library of Indiana University, a major resource of rare books and manuscripts for teaching and study, which attracts scholars from all over the world. The Lilly Library is named for the distinguished family that founded the Indianapolis pharmaceutical firm. I am honored to have been asked by the library to place my manuscripts, cookbooks and papers in its care.

A Dedication . . .

To my wife, who tasted and judged all of the pastries in the book—first on location, whether in Budapest, San Francisco, Brussels, Cornwall, Copenhagen, Monaco or Williamsburg; and then again in the kitchen at home. Yet, three years later, she swore she never gained a pound.
    I believe her.

B. C., Jr.

Contents

Preface

After having written two best-selling cookbooks, one of which has been translated into French and Spanish, I knew the art of bread making could be demonstrated and described in a way that would give confidence to the home bread baker. Why not pastries? I was asked to try. And in the process I learned a lot. For one thing, I discovered very quickly that one cannot move into the pastry field with the same swashbuckling fervor that goes so well with bread. I found it asks for a more tender approach. Pastry dough is not slammed down against the work surface. Most of it is rolled gently and lifted with care.

Experience begets confidence. I found it a good idea, and I think you may too, not to try a new recipe for the first time when guests are coming for tea. Introduce it first to the family or compassionate friends.

How best to do a book on pastries that would embrace the entire spectrum of the art—and describe how each basic pastry is made?

For more than a decade I had been traveling in the United States and in Europe collecting recipes and learning the techniques of bread making. Although I had collected some pastry recipes as well on those trips, it was bread that had received my attention. After *The Breads of France* was published and well received, I decided to spend a summer in Europe concentrating on pastries.

Being with and listening to *pâtissiers* and home pastry bakers in a dozen countries is an exciting experience. After a five-hour trip by hydrofoil on the Danube River to Budapest, with a certain apprehension that attends one's first visit behind the Iron Curtain, I sat at tea with the managing director of one of the great hotels of the world, the Grand Hotel Margitsziget. He leaned across the pastry tray and, with a small smile, said, "Please tell me, Monsieur Clayton, did you *really* come all the way to Hungary just to learn to make strudel?"

Yes, I did. I now call the director's attention to Madame Jánosné's recipe on page 228.

My pastry trail led to the coast of Cornwall, where I stood in the kitchen of a three-centuries-old tavern (now the pleasant Lugger Inn) to listen to the granddaughter of a smuggler, who had used the tavern as a base for his operations, describe in detail the steps necessary to make an authentic Cornish pasty.

Aboard the hotel barge *Palinurus*, on the Canal de Bourgogne, near Dijon, I watched a young French chef prepare puff paste as the vessel rose silently in the lock—and then looked up, startled, to meet the eyes of the lock keeper's milk goat watching us both.

Italy's Borghese family, once owners of a quarter of all of Michelangelo's works, has an exquisite taste for food. In a town house in Rome, on the via Monte Brianzo, near the Tiber, I was served an apple flan prepared by Signora Giangelo Borghese whose husband retains strong ties to Indiana University in my small city, where he was a student after World War II. The flan was light, delicious and surprisingly like the *tarte aux pommes Normandie* (page 332) I had found a fortnight earlier in France. She, too, had found the flan in her travels in Normandy.

In the family's living quarters on the upper floor of a 350-year-old building near Berne's famous clock tower, the manager of Tschirren, one of the city's finest *confiseries*, said it pleased him that the trend in Switzerland is toward lighter pastries. His bakers, for example, are using more yogurt and less pastry cream for fillings.

My first *empanada*, a turnover filled with a lovely light salmon mixture, was from La Mallorquina, near the subway entrance on the bustling Puerto del Sol in Madrid. Here the clerks were so gracious they stopped all business in the shop to pose for a group photograph behind the big pastry-filled counter. My second *empanada* was of Argentine descent and was filled with beef (page 138).

The largest overseas contribution to recipes and techniques in this book is from England and the Continent, where I visited, talked and baked with pastry chefs in Madrid, Vienna, Munich, Athens, Zurich, Paris, London, the Cornish coast of England, Brussels and Copenhagen —and a few along the Canal de Bourgogne, not to mention *pâtissiers* aboard the S.S. *France*.

The American contribution to this book is enormous. Recipes came from every part of the United States, and many are regional favorites. They came from fellow cookbook authors interested in a definitive work on the subject of pastries, from collections of old cookbooks as well as newer ones and from pastry chefs in the United States and in Canada —literally, from almost everywhere.

Thus a book on pastries came together. There would be still other travels on the Continent and in the United States.

While the pastry recipes in this book came from many places, all found a home in my studio kitchen in Bloomington, Indiana, where many times during the months of testing recipes I had pastries and breads baking simultaneously in all six ovens. Each recipe has been taken apart, tested, tasted, judged, adapted and put back together in a way that is wholly compatible with the American kitchen.

Each family of pastries, whether pies (both dessert and entrée) or Danish pastries or pizza or puff pastries, is thoroughly explained. The whys and wherefores of every step are fully detailed; there are no secrets, no gray areas that might puzzle or dismay. The full measure of every recipe was taken before it was added to this comprehensive collection. No untried recipe has slipped in. There was no need, for good recipes abound—and they are here.

The recipes for basic doughs and the techniques used in their preparation are followed by the pastries that are made from those doughs. There often is a choice of doughs for a certain pastry; one, two or even three doughs are sometimes suggested—with cross references that will take you to your choice immediately.

There are three basic ways to make doughs—by hand, by electric mixer and by the new food processors. The instructions for each are given in each recipe so that there is no need to search frantically through the book for instructions given only once.

The steps for preparing each recipe are timed to the minute so that you will know exactly how much time to devote to preparation, in part and in total.

At no point will you be left alone with a rolling pin and a ball of chilled dough to wonder what to do next. The book is at your side from the moment you begin to think of a pastry until a flaky golden puff or a hot bubbling pie is taken from the oven and rests on a rack.

It is my hope that this book will present pastry in all of its shapes, forms and uses. If you are an experienced pastry maker, you will find new ways to enhance your skills with this collection of classical, traditional and innovative recipes developed by scores of fine pastry makers over many decades.

If you are new to pastry making, or need encouragement after some not-too-successful attempts, try this book. It is meant to give you the confidence you need to venture, at your own pace, from that first satisfactory pie or tart into exciting variations. I hope the book will lead you, as it has many readers of my bread books, to share the pleasures of pastry-baking with me.

Introduction

"The greater desideratum a person can wish to attain
in this art is the making of good puff paste."
—Iwin P. Beadle,
The Ten Cent Cook Book, 1863

Apicius, a Roman gourmand who, during the reign of Tiberius Claudius
Nero Caesar, could command battalions of chefs, bakers, cooks and
assistants, is accepted as the author of the first cookbook. He left this
modest recipe for a fritter-like dessert, which also illustrates that pastries
can be fried as well as baked and boiled: "Cook the finest flour in some
milk, of which make a tolerably stiff paste: spread it on a dish: cut it in
pieces, which, when you have fried in very fine oil, cover with pepper
and honey."

It is modest indeed for a period in Rome when the ideal number at
the table was nine and the feast, while sumptuous and magnificent,
could hardly be called refined, with live birds, animals and small people
bursting through pastry crusts.

In a span of sixteen centuries pastry moved across Europe to the
Americas, where an abundance of sugar (rather than honey) and cocoa
lifted the art of pastry making to new heights on both sides of the
Atlantic.

In Paris the first school of baking opened and, following the French
Revolution, chefs formerly employed by the aristocracy opened their
own *pâtisseries* to spread their influence far beyond the palaces and the
grand *châteaux*.

21

In the colonies, however, the first pastry making was done in the home, but with results that Carême, the famed eighteenth-century pastry maker and author of great works on cooking, would have praised.

Pastry making was not an easy matter even in the big houses in colonial America. The brick oven, whether adjacent to the hearth in the kitchen or in a separate building outside, was designed exclusively for bread, cakes and pastries. The fire was built on the oven floor, and because there was no flue, the door was left open to allow the smoke to escape. When the cook judged the oven to be hot enough, the ashes were raked out. Breads went into the oven first and were dropped from a long-handled wooden peel directly onto the hot floor stones. The door was closed to trap the heat and not opened until the yeast-raised bread was done. Then, in the milder heat, pastries and cakes were baked.

The all-purpose crust of the colonies was puff paste. From a 1747 cookbook published in London that was quick to find its way to America, *The Art of Cookery Made Plain and Easy . . . by a Lady*, Mrs. Hannah Glasse's recipe could be used today: "Take a quarter of a peck of flour, rub fine half a pound of butter, a little salt, make it up into a light paste with cold water, just stiff enough to work it well up; then roll it out and stick pieces of butter all over, and strew a little flour; roll it up, and roll it out again; and so do nine or ten times, till you have rolled in a pound and a half of butter. This crust is mostly used for all sorts of pies." While Mrs. Glasse's nine or ten turns of dough is more than double that now required, her proportion of flour to butter is similar to that in today's puff paste recipes.

"Pastry coffins" to hold a wide range of fillings are to be found in *The Martha Washington Cook Book*, a collection of recipes put together by a famed colonial hostess, Frances Parke Custis. The "coffins" were made with a strong, firm pastry mixed with egg yolks, butter and suet melted in hot water, rolled only one time. Recipes for coffin fillings were both simple and elaborate, made with beef, pork, veal, mutton, venison, rabbit, fowl, fish and shellfish.

In the Custis cookbook there are also directions "To keepe cherries yt [so that] you may have them for tarts at Christmas without Preserving." The fruit was to be wiped with a linen cloth and placed between layers of straw in a box. "Then set them under a fether bead where one layeth continually for ye warmer there are kept ye better it is soe they be neere no fire."

Later, an immigrant would write to his friends in Norway that in America strawberries, raspberries and blackberries thrive. "From these," he wrote, "they make a wonderful dish combined with syrup and sugar which is called pai. I can tell you that pai is something that glides easily down your throat. . . ."

Pastries had indeed arrived in America.

The Complete Book of
PASTRY
Sweet and Savory

Ingredients to Make Fine Pastries

Many students in my bread-making classes and many readers of my bread books had never baked before and, as a consequence, knew almost nothing about ingredients and their importance to the creation of good loaves of bread. But they quickly learned to appreciate the whole range of foodstuffs, from flours and shortenings to nuts and spices.

From tarts and pies to *baklava* and strudel, top-quality pastries must have top-quality ingredients. No pastry can rise above its ingredients. Most of the time you will be saving money by making pastries yourself, so don't skimp on materials. During the fresh fruit season, for instance, don't buy canned pie filling when the one you make will contain substantially more fruit per cubic inch—and less liquid. At the same time, don't overlook good materials because they are inexpensive. Lard is a relatively cheap shortening and deserves a higher standing in today's kitchen than it has.

I don't think it is necessary to buy nationally advertised flours when I can get less well-known but equally good flours from mills in my part of the country or those packaged under a supermarket name. Milling standards are so high in this country that you can be certain the sacks contain what the labels claim they do.

FLOUR

North America's reputation for bountiful harvests rests in a large measure on the magnificent wheat crops grown on millions of fertile acres in the northern tier of states of the United States and in the western

25

provinces of Canada. This is a boon to America's home bakers and the envy of much of the rest of the world, including France, where U.S. and Canadian flours are admired by both the *pâtissier* and the *boulanger*.

There are essentially two kinds of wheat grown by farmers and ranchers: hard and soft. (A third wheat, important to the American diet but not to pastry, is a hard wheat variety called durum, which is used in making pastas such as macaroni, spaghetti and noodles as well as poultry and livestock food.) Both share an important element, in varying degrees, that makes wheat unique among cereal flours. This element is gluten, a plant protein prized by bakers because when mixed with water it forms an elastic dough that catches the gas (from yeast) and/or steam from a moist blend of ingredients to raise and expand the dough.

Hard wheat, grown on western prairie land, has a high gluten content and is milled into "bread" flour. Hard wheat flour has great elasticity that allows it to be stretched and rolled into an incredibly thin sheet for strudel or *phyllo*, or folded and rolled again and again to make puff paste and Danish dough with hundreds of thin layers.

Bread flour has now returned to the shelves of the neighborhood market after an absence of two generations. When bread making was part of the tempo of life in the American home, especially on the farm, the big cotton sacks printed with pretty patterns for making dresses, curtains and towels could be found stacked in every grocery. They still are found in ranch country in the West. Bread flour is back, thanks to the renaissance in home bread baking; but in most parts of the country it is no longer put in cotton sacks but in much smaller paper ones.

If bread flour is scarce in your markets, you may substitute "unbleached" flour. Despite its name, the flour is bleached in an aging rather than a chemical process, and it is milled from a blend of hard wheats. It can be substituted for bread flour in all recipes that call for the latter in this book.

Soft wheat, grown in the milder regions of middle and eastern America, produces a flour lower in gluten, one that is ideal for baking such products as pastries, crackers, pretzels, cookies and cakes. At the bottom of the gluten scale is cake flour, which has only enough of the protein to hold the cake together in the oven while a delicate and tender, yet stable, structure of cells is formed. A little higher up the gluten scale is pastry flour, which is ideal for pie and tart doughs because it can tolerate a considerable amount of fat, such as butter, lard or margarine, without becoming tough (actually difficult to bite). If your grocer or specialty food shop does not have pastry flour, a satisfactory substitute can be blended at home with 60 percent cake flour and 40 percent bread or unbleached flour. Mix them together well.

At mid-range is the versatile all-purpose flour, a blend of hard and soft wheat flours which has been developed by the nation's millers to take care of a wide range of home baking needs with one flour—from breads and biscuits to pies and doughnuts.

"Instant" flour, a product that is free-pouring and disperses instantly in cold water, is in the all-purpose category. I have not used it because it is almost double the price of other flours, and the advantages don't seem to be worth the cost.

All-purpose flour can be substituted for other flours in recipes that call for bread flour at the top of the gluten scale or pastry flour at the lower end. It will not rise as high as bread flour or be as tender as pastry flour, but it is a worthy substitute nevertheless.

Whole wheat or graham flour, which is made from the entire kernel of wheat, is used in several pie and tart dough recipes in the book. I have successfully substituted a portion of whole wheat in other recipes with good results.

In many recipes in this book, alternate flours are given in the list of ingredients. The first is preferred in the recipe, but the second can be substituted with good results.

It is easy to check the protein or gluten content of a flour by looking at the paragraph of nutritional information on each package. Although figures vary somewhat from brand to brand and mill to mill, here is the range: bread flour, 14 percent; unbleached, 12 percent; all-purpose, 11 percent; pastry, 8 percent and cake, 7 percent.

Flour freezes and keeps well for periods of a year or more. If you have extra freezer space at 0° F., watch supermarket shelves for bargains or for flours that appear for a short while and then are gone for long periods. Buy the bargain and freeze it.

In preparing pastries, the flour, especially pastry and cake types, should be sifted to break up clumps or lumps which often occur in these soft wheat flours. Attempting to mash or stir away lumps later during the mixing process can cause overmixing—and a tough dough. Measure the quantity of flour called for in the recipe before sifting, unless the recipe directs otherwise. Sifting isn't important in preparing yeast-raised doughs because the kneading quickly breaks up the lumps. Not so with the gentle handling of many pastries.

Be sparing in dusting the work surface with flour. More flour than necessary will toughen the dough. A minimum of flour is all that's needed to keep the dough loose on the work surface and under the rolling pin. A tidy and economical way to spread an even dusting of flour is with a wide 2- or 3-inch pastry brush dipped into a cup of flour. Brush it across the dough as well as the work surface when flour is needed.

A final and important note about flour: For all doughs, the measurement of one of two ingredients must be taken as approximate—the flour or the liquid, one or the other. The ability of the flour to absorb liquid varies from harvest to harvest, sack to sack, as well as month to month as the humidity changes and the flour absorbs or releases moisture.

If the recipe calls for a precise amount of flour, the liquid must be added carefully so as not to overload the flour. If the recipe calls for a precise amount of water, add the last portion of the flour slowly and carefully. Approach the final judgment with care. It is better, however, to have a moist dough that will stiffen in the refrigerator than a hard and unforgiving cannonball for which there is no hope.

(Only in batter can the measurement of flour and liquid be precise and foretold. The determining factor then becomes the length of time the dough will be in the oven. The burden rests on the temperature and the length of oven time to correct any imbalance there is in the moisture of the dough.)

Yeast and Other Leavenings

Almost all doughs are leavened; if they weren't, they would bake flat as a pancake, literally. Leavening can come from yeast cells producing carbon dioxide to raise bread dough, or from the moisture in butter or other fats becoming steam and expanding between layers of dough to create flaky pastry. It may be the ballooning action of heat on beaten eggs in *pâte à chou*, or of egg whites alone in an angel food cake batter.

Baking soda, which was the first chemical leavener, is little used in pastry doughs. It reacts with sour cream or buttermilk to produce carbon dioxide. Baking powder was a later development. Its multiple action releases a small amount of gas while the ingredients are being mixed, but the main thrust comes from the heat of the oven.

While yeast is used in this book only in Danish pastry, pizza and the crescent-shaped *kipfel*, its role should be understood by the pastry maker. The yeast cells, feasting on the natural sugars in the batter as well as on sugar or honey that may be introduced by the cook, grow and flourish in fantastic numbers. The 130 billion living cells in one package of yeast will double in number in about 2 hours. It is this potent force that throws off carbon dioxide gas, which in turn pushes against the elastic framework formed by the gluten in the flour—and expands and raises the dough.

The recipes in this book call for active dry yeast because I have found it much easier to store and use than the foil-wrapped cakes of compressed yeast, which must be refrigerated. The packets are easy to keep anyplace in the kitchen and can even be slipped into luggage if you expect to be importuned by your host to bake a little something for tomorrow's brunch. The packets are age-dated and have a shelf life of many months. The 4-ounce bottles of yeast granules that are available in some regions of the country are equivalent to sixteen envelopes, but they must be refrigerated after opening. The compressed cakes may be substituted for active dry yeast, of course.

FAT

Fat is the generic term for one of the most important and essential ingredients used in pastries, whether it be butter, lard, margarine or oil, or a combination. In pastry making, fat imparts richness and tenderness. It also leavens and raises the crust. Fat, especially butter and lard, contributes a unique flavor to pastries. It also lubricates the gluten in the dough so that it is free to rise and puff.

Butter continues to be the most highly regarded fat for pastries because of its delicious flavor and rich aroma. Sweet or unsalted butter is preferred because it indicates a fresher product than salted butter, which has a longer shelf life. Butter has a low melting point and is often blended with other fats, such as vegetable shortening or lard, to allow high oven temperatures without burning.

Lard is the most widely used fat for pies because it makes a delicious crust with a distinctive taste. It is readily available on the market, as it has been since pigs first ran loose down village streets in colonial America. It has an attractive low price.

Lard has a distinctive flavor and odor which vary somewhat with the way it is rendered. "Farm" or "country-style" is cooked in an open kettle (as opposed to cooking by steam in a closed tank) and closely resembles the kind made by farm families at butchering time. The old-fashioned unprocessed kind is now difficult to find except in rural areas, where it can be found occasionally in a country store. It must be kept refrigerated. Most store-bought lard, on the other hand, is a blend of several lards to achieve uniform quality and is highly refined so that it can be kept on store shelves and at home at room temperature.

While kettle lard has a distinctly cooked flavor, more so than steam-rendered lard, many people prefer it. Equally delicate crusts can be baked with either.

To make a fine high-quality lard in your own kitchen, see page 380.

Margarine is intended to simulate butter at a much lower price. It is made with vegetable or animal fats churned with milk or cream. It can also be made without animal fat to meet specific dietary requirements. Margarine has a higher melting point than butter and may be used as a roll-in fat for puff pastry or Danish doughs. A creation of the chemist, margarine does not have butter's texture or taste.

Solid vegetable and animal fats are made with oils through which hydrogen gas has been forced under pressure to produce a creamy solid —hence the word *hydrogenated*. Vegetable shortening is a good-tasting compromise for those who wish a medium-flaky crust—for a pie, for example—without a pronounced taste that can overwhelm a delicate custard filling. It is less expensive than butter and a good choice for those who eschew animal fat because of dietary or religious considerations.

MILK

Milk complements the nutrients of many doughs to produce a pastry of near-perfect dietary quality. It also gives color to the crust and prolongs the freshness of the pastry.

Most recipes in this book specify non-fat dry milk because it is easy and convenient to use. All one adds is water. When warming or heating this reconstituted milk, there is no danger of scorching—a common hazard with whole milk. And it is non-fat!

If you prefer whole milk, use an amount equal to the water listed with the non-fat milk.

SALT AND SPICES

Salt controls the action of yeast in doughs and strengthens the gluten. Salt accents the flavor of other ingredients. Sugar, for example, tastes sweeter with the addition of salt. Salt has a positive action on egg whites and, when whipped, gives them more body.

Don't guess as to the amount of salt to be added to a mixture. Measure it precisely.

One stick of salted butter contains about ½ teaspoon of salt; therefore allow for this amount in following a recipe that calls for salt if you use salted butter.

Spices contribute to the taste and aroma of pastries. The most commonly used are cinnamon, nutmeg, caraway, anise, allspice, poppy, ginger and clove. Spices freshly ground at the time they are to be used are invariably superior to their commercially ground counterparts. Spices keep best in tightly sealed glass bottles and should be kept away from heat, preferably in cool places. I frequently freeze poppy and sesame seeds, which I buy in quantity and store until I need them four or five months hence. These two seeds are used often to sprinkle over pastries. Apply them carefully and sparingly. Don't overload. It is not only costly but unsightly.

LEMON JUICE AND VINEGAR

Lemon juice and vinegar are often listed among ingredients in a way that could be puzzling if you did not know that apart from flavoring, their acidity mellows the gluten in the flour. This allows the dough, especially for puff paste, to relax more quickly so that it doesn't pull back when rolled. Cream of tartar also serves this function.

Sugar

Granulated sugar imparts a rich brown color to the crust through caramelization. The fineness of confectioners' sugar, which contains cornstarch to retard lumping and crystallization, makes it easy to blend with other ingredients and is used primarily in icings and to dust the tops of pastries.

Confectioners' sugar placed in a dredger can be attractively and uniformly sprinkled over a pastry, or the sugar can be spooned into a small 1-cup fine-mesh sieve. Hold the sieve over the pastry and tap the handle to release a dusting of sugar.

Eggs

Eggs leaven and lighten batters and doughs, glaze, insulate against sogginess, give structural strength as well as provide additional richness, flavor and color. For baking, hard-cooking and beating, eggs should be at least three days old. Fresh eggs have a greenish tinge when hard-cooked and are difficult to peel. Beaten new eggs will not give the volume of older ones.

A large egg (2 ounces) is the size used in these recipes. The yolk of a large egg is about 1 tablespoon plus a teaspoon; the white, about 2 tablespoons. If you substitute egg size, remember that two large eggs will nearly fill a ½-cup measure, while it takes three medium eggs to do the same. (For more about eggs, see "Standard Weights and Measures," page 385.)

Nuts and Almond Paste

Nuts provide flavor and texture for inspired fillings and handsome decorations. They are used whole, sliced, slivered, chopped and ground. The principal nuts used in pastry making are almonds, pecans, walnuts, filberts (cultivated) and their related species, hazelnuts (picked wild) and pistachios. Peanuts are never used.

One pound of nuts in the shell yields about ½ pound of meats. Always buy nuts fresh, and if shelled, unsalted. Keep them in a closed container at 34° F. to 36° F. in the refrigerator. Nuts will keep for several years frozen without getting stale or rancid. Even unopened vacuum-packed shelled nuts should be stored in the refrigerator.

To blanch shelled almonds, drop into boiling water for 1 minute. Drain and squeeze each nut out of its skin. Place them in a 350° F. oven for 5 minutes, or let them dry for a day or two, spread on a rack or pan.

Toast almonds in a 350° F. oven until they are a light brown, about 12 minutes. Almond slices take less time, about 6 minutes.

Hazelnuts, filberts or the similar French *noisettes* are used with the skin for flavor, color and texture unless indicated otherwise. To remove the brown skin, spread the nuts on a baking sheet in a 350° F. oven for about 15 minutes. Remove the nuts and rub in a folded towel.

Shelled pistachios are almost prohibitively expensive, but one can make do with less costly pistachios still in the shell. It is a tedious chore, but shell them and drop the meats in boiling water for 1 minute. Peel off the skin.

English walnuts are indigenous to every part of the globe (California grows half the world's supply), and like that of other nuts, their taste is considerably heightened by roasting. Black walnuts, native American nuts grown in the central and eastern states, have a strong, dusky flavor that does not disappear during the cooking process. (My annual Christmas gift to my sister who lives in France is a pound of black walnuts from southern Indiana.) If substituting black for English walnuts, reduce the quantity at least by half. Remember, too, it is an entirely new flavor —but good.

(For catalog sources, see "Sources of Supply," page 47.)

Chop nuts by hand to have better control over the size of the pieces. Use a nut chopper, such as the Mouli grater with its several drums with different cutting edges, or a curved chopping knife and bowl.

To grind, use a special nut grinder, food processor or blender. Be careful not to operate machines too long, or you will have nut butter! Grind in short bursts and watch closely. Don't attempt to use a meat grinder, which will press the oil out of the nut and destroy its body. Ground nut meats must be light and airy, not mealy and mashed.

Almond paste, an important ingredient in many pastries, is made primarily with blanched almonds and should not be cloyingly sweet or overpungent. It should only subtly hint of almonds.

A pure almond paste, called SOLO, distributed by Soko & Co., Countryside, Illinois, is on many market shelves in ½-pound cans. It is a solid and must be cut into pieces and thinned with egg whites and sugar before use. Almond paste is sometimes referred to as marzipan paste.

A recipe for homemade almond paste can be found on page 305. It is a thick paste that can be kept refrigerated for five or six months.

Equipment to Make Fine Pastries

In order of their appearance—

WORK SURFACES

A place to work need not be larger than 24 inches by 24 inches   or enough room to maneuver a large rolling pin. The ideal work surface, however, would be large enough to assemble all the ingredients and do the mixing, kneading (if the dough is yeast-raised), rolling, cutting and shaping.

My favorite table is 9 feet long, but I seldom work outside a 30-inch square. The actual size is determined finally by the size of the piece of dough being rolled. If it gets too big for the work surface, cut it into two or more pieces. Or move to the dining table.

Formica is the most commonly used work surface in today's homes, and it is good for pastry making. The only caution: it can be scratched by a knife or dough scraper. Stainless steel counter tops are also excellent.

My maple tables are scrubbed beauties, but wood must be scraped clean and washed after each pastry-making session. I think wood is worth the extra effort for the warmth it gives my kitchen.

The height of the work table is of paramount importance. Don't antagonize your back and arm muscles. Rolling, kneading and shaping dough are easy when the work surface nearest you rests under the palms when your arms are extended in front of the body. If the work surface is too high, you cannot push down on the dough without straining. Too low, and the muscles in the back will call for help.

Work surfaces in my kitchen are 36 inches high to accommodate my tall frame, which means that some of my students in the 5-foot range must stand on boxes.

The entire pastry-making operation can be carried out directly on these surfaces if a light dusting of flour is kept between the surface and the dough. Many bakers, however, roll their pastry doughs on a canvas cloth held taut by wires and springs. The cloth must be kept clean and dry or it will take on a sour and musty odor. Small 20-inch cloths are too small to be effective. Get one that is at least 30 or 36 inches square.

An old damask tablecloth or an old sheet, well washed and soft, is an ideal surface on which to roll and stretch a large piece of strudel dough. The cloth is lifted to coax the strudel into a long roll (sometimes 6 feet or longer).

Look to marble to augment your work surfaces if your kitchen is unusually warm and the butter in puff paste oozes out when rolled. Marble makes pastry making possible in summertime. Nothing chills a piece of dough as quickly and as effectively as the cold radiating from a 1-inch-thick slab of marble that has rested overnight in the refrigerator. Mine has a permanent home on a refrigerator shelf, and I use it often there to give a quick chill to a ball of dough or a pan of pastries, knowing that the cold will transfer more quickly from the marble than it will from the surrounding air. Marble does not absorb fat or moisture and always remains cool and dry. The surface must be polished, but the edges can be ragged just as were those on my marble slab when I picked it out of the rubble of an old house that had collapsed.

A highly recommended auxiliary work surface is the 18 by 24-inch acrylic anti-stick pastry board, with a wide lip to hold it against the table and another lip on the far side to contain sprinkles of flour. A series of concentric circles, ranging from 4 to 14 inches, is marked on the surface as a helpful guide for cutting a circular piece of dough. I carry one with me when I travel on demonstration tours because television studios and department stores can offer outrageous surfaces on which to work (blue velvet was one extreme). One day I stood in a store earnestly demonstrating bread making from my first book to an audience of one. (Everyone else was watching a Vikings football game on television sets two aisles away.) She let me go through my entire performance, and when I finished, she offered that I made a good loaf of bread but "where can I get one of those nifty plastic boards you're working on?"

Measuring Devices

Pastry making is an exacting art that calls for precise measurements of volume, weight and temperature.

A set of stainless steel cups, ¼ through 1 cup, and four spoons, ¼ teaspoon through 1 tablespoon, are the basic measuring devices in the American kitchen; large 4-, 5- and 10-cup clear plastic cups (actually bowls with handles) that are marked in both American and metric measurements are optional.

All of the recipes in this book call for American measurements for both dry and liquid ingredients. While it is the Europeans, not the Americans, who measure dry ingredients by weight, a scale in the kitchen will quickly win its way into a baker's heart by measuring things that are more easily and quickly done by weight—such as a ¼ pound of bulk lard—than by the spoonful. While not an absolute necessity, a beam balance scale is a relatively inexpensive and versatile helper ($25–$35).

If you need to convert a volume measurement into a weight measurement without scales, kitchenware shops have a cone-shaped plastic container with markings for the volume and approximate weight of all common ingredients.

A device for converting U.S. cup measurements for flour and sugar into pounds and ounces, fluid ounces, United Kingdom cups, kilos and grams and litres was developed for me by a friend, Ramsay St. George, of Pembridge in Herefordshire, England. It is a form of Nomogram which has been used by engineers and scientists for many years to provide a simple means of converting one set of values directly into another form.

The pastry Nomogram consists of a set of scales printed at the top and bottom of a sheet of paper. The straight edge of a rule is laid on the center point which connects all of the equivalents, i.e., five U.S. cups of flour equals four U.K. cups equals 1 pound four ounces equals 580 grams.

The Nomogram is on page 381.

Fluid and weight measure equivalents in metric, U.S. and U.K., as well as weights and measures of ingredients important to home bakers, are on page 389.

Bowls

A selection of bowls, ranging from a medium 10-inch to a small 5-inch one, that are close at hand when preparation begins makes pastry making a joy. As the ingredients are mixed, chopped, whipped or strained a bowl should be there to receive the material as it awaits its turn to go into the final blend. There are containers other than bowls that can be used (a bottle, a glass or a plastic box), but none has the graceful, sloping sides of a bowl that make stirring and mixing a pleasure and cleaning no less so.

Stoneware, earthenware and heavy ceramic bowls, accumulated at farm sales, antique shows and from friends' cupboards, are favorites in my kitchen. They are easy to hold and heavy enough to maintain an even temperature. Stainless steel bowls, such as those used with an electric mixer, and plastic bowls are usable, but be aware that they reflect temperature changes more readily than most others.

FLOUR SIFTER

Once upon a time when mice and other small creatures were a part of every *ménage*, it was customary to sift flour. No longer—not for sanitary purposes, at least.

Pastry and cake flours, ground from soft wheat, clump and pack more than do bread, unbleached and all-purpose flours. A flour sifter will break up these dense flours and aerate them. The single-screen sifter is the best and least complicated. Those with several layers of screen trap particles that are impossible to remove short of disassembling the whole thing.

There is no need to sift bread, unbleached and all-purpose flours, unless the recipe calls for it.

PASTRY BLENDER

Nimble finger rubbing and tossing the butter into the flour so quickly that the heat of the hand cannot melt or soften the fat, which would allow it to be absorbed into the flour, is an accepted technique used by many experienced pie bakers. Others use two knives, crossed like scissors blades. I recommend a hand-held pastry blender with six curved wires to chop the butter into smaller and smaller flour-covered particles. The important thing is that the flour and fat be tossed together only until they resemble coarse meal. They are never completely blended together unless the recipe calls for it.

My concern with machines is always that the mixing of the pastry dough will be carried too far—the flour and fat will become paste and the ability of the tiny individual flour-coated pieces to expand and take shape in the heat of the oven will be lost. For this reason I tell my pastry classes to become proficient mixing by hand—with the pastry blender —so that they will know what the mixture is supposed to look like before allowing the machine to do it.

MIXERS

Fine pastry doughs can be made in a bowl using only your fingers or a pastry blender and a fork. It was true for years and remains so now. Today, however, there are two different machines that can take over the mixing chores and do them with thoroughness and dispatch: the electric mixer and the food processor.

A portable or lightweight mixer should be used only for light beating and mixing jobs, such as thin batters. Most pastry doughs demand a kitchen heavyweight, of which several are now available. Dough puts a strain on small motors, and even large machines get hot during the several minutes it takes to mix a batch of heavy dough. There are also attachments available for grinding nuts, grating cheese or chocolate and doing a dozen other chores.

The electric mixer is a scaled-down version of the mixer used in commercial bakeries and pastry shops. The food processor, on the other hand, sprang full-blown into the American kitchen (by way of France), and it has created a revolution. It does an amazing job with pie and tart doughs. If I have a criticism of the processor it is that the machine does things too fast and can quickly take food preparation past the point of no return. You must train a fast trigger finger. Do things in short bursts, and inspect often until you know how the processor is going to perform under different conditions.

I may never again mix some pie and tart doughs by hand, unless, of course, the electricity is off. Yet I have not fully committed myself to the processor for yeast-raised doughs, which I like to feel with my hands to judge their texture. Dough does not seem to spring to life in a machine with the same robust vitality it does when kneaded by hand. Perhaps it feels deprived of the warmth of the hands. The cold machine gives little in return.

Finally, when I make pastries by hand I have only smooth, curved surfaces to wash and clean. Machines have hard angles, hidden recesses and springs and things that trap bits of dough, which I find vexing. But for speed and taking the toil out of preparation, machines are to be reckoned with.

REFRIGERATOR/FREEZER

The serious pastry maker is as concerned about the cold-keeping qualities of the refrigerator and freezer as about the heat-making ability of the oven. Although bread doughs are seldom refrigerated except for conveniently delaying the process for an hour or so or overnight, cold is important to pastry because chilled fat cannot be absorbed into the flour, which it would do at room temperature. The cold keeps the fat separate and discrete. During the respite in the refrigerator, the dough also relaxes so that it can be rolled and fashioned without drawing back. To control the temperature, use a thermometer. Change dial settings on the machines, if needed, to bring temperatures into line.

The ideal temperature for chilling pastry doughs, before and after filling or shaping, is 40° F. The best temperature for layering butter and dough for puff and Danish pastries is 60° F. A variation of 10° up or down will not give the same results. Rely on a thermometer.

There is an excellent Taylor freezer thermometer that can be used in the refrigerator as well. For a description of the Taylor Bi-Therm thermometer in making puff pastry, see "Butter Temperature," page 161.

A ball of dough can be tucked onto a cluttered refrigerator shelf to chill, but a large pastry-filled pan demands some advance planning. Either clear off a shelf, or give the pan a stable base on top of some of the other containers where it can rest for the chilling period.

A piece of marble, as described under "Work Surfaces," is unexcelled for holding the cold in the refrigerator. Leave it in place as part of the shelf when it is not being used for pastries. Clear off as needed, or bring it out into the room where it will keep its chill for an hour or more.

ROLLING PIN

Pastry dough demands far more rolling and rerolling than do other doughs. The proper rolling of dough to get the required shape and thickness is a skill that comes with experience—and a good rolling pin.

A heavy pin, upwards of 6 pounds and with roller-bearing handles, will make the job a lot easier than using a spindly light pin that cannot push down the dough. A yeast-raised dough (as for Danish) will fight back. A heavy pin dares chilled dough not to behave as it should.

Puff pastry and other layered doughs have their own imported rolling pin that does a masterful job of spreading the chilled butter beneath the dough. It has ³⁄₁₆-inch grooves running lengthwise on the 4-pound

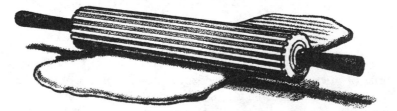

TUTOVE ROLLING PIN

plastic roller and is made by a French firm, Tutove. It is very expensive, but worth it if you are deep into puff pastries. The twenty-two rounded ribs separating the grooves push the butter ahead as the pin is rolled. With it there is less wear and tear on both the dough and the butter. The butter always seems to be better behaved under its influence.

Forsake all lightweight plastic or glass pins, especially those that have hollow centers into which ice cubes are inserted. They sweat, which is a disaster for pastry doughs. Porcelain pins are pretty but fragile. The graceful French rolling pins of tapered wood are all right for unleavened doughs but too light to roll out yeast-raised dough.

A Maine inventor, Guenther Brandes, has made "Rolleraid"—a 19-inch rolling pin of polished maple that has settings that allow it to roll dough to one of four selected thicknesses: ⅟₁₆, ⅛, ³⁄₁₆ or ¼ inch. The pin is held above the dough on small Teflon wheels set in plastic squares at the handles. The wheels carry the pin at the selected distance above the

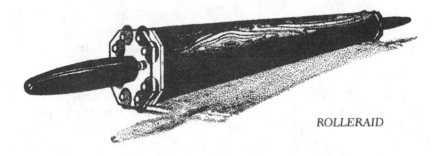

ROLLERAID

dough. I use one in my kitchen to check the thickness of a dough which I have often rolled out with a heavier pin. It is a precise way to measure it. To order, see "Sources of Supply," page 47.

Another way to control the thickness of the dough is to place strips of wood or cardboard, of whatever thickness you desire the dough to be, as tracks on the work surface. These hold the ends of the rolling pin at this predetermined height as it rolls over the dough.

YARDSTICK AND RULER

Most pastries must be cut and tailored to a particular size to be rolled into a particular shape, or to fit a particular pan or tin. The ubiquitous yardstick given away by feed companies and tractor manufacturers at state and county fairs is an unexcelled measuring device for the pastry maker as well as a marker against which to hold a knife or rolling pastry blade when cutting dough. You can buy a washable 24-inch metal rule, but it is not as much fun as a wooden one from the feed store.

ROLLING PASTRY PIERCER

This is an exotic instrument with a half-dozen rows of sharp metal pins driven into a wooden roller that does a down-to-earth job in the pastry kitchen: pricking tiny holes in dough so that it does not rise in the oven. It is also a marvelous conversation piece, but the tines of a fork will do as well.

PASTRY CRIMPER

Filled pastries—pies and Cornish pasties among them—must have a tight seal between the two layers of crust. Most times the fingers or the tines of a fork are sufficient to do the job, but a professional way to go is with a stainless steel pastry crimper.

PASTRY BAG

A pastry bag with the appropriate tubes or tips is much used in pastry making for decorating filled pies and tarts, laying down strips of filling in Danish pastries, squeezing *pâte à chou* into cream puffs and eclairs and so on.

There are nylon- and plastic-lined fabric bags which must be cleaned and scrubbed after each use—a bother easily sidestepped when you learn the trick of folding throwaway cones of parchment paper. I watched fascinated in the kitchen of the Hotel d'Angleterre in Copenhagen while a pastry chef folded, filled and squeezed dry a parchment cone at the rate of about one a minute. He didn't use a metal tip or tube. He simply cut with scissors the diameter he wanted. Later he did use metal tips for fancy flowers.

Housewares departments or shops that sell cake-decorating equipment have ready-made parchment triangles and sets of assorted metal tips. If you use a metal tip, simply drop it into the neck of the paper cone, fill and decorate. Afterward, cut out the metal tip before you throw the cone away.

Shop clerks will show you how to wrap the parchment triangle into a cone. With experience you can do it faster than a cowboy can hand-tailor a smoke.

PARCHMENT PAPER

Line every baking sheet or tin with parchment paper before the pastries are set on them and you will never have a sticking problem. "Quick 'N Clean" Kitchen Parchment, made by Brown Co., Parchment, Michigan, is 15 inches wide and comes in 16-foot rolls. It is sold in gourmet cookware shops and housewares departments. Large 16 by 24-inch flat sheets of parchment paper can be bought, but only in quantities, at bakery supply houses. Either the rolls or the sheets can be cut into triangles to shape the throwaway pastry bags described above.

BAKING SHEETS, PANS AND TINS

The important consideration about all sheets and pans that carry pastries and breads into the oven is whether they are bright, shiny and reflective (poor) or dark, dull and absorptive (good). The bright, shiny surfaces reflect the heat away from the dough, which takes longer to bake and brown. Dark metal and Teflon (and Pyrex) absorb the heat and bake and brown the pastry rapidly. This is true of baking sheets and large baking pans on which one or more individual pieces are placed to bake, as well as of containers that encase all but the top of pastry such as tart and pie pans and their smaller counterparts. But don't discard bright sheets and pans; allow more time to bake and brown.

Get the largest and heaviest baking sheet your oven will accommodate, leaving a 1-inch clearance around all sides for the free circulation of hot air. Many pastries can be baked on a flat sheet, but butter-layered and filled pieces should be baked on a sheet or pan with a solid edge or bead to prevent fat and syrup from dripping to the floor of the oven and burning. A jelly-roll pan with narrow sides, less than 1 inch, is also suitable for most pastry baking. A high side, however, will reflect heat away from a small piece in its lee.

Grandmother's almost black metal pan, encrusted by a thousand pies, was a superb pie baker. So is Pyrex, and it is not expensive.

The shiny aluminum throwaway pans, large and small, that are bought in packages at the supermarket have only one thing going for them: disposability.

Pie pans have sloping sides and, commonly, come in 8-, 9- and 10-inch sizes, measured from the inside of the top of the rim to the opposite side. These are not standardized for the dough—the same amount can be rolled and extended to fit any size—but to insure the recipes for fillings will make the right amount.

Traditional flan forms are square, rectangular and round. They are nothing more than metal hoops, with no bottoms, that are placed on a baking sheet, filled and then baked. Most have smooth sides but a few are fluted. In the hot oven the pastry dough shrinks from the sides of the form, which is then easily lifted off—and the tart stands in unsupported splendor. Forms range in diameter from 6 inches to 11½ inches.

Tart and tartlet pans, on the other hand, are made with bottoms,

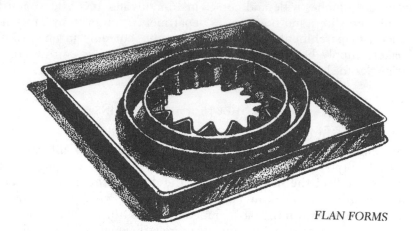

FLAN FORMS

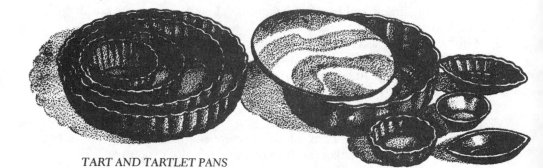

TART AND TARTLET PANS

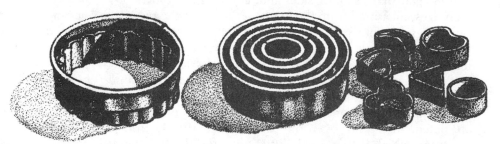

CUTTERS

some of which are loose. This makes it easy to push out the pastry after it is baked. They are made in all sizes, from 1½ inches up to 12 inches. Most of the very small tartlet and *barquette* tins are made individually (which I find convenient), but a few are stamped into a single piece of metal much like a muffin tin.

Quiche pans, unlike flan rings and loose-bottomed tart pans, have a dual purpose. They are for both baking and serving. They may vary in size and fluting, and they are opaque, with straight 1- to 2-inch sides.

One of the classic uses of puff paste is for shells and cases. No pans are needed. No tins. No molds. They are assembled to stand alone during the baking process. The principal requirement, however, is a sharp cutting edge that will not compress and jam the layers together as they are being cut. To do this, there are plain and fluted cutters, especially well made and sharp as a razor, that come in sets for creating ovals, rounds or crescents—traditional shapes for this pastry. There is also a square cutter for this purpose. The cutters are described in the chapter on puff pastry, page 159.

Pastry Brushes

To get started in pastry making, acquire a collection of four pastry brushes: one flat, with a 2-inch-wide brush, to use only for dusting flour across the work surface or the dough as you roll and shape it; a 1-inch-wide brush to coat large areas with butter (for strudel and *phyllo* leaves) or glaze; a soft round one, about ½ inch in diameter, that will allow you to be selective in applying glaze and do other delicate chores; plus a goose-feather brush (more rugged than it looks) for an especially light touch in glazing a dainty tart.

Dough Scraper—Soft and Hard

A soft rubber or plastic dough scraper to follow the contours of the bowl will save expensive fragments of a mixture, whether a filling or a dough.

The metal dough knife or pastry scraper *(coupe-pâte)* will lift, turn and work a variety of doughs. Soon you will come to think of it as an extension of your hand. I prefer the thin, flexible blade of the inexpensive made-in-France scraper to a heavy, stiff one of stainless steel. My French blade has a tendency to discolor, but I know this and keep it polished with steel wool. It is also excellent for scraping clean the work surface. Check a new blade for burrs that might scratch the work surface and, if present, file the blade smooth.

Metal dough knives are sold in gourmet equipment sections of department stores and specialty shops. A 4-inch putty knife from the local hardware store is an excellent substitute.

TIMERS

A timer is as essential to the baking process as an accurate thermometer. There are many good timers on the market, and one comes with most ovens, but there is one I treasure above all: a round, ivory-colored timer about the size of a child's yo-yo which hangs around my neck on a soft

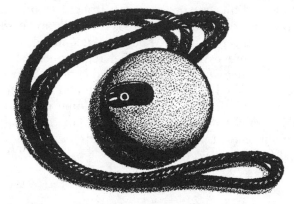

cord. It goes with me to other parts of the house or into the yard to remind me that something is baking in the oven or rising in a bowl. I have also used it to break up an unwanted conversation: "Pardon me, I must go. The bell. The pie." It works on everyone but my wife, who gave it to me as a gift.

For those who wish to give it or receive it as a gift, it is made by Terraillon and sold in most gourmet cookware shops and by catalog.

THE OVEN

It is best to assume that the oven thermostat is not accurate until proven otherwise. A good oven thermometer, the mercury-filled columnar by Taylor, is a good investment when you consider simply the cost of the ingredients, to say nothing of your time.

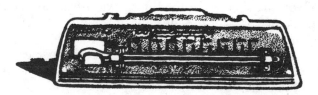

I ask my students to check their home ovens and report back. Nine out of ten report faulty readings that vary from as much as 150° F. too cool to 50° F. too hot. It is impossible to bake good things under these conditions. A too-hot oven will burn the pastries. A too-cool oven will not bake them. An oven that is just right will produce a masterpiece.

Even though the utility company will usually adjust your oven at no cost, continue to use the thermometer to keep the thermostat honest.

The heat in an oven varies in intensity from side to side, front to back and top to bottom. Move the pans and turn them at least once during the baking period to compensate for these variations. Also remove pastries on the outer perimeter of pans first because they bake faster than those in the interior.

I have six ovens in my studio kitchen, electric, gas and wood-fired. I have found almost no difference between electricity and gas in the quality of pastries and breads. My wood-fired oven, in which I bake directly on the stone floor after it has been swept clean, produces a thick bottom crust on loaves of bread and pizza that can't be duplicated any other way except with a baking stone (see below).

The only use I can think of for a microwave oven (I don't have one) in a baker's kitchen is to quickly thaw frozen ingredients or pastries baked in a conventional oven.

Professional cooks and bakers have been using convection ovens with excellent results for many years. The home models do good work, I am told, though I haven't found space in my kitchen that I want to give up to yet another oven.

BAKING STONE

A first-rate substitute for the floor of a baker's oven is a baking stone. Developed in the past few years, it allows you to duplicate in the home oven the same conditions found in the bake shop. Drop pizzas and pastries, especially those with moist fillings, onto the hot stone, and you have the thrust of heat from the bottom that ambient air can never provide. Stones are made both circular and rectangular and are at least ¾ inch thick. The oven is a good place to store the stone, and it can be left there when using the oven for other baking. Tiles are often used for the same purpose. (See "Sources of Supply," page 47.)

KNIFE

Pastries that are to be cut and sliced deserve a sharp knife. Don't butcher and tear, with a dull knife, a lovely and delicate pastry that you have brought this far with such success.

A sharp knife adds a touch of professionalism that fine pastry and bread deserve. I use a stainless steel Swiss knife with a long serrated blade that allows me to cut with a rhythmic motion. Now about fifteen years old, the knife has cut hundreds of loaves, pies, tarts, flans, strudels and *baklavas*—and it is still sharp as a razor. I respect the blade and use it only for baked things in my kitchen. I never allow it to commingle with other things being washed. It gets my complete attention from the moment I wash the blade until it is dried and put away.

For where to get a fine pastry and bread knife, see "Sources of Supply."

Sources of Supply

The renaissance in home baking has made yesterday's specialties commonplace on shelves across the country. It is certain to continue.

Today's supermarkets, gourmet food shops, specialty cookware establishments and hardware and housewares stores carry almost anything that a home baker needs in the way of ingredients and equipment. If you live on a farm in Wisconsin or a ranch in Texas you can get everything you need by mail order.

A basic book for someone putting together a kitchen is the encyclopedic 565-page *Cook's Catalogue*, which is a "critical selection of the best, the necessary, and the special in kitchen equipment and utensils." Prices change, but the book will point you in the direction of what you need. It will also help you put a name on "that thing" you have hankered after but couldn't describe to the clerk. The book is published by Harper & Row, and if your bookstore doesn't have it or can't order it, you may write the publisher, 10 East 53rd Street, New York, New York 10022.

There is also *The Cook's Store*, 192 pages on how to buy and use gourmet gadgets—from a Mouli rotary grater to pie weights—by the editors of *Consumer's Guide*, a Fireside Book published by Simon & Schuster.

The Complete Food Catalogue is a 255-page inventory of mail-order sources from all over the world for foods, recipes, cooking tips and equipment and gadgets, by Jose Wilson and Arthur Leamon, published by Holt, Rinehart and Winston, New York, New York.

There are also many fine mail-order catalogues, but one of my favorites is Williams-Sonoma, P.O. Box 3792, San Francisco, California 94119.

FLOUR

Supermarkets and groceries have or will order for you all the basic flours —bread, unbleached, all-purpose, cake and whole wheat. Pastry flour is not easy to find. I buy mine in 25-pound bags at a large mill in Indianapolis or make do with a blend of 60 percent cake (soft wheat) and 40 percent bread or unbleached (hard wheat) flours. Cake flour can also be ordered by mail.

Be prepared to buy flours when you see them on the shelves. Baking in the United States slacks off in the summer, and stores, in anticipation of this, begin to cut back on inventory in the late spring. Also, buyers often make a one-time-only purchase of a boxcar or two of a certain flour at a special price, and for a while it is stacked in the aisles. Then it is gone, not to reappear for months, if ever. Buy flour when you see it. Drop it into a plastic bag and freeze it until you need it.

Flours in 1- and 2-pound bags and boxes at premium prices (some more than double the usual price per pound) may be purchased in health food stores, gourmet sections of department stores and special food sections of supermarkets, but they are no better than national brands such as Gold Medal and Robin Hood, which, in turn, I find bake no better than store brands milled and packaged (at lower prices) for the big supermarkets.

If you have exhausted local suppliers, here is a list of mail-order sources. Write for catalogs and prices.

Byrd Mill Company
P.O. Box 5167
Richmond, VA 23220

Basic flours and mixes can be found in most supermarkets and gourmet shops, but at premium prices.

The Birkett Mills
P.O. Box 440-A
Penn Yan, NY 14527

Unbleached pastry flour in 5-pound sacks and stone-ground flours.

Elam's Flours
Elam Mills
2625 Gardner Road
Broadview, IL 60153

Elam's striped yellow and red boxes of basic flours are in many stores. No mail order. Expensive.

The Great Valley Mills
Quakertown
Bucks County, PA 18951

Stone-ground flours since 1710. Unbleached bread flour, pastry flour, oatmeal flour, brown rice flour and others in 3-pound bags or more.

Lekvar-by-the-Barrel
H. Roth & Son
1577 First Avenue
New York, NY 10028

Many flours, including pastry and bread flours and other baking supplies, including nuts.

Arrowhead Mills, Inc.
P.O. Box 866
Hereford, TX 79045

This Deaf Smith County mill has a complete line of basic flours, all from organically grown grains, as well as a complete line of natural food staples. Write for their impressive price list.

The Vermont Country Store
Weston, VT 05161

The catalog costs 25 cents but the store has nine different stone-ground flours and meals: bread flour, pastry flour, rye flour, oat flour, buckwheat flour, soy flour, yellow and white cornmeal and muffin or pancake meal.

NUTS

Nuts are an expensive ingredient in pastry making, so it is good to know where to go for better buys than those puffed-with-air plastic bags hanging from the walls in the market. These suppliers will send a catalog on request:

Riggs Pecans
P.O. Box 428
Camden, AL 36726

Pecans only.

Sunnyland Farms Inc.
Route 1
Albany, GA 31702

Black walnuts, almonds, Brazils, filberts.

Torn Ranch Grove
1122 Fourth Street
San Rafael, CA 94901

Walnuts, almonds, Brazils, filberts, pecans, black walnuts.

Paprikas Weiss Importer
1546 Second Avenue
New York, NY 10028

Nuts here are sold shelled and whole, ground, sliced or slivered. Almonds, walnuts, hazelnuts, pignolias, pistachios and bitter kernels for marzipan.

Almond Plaza
California Almond Growers Exchange
1802 C Street
Sacramento, CA 95808

Almonds, of course.

DATE CRYSTALS

A little-known specialty product, date crystals, has been an important ingredient in my baking for more than a decade. No messy, sticky dates. Now I use only Mrs. Shield's dry date crystals, which resemble a hard, crunchy breakfast food. They are made from tree-ripened dates and can be stored for several years in an airtight tin. Sold only by mail. Write for a price list to:

Shields Date Gardens
Indio, CA 92201

ANTI-STICK PASTRY BOARD

The Lucite pastry board described on page 34 came from:

Krystal Kitchens
#PB 7 Rialto Products
Brooklyn, NY 11201

ROLLING PIN

The inventive Guenther Brandes and his polished maple pin that rolls —on command—four different dough thicknesses (see page 39) is from:

Rolleraid
Down Yeast Products
3 Wilson Avenue
Camden, ME 04843

The Down Yeast shop has a supply of lovely squares of woolen blankets (scraps from the town's mills) to place over Danish and bread doughs as they rise. There is nothing better, as wool does not stick. Write for prices.

The Tutove pin (see page 39) is available from many catalogs and specialty cookware shops. If unsuccessful locally, write for prices to:

Bazar Français
666 Avenue of the Americas
New York, NY 10010

Baking Stone

There are now many baking stones and tiles on the market. For a particularly good one—circular or rectangular—write for names of stores in your area or order directly from:

Old Stone Oven Corporation
6007 Sheridan Road
Chicago, IL 60660

Knife

A sharp knife at the table and in the kitchen is a blessing. A pastry cut cleanly without being torn apart by a dull knife is a sure sign of a cook who cares. One of the best for slicing pastries and breads is a Swiss blade, No. 460-9, stainless steel. Restaurant supply houses and culinary departments of retail stores carry them. If you can't find a local outlet, write:

R. H. Forschner Company
324 Lafayette Street
New York, NY 10012

Thermometers

Specialty cookware shops and hardware stores carry the Taylor oven and freezer/refrigerator thermometers. You may have to call the Taylor representative in your area (see the yellow pages) to find out where to buy the Bi-Therm Pocket Dial Thermometer (0° F. to 220° F.), No. 6072, which is used to determine the temperature of the butter before it is rolled into the dough to make Danish and puff pastries. Or write to:

Sybron/Taylor
Consumer-Industrial Products
Arden, NC 28704

BUTTER THERMOMETER

Phyllo and Strudel Leaves

Even in Greece, the *zacharoplasteia* (pastry shops) buy rather than make their own paper-thin *phyllo* leaves. In large U.S. cities they can be found freshly made or frozen in Armenian, Syrian, Greek and other Middle Eastern groceries and supermarkets. The quickest and easiest way to find a source near you is to call or write the area's Greek Orthodox church, the center of Greek ethnic and cultural life. The yellow pages list the churches.

Phyllo are also marketed as strudel leaves. In my small Indiana city I can get 1-pound boxes of "Filo Krousta/Strudel Leaves," made in Newark, New Jersey, as well as "Fillo/Strudel Leaves" from Cleveland. There are about twenty-five leaves in a box, sufficient to make about two dozen *baklavas*.

The *phyllo*/strudel leaf is somewhat thicker than the Greek-made single-purpose *phyllo* leaf of which there are about fifty sheets to the pound. Some are labeled for thinness (No. 4 is considered the best for *baklava*).

Pie Bird

The pie bird is fun—and useful. Its open beak pointed to the heavens allows the steam to escape from underneath the crust. There is a more elegant bird of flame-proof porcelain by Royal Worcester that gracefully rises off its perch to allow the steam to escape at its feet. Both are functional and fun. Kids love the bird, as do all adults who ever recited "Four and twenty blackbirds . . ." Most gourmet cookware shops carry it. If you can't find one in a nest, write:

Edwin Jay, Inc.
20 Cooper Square
New York, NY 10003

PIE SPATULA

The person who thought of the pie spatula probably invented the wheel in his or her spare time. Both are so simple yet were so long in coming.

The pie spatula is a triangle of metal with a handle that is positioned in the pie plate before the dough is put in. When the pie is baked, the spatula is underneath, ready to lift out the first piece. And from then on lifting out the pieces is a piece of cake. (I have since discovered that the inventor is Louise Bateman who will be pleased to tell you where to buy one if your store does not have it. Her address:

> P.O. Box 182
> HoHoKus, NJ 07423

Why Pastries Rise

Puff pastry rises elegantly. Pie crust browns and becomes flaky and tender. Pizza dough expands and lifts the rich covering of tomato sauce and cheese. The tiny ball of *pâte à chou* balloons into a golden puff.

In each instance the dough expands in the heat of the oven because one or more leavening agents are at work. In varying degrees, air, steam and carbon dioxide leaven all baked goods. Air beaten into egg whites raises an angel food cake. Bread (and pizza) are raised and expanded by the gas from fermenting yeast or the chemical action of baking powder or baking soda (interacting with an acid such as buttermilk).

The critical factor in making pie doughs is the manner in which the fat—lard, butter, margarine, oil or a solid vegetable shortening—is mixed or "cut" into the flour. The fat is either blended completely into the flour so that the two become one, or the shortening is left in small particles—often described as looking like coarse meal. At times the fat is left in even larger pieces (pea-size) in the dough, which is then rolled and turned (as for puff pastry) several times. Each produces a delicious but different kind of crust.

Doughs for tarts and *quiches* are made with the four basic pie dough ingredients—flour, salt, fat and water—but with other things added, principally sugar and eggs, to enrich and strengthen the crusts. The doughs for entrée pies and turnovers are leavened in the same way.

Three doughs without leavening—puff paste, strudel dough and *phyllo* leaves—are prepared with bread or unbleached flour to withstand the extremes of stretching and rolling without breaking up.

The several hundred sheets of unleavened dough in puff pastry are formed as the layers of dough and butter are built up, one on top of the other. The small lump of strudel dough is stretched into one incredibly thin sheet before it is covered with a filling. It is then rolled into a long piece in which the layers of filling become interweaved with the layers of dough. The *phyllo* leaves, brushed with melted butter, are laid down one by one in a pan for *baklava* or wrapped around a cheese bit and folded into a triangular morsel for *tiropetes*.

Each of these pastries, while made with dough that cannot rise by itself, does so dramatically in the oven when the moisture in the dough, fat and filling becomes hot and expands. For the piece of puff pastry, this means hundreds of flaky layers. For strudel, it means several dozen layers, and for *baklava*, perhaps twenty or thirty crisp leaves.

Danish pastry and pizza begin life as yeast-raised doughs. Danish takes a peculiar turn, however, because it is rolled flat, spread with butter or margarine and then treated as puff pastry—rolled and turned several times to increase manyfold the layers of dough and butter. Danish, therefore, is doubly blessed. The yeast-raised dough rises and expands in the oven as would a loaf of bread. But it has the added incentive of steam between the layers of dough to form a pastry that is not only flaky and short but soft and porous, a unique and delicious combination.

Pâte à chou, cream puff dough, starts with a cooked batter-like blend of flour, fat, water and salt. Bread or unbleached flour is used to enable the paste to expand to three or four times its size. Beaten eggs, stirred into the cooked batter, combine with the flour to form a tight but elastic shell that traps the steam and puffs it grandly.

Pie

Pie.

A three-letter word with the power to call back memories as old as childhood or as fresh as yesterday's picnic in the park. Pie. It means grandmothers, mothers and Aunt Marthas, harvests, Christmas, good table companions, a birthday, a cup of coffee, a school box lunch, a piece of cheese, a scoop of ice cream and, above all, good eating. That's the power of pie.

Pie, our kind of pie—covered wholly with a crust or under a lattice of delicate pastry strips—is quintessentially American. Pie to the Scots, for example, means a filling of mutton or pigeon. In France the term would draw a blank look, even though the same crust, with some modification and without a top, is known everywhere on the Continent as a tart or flan.

Only in America is pie, well, pie, and with so many offerings. In *The Hoosier Cookbook*, a fine collection of dishes from the best of Indiana cooks, there are 112 recipes for pie, from Impossible and Millionaire to Apple Pizza and Green Tomato.

There are fifty-one different pie recipes in an eighty-year-old cookbook written by the women of the Brethren Church. These Brethren "sisters" are as famous in their kitchens as are their more celebrated Pennsylvania Dutch cousins. Funeral Pie, a raisin pie with a squeeze of lemon, served to mourners at a big meal following the service, by Sister Etta Eckerle, an Illinois farm wife, is included in the book along with carrot, syrup and vinegar pies.

Sister Mary E. Crofford, of Pennsylvania, said this about her Rich

Man's Pie: "Take 4 tablespoons of melted butter spread on a pie crust, spread over it ½ cup of sugar, grate on a little nutmeg, then spread on top of all 2 tablespoons of flour. Now set the pie in the oven and pour over enough sweet milk to make it full enough, and bake. Put in the ingredients just as they are written, beginning with the butter and ending with milk. It will make a queer-looking pie to those who have never seen it, but it will taste far better than it looks. Try it."

I did, Sister Crofford, and it was delicious!

The pies chosen for this book are to be found on about everyone's list of the ten favorite pies in America. Seventeen are presented here to be certain the ten are represented. Five of the pies repeat a chief ingredient—rhubarb, lemon and strawberries. I didn't plan it that way. I was determined to choose between lemon and Shaker lemon and between rhubarb and strawberry-rhubarb, but I could not. All four are here.

There are literally hundreds of other pies made with other ingredients in thousands of combinations. Each is one of four kinds, essentially.

The first kind is fruit and berry. Almost everything from the orchard or berry patch can be made into delicious fillings for pies. Plan first to use fruit that is fresh and seasonally abundant. Between harvests, substitute frozen fruit and berries from your own freezer, or choose from a wide variety found at the store. Not to be overlooked, of course, is canned fruit. The recipes here are for traditional apple pie, cherry, rhubarb, Shaker lemon, rhubarb-strawberry, blackberry and strawberry. I have included mincemeat in this category as well.

The second kind is pies with custard, cream and meringue, the soft-filled pies. These have a cool, satiny texture and delicately sweet flavor. Many have fillings that are cooked separately and poured into a baked shell. The recipes for these include chocolate, lemon meringue, coconut cream, pumpkin, custard, chess and pecan.

The airy, foamy chiffon pies comprise the third grouping—served without topping or surrounded with peaks of whipped cream. Lime chiffon is presented here as representative of the group which includes lemon, orange, strawberry, Nesselrode, Black Bottom and mocha chiffon, to name but a few.

Then there are the refrigerated or frozen pies, which range from the exotic Grasshopper and Alexander to those filled with softened ice cream and topped with fruit or nuts, or syrup, or a touch of each. They can be made well in advance and simply whisked out of the refrigerator or freezer at dessert time.

To get to the heart of good pie making, however, it is necessary only to bake the seventeen (plus variations) in this book, which represent the best there is to be found in kitchens across the country. With this solid background in pie making, the home baker can move with confidence to scores of other pies, America's favorite dessert.

The Crust

A great part of the pleasure of eating pie should be the delight of a bite of crust. A moment to anticipate should be the instant the fork parts the tender crust. Alas, not always so. An appalling number of soggy crusts are left behind after the fillings have been scooped out.

A friend, Cecily Brownstone, food editor of the Associated Press, said to me, "Pie is probably the most widely made of all American pastry desserts—and people do it so badly!" She was referring, of course, to the crust.

If the crust is tender, flaky, crisp and above all (or below all) not soggy, the crust can add a dimension that ranks pie with the best pastry creations in kitchens both here and abroad. A favorite filling may be the excuse to eat pie, but it should be the crust that makes the occasion memorable.

Several crusts have evolved in the American kitchen over the past two hundred years. They reflect regional and ethnic preferences, the availability and cost of ingredients, as well as dietetic and religious considerations.

Pie crust dough in its simplest form is made with four ingredients: flour, salt, fat and water. It is low in moisture and high in fat to prevent the formation of the gluten network so prized in bread making. Because it must support and retain fillings without leaking, it cannot be porous.

One of the principal reasons that many pie crusts are poor is that the dough has been rushed into the oven without a proper period of rest. Some pie makers have their pies in the oven 30 minutes after they have started to prepare the dough. This should not be. Good pie crust cannot be made in haste. It must not be rushed.

For a fine crust, the dough must be allowed to rest for a minimum of 4 hours and a maximum of 24. During this time the gluten in the flour is mellowed by the enzymes in the flour, which permits the flour to absorb the moisture fully. It is this critical period of rest and conditioning that eliminates toughness, shrinkage and the possibility of a crust's being soaked by the filling.

If it annoys you (as it does me) not to be able to produce a pie late in the afternoon for a suddenly scheduled dinner party, keep a supply of conditioned dough or one or two partially baked shells in the refrigerator or freezer with which an outstanding pie or two can be made within the hour.

It becomes a joy to begin a project that has every chance of success if, for example, you know before you begin why the particles of fat are left discrete in a medium-flake pie dough and not smeared together.

There are three kinds of crusts made with the same ingredients, but the difference lies in the manner in which the fat is introduced into the dough. To bakers, they are known as "medium-flake," "long-flake" and "short-flake" or "mealy." Crumb crust, with its many variations, is a fourth type.

Medium and *long* refer to the relative size of the particles of fat as they are rolled and elongated in the dough. Short-flake dough is almost not a "flake" at all, since the fat is allowed to blend with and become part of the dough.

Short is a word often used to describe pie dough. "My, this dough is short," my grandmother would say as she tasted one of my aunt's pies at the family picnic. What she meant was that the crust was tender under the fork and in the mouth. The fork cut a precise line as it cleaved the crust—no flaky fragments.

If a bite of crust does not reveal the true nature of the dough, break a piece with your fingers. If the break is clean, the crust is short. If the crust shatters or comes apart in layers, it is a medium- or long-flake crust. All should be tender and a delight to eat.

The versatile "medium-flake" crust has long been one of the most popular pie crusts in America. It is tender, flaky, easy and quick to make. If I could have only one crust for all pies it would be this one.

The fat is first cut into the flour by hand or machine until the mixture resembles coarse meal. Some have likened its appearance to damp sawdust, grains of rice or small peas. Cold water is added. The mixture is stirred, but only enough to mix all the ingredients into a rough mass that will hold together and not fall apart when it is picked up. Don't smear the particles together or make a paste of the dough. Everything should be kept cold to protect the tiny particles. In the oven each tiny flour-covered bit of moist fat will create a small burst of steam to expand and flavor the dough and make it flaky.

The "long-flake" crust is esteemed for its flakiness and crispness, but it is fragile and must be handled with care. It is usually reserved for small pies, turnovers and tartlet shells that are less rich than those made with the usual tart doughs. The particles of fat are left in large pieces (the size of small whole walnuts) when they are dropped into the flour. With the addition of chilled water, a rough mass is formed which is rolled and folded a total of three times. Each time the fat gets thinner and more scattered throughout the dough as layer mounts on layer, as with puff pastry. The crust will lift in the oven to three or four times its original thickness.

The third favorite in the family of pie crusts is made with "short-flake" or "mealy" dough in which chilling the ingredients beforehand becomes unimportant; the flour and fat are blended to lose their identities and become one. A similar dough can be made by reducing the amount of fat so that there are few flour-covered fat particles in the mixture. When baked, the crust is more substantial and less flaky. It is excellent for liquid fillings such as custard, pumpkin and pecan. The crust is highly favored by bake shops for its ability to be trucked around without breaking up, and by busy restaurants where a waiter can quickly cut a wedge of pie without fear of shattering a less sturdy shell. Jostling in a picnic hamper won't harm it either.

The fourth type of crust, made with crumbs or nuts mixed and patted into place in the pan, is a shortcut in the pie-making process.

DOUGH PREPARATION

The fat is "cut" or broken into the flour in several ways. It can be done with nimble fingers, rapidly so that body heat does not soften the fat. When making medium- and long-flake dough, the concern is that the fat will soften and be absorbed by the flour rather than remain as *flour-coated* particles. The job is usually done with a pastry blender or two knives, one held in each hand. Let me repeat: this cutting is not done to blend the flour and fat into a homogeneous mass but to break it into hundreds and thousands of small granules, each retaining its own identity.

Don't rush the addition of the liquid; sprinkle it slowly over the flour-fat mixture while lightly lifting and tossing the particles together with a fork. It may take two or three minutes before the fork has gathered all the mixture into one mass. Feel it. It will be moist but not wet. It should not be sticky. If it is, add sprinkles of flour, but do so sparingly. Pat the dough gently into a ball. Cover it, place it in the refrigerator and let it chill.

The fingers, a pastry blender and knives have been the accepted equipment for decades of baking. Today, however, kitchen machines can do all or part of the job. The electric mixer, one powerful enough not to be stopped by a heavy blend of ingredients, has been in the kitchen for some time. The food processor, with its ability to perform almost instantaneous miracles, is newly arrived.

Detailed instructions for preparing each recipe in three ways—by hand, electric mixer or food processor—are given as part of each crust recipe.

With this machinery beckoning in the wings, don't forget how to use the hands. The fingers, best of all, can tell you when the dough is exactly right.

SHAPING

The dough is shaped and baked in several ways. It may be formed *inside* a pie pan to be chilled and filled, or baked partially or wholly to be filled later. The latter is called a "blind" crust. The baked-beforehand shell is for cream and chiffon fillings, open pies to be filled, chilled and served.

The partially baked shell is taken from the oven before it begins to color, after about 15 minutes, and allowed to cool. It is filled and returned to complete the baking process. This is done to assure that the bottom crust will be crisp and flaky no matter how moist the filling it holds.

If the crust is to be baked "blind" beforehand, there are several ways to keep the bottom and sides from bubbling and ballooning out of shape or unduly shrinking. The most satisfactory way is to press a piece of aluminum foil down into the crust-lined pan. Do this when the dough has been chilled so that it can't be pushed out of shape. Fit it around the sides and fill to the brim with weights—dried beans, rice or aluminum pellets especially packaged for the purpose. After the crust has been in the oven about 15 minutes, remove, lift out the foil and weights and return the crust to the oven for a few minutes to bake out the moisture that may still be evident in the bottom, or for the full baking period if the crust is not to be returned to the oven for further baking.

Save the weights to use again. I have a big glass jar filled with dried beans, now discolored, which have been baked times without number. I also save the aluminum pieces just as they are when I lift them out of the pans so that next time they can be slipped into the same pie tins with no fuss.

The crust may also be pricked beforehand to allow the steam to escape during baking, but sometimes the tiny holes get clogged and the crust bubbles up anyway. If it does, prick the crust again and press it to the bottom of the pan with the flat of the fork.

A third way is to butter the bottom of an identical pan and fit it into the dough-lined pan to hold the dough in place while it is baking, but I find this less than satisfactory.

TO ROLL DOUGH

Sprinkle the work surface lightly with flour before taking the chilled dough from the refrigerator. Place a cup of flour for dusting to one side. I dust with a large brush as described in the chapter on equipment (page 43).

Flatten the dough by pressing it down firmly with the hands. Dust both sides with flour. Roll from the middle of the dough to the upper edge, away from you. Turn the dough 180 degrees and again roll from the middle to the upper edge. Turn the dough over; dust it and the work surface. Turn the dough 90 degrees so that the third and fourth rollings are crosswise of the length of dough.

After each rolling, loosen the dough by slipping a spatula or dough blade under the edges before turning. Continue the turning and rolling until the dough is the desired shape, whether circular or elongated.

Refrigerate whenever the fat particles in the dough begin to soften.

PREPARING SINGLE CRUST

PREPARATION
6 min.

Remove the dough from the refrigerator 1 hour beforehand to make it less difficult to work. Divide into the number of single shells to be made. While preparing the first crust, reserve the balance of dough in the refrigerator.

Roll dough into a rough circle on a lightly floured work surface. Move the dough after each rolling to be certain it is not sticking, especially if the room is warm. (A chilled marble piece is ideal to work on.) Brush or dust lightly with sprinkles of flour if necessary.

Doughs for single-crust pies should be rolled to the thickness of ⅛ inch. Place an inverted pie tin over the dough to determine its diameter. Allow an addi-

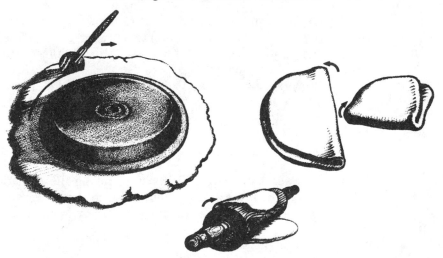

tional ½- to 1-inch margin for the border. Trim with scissors, knife or rolling pizza cutter.

Fold the dough into quarters or drape carefully over a rolling pin and lift to the pan. Smaller pieces can be lifted directly from the work surface and placed in pans. Gently press into the sides of the pan without stretching or pulling the dough. A small wad of scrap dough, dipped in flour, is useful to pat the dough into the deep recesses of the pan, especially a fluted one.

Leave a margin of dough around the rim for the edging (page 65). Fold the overhanging dough under to make a thicker rim, if desired. When fluted, it will provide a high rim to contain more filling than otherwise possible.

If the shell is to be formed *over* an inverted pan, grease the pan lightly. Gently press the dough to fit the shape of the pan. Trim. Prick with the tines of a fork over the entire surface of the crust. Place the inverted pan (and crust) on a baking sheet for ease in moving to the oven. A second and identical form may be placed over the inverted pan to hold the dough in place during the first 15 minutes of the baking period so that the dough does not balloon or pull away from the edges; first butter the inside surface of the pan that will fit over the dough. Or a heavy pan or baking sheet, buttered on the bottom, can be laid on top of the dough.

REFRIGERATION 20 min. or longer

When the dough has been shaped in or on the pan, place in the refrigerator to chill and relax for at least 20 minutes.

Preheat oven to 425° F.

BAKING 425° F. 15 min. 20 min.

Shells to be only partially baked should be taken from the oven before the exposed edges begin to brown, about 15 minutes. Later these will be baked completely when filled and returned to the oven. Carefully lift out the foil and weights. Allow the shells to cool before filling.

After removing the weights, return shells that are to be baked completely to the oven for an additional 20 minutes to allow the dough to become a light golden brown. Watch carefully. Don't let the crust scorch.

FINAL STEP The baked shells may be used immediately or held in the refrigerator, wrapped in plastic or tucked into a plastic bag, for another day. If a shell is to be frozen, place it in a pan or pie box to protect it from being jostled. Wrap the container with freezer paper.

TWO CRUSTS FOR COVERED PIES

PREPARATION
8 min.

Remove the dough from the refrigerator 1 hour beforehand to allow it to soften somewhat. Divide the dough into two pieces, one slightly larger for the bottom crust. Reserve the dough for the top crust in the refrigerator.

Dust the work surface lightly with flour. Roll the larger piece into a circle ½-inch larger than the diameter of an inverted pie pan. Keep a light dusting of flour under and on the dough so that it does not stick when rolled.

Fold the dough in half or quarters so that it can be lifted and moved to the pan without tearing. Carefully unfold. Loosely drape the dough over the sides of the pan so that it can be pushed against the sides and the bottom without being stretched or put under tension.

Trim the dough around the rim, leaving a ½-inch margin to be folded over the top crust when it is in place, or tucked under the rim dough to make a thicker and higher crust around the pie, especially if the filling is juicy.

FINAL STEP The bottom crust is now ready to be filled according to the recipe. It may be filled immediately or kept wrapped in the refrigerator for several days, or frozen for a longer period.

It may also be convenient to roll out the top crust at this point rather than to store the dough in a ball. If so, cover the rolled-out dough with a sheet of wax paper. Lift half the circle of dough and lay it back on the paper so that the wax paper is between the two halves. Fold in quarters and separate with wax paper. Lay the folded dough on top of the lower crust in the pan, wrap both together and store.

The prepared crusts may be frozen for three months.

EDGES

When a single-crust recipe calls for a ½-inch edge of dough to extend beyond the pan, it is done to provide extra dough to be folded under to build up the rim. For a covered pie, the edge of the top crust is folded under the bottom crust (rather than over, for neatness) to seal the two together—and, again, provide a thickness of dough that can be fluted and decorated in several ways.

The simplest decorative pattern is made with the tines of a fork. First, trim the dough and, if wanted, turn the edge under. Press around the edge with the fork to decorate (and to seal, if using a double crust or lattice strips).

A series of delicate V's around the rim may be made by placing the right index finger on the inside of the rim, left thumb and index finger on the outside of the pastry. Push dough into a V shape. Pinch gently to sharpen the points.

The effect of a tiny rope laid around the rim can be achieved by pinching dough between the index finger and thumb. Do a second time to sharpen the lines.

For a ruffle, place the left thumb and index finger ½ inch apart on the pastry rim. With the right index finger pull the pastry between the fingers and toward the outer edge of the pie.

All of these edges can be done either on a single crust or after a top crust has been placed over the filling. One-crust pies can also be decorated with pieces of scrap dough cut with small cutters into hearts, stars, circles and leaves. Brush the rim with water before placing cutouts, which should slightly overlap each other. Press firmly into place.

LATTICEWORK

Interweave lattice strips before moistening the edge of the lower crust because the strips may stick to the dough and resist being picked up and laid down in the weaving process.

There are several lattice designs other than those laid out at right angles. Try diamonds, made by weaving the second half of the strips diagonally across the first strips.

Lattice strips may also be twisted as they are laid across the pie. Or the twisted strip can begin in the center of the pie and be laid in a spiral toward the outer edge, where it is fastened.

For a fruit pie that is particularly juicy and may bubble over during baking, trim the lower crust but leave a 1-inch margin of dough. Put down the lattice strip (or a top crust) and fold the lower crust edge over

SINGLE CRUST

FOR COVERED PIE

FOR JUICY PIE

FORK-FLUTED EDGE

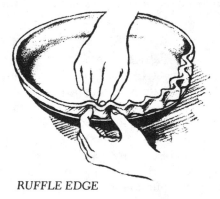

RUFFLE EDGE

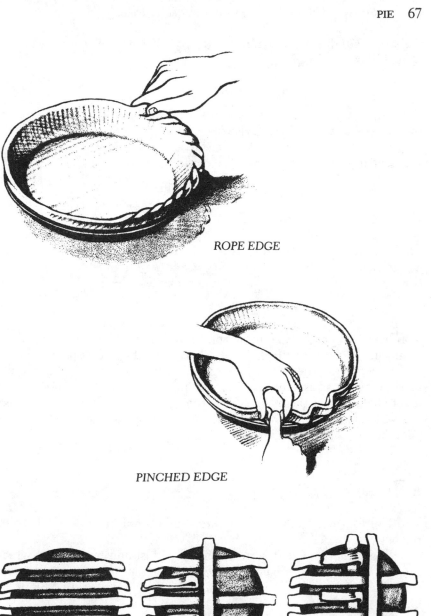

ROPE EDGE

PINCHED EDGE

LATTICE TOP

the strips, building up a high retaining side. Press firmly with the fingers to seal. Flute.

COLOR OF CRUST

For a shiny crust, brush with plain milk before baking; for a glazed one, brush with a mixture of 1 egg yolk and 1 teaspoon milk. For a light brown crust, brush with melted butter and sprinkle with 1 tablespoon granulated sugar before putting the pie in the oven.

HOW MUCH DOUGH?

Here are some handy though approximate measurements:

Approximately 1 cup unsifted or 1¼ cups sifted flour in a recipe will produce one large 8- or 9-inch shell or crust. Two cups, or a little less, will make a two-crust pie—remember that the top crust is rolled a little thinner than the lower one—or it will make two shells.

PIE SPATULA

You have just baked a pie masterpiece and there it sits in all its golden grandeur, as yet unscathed. But how to get out the first piece without making a mess of the beauty? The pie spatula, of course. The triangular piece of metal is baked under the crust and, when the time comes, there it is to help lift out the first piece. It then slips along underneath, assisting with other pieces. It is equally good for tarts and the like. (See "Sources of Supply," page 47.)

A Collection of Crusts

The four basic crusts for pie are represented in this book by nine recipes.

The Basic Pie Crust, a medium-flaky crust and one against which most other crusts are judged, is joined by two unusual and very delicious natural crusts: Whole Wheat Pie Crust and Whole Wheat–Oat Flour Pie Crust.

There is one recipe for long-flake crust, the Layered Crust, which has its antecedents in puff pastry.

The short-flake crusts (bakers call them the "mealy" type) are Half-and-Half, Hot Water, No-Roll and another natural delight, All-Rye.

Crumb crust and its variations, including the use of nuts rather than crumbs, follow.

There are literally hundreds of variations on these themes. Some may have more salt or a few grains less sugar, or vice versa, or call for milk instead of water. On and on. The fundamentals for them all are detailed here. Nevertheless, you are urged to move from here with variations of your own choosing that will make pie making—and eating —an even greater pleasure.

THE *BASIC PIE CRUST*

One of the finest pie crusts—and one of the most widely made in kitchens across the country—is an easy-to-prepare dough using lard or vegetable shortening or a combination of the two. It deserves to be called *the* basic crust because the recipe is so widespread that it is usually known as Auntie Skoog's Best Pie Dough or Mrs. Snoeberger's Favorite Crust or even Dad's Delight, so named to honor a family cook or neighbor who created a memorable pastry with it.

This does not mean that all home bakers make it well. Many don't. But it can be made so with a little thought and advance planning that will allow the dough time to rest and relax along the way. It will be tender under the fork and delicious on the tongue when done properly.

The dough makes a "medium-flaky" crust in which the lard or shortening is cut into tiny flour-covered particles that retain their identity throughout the process. Butter can be used to give the crust its delicate flavoring, but it must be blended with lard or shortening in the ratio of one part butter to two parts shortening. Butter alone in this type of dough produces a hard crust with none of the shortness or tender crispness imparted by lard or solid shortening.

Although the basic recipe is usually made with only four ingredients —lard or a solid fat, salt, flour and liquid—a more delicate and somewhat richer version is made with the addition of egg (for extra crispness and richness), sugar (a touch of sweetness and color) and vinegar (tenderness). If the optional vinegar and egg are added, reduce or eliminate cold water.

All the good things I knew about this recipe were confirmed one day when I discovered it taped to the big refrigerator door in the test kitchen of the Louisville (Kentucky) *Courier-Journal*. This alone was an impressive measure of its value, because Kentuckians know and demand fine food just as they know and demand fine horses. It is known there as Mrs. Crosier's Perfect All-Purpose Pie Crust. Whenever there is a pie to be baked in the newspaper's test kitchen with an unspecified crust, the lot falls to Mrs. Crosier's recipe to help the soon-to-be-tested pie become something just as great as the aspiring home baker said it is and hopes it will be. "It's a perfect crust for almost every kind of pie," said Lillian Marshall, for many years the paper's esteemed food editor, who peeled the recipe off the door and gave it to me.

Poignant note: While the memory of Mrs. Crosier and her fine recipe lives on in Kentucky, and in surrounding states as well as in my kitchen, the food editors don't know what became of the lady who submitted the version of this winning recipe so many years ago.

One of my pie-baking mentors who uses only lard in this basic dough is eighty-year-old Katherine Records, who with her late husband operated a feed store and hatchery for many years in my southern Indiana town. Her pies have been consistent blue ribbon winners at the county fair for generations. Rather than store either dough or an unbaked shell, Mrs. Records keeps a bag of "crumbs" in her refrigerator to be made into a crust at a moment's notice with only the addition of 3 or 4 tablespoons of cold water. The "crumbs" are the tiny particles of flour, salt and lard that have been cut with a pastry blender. They keep refrigerated almost indefinitely.

INGREDIENTS
For one single 8- or 9-inch shell or approximately four tartlet shells:
1 cup all-purpose flour
½ teaspoon salt
6 tablespoons lard or vegetable shortening, chilled
　(or 4 tablespoons lard or vegetable shortening and
　2 tablespoons butter, chilled)
¼ cup ice water, approximately

Optional:
1 teaspoon sugar
1 teaspoon vinegar
2 tablespoons egg (half of 1 slightly beaten egg)

For one two-crust 8- or 9-inch pie:
2 cups all-purpose flour
1 teaspoon salt
¾ cup (6 ounces) lard or vegetable shortening, chilled
　(or ½ cup (4 ounces) lard or vegetable shortening
　and 4 tablespoons butter, chilled)
½ cup ice water, approximately

Optional:
2 teaspoons sugar
2 teaspoons vinegar
1 egg

PIE PAN(S) PREPARATION	Pans of choice, large (9- or 10-inch) or small (8-inch). *Note:* 1. If the blend of butter and lard or shortening is to be used, allow both to come to room temperature before mixing them together. The mixture must be chilled before it is cut into the flour, however. 2. If the optional vinegar and egg are used, reduce water by half. 3. The volume of one large egg is about ¼ cup; hence, half is 2 tablespoons.
● BY HAND 5 min.	Into a medium bowl measure flour and salt. With a knife cut the fat into several small pieces and drop into the flour. Toss and work the fat and flour together with a pastry blender, two knives or fingers working quickly, until the mixture resembles coarse meal, with irregular particles ranging in size from tiny grains of rice to small peas. (These are Mrs. Records's "crumbs.") Add sugar, vinegar and egg, if desired. Pour each ingredient into the flour mixture and stir to blend before adding the next. Sprinkle in the water, a tablespoon at a time, and stir with a fork held lightly. Gently toss the loose particles around the bowl to absorb moisture. Add water as needed to bring the particles together in a moist (not wet) mass that holds together with no dry or crumbly places apparent.
▲ ELECTRIC MIXER 4 min.	Measure flour and salt into mixer bowl. Cut fat into several small pieces and drop into the flour. Start mixer at slow speed and stir until flour-covered fat particles are the size of small peas, about 1 minute. Add sugar, vinegar and egg, if desired. Add water, a tablespoon at a time, until the mass is moist and forms a rough ball. Stop. Don't overmix.
■ FOOD PROCESSOR 3 min.	With the metal blade attached, add flour, salt and fat to the work bowl. Process with two or three short bursts, or until the mixture has the consistency of coarse meal. Stop the machine. Add sugar, vinegar and egg, if desired. (Operate the machine in short bursts so as not to overmix.) Pour ice water through the feed tube. Stop as soon as dough begins to form a rough, moist mass.

REFRIGERATED REST 4 hours or longer	Wrap the ball of dough in plastic wrap or foil and place in the refrigerator to mature and chill, 4 hours or longer.
ROLLING/ SHAPING	Beforehand remove the dough from the refrigerator about ½ hour before rolling or it will be difficult to work. 　　To shape for pie pans, see page 61.
BAKING Times vary	If the shell(s) is to be baked before filling, see page 61. 　　If the shell(s) is to be filled before baking, follow instructions for the specific pie recipe.
FINAL STEP	See specific pie recipe. If the pie is to be frozen, see page 372.

WHOLE WHEAT PIE CRUST

A pie crust made with whole wheat dough has the dark brown color and true wheaty flavor that comes only from the whole wheat berry. Because the wheat particles are large by comparison with finely milled white flour (though both are from the same grain) and contain a full ration of fiber and wheat germ, whole wheat bakes into a less tender crust than white flour, but it is crisp and delicious nevertheless. There is no sugar in the recipe, which makes it even more attractive to one looking at a diet.

For a medium-flaky crust, the lard is cut into the whole wheat flour I would expect to find at a country dinner prepared by the family's best cook and baker.

For a medium-flaky crust, the lard is cut into the whole wheat flour until the particles in the mixture are the size of grains of rice.

The large particles in regular whole wheat flour are slow to absorb moisture, so allow the mixture to rest 4 or 5 minutes after all the liquid has been added. Stone-ground whole wheat flour is even coarser, so allow a moment or so longer for the absorption process. If the mixture then seems to have dried out somewhat, add one or two additional spoonfuls of liquid before chilling the dough.

INGREDIENTS	*For one single 8- or 9-inch shell or approximately four tartlet shells:* 1¼ cups whole wheat flour ¼ teaspoon salt

½ cup (8 tablespoons) lard or other fat, chilled
½ teaspoon lemon juice
¼ cup ice water, approximately

For one two-crust 8- or 9-inch pie:
2½ cups whole wheat flour
½ teaspoon salt
1 cup lard or other fat, chilled
1 teaspoon lemon juice
½ cup ice water, approximately

PIE PAN(S)

Pans of choice, large or small.

PREPARATION
● BY HAND
6 min.

Measure (don't sift) the flour and salt into a large mixing bowl. Drop in the pieces of chilled fat and cut into the flour with a pair of knives or a pastry blender. Fingers may also be used if they are nimble and get the job done without softening the fat pieces. The particles should be about the size of rice grains.

Pour the lemon juice into the chilled water and carefully add the liquid by the tablespoonful so that the flour is not suddenly flooded. Stir and toss with a fork, being careful not to mash the particles.

RESTING
4–5 min.

When the mixture appears ready to be shaped into a ball, allow it to rest so that the whole wheat has an opportunity to absorb its quota of liquid. After the rest, stir the mixture into a rough mass. If it crumbles and falls apart, add 1 or 2 more teaspoons of chilled water.

▲ ELECTRIC
MIXER
5 min.

Measure unsifted whole wheat flour and salt into the mixer bowl. Cut the fat into several small pieces and drop into the flour. Attach bowl and beater. Start at slow speed and stir until the lumps of flour-covered fat are the size of small peas, about 1 minute. Add lemon juice and water, 1 tablespoon at a time, until the particles are moist. Stop the machine and allow dough to rest 4 to 5 minutes. Press dough with a finger. If it crumbles or falls apart, add sprinkles of water. But don't overmix.

■ FOOD
PROCESSOR
4 min.

With the metal blade attached, put unsifted whole wheat flour, salt and fat, cut into 1-inch pieces, into the work bowl. Process with two or three short bursts, or until the mixture is the consistency of coarse meal. Stop the machine. Add lemon juice and 1 tablespoon water followed with a short 3-second pulse. Repeat pattern with additional tablespoons of water. Stop the machine the moment dough comes together in a mass. Let it rest for 3 or 4 minutes so that it may absorb its full quota of moisture. Press with a finger. If moist and soft, the dough is finished.

REFRIGERATED
REST
4 hours or
longer

Wrap the dough in plastic wrap or foil and place in the refrigerator to chill and relax, 4 hours or longer.

ROLLING/
SHAPING

Beforehand, remove the dough from the refrigerator 1 hour before rolling or it will be difficult to work.
　　To shape for pan(s), see page 61.

BAKING
Times vary

If the shell(s) is to be baked before it is filled, see page 61.
　　If the shell(s) is to be filled before baking, follow instructions for the specific pie recipe.

FINAL STEP

See specific pie recipe. If the pie is to be frozen, see page 372.

WHOLE WHEAT–OAT FLOUR PIE CRUST

Equal amounts of whole wheat and oat flour are the basic ingredients of this nutritious and delicious crust with a pleasant nutty flavor. Although oat flour isn't on everyone's kitchen shelf, oatmeal usually is. Put a cup of oatmeal in the food processor or blender and spin it until finely ground.

　　This is a medium-flaky crust. When baked it is not quite as tender under the fork as one made with white flour because of whole wheat's larger particles.

INGREDIENTS

For one single 8- or 9-inch shell or approximately four tartlet shells:
½ cup oat flour or finely ground oatmeal
½ cup whole wheat flour, stone-ground or fine
½ teaspoon salt
⅓ cup vegetable shortening or lard, chilled
3–4 tablespoons ice water

For one two-crust 8- or 9-inch pie:
1 cup oat flour or finely ground oatmeal

1 cup whole wheat flour, stone-ground or fine
1 teaspoon salt
⅔ cup vegetable shortening or lard, chilled
6–8 tablespoons ice water

PIE PAN(S)

Pans of choice, large or small.

PREPARATION

Working note: Beforehand, if necessary, process oat-meal into fine meal in a food processor or blender. The latter will produce a fine flour.

● BY HAND
8 min.

Into a large bowl measure the two flours and salt. Drop in pieces of the butter or margarine. Use hands, a pastry cutter or knives to toss and cut the flour and shortening together. The mixture will resemble coarse meal.

Carefully add the ice water by the single table-spoonful so that the flour is not suddenly flooded. Stir with a fork only enough to make a rough ball of dough.

▲ ELECTRIC
MIXER
5 min.

Pour the two flours and salt into the mixer bowl. Cut the shortening into several small pieces and drop into the flour. Attach beater and bowl. Start at slow speed and stir until the lumps of flour-covered fat are the size of small peas and rice grains, about 1 minute. Add ice water, 1 tablespoon at a time, until the particles are moist. With the fingers gather them into a rough mass that is moist but not wet. Don't overmix.

■ FOOD
PROCESSOR
4 min.

Attach the metal blade and add the two flours, salt and shortening cut into several small pieces. Process with two or three short bursts, a total of about 4 seconds, or until the mixture resembles coarse meal. Stop the machine. Pulse the machine on and off, adding a tablespoonful of water each time. Stop as soon as dough comes together in a moist (not wet) mass.

REFRIGERATED
REST
4 hours or
longer

Wrap the ball of dough in plastic wrap or foil and place in the refrigerator to chill, 4 hours or longer.

ROLLING/
SHAPING

Beforehand, remove the dough from the refrigerator 1 hour before rolling or it will be stiff and difficult to work.

To shape for pan(s), see page 61.

BAKING   If the shell(s) is to be baked before filling, see page 61.
Times vary   If the shell(s) is to be filled before baking, follow
                 instructions for the specific pie recipe.

FINAL STEP   See specific pie recipe. If the pie is to be frozen, see
                 page 372.

LAYERED CRUST

Layered pie crust has its genesis in puff pastry, which is layer upon layer
of dough, butter, dough, butter—and on and on—building into several
hundred layers.

In this unusual long-flake crust, the chilled fat is dropped into the
flour in pieces the size of ½-inch marbles. Each piece is left whole.
Liquid is added, and the mixture is carefully tossed into a rough mass in
which the chunks of fat retain their identity. The ball of dough is chilled
and then rolled out into a rectangle. It is folded into three layers and
rolled again. This is done three times. Each time the fat gets thinner as
layer is piled on layer. The flattened and discrete pieces of fat can be
seen as irregular shapes beneath the thin film of dough.

In the oven, the pockets of moist fat puff out to create a flaky and
delicious crust. There is also a small portion of baking powder among
the ingredients to bolster the leavening action of the steam. The fat
mixture is one part butter or margarine and two parts lard or vegetable
shortening.

Once baked, this is a fairly fragile crust and should be used principally for small pies and turnovers. It is an excellent crust, too, for tarts,
tartlets and flans.

The layered crust is made in much the same way as Three-Minute
Puff Paste (page 168) is made for tarts and flans. The latter, however, is
made with butter rather than a blend of butter and lard or vegetable
shortening.

INGREDIENTS   *For one single 8- or 9-inch shell or approximately four
                 tartlet shells:*
                 3 tablespoons unsalted butter or margarine, room tem-
                     perature
                 6 tablespoons lard or vegetable shortening, room tem-
                     perature

                 1¼ cups pastry or all-purpose flour
                 ½ teaspoon salt

¼ teaspoon baking powder
½ teaspoon lemon juice or vinegar
3 tablespoons ice water, approximately

For one two-crust 8- or 9-inch pie:
6 tablespoons unsalted butter or margarine, room temperature
12 tablespoons (¾ cup) lard or vegetable shortening, room temperature

2½ cups pastry or all-purpose flour
1 teaspoon salt
½ teaspoon baking powder
1 teaspoon lemon juice or vinegar
6 tablespoons ice water, approximately

PIE PANS — Pans of choice, large or small.

PREPARATION — Beforehand, bring the two fats to room temperature. Cream together and shape into a ½-inch-thick rectangle. Wrap and chill before using, about 30 minutes.

● BY HAND
(only)

Special note: There is so little mixing involved in this recipe that I never use either the electric mixer or the food processor to make it. The cleanup of bowls, beaters and blades is simply not worth it. But, more important, it is easier to control the size of the pieces of chilled shortening when done by hand rather than by machine.

8 min.

Into a medium bowl sift the measured flour, salt and baking powder. Remove the block of fat from the refrigerator and score it into ¾-inch squares. Cut and drop into the flour. Stir to be certain all pieces are flour-covered.

Mix the lemon juice or vinegar with the chilled water and sprinkle 2 tablespoons, one at a time, over the flour-fat mixture. Each time gently toss the mixture with a fork. The mixture will vary in its ability to absorb water, so add the third tablespoon only if needed to hold together in a moist mass that can be lifted from the bowl without crumbling.

REFRIGERATED
REST
2 hours or
longer

Wrap the ball of dough in foil or wax paper and refrigerate to chill and relax the dough, 2 hours or longer.

LAYERING
3 min.

Remove the dough from the refrigerator. Lightly dust the work surface with flour. Roll dough into a rectangle, about ½ inch thick and 10 inches long.

TURNS
3 min.

Fold the dough into three layers, as with a letter. Turn the ends to 12 and 6 o'clock. Roll the dough into a rectangle. Repeat this twice more, or a total of three turns.

REFRIGERATED
REST
4 hours or
longer

Cover the rectangle and refrigerate for at least 4 hours or longer.

ROLLING/
SHAPING

To shape in pans, see page 61.

BAKING
Times vary

If the shell(s) is to be baked before filling, see page 61.
    If the shell(s) is to be filled before baking, follow the instructions for the specific pie recipe.

FINAL STEP

See specific pie recipe. If the pie is to be frozen, see page 372.

HALF-AND-HALF PIE CRUST

Pies with liquid fillings—custard, pumpkin or pecan, for example—should be baked in a crust that retains its crispness without a hint of sogginess. This is one of the special qualities this crust shares with tart and flan doughs for which this dough can be substituted.

Half-and-Half dough is half "sugar dough," which in itself is rich in sugar and eggs and is used for small tartlet shells, and half short-flake or mealy dough. The crust has the crispness reminiscent of a sugar cookie. For a pie with an already sweet filling, such as a pecan, the sugar in the dough can be reduced by half.

This recipe combines the two doughs into one and is the creation of Dominique D'Ermo, for many years executive pastry chef of the Americana Hotel at Bal Harbour, Florida, and now chef-owner of a Washington, D.C., restaurant. It is a short-flake dough in which the ingredients are creamed, so the shortening and liquid need not be chilled beforehand. The soft dough, of course, is refrigerated for rest and chilling after it is made and before it is rolled and pressed into pans.

INGREDIENTS

For one 8- or 9-inch shell or approximately four tartlet shells:

2 tablespoons unsalted butter, room temperature
4 tablespoons vegetable shortening, room temperature
2 tablespoons granulated sugar
¼ teaspoon salt
1¼ cups pastry or all-purpose flour
Pinch baking powder
2 tablespoons milk
½ teaspoon lemon juice

For one two-crust 8- or 9-inch pie:
¼ cup unsalted butter, room temperature
½ cup vegetable shortening, room temperature
¼ cup granulated sugar
½ teaspoon salt
2½ cups pastry or all-purpose flour
⅛ teaspoon baking powder
¼ cup milk
1 teaspoon lemon juice

PIE PAN(S)

Pans of choice, large or small.

PREPARATION

Working note: Beforehand have butter and vegetable shortening at room temperature, as they will be creamed together during preparation.

● BY HAND
8 min.

Into a medium bowl drop butter, shortening, sugar and salt. Stir with a wooden spoon until well blended and smooth (unlike medium-flake doughs, which are left in coarse particles). Add ½ cup flour and a pinch of baking powder. Follow with a portion of the milk and lemon juice. Stir to blend. Continue adding flour and milk alternately. The mixture will be smooth and soft but will stiffen when chilled.

▲ ELECTRIC
MIXER:
5 min.

Drop butter, shortening, sugar and salt into the mixer bowl. Beat with the flat blade until creamy. With beater turning, add ½ cup flour and pinch of baking powder. Add a portion of the milk and lemon juice. Stop the machine when the dough is smooth. It will be a soft mixture that will harden when chilled in the refrigerator.

■ FOOD
PROCESSOR:
3 min.

With the metal blade in place, add butter, shortening, sugar, salt, flour and baking powder. Blend with a short burst of power, about 4 seconds. With the processor running, pour 1 tablespoon milk and lemon juice through feed tube. Follow this with additional milk, 1, 2 or 3 tablespoons—or until the dough forms on top of the blade and is smooth.

REFRIGERATED
REST
4 hours or
longer

Wrap the dough in foil or plastic wrap and chill to relax for at least 4 hours before shaping.

ROLLING/
SHAPING

Beforehand, remove dough from the refrigerator 1 hour before rolling to make it less difficult to work.
    To shape in pans, see page 61.

BAKING
Times vary

If the shell is to be baked before it is filled, see page 61.
    If the shell(s) is to be filled before baking, follow instructions for the specific pie recipe.

FINAL STEP

See specific pie recipe. If the pie is to be frozen, see page 372.

HOT WATER PASTRY

The pastry maker is constantly admonished to keep the dough cool or chilled. It comes as a surprise, therefore, to find a crust recipe that begins by having you pour boiling water over lard or butter. The dough is later refrigerated, but nevertheless it begins life in hot water.

The effect of the hot water is to liquefy the lard or butter to make a short-flake dough (one without grainy particles). It has all the fine taste characteristics that come with either butter or lard, yet it achieves a solid crust that is particularly suited for soft fillings. A solid vegetable shortening can be used in this recipe, but it does not have the natural flavor of either butter or lard.

Many country cooks in the United States use lard, and a friend in southern France makes the same delicious crust with butter. I use both with marvelous results.

INGREDIENTS

For one 8- or 9-inch shell or approximately four tartlet shells:
6 tablespoons lard or butter, room temperature
3 tablespoons boiling water
1 cup pastry or all-purpose flour
¼ teaspoon baking powder
½ teaspoon salt

For one two-crust 8- or 9-inch pie:
12 tablespoons (¾ cup) lard or butter, room temperature
6 tablespoons boiling water
2 cups pastry or all-purpose flour
½ teaspoon baking powder
1 teaspoon salt

PIE PAN(S) Pans of choice, large or small.

PREPARATION Beforehand, place the preferred shortening in a medium bowl and pour hot water over it. With a fork, stir to a creamy consistency. Allow the liquid to cool until it feels tepid (no sensation) to the finger. Hot liquid in flour will harden the dough.

● BY HAND:
8 min.

Sift the flour, baking powder and salt onto a piece of wax paper from which to spoon the dry ingredients as needed. Sprinkle a spoonful of flour mix into the shortening and stir to blend. Continue with sprinkles of flour mix until the mixture becomes smooth, soft and moist and can be lifted from the bowl with the fingers. Dust with flour if sticky. The oiliness on the surface will disappear when the dough has been chilled.

▲ ELECTRIC
MIXER:
5 min.

Pour the melted shortening into the work bowl. Attach beater and bowl. Start the mixer at slow speed and pour in flour, a cupful at a time. Spoon in the final portion slowly so as not to add too much suddenly. Stop the machine and inspect dough; it should be moist, soft and smooth. Add sprinkles of flour if sticky. The oily appearance will disappear when dough is chilled.

■ FOOD
PROCESSOR:
3 min.

Working note: Reverse the order of ingredients.
    Attach the steel blade. Place the sifted flour, baking powder and salt in the work bowl.
    Pulse machine on/off while pouring melted shortening through the feed tube. Stop when liquid has been absorbed and dough is moist, smooth and soft. If sticky, add 1 or 2 teaspoons additional flour. Pulse to blend.

REFRIGERATED REST 4 hours or longer	Wrap the dough in plastic and put in refrigerator for at least 4 hours to chill and relax.
ROLLING/ SHAPING	Beforehand, remove dough from the refrigerator about 1 hour before needed or it may be too difficult to roll. To shape in pans, see page 61.
BAKING Times vary	If the shell(s) is to be baked before filling, see page 61. If the shell(s) is to be filled before baking, follow the instructions for the specific pie recipe.
FINAL STEP	See specific pie recipe. If the pie is to be frozen, see page 372.

NO-ROLL PIE CRUST

There is an economy of movement and space in this recipe as the dough is mixed in the pie pan and spread and patted into place with the fingers.

It seems almost too easy simply to stir oil into flour, after one has been accustomed to cutting in hard fat with a pastry cutter or a pair of knives. This is a short-flake or mealy crust that is especially good for liquid fillings because it has little porosity.

(If you wish to make this a covered pie, the top can be rolled between sheets of wax paper and lifted to the pan. Double the ingredients if a second crust is to be prepared.)

The last portion of the oil-milk liquid should be added slowly and carefully so that the dough is not suddenly overwhelmed with oil. Add only enough liquid to moisten the flour and hold it together. Too much oil weakens the crust.

Because of the unusual method of mixing the ingredients, this dough is usually prepared only in the pan(s) in which it is to be baked.

INGREDIENTS	*For one large 8- or 9-inch shell:* ½ cup oil—corn, peanut, soya or other 2 tablespoons milk 1½ cups pastry or all-purpose flour ½ teaspoon *each* salt and sugar
PIE PAN(S)	One 8- or 9-inch pie pan.

PREPARATION
15 min.

In a cup or small bowl whip together, with a fork, the oil and milk until they are blended and the oil is suspended in the milk.

Sift the flour, salt and sugar directly into the pie pan. Spread the flour mixture over the bottom of the pan. Pour about three-quarters of the liquid onto the flour and stir with a fork to mix. Carefully add oil 1 teaspoon at a time to be certain not to add too much. When the flour is barely moist, stop adding oil. Mix well with a fork.

Spread the moist dough over the bottom of the pan, pushing it toward the sides from the center with the fingertips. The dough will probably be thickest where the sides meet the bottom; thin this out with the fingertips, but don't rob the bottom as you push the dough up the sides. Try for a balanced spread.

If you choose to roll the dough, do so between sheets of wax paper. Tape two pieces together if the extra width is needed for a large crust. Wipe the table with a moist cloth to prevent the paper from slipping while you roll.

Place dough between sheets of wax paper and roll 2 inches larger than the inverted pie pan. It is helpful to lift the paper once or twice during the rolling process if the dough does not move freely under the paper. When finished, peel off the top paper.

The bottom paper makes it easy to invert and position the dough over the pan. Peel off paper.

REFRIGERATED
REST
1 hour or
longer

Chill the crust for 1 hour or longer.

BAKING
Times vary

If the shell(s) is to be baked before filling, see page 61.

If the shell(s) is to be filled before baking, follow instructions for the specific pie recipe.

FINAL STEP

See specific pie recipe. If the pie is to be frozen, see page 372.

ALL-RYE PIE CRUST

This rye crust made without wheat flour is not only an allergist's delight but a delicious surprise that offers a piquancy not found in many other doughs. It is faintly sour with a hint of cheese. Cottage cheese, yes, and butter or margarine. It can be used as a substitute for all crusts made with white flour, although it seems even more happily at home with a savory filling (a meat pie, for instance) or a *quiche*.

Scraps cut into small squares can be served as hors d'oeuvres that will puzzle and please the palate.

The ingredients are thoroughly blended and creamed into a short-flake dough which bakes into a solid and not very flaky crust. It is a fragile dough even when it is chilled, so rather than attempt to fit the unbaked crust on top for a covered pie, cut the top crust to shape, place it on a baking sheet and bake or partially bake it. Later, when the pie is filled, drop the top crust into place.

INGREDIENTS

For one single 8- or 9-inch shell or approximately four tartlet shells:
½ cup cornstarch
½ cup rye flour (not coarse or stone-ground)
½ teaspoon salt
½ cup dry cottage cheese
½ cup (1 stick) unsalted butter or margarine, room temperature
1 tablespoon milk, room temperature, if needed

For one two-crust 8- or 9-inch pie:
1 cup cornstarch
1 cup rye flour (not coarse or stone-ground)
1 teaspoon salt
1 cup dry cottage cheese
1 cup (2 sticks) unsalted butter or margarine, room temperature
2 tablespoons milk, room temperature, if needed

PIE PAN(S)

Pans of choice, large or small.

PREPARATION

Working note: If small-curd, dry cottage cheese is unavailable, squeeze the moisture out of regular cottage cheese through a piece of cheesecloth. Push the dry curds through a sieve to make fine.

6 min.	Place the cornstarch and rye flour in a flour sifter and sift at least four or five times.
● BY HAND: 10 min.	Sift the cornstarch, rye flour and salt into a medium bowl. Stir in the cottage cheese. Cut the butter or margarine (at room temperature) into several small pieces and add to the mixture. Stir with a wooden spoon or solid spatula to cream. If by chance the cottage cheese is too dry and the mixture is slow to cream, add a few drops of milk. The dough will be soft but will become firm when chilled.
▲ ELECTRIC MIXER: 7 min.	Sift the cornstarch, rye flour and salt into the work bowl. Drop in the cottage cheese. Attach bowl and beater and mix to blend at slow speed. Add the butter or margarine (at room temperature) and stir to cream. If the mixture is slow to cream, add a teaspoon or two of milk. The dough will be soft and moist but will become firm when chilled.
■ FOOD PROCESSOR: 3 min.	Attach the steel blade and pour the sifted cornstarch and flour into the work bowl. Add salt. Drop in the cottage cheese and blend with two or three short bursts of power. Cut the butter or margarine into several small pieces (about six to a stick) and add to the mixture. Process for about 15 seconds, or until well blended.
REFRIGERATED REST 2 hours or longer	Wrap the dough in foil or plastic and place in the refrigerator to chill for at least 2 hours or overnight.
ROLLING/ SHAPING	Beforehand, remove dough from the refrigerator 1 hour before rolling or it will be difficult to work. This dough rolls best between two sheets of wax paper. To shape for pie pan(s), see page 61.
BAKING Times vary	If the shell(s) is to be baked before filling, see page 61. If the shell(s) is to be filled before baking, follow instructions for the specific pie recipe.
FINAL STEP	See specific pie recipe. If the pie is to be frozen, see page 372.

CRUMB CRUST

Before there can be a crumb crust there must be a crumb that began life as part of a graham cracker, a piece of zweiback, a gingersnap or perhaps a vanilla or chocolate wafer. Crumb crust is the easiest crust to make because most of the baking has already been done. The crust goes into the oven for a few minutes, not to bake the crumbs again but to allow them to absorb wholly the hot butter or margarine. When the crust cools, the crumbs will have been baked into place.

Although crumb crusts can also simply be chilled before filling, the briefly baked crumb crust is less fragile. It also tastes more buttery.

A crumb crust is a fine vehicle for many delicious fillings—velvety creams, fluffy chiffon, fruit and ice cream. Almost any crumbs can be made into a crust, but high on the preferred list are those made with graham crackers, gingersnaps, vanilla or chocolate wafers, corn flakes, rusks and zweiback.

INGREDIENTS	*For one 8- or 9-inch shell or an assortment of smaller ones:* 1½ cups (6 ounces) fine crumbs ½ cup granulated sugar ½ cup butter or margarine, melted
PIE PAN(S)	One medium or large pie pan or an assortment of smaller tins.
PREPARATION	*Working note:* Reserve a quarter of the prepared crumbs for topping after the shell is filled, if desired.
6 min.	Into a medium bowl measure the crumbs and sugar. Melt the butter and slowly pour into the crumb-sugar mixture while stirring with a fork.
SHAPING 5 min.	Pour the crumb mixture into the pie plate(s). Press it firmly against the bottom and sides of the pan with the back of a large spoon. Another pie pan may be fitted down into the crumbs to help shape the crust. Do so with care.
REFRIGERATED REST 1 hour or longer	Chill in the refrigerator for 1 hour or longer. Preheat oven to 400° F.

BAKING 400° F. 5 min.	To prevent the butter-rich crumbs from scorching, carefully fit a piece of aluminum foil over the crust. Do not fill it with weights, however. The bright foil will reflect and moderate the heat on the inside of the crust. Bake on the middle shelf of the hot oven for 5 minutes. Watch carefully so that the edges and bottom do not burn. Lift the foil and check progress after 3 minutes.
FINAL STEP	Place the shell on a rack to cool before filling. It will stiffen as it cools.

VARIATIONS

Nut Crumb Crust

Ground almonds or chopped Brazil nuts (1½ cups) mixed with 1 beaten egg white and ¼ cup granulated sugar make an excellent crust for a butterscotch or chocolate chiffon pie. Bake at 375° F. for 5 minutes.

Coconut Flake Crust

An exceptional crumb-type crust is made with 2 cups coconut flakes patted and pressed against the side of a pie pan that has been spread with 3 tablespoons butter or margarine. Bake in a 350° F. oven 20 to 30 minutes, or until golden brown. It is a fitting case for a lovely coconut cream filling.

The Filling

TRADITIONAL APPLE PIE

[ONE 8- OR 9-INCH TWO-CRUST PIE]

Famous though it is, there is no one recipe for apple pie, no national recipe. It can be made in almost as many ways as there are American pie bakers.

This one is traditional (one of many, of course), but apple pies are also made with a sprinkling of nuts and raisins, mixed with green tomato slices, topped with syrup, scattered with streusel, seasoned with Chinese five spices, fennel, orange or lemon—and on and on. Some are called Dutch; others, French. Some apple pies are made with a full top crust.

Some are made with none, and others have strips of dough laid in lattice fashion over the apples. Some are deep-dish; some are not. While some recipes call for the apples to be partially cooked before hand in seasoned juice, this recipe is for the thinly sliced apples to go uncooked into the shell.

Apple pies are best when made with a tart apple such as a Rhode Island Greening, Rome Beauty, Jonathan or Baldwin, but they are almost as good made with Golden Delicious, which the markets carry most months of the year. The orchardist in your region harvests a variety of apples. Ask him to suggest his best pie apple and then lay by a half bushel to have weeks and months of delicious pie eating ahead.

SUGGESTED CRUST	The Basic, Whole Wheat or Hot Water (pages 69–82)
INGREDIENTS	Pastry for two-crust pie

Filling (double amounts for two pies):
4 cups thinly sliced tart apples (about 5 large apples)
½ to 1 cup granulated sugar
1 to 2 tablespoons quick-cooking tapioca or cornstarch
¼ teaspoon salt
½ teaspoon cinnamon, optional
1 teaspoon lemon peel, grated or chopped fine
1 teaspoon lemon juice

2 tablespoons butter, to dot
1 tablespoon cream or milk, to brush
1 tablespoon granulated sugar, to sprinkle

PIE PAN	One pie pan of choice.
PREPARATION	*Crust:*

Prepare bottom crust according to instructions, page 64. Top crust may also be rolled in advance and covered with plastic wrap to prevent it from drying.

Filling:
Working note: Very tart apples may require the larger amount of sugar, and very juicy ones may call for the larger amount of tapioca or cornstarch.

25 min.   Peel, core and slice apples into a medium bowl. Stir in sugar, tapioca, salt, cinnamon, lemon peel and lemon juice. Let stand for 15 minutes. Arrange a row of slices around the outer edge of the bottom crust. Put down other rows in concentric circles. Pile remaining slices

over the rows, building the center higher than the sides. Pour lemon juice over the slices. Dot with butter.

Preheat oven to 425° F.

5 min.

Roll out the top crust, if it has not been prepared earlier. Cut a decorative pattern to allow steam to escape. (This may be cut after the crust is on the pie.)

Trim and moisten the edge of the bottom crust with water or beaten egg white to seal the crusts together.

Fold the top crust in half and carefully lay it in place over the apple filling. Seal edges between the fingers. Crimp with a fork or pie crimper.

BAKING
425° F.
15 min.
375° F.
35 min.

Place pie on the lower shelf of the hot oven. After 15 minutes reduce heat to 375° F. and continue baking for 35 additional minutes, or until juice bubbles from the center vent cuts. Five minutes before the pie is finished baking, brush the top with cream or milk and sprinkle with sugar.

FINAL STEP

Remove from the oven and place on a rack to cool. Serve warm or at room temperature. Cheddar cheese and ice cream are traditional as well as inspired accompaniments.

VARIATIONS

Dutch Apple
Make large slits in the top crust, and 5 minutes before the pie is completely baked, pour ½ cup heavy cream through the openings. Bake 5 more minutes.

French Apple:
Omit the top crust and top with a crumb or streusel mixture made with ¼ cup brown sugar, ½ cup flour and ⅓ cup butter or margarine. Mix till crumbly. Increase baking time 10 minutes.

Cheese Surprise:
After half of apples have been spread in the pan, cover with thin slices of Cheddar cheese and top with remaining apples. Bake and serve warm.

LATTICE-TOP CHERRY PIE

[ONE 8- OR 9-INCH TWO-CRUST PIE]

There are several reasons why a cherry pie to me is the epitome of fine pie making. It is a much prized fruit in my small orchard, for I am always doing battle with the robins for its possession. It is the first pastry my bride made, and it was served and received with love. It has remained a good-natured token of our affection for four decades.

Cherry pie, juicy and packed with fruit, is delicious. It has just the right combination of tang and sweetness. And the color is so right. It is a mockery to serve a pie professing to be cherry in which cherries, suspended in a red thickening, are too few even to touch skins.

This is a big cherry pie filled with lots of cherries. It will bubble and gurgle in the oven, and it may even run over the sides now and then, but it will all be done in the name of love and good eating.

I like to bake the fruit filling partially before it goes into the unbaked or partially baked shell. My mentor on this has been an Indiana farm woman, Arnola Beck, whose lovely fruit pies I have had the good fortune to eat for more than four decades. She cooks—but never overcooks—the fruit for all pies beforehand. The pie with a precooked filling needs to be in the oven about one-third less time. The filling bubbles through the center holes, but the pie is immediately taken out before the juice has a chance to drip over the sides and down into the oven.

Arnola's precooked Montmorency cherry filling is used in this recipe.

The pie can be made with fresh or frozen fruit, or with canned cherries. The latter takes an extra step in preparation; see below.

For frozen cherries, I prefer the fruit that is packaged loosely rather than compressed into a box. Partially thaw to allow all the fruit to separate, and then prepare.

This recipe can also be used for other berry pies—gooseberry, currant, blackberry, raspberry, strawberry, blueberry, huckleberry or loganberry. Half a teaspoon of cinnamon may be added to the ingredients rather than lemon juice. The pie can also be made with a full crust rather than with lattice strips, which I like because they show off the handsome fruit underneath.

SUGGESTED CRUST	The Basic, Half-and-Half or Whole Wheat–Oat Flour (pages 69–80).
INGREDIENTS	Pastry for two-crust pie

Filling (double amounts for two pies):
4 cups fresh or frozen tart cherries, pitted
   (*or* 2 16-ounce cans tart cherries, pitted)
1 to 1½ cups granulated sugar
3 tablespoons quick-cooking tapioca
   (*or* 3 tablespoons cornstarch, if cherries are canned)
½ teaspoon lemon juice
¼ teaspoon salt
⅛ teaspoon almond extract

1½ tablespoons butter, to dot
1 tablespoon granulated sugar, to sprinkle

PIE PAN   One pie pan of choice.

PREPARATION   *Crust:*
Prepare bottom crust according to instructions, page 64. Top crust may be rolled in advance and lattice pieces cut. They should be covered with plastic wrap or wax paper to keep them from drying.

5 min.   *Filling:*
Fresh or partially thawed cherries: Place the pitted cherries in a large bowl; stir in 1 cup sugar, tapioca, lemon juice, salt and almond extract. Taste the mixture. Add sugar if desired. Set aside for 30 minutes.

    To partially cook the cherries before they are put into the shell and thereby reduce the time the fruit filling needs to cook *inside* the shell, put the fruit in a medium saucepan and place over heat. Cover. Within 3 or 4 minutes the cherries will have given off considerable juice. Remove from heat. In a small bowl mix sugar, tapioca, salt and almond extract. Pour this into the hot cherries. Stir to blend. Add the lemon juice. Place over low heat and cook until thickened, about 3 minutes. Allow the cherry filling to cool before pouring into the pie shell.

    Working note: If, after the cherry filling has cooled, it is too thick, add several tablespoons of water; if too thin, add cornstarch. Also, if the cherries have been picked before they have reached full color, you may wish to add a few drops of red coloring.

10 min.   *Canned cherries:* Drain the canned cherries into a medium saucepan. Set aside for a few minutes while the liquid is prepared. Stir 1 cup sugar, cornstarch, lemon

juice, salt and almond extract into the drained juices. Bring the liquid to a boil over medium heat. Stir constantly while it thickens. Remove from the heat and combine with the reserved cherries.

Preheat oven to 400° F.

ASSEMBLY
15 min.

Pour the cherry mixture into the prepared crust. Dot with butter.

Roll the remaining dough into a rough rectangle, ⅛ inch thick and long enough to provide lattice strips to cross the pie. Cut six or eight strips ½ inch wide with a pastry cutter or sharp knife. A pastry cutter with a special blade, called a jagger, cuts an attractive lattice strip. Arrange strips in a latticework pattern, weaving over and under, if desired. Strips may be twisted when laid down. Moisten the edge of the bottom crust. Pinch ends to seal. Strips may also be pressed around the edge of the pan and over the ends of the crossed lattice pieces. Flute edge of crust (see "Edges," page 65). Sprinkle lattice with sugar.

BAKING
400° F.
15 min.
350° F.
40 min.

Place the pie on the lower shelf of the hot oven for 15 minutes. Reduce heat to 350° F. and move pie to the middle shelf to continue baking until filling in center of pie is hot and bubbling, about 40 minutes more. If edges should brown too rapidly, cover with a narrow strip of foil.

Because cherry pies are notorious for bubbling over the sides of the pan, it is wise to place a length of foil on the shelf below to catch any spills.

FINAL STEP

Remove from the oven and place on a rack to cool. This pie freezes well.

VARIATION

Orange-Glazed Cherry Pie
When the crust is being prepared, include among the ingredients 1½ teaspoons finely shredded orange peel. When the lattice-covered pie comes hot from the oven, spoon orange glaze over the center and garnish with a twisted orange slice. Glaze: Blend ½ cup confectioners' sugar, 2 teaspoons finely shredded orange peel and 1 tablespoon orange juice. Tangy!

RHUBARB PIE

[ONE 8- OR 9-INCH TWO-CRUST PIE]

A familiar sight on many farms and in small towns at the turn of the century was clumps of green leafy rhubarb growing on the south side of the woodshed, where the warm sun would encourage early spring growth. Pulling rhubarb still remains one of the rites of spring in rural America, like soda tablets and sassafras tea. Rhubarb is pulled with a satisfying "pop" when it lets go, and the long stalk comes cleanly out of the ground.

Both the flavor and the color are in the skin, so don't peel it off. Later in the summer it may get tough and stringy. Then be more selective—search for the new, slender stalks.

A bite of rhubarb taken blindfolded would send up all the colors of the rainbow, with a tangy ZOW at the end. Yet to look at it—a warm green! There is some red in mine (Stark's Valentine), and I strengthen this with two or three drops of red coloring.

Rhubarb is mostly water (95 percent) and contains a healthy portion of vitamin A, calcium and potassium. It has very few calories—16 for each 3½-ounce serving. It is the sugar to sweeten it that boosts the calorie count of the pie.

Although rhubarb is a vegetable, a member of the buckwheat family, a court of law in 1947 reclassified it as a fruit to reduce the export duty on stalks brought in from Canada.

The words alone—*rhubarb* or *pieplant*—simply do not have the power to raise under the tongue of the uninitiated the tingling sensation that comes when one thinks about a slice of one of America's best pies and England's best tarts.

SUGGESTED CRUST	The Basic, Whole Wheat or Half-and-Half (pages 69–80).
INGREDIENTS	Pastry for two-crust pie

Filling
1½ pounds fresh rhubarb
1¼ cups granulated sugar
⅓ cup all-purpose flour
1 teaspoon grated orange peel or zest
½ cup orange juice

2 tablespoons butter or margarine, to dot
¼ cup granulated sugar, to sprinkle

PIE PAN	One pie pan of choice.
PREPARATION	*Crust:* Prepare bottom crust according to instructions, page 64. Top crust may be rolled in advance and, if desired, lattice strips cut. They should be covered with plastic wrap or wax paper to keep them from drying out.
6 min.	*Filling:* Cut the long stalks of rhubarb into ½-inch or smaller pieces (4 cups). (It takes only seconds to push a cluster of stalks through the slicing blade of a food processor.) Stir together the sugar, flour and orange peel in a small bowl. Pour the orange juice over the rhubarb pieces. Preheat oven to 425° F.
ASSEMBLY	Spread half the rhubarb pieces over the crust; sprinkle with half the sugar mixture. Repeat with the remaining rhubarb and sugar. Dot with butter. Roll out the remaining dough into a circle slightly larger than the diameter of the pan. Cut decorative slits in the dough. Fold to move, or roll onto a rolling pin to carry. Dampen the edge of the lower crust with moisture from the pie or with water. Cover pie with top crust. Seal with the fingers. Flute a decorative edge between forefingers or with a fork (see "Edges," page 65). Sprinkle sugar over the crust.
BAKING 425° F. 15 min. 375° F. 45–50 min.	Place the pie on the lower shelf of the hot oven. Reduce heat after 15 minutes to 375° F. and continue baking for 45 to 50 minutes. If crust edge browns excessively during the later part of the baking period, wrap a length of 3-inch-wide foil around the edge to protect it. Bake until the crust is brown and juices begin to bubble through the slits in the crust, about 1 hour.
FINAL STEP	Remove from the oven and place on a rack to cool. Ideally, rhubarb pie should be served slightly warm and perhaps topped with a small scoop of ice cream or a large dab of whipped cream. Spring is here!

VARIATIONS

Pear-Rhubarb Pie:
Place a layer of chunked pear halves over the bottom layer of rhubarb. Repeat with remaining pieces of rhubarb and pears and sugar before adding the top crust. Serve warm, topped with ice cream.

Rhubarb Tart or Flan:
To use as a delicious filling in tarts or flans as well as tartlets, see page 330.

SHAKER LEMON PIE

[ONE 8- OR 9-INCH TWO-CRUST PIE]

There is something especially refreshing, and a bit surprising, when biting into a wedge of lemon pie and actually finding a slice of lemon. Too often the lemon filling is bland, without the zest and tang of the real thing. Not this one, which contains three lemons sliced paper-thin. There are few recipes with so few ingredients. This fact is worth noting.

This pie is part of the Shaker tradition of fine food in evidence in the restored village of Shakertown, near Harrodsburg, Kentucky. Founded in 1805, it was a thriving colony of 500 industrious but celibate persons, the last of whom was gone by the mid-1920's. The simple goodness of their food was known all over the region, as was their ability to craft furniture.

The crust suggested is from Kentucky, too—one of Mrs. Crosier's Perfect Pie Crusts as detailed under the Basic Crust.

SUGGESTED CRUST	The Basic, Layered or Half-and-Half (pages 69–80)
INGREDIENTS	Pastry for two-crust pie
	Filling 3 lemons, sliced paper-thin 2 cups granulated sugar 4 eggs, beaten
PIE PAN	One pie pan of choice.
PREPARATION	*Crust:* Prepare bottom crust beforehand according to instructions, page 64. Top crust may be rolled in advance.

Cover with plastic wrap or wax paper to keep from drying.

Filling:
Working note: An extremely sharp knife is a necessity. Try slicing lemons on an old-fashioned slaw cutter (adjustable) or a somewhat similar French device, a mandoline. The slicing blade of a food processor cuts too thick, but the steel blade can do small bits. I often slice two lemons by hand, then process the third (and the hard-to-cut ends of the others) and mix them together.

8 min.

Slice the lemons on a cutting board placed over a large bowl, to catch the juice. Place the slices and the juice in the bowl and pour in the sugar. Mix well and let stand for 2 hours or more.
Preheat the oven to 425° F.

ASSEMBLY

Beat the eggs together, add the sugared lemons and stir together. Pour or spoon the filling into the prepared pie shell.
Roll the crust for the top slightly larger than the pie pan. Cut decorative vents in the crust to allow the steam to escape.
Moisten the rim of the crust with water or juice from the mixture. A finger does nicely as a brush. Carefully lift the top crust and place it over the filling. Press gently but firmly to seal. Make a decorative trim or fluting with the fingers or the tines of a fork to further secure the edges.

BAKING
425° F.
15 min.
350° F.
40 min.

Place pie on the lower shelf of the hot oven. After 15 minutes reduce heat to 350° F. and continue baking for about 40 minutes, or until the crust is a light golden brown and juices bubble through the vents. Insert a silver knife through a slit in the crust to test the custard. If the knife comes out clean, the pie is done.

FINAL STEP

Place on a rack to cool. The aroma of this pie baking and cooling in the kitchen is, in itself, worth the doing.

RHUBARB-STRAWBERRY PIE

[ONE 8- OR 9-INCH TWO-CRUST PIE]

Strawberries and rhubarb, joined with orange juice and bits of orange peel, seem improbable companions in anything as delicious as this pie. It takes the first bite, followed by the second, for one to be wholly reassured that, yes, the burst of flavor on the tongue did indeed come from this happy combination.

When the rhubarb is stirred with the fruit and juices, the colorful mixture has the appearance and the bouquet of an enticing fruit salad. Forbear for an hour or so. The rhubarb bits must first be baked.

In the springtime when the rhubarb (or pieplant) stalks are slender and fresh-sprung from the earth, they are at their best. Later in the summer, if the stalks are tough or stringy, peel away the outer skin. The vegetable/fruit freezes well for a surprise midwinter delight.

SUGGESTED CRUST	The Basic, Hot Water or Whole Wheat (pages 69–82).
INGREDIENTS	Pastry for two-crust pie
	Filling (double amounts for two pies):
	1½ pounds (4 cups) fresh rhubarb
	2 cups (1 pint) fresh strawberries
	1¼ cups granulated sugar
	⅓ cup orange juice
	2 teaspoons grated or freshly chopped orange peel
	2 tablespoons quick-cooking tapioca
	½ teaspoon salt
	2 tablespoons unsalted (sweet) butter, to dot
	2 tablespoons granulated sugar, to sprinkle
PIE PAN	One pie pan of choice.
PREPARATION	*Crust:* Prepare bottom crust beforehand according to instructions, page 64. Top crust may be rolled in advance and, if desired, lattice strips cut. Cover with plastic wrap or wax paper to keep from drying.
10 min.	*Filling:* Cut rhubarb into ½-inch pieces, and strawberries in half.

20 min.

In a bowl combine the rhubarb and strawberries, and add sugar, orange juice and peel or zest, tapioca and salt. Let stand for 20 minutes while pastry is shaped.
Preheat oven to 425° F.

ASSEMBLY

Spoon the rhubarb mixture into the pie shell, higher in the center than on the sides. Dot with butter.

Roll remaining dough into a rectangle about 11 inches long, the length of the longest lattice piece you will need.

Cut the rectangle into six or eight strips about ½ inch wide. This can be done with a knife or pastry cutter. An attractive cut can be made with a jagger wheel.

Brush the edge of the crust with water to secure the strips when they are laid on.

These long pieces are fragile, so slip a narrow spatula under each as you lift and position it on the pie.

Crimp the edge into a decorative trim or, if sufficient long strips remain unused, twist and lay them around the edge. This will give a handsome layered look to the pie when it is baked.

Sprinkle 2 tablespoons granulated sugar over the lattice top.

BAKING
425° F.
20 min.
375° F.
35–40 min.

Place the pie on the lower shelf of the hot oven. After 20 minutes reduce heat to 375° F. and continue baking for another 35 or 40 minutes, or until the crust is brown and flaky and juices bubble through lattice openings, about 1 hour.

FINAL STEP

Cool on a wire rack. This pie freezes especially well.

VARIATIONS

There are many combinations of fruit that might strike one as improbable pie mates, but after sampling many pies I find these two hold true: one-third gooseberry and two-thirds strawberry, or half cherry and half rhubarb.

BLACKBERRY PIE

[ONE 8- OR 9-INCH TWO-CRUST PIE]

The words *berry pie* mean something special in taste as well as in color —a slash of deep red or purple across a golden crust. Or a vivid and delicious blend of a pie wedge and a pouring of thick country cream.

One of the choice berries is the blackberry, but this has not always been so. Until the middle of the last century the blackberry was frowned upon as a weed, and it was only after it was cultivated for its supposed medicinal qualities that the scrawny fruit started to swell and blossom into the luscious fat berry it is today.

Two crusts are recommended. I especially like blackberry filling poured into a whole wheat crust, but because it is dark brown much of the visual effect of purple against gold is lost. The good taste of both the whole wheat crust and the berries more than compensates for the loss, however. For a dramatic appearance—The Basic Crust.

SUGGESTED CRUST	(See above.) Whole Wheat or The Basic (pages 69–74).
INGREDIENTS	Pastry for two-crust pie
	Filling (double amounts for two pies): 2½ tablespoons cornstarch 1 cup sugar 3 cups fresh or 1 12-ounce package frozen blackberries 1 tablespoon lemon juice
	1 tablespoon butter, to dot 1 tablespoon granulated sugar, to sprinkle
PIE PAN	One pie pan of choice.
PREPARATION	*Crust:* Prepare bottom crust beforehand according to instructions, page 64. Top crust may be rolled in advance and, if desired, lattice strips cut. Cover with plastic wrap or wax paper to keep from drying.
20 min.	*Filling:* In a medium bowl mix cornstarch and sugar. Drop in the berries and stir to coat fruit. Sprinkle lemon juice over the mixture and allow to stand for 15 minutes. Be certain berries are separated and not frozen together

before spooning them into the pie shell. Dot with butter.

Preheat oven to 425° F.

Roll out the top crust, if it has not been prepared earlier. Cut a decorative pattern to allow steam to escape. (This may be cut after the crust is on the pie.)

Trim and moisten the edge of the bottom crust. Fold the top crust in half and carefully lay it in place. Seal edges between the fingers. Crimp, if necessary, with a fork or pie crimper. Sprinkle sugar over the crust.

BAKING
425° F.
15 min.
375° F.
40–50 min.

Place the pie on the lower shelf of the hot oven. After 15 minutes reduce heat to 375° F. and continue baking for an additional 40 to 50 minutes. If crust edge browns excessively during the later part of the baking period, wrap a length of 3-inch-wide foil around the edge to protect it. Bake until the crust is brown and flaky and juices begin to bubble through slits in the crust, about 1 hour.

FINAL STEP

Remove from the oven and place on a rack to cool. Serve warm with a scoop of ice cream or a pouring of thick or whipped cream.

VARIATIONS

Every berry can be made into a delicious pie with this simple-to-make recipe—red and black raspberries (also known as black caps), currants, gooseberries, huckleberries, blueberries and loganberries. Strawberries carry the berry name, but they have different qualities and are not included here.

GLAZED STRAWBERRY PIE

[ONE 8- OR 9-INCH SINGLE-CRUST PIE]

The striking thing about this strawberry pie is the peaks of red berries rising above the deep glaze of the crushed fruit—and the topping of whipped cream. It is as delicious as it is handsome.

A measure of its appeal is the pie's effect on my wife. It is her favorite. Absolutely. Normally she is an unselfish woman, but when this pie is in the house she will not share it with the neighbors as we do every other pie. I have not yet accused her of marrying into the family to get my mother's recipe, which this is. Someday I may.

I have added a step not in the original recipe—a layer of cream cheese thinned with strawberry juice and spread over the crust before the filling goes in.

Both mashing the berries for the glaze and blending some of the puree with the cream cheese are great jobs for a food processor.

SUGGESTED CRUST

Half-and-Half or Crumb (pages 78–87).

INGREDIENTS

Pastry for one-crust pie, to be baked beforehand

Filling (double amounts for two pies):
1 quart strawberries, hulled
1 cup granulated sugar
2 tablespoons cornstarch
¼ cup water
1 tablespoon butter
2 or 3 drops red coloring, if needed
3 ounces cream cheese

Whipped cream, optional

PIE PAN

One pie pan of choice.

PREPARATION

Crust:
Prepare and bake single crust beforehand according to instructions, page 62.

Filling:

15 min.

Wash and hull berries.

Select about twenty-five to thirty strawberries to be placed later on the crust, large end down. (The remainder are to be mashed or pureed and cooked into a thick glaze or filling.)

Put the choice berries aside. In the food processor (or by hand with a food chopper) puree the remaining berries, about 1½ cups.

Place the strawberry puree in a saucepan. Heat slowly to a boil. Add sugar. Mix cornstarch and ¼ cup water into a smooth paste in a small bowl and add to the strawberry-sugar mixture.

5–8 min.

Allow to cook to the clear stage, bubbling slowly, over medium heat for about 5 to 8 minutes. Stir frequently so that the mixture doesn't stick to the pan. Remove from heat. Add butter, and drops of red coloring if the mixture needs brightening. Set aside.

ASSEMBLY
5 min.

In the food processor place the cream cheese and 1 tablespoon of the cooked puree. Blend with the steel blade until the mixture is smooth, about two bursts. If you do this by hand, mash the cream cheese in a small bowl and mix in the cooked puree. Stir until well blended. Spread cream cheese mixture over the pie crust and arrange berries in a design with the largest fruit in the center, the smaller berries around the sides.

Spoon the cooked glaze over the berries.

FINAL STEP

When the glaze has cooled somewhat, in 15 or 20 minutes, place pie in the refrigerator to chill before topping with whipped cream and serving.

VARIATIONS

Black and red raspberries (in that order) are high on my list of preferred glazed pies, but other berries assembled in the same manner, notably blueberries and blackberries, are very close behind.

All these berries, plus the strawberry, of course, make outstanding flans, tarts and tartlets.

MINCE PIE

[ONE 8- OR 9-INCH TWO-CRUST PIE]

A Thanksgiving or Christmas feast is really not a feast without a mince pie waiting on the sideboard to be cut. When the meat in the mincemeat is venison, it becomes very special indeed. But then not everyone has a friend like Charley Hardy, who hunts with a bow in the Hoosier National Forest. He supplies the meat. I supply the pies.

This is an excellent mincemeat recipe. If you do not have a hunter in the woods, substitute an equal amount of lean rump of beef.

The English mince pie, a great British Yuletide favorite, is not made with meat. It is much like our mock mincemeat, which includes, among other things, green tomato slices.

Mince pie is not an impulse item unless a can of mincemeat at the grocer's strikes your fancy. Homemade mincemeat should be aged three weeks to a month before it is used.

Canned or frozen, mincemeat will keep for many months. This recipe may be changed in quantity to fit the need. Ingredients may be substituted to fit personal taste and preference.

SUGGESTED
CRUST

First choice is The Basic Pie Crust made with lard or with vegetable shortening, or Whole Wheat (pages 69–74).

INGREDIENTS

Pastry for two-crust pie

Filling (makes 3 quarts for 3 pies):
1½ pounds venison or rump of beef
½ pound suet
4 pounds tart apples, unpeeled, cored and finely chopped
1 pint (2 cups) sweet cider
2½ pounds granulated sugar
1 tablespoon *each* cinnamon and nutmeg
1½ teaspoons *each* salt, allspice, and mace
¼ teaspoon white pepper
1 pound *each* raisins and currants
¼ pound *each* candied citron, orange peel and lemon peel
1 tablespoon pitted and chopped olives
1 quart Sherry
1 pint brandy

PIE PAN

One pie pan of choice.

PREPARATION

Filling:
This should be done days, if not weeks, in advance to give it time to age. Mincemeat purchased in the store can immediately be made into pie.

1½ hours

Place venison in a saucepan. Cover with water and boil over medium heat until tender, about 30 to 40 minutes. Leave the meat in the water to cool. Cut venison and suet into pieces that can be fed through a food chopper. Use the finest blade. Place the ground meat in a large bowl and mix in the unpeeled but cored and finely chopped apples.

Pour cider and sugar into a large pan and bring to a boil. Add the ground venison and apples, and return to a boil. Reduce to a simmer and cook for 5 minutes.

Remove from heat and add the spices: cinnamon, nutmeg, salt, allspice, mace and white pepper. (It may be convenient to measure them together onto a piece of wax paper and pour into the hot mixture at one time.)

Measure in the raisins, currants, candied citron, orange and lemon peel and chopped olives.

Add Sherry and brandy. Stir mincemeat to blend.

AGING
3–4 weeks

Pour the mincemeat into sterilized jars, cover tightly and keep in a cool place.

Shake or stir the mincemeat daily for three weeks. The mincemeat may also be kept in a crock, covered with plastic wrap stretched over the top.

Working note: On baking day prepare dough for a covered pie, page 64.

ASSEMBLY
10 min.

Fill the shell to the top with mincemeat. Roll the second piece of dough into a circle ⅛ inch thick for the top crust, or cut into strips for a latticework of pastry.

Preheat oven to 400° F.

Moisten the edge of the lower crust. Place top crust over filling. Pinch the upper and lower crusts together to seal. Or interweave strips of dough in a latticework pattern. Press ends tightly to bottom crust to secure. Flute edge of crust (see "Edges," page 65).

BAKING
400° F.
40–50 min.

Place pie on the lower rack of the hot oven. Pie is baked when the filling in the center is hot and bubbles through the vent holes or around the lattice strips, about 40 to 50 minutes.

FINAL STEP

Place pie on a rack to cool.

Freezing the extra supply of mincemeat in several containers is the easiest way to store it for later use.

VARIATION

Mock Mince Pie:
No aging is needed for this filling in which there is no meat: In a saucepan mix 1½ cups chopped raisins and 4 tart apples or green tomatoes (or both), sliced. Blend with the grated rind and juice of 1 orange and ½ cup cider or other fruit juice. Cover and simmer until apples and/or tomatoes are soft. Stir in ¾ cup sugar, ½ teaspoon *each* cinnamon and cloves and 2 tablespoons crushed soda crackers. Add 1 to 2 tablespoons brandy, if desired.

CHOCOLATE PIE

[ONE 8- OR 9-INCH SINGLE-CRUST PIE]

This pie is for chocolate lovers. Nothing is understated here. The squares of unsweetened or bitter chocolate assert themselves without reservation.

Layered dough, suggested here, rolled out and folded three times, is unusual for pie crust which normally demands almost no movement at all before placing in the pan.

SUGGESTED CRUST	Layered, Crumb or Half-and-Half (pages 76–87).
INGREDIENTS	Pastry for one-crust pie, to be baked beforehand *Filling:* 3 egg yolks (reserve whites for meringue) 1½ tablespoons cornstarch ¾ cup granulated sugar 1½ cups milk ¼ teaspoon salt 1 tablespoon butter 2 squares (2 ounces) unsweetened chocolate 1 teaspoon vanilla extract *Meringue:* 3 egg whites ½ teaspoon salt Pinch cream of tartar 6 tablespoons granulated sugar
PIE PAN	One pie pan of choice.
PREPARATION	*Crust:* Prepare and bake single crust beforehand according to instructions, page 62.
4 min.	*Filling:* In a saucepan beat the egg yolks and mix in cornstarch and sugar. Stir in milk, salt and butter.
COOKING Medium heat 5–6 min.	Cook slowly over medium heat, stirring constantly, about 5 to 6 minutes. Break or grate the chocolate squares into a dozen small pieces and drop into the

bubbling mixture until melted and blended. Stir in vanilla.

CHILLING
2 hours or
overnight

Place plastic wrap against the surface of the chocolate filling so that a film will not form as it cools. Refrigerate.

4 min.

Meringue:
Beat egg whites, adding salt and pinch of cream of tartar, until a soft peak forms when the beater is lifted. While the beater is turning, pour in sugar a tablespoonful at a time—6 tablespoons for 3 egg whites—until meringue is thick and stands in a firm, glossy peak, about 1 minute. Put aside for a few moments.
Preheat oven to 375° F.

ASSEMBLY
5 min.

Spoon chilled filling into cooled pie shell. Spoon meringue over the filling, making sure it touches the crust edge at all points so that the meringue will not shrink in the oven's heat. Do not smooth meringue into a flat slab—leave it in swirls and small mountain peaks to give it a lush, decorative look.

BAKING
375° F.
10–12 min.

Place meringue-covered pie on the middle shelf of the 375° F. oven for 10 to 12 minutes, or until it is delicately browned.

FINAL STEP

Cool and refrigerate for 1 or 2 hours before serving.

VARIATIONS

Vanilla Cream Pie:
Omit chocolate.

Banana Cream Pie:
Omit chocolate. Cool filling to room temperature with plastic wrap placed across the surface to prevent a skin from forming. Slice two medium bananas into the baked shell and cover with cooled filling.

Butterscotch Cream Pie:
Substitute 1 cup brown sugar (packed into cup) for the granulated sugar and chocolate.

LEMON MERINGUE PIE

[ONE 8- OR 9-INCH SINGLE-CRUST PIE]

Lemon is highly regarded by all cooks and bakers for its important and assertive role in lifting so many dishes out of the ordinary. Highly regarded is this pie, which is not timid in declaring its delicious nature with ⅓ cup lemon juice and 5 teaspoons lemon zest.

This is one of the great pastries handed down from colonial America via Colonial Williamsburg's Inn in a recipe adapted by its talented executive pastry chef, Rolf Herion.

SUGGESTED CRUST	Half-and-Half, No-Roll or All-Rye (pages 78–85).
INGREDIENTS	Pastry for one-crust pie, to be baked beforehand
	Filling: 1¼ cups granulated sugar ½ cup cornstarch ¼ teaspoon salt 1½ cups water 3 egg yolks (reserve whites for meringue) ⅓ cup lemon juice 5 teaspoons lemon zest 2 tablespoons butter 1 or 2 drops yellow food coloring, optional
	Meringue: 3 egg whites ¼ teaspoon salt 6 tablespoons granulated sugar
PIE PAN	One pie pan of choice.
PREPARATION	*Crust:* Prepare and bake single crust beforehand according to instructions, page 62.
12 min.	*Filling:* In a medium saucepan mix together the sugar, cornstarch, salt and water until dissolved and blended. Cook over medium heat, stirring constantly, until the mixture is smooth, about 3 to 4 minutes. Remove from heat.

Beat the egg yolks and lemon juice together in a small bowl. Stir ½ cup of the hot mixture into the yolks to bring up their temperature gradually. Pour the warmed yolks into the hot cornstarch mixture. Return the saucepan to medium heat and stir constantly until the mixture is thick, about 4 to 5 minutes. Add the zest and butter. Stir well. Drop a piece of plastic wrap onto the surface of the lemon filling to prevent a film from forming while it is refrigerated, 1 hour or overnight.

When cool, stir and spoon into the pie shell.

Preheat oven to 375° F.

6 min.

Meringue:

Beat together egg whites and ¼ teaspoon salt until soft peaks form under the beaters when lifted. Gradually add the 6 tablespoons sugar and continue beating at high speed until firm, glossy peaks form.

Pile meringue on top of the lemon filling, spreading it to touch the edge of the crust so that it will not draw back or shrink in the oven. Swirl meringue with the back of a spoon to create lush, decorative peaks.

BAKING
375° F.
10–12 min.

Place in the oven and bake 10 to 12 minutes at 375° F., or until the meringue is delicately browned.

FINAL STEP

Allow pie to cool at least 2 hours before serving. I often place mine in the refrigerator for several hours before cutting. Delicious.

VARIATION

Lime Meringue Pie:
Decrease cornstarch to ⅓ cup and omit butter. Substitute 2 teaspoons grated lime peel and ¼ cup lime juice for lemon zest and juice. Green coloring may be substituted if desired, but use a light touch!

COCONUT CREAM PIE

[ONE 8- OR 9-INCH SINGLE-CRUST PIE]

Toasted coconut shreds on a mountain of meringue in all shades of brown not only is a visual triumph but leads directly to a bite of one of the finest (to my taste) cream pies. I have most of my mother's pie recipes but not the one for this pie. This is a re-creation of her creation as I remember it, with the help of several fine pie makers of my generation.

I also have memories of thick and creamy slices of coconut cream pie at the Willows in Honolulu. The coconut used for this pie may not be fresh-grated from a coconut picked earlier in the day from a tree along the beach, but this version is its equal, I believe.

SUGGESTED
CRUST

Coconut Flake (page 87) or Half-and-Half (pages 78–80).

INGREDIENTS

Pastry for a single shell, to be baked beforehand
(If the coconut flake crust is chosen, allow for an additional 2 cups coconut plus 3 tablespoons butter or margarine.)

Filling:
½ cup granulated sugar
¼ cup cornstarch
2½ cups milk
3 egg yolks (reserve whites for meringue)
2 tablespoons butter, room temperature
4 ounces coconut flakes (reserve 1 ounce for topping)
1 teaspoon vanilla extract

Meringue:
3 egg whites
¼ teaspoon cream of tartar
¼ teaspoon cornstarch
Pinch salt
4½ tablespoons granulated sugar

PIE PAN

One pie pan of choice.

PREPARATION

Crust:
Prepare and bake single crust beforehand according to instructions, page 62.

15 min.

Filling:
In a medium saucepan mix sugar and cornstarch. Pour in the milk and cook over medium heat until it coats a spoon thickly. In a small bowl beat the egg yolks lightly. Stir a portion of the hot liquid into the yolks. When the yolks have been warmed, pour them into the hot liquid, stirring until it is as thick as mayonnaise.

Remove from heat and blend in butter. Stir in

three-quarters of the coconut and vanilla. Allow the mixture to cool before pouring into the shell.
Preheat oven to 325° F.

3 min.

Beat the egg whites until foamy. Add the cream of tartar, cornstarch and salt. Beat at medium speed until whites come to a soft peak when the beater is lifted. Add sugar 1 tablespoon at a time while beating constantly. The whites should form stiff, glossy peaks.
Pour cooled filling into the baked shell.
Pile meringue on the pie, touching it to the crust edges to seal. Give it all a great swirl and leave several peaks standing to culminate a culinary triumph! Sprinkle on the reserved coconut.

BROWNING
325° F.
10–12 min.

Place the pie in the oven to brown the meringue, about 10 to 12 minutes.

FINAL STEP

Cool on a wire rack before serving.

PUMPKIN PIE

[ONE 8- OR 9-INCH SINGLE-CRUST PIE]

Although pumpkin pie may not have the year-round stature of apple pie, it does have its supreme moments in the autumn when the harvesting begins across the land, through the crisp cold days of late fall and winter. It has a reputation as an outstanding cold-weather dessert. Personally, a slice thrills me just as much on the Fourth of July.

Others have sung its praise: "With the pastry light, tender, and not too rich, and a generous filling of smooth spiced sweetness—a little 'trembly' as to consistency, and delicately brown on top—a perfect pumpkin pie, eaten before the life has gone out of it, is one of the real additions made by American cookery to the good things of the world" (from *The House Mother*).

A pumpkin in the flesh deserves more than just the attention it gets from the kids at Halloween. With very little effort in the kitchen, it becomes the stuff from which this great pie is made. Squash, too. Small pie pumpkins, grown specially, are better than the huge monsters that win prizes at the county fair. Wash and cut the pumpkin in half. Scrape out the seeds and fibers that are attached. Place the halves upside down on a baking pan in a 350° F. oven. Bake for an hour or more, or until the meat is tender and falls out of its skin. Put the pumpkin through a ricer or strainer. Use the pulp immediately, or freeze it in plastic bags or boxes. It will keep frozen from one harvest to the next.

SUGGESTED
CRUST

The Basic, All-Rye or Hot Water (pages 69–85).

INGREDIENTS

Pastry for a single shell, to be partially baked beforehand

Filling:
1½ cups fresh, frozen or canned pumpkin
1 tablespoon flour
⅓ cup granulated sugar
2 tablespoons dark brown sugar
1½ teaspoons cinnamon
½ teaspoon nutmeg
¼ teaspoon allspice
1⅔ cups milk
½ teaspoon salt
2 eggs, beaten slightly

PIE PAN

One pie pan of choice.

PREPARATION

Crust:
Prepare and partially bake single crust beforehand according to instructions, page 62.

Filling:
Working note: The filling, without the eggs, is allowed to rest for 1 hour so that the pumpkin is totally absorbed into the liquid mixture. The eggs, however, are added later. This avoids their coagulation during the rest period and permits them to better bind and provide body for the filling during baking. The filling (without the eggs) can be prepared the night before and refrigerated.

10 min.

Into a large bowl measure the pumpkin, flour, granulated sugar, brown sugar, cinnamon, nutmeg, allspice, milk and salt (eggs to come later).

RESTING
1 hour or
overnight

Blend and put aside for an hour or longer to allow the pumpkin and liquid to blend fully.
        Prepare the shell, if you have not done so earlier.

Partially bake beforehand for 20 minutes and allow to cool before filling.

Preheat oven to 425° F. 15 minutes prior to baking.

Lightly beat the eggs and add them to the pumpkin mixture.

BAKING
425° F.
15 min.
375° F.
40–45 min.

Fill the pie shell half full and place it in the oven. Allow 5 minutes before filling the pie to the brim. This double filling ensures a better bake and eliminates curdling and separation. Use a ladle or measuring cup with a long handle to pour the liquid.

After 15 minutes reduce heat to 375° F. and continue baking for an additional 40 to 45 minutes.

Working note: Some pie bakers object to the gash left in the face of an otherwise perfect pie when a silver knife is inserted to test doneness. The pie is baked when it feels jelled or firm in the center. Touch it gently or shake the pan. It should move and quiver but not violently, as if threatening to break the surface.

FINAL STEP

Place on a rack to cool.

VARIATIONS

Squash Pie:
The pulp of squash can be substituted for pumpkin without changing the recipe in any way—except the name. The taste and texture are almost identical.

Pumpkin Pecan Pie:
Arrange 1 cup chopped or whole pecans over the bottom of the crust before the filling is poured in.

Nut Pumpkin:
Sprinkle the top of the pie with sliced Brazil nuts, almonds, hazelnuts, pecans or walnuts about 10 minutes before the pie is finished baking.

CUSTARD PIE

[ONE 8- OR 9-INCH SINGLE-CRUST PIE]

Custard pie is a special kind of pie which requires special care while it is being baked. Properly made, the crust of a custard pie is tender and flaky underneath while the filling is soft and custardy, not wet, with just a hint of nutmeg about it.

The crust is prebaked for 15 minutes before filling. When the shell is ready to be filled, it is placed on the oven shelf and the filling is ladled into it there. This saves spills on the kitchen floor and allows you to fill the crust to the very brim. Finally, make a small hole in the center of the pie after a thick skin has formed and carefully add more custard mixture to plump the pie.

SUGGESTED CRUST	Half-and-Half, No-Roll or Hot Water (pages 78–83).
INGREDIENTS	Pastry for a single shell, to be partially baked beforehand

Filling:
4 eggs, beaten
⅔ cup granulated sugar
½ teaspoon salt
¼ teaspoon nutmeg
1 teaspoon vanilla extract
2⅔ cups milk

PIE PAN	One pie pan of choice.
PREPARATION	*Crust:* Prepare and partially bake single crust beforehand according to instructions, page 62.

5 min.

Filling:
With a wire whisk or hand rotary beater lightly beat the 4 eggs in a medium bowl. Gradually add the sugar while beating. Add salt, nutmeg, vanilla and milk. Blend well.

Preheat oven to 450° F.

Working note: The shell should be placed on the oven rack before it is to be filled. Use a long-handled ladle (be certain it can be maneuvered between the shelf and the top) or a metal 1-cup measure (which has its handle in the right place) for reaching into the hot oven to pour.

BAKING
450° F.
20 min.
350° F.
35 min.

Place the shell on the middle shelf of the hot oven. Ladle in the custard filling to the very edge of the crust. Bake for 20 minutes before reducing heat to 350° F. for an additional 35 minutes.

Optional: At this point a small hole can be made in

the center of the custard and liquid added to plump the pie. A small funnel or spoon may be used. Do not remove the pie from the oven for the plumping addition.

The pie is baked when a silver knife inserted near the center comes out clean. There will be movement in the hot custard, but it will not shake as if the skin on top were about to break. It will continue to bake for a few minutes after it has been taken from the oven and will firm as it cools.

FINAL STEP   Place pie on a rack to cool. Sprinkle the top with a pinch of nutmeg. Delicious!

VARIATIONS

Slip-Slide Custard Pie:
Have ready one fully baked "blind" (unfilled) pie shell. Select an identical pie pan and butter it well. Pour in filling and bake until just firm. Cool to lukewarm. To slip custard into the shell: Loosen custard around the edge with a knife; shake the pan gently to loosen custard completely; slip custard into the shell. Let settle for a few moments before serving.

Coconut Custard Pie:
Sprinkle 1 cup lightly toasted shredded coconut in the bottom of the pan. Use unsweetened flakes, which are less likely to burn.

Coffee Custard Pie:
Dissolve 1½ tablespoons instant coffee in heated milk before adding to the other ingredients.

Chocolate Custard Pie:
To heated milk add 4 ounces melted unsweetened chocolate and 3 ounces melted semisweet chocolate.

CHESS PIE

[ONE 8- OR 9-INCH SINGLE-CRUST PIE]

Originally this English pastry was made with cheese. Someone stopped using cheese and shuffled the name, but it remains a favorite nevertheless. More elaborate chess pies are made with whipping cream, dates and walnuts, but this fine basic dessert pie is made with cornmeal and buttermilk. It can also be flavored with lemon or orange.

SUGGESTED CRUST	The Basic, Hot Water or Half-and-Half (pages 69–82).
INGREDIENTS	Pastry for a single shell, to be partially baked beforehand

Filling:
½ cup (1 stick) butter, melted
2 cups sugar
Pinch salt
2 tablespoons all-purpose flour
2 tablespoons cornmeal, white or yellow
3 eggs
2 teaspoons vanilla extract
½ cup buttermilk

PIE PAN	One pie pan of choice.
PREPARATION	*Crust:* Prepare and partially bake crust beforehand according to instructions, page 62.
8 min.	*Filling:* Melt butter in a small saucepan and set aside.

In a medium bowl blend sugar, salt, flour and cornmeal. Make a well in the flour and break in the eggs. Stir with a fork to blend. Stir in the warm butter, vanilla and buttermilk. Pour the flour into the liquid and mix all ingredients into a smooth batter.

(If lemon or orange flavoring is desired, add 2 tablespoons grated lemon or orange peel plus 2 tablespoons lemon or orange juice.)

Preheat oven to 400° F.

Pour filling into the partially baked pie shell.

BAKING 400° F. 5 min. 350° F. 35–40 min.	Place the filled pan on the center shelf of the hot oven. After 5 minutes reduce heat to 350° F. and continue baking for 35 to 40 minutes, or until the pie is firm except for a small area in the center. The heat in the pie will finish the cooking. You may also test it with a silver knife inserted near the center. If it comes out clean, the pie is baked.
FINAL STEP	Place on a cooling rack. The pie is better if it is allowed to "ripen" for several hours before serving. It may be served plain or topped with whipped cream.

Jefferson Davis Pie:
Substitute brown for granulated sugar and add ¾ cup *each* date pieces and chopped pecans.

PECAN PIE

[ONE 8- OR 9-INCH SINGLE-CRUST PIE]

All resolve collapses at the mention or sight of pecan pie. My will is destroyed. I love it. I dare not venture often below the Mason-Dixon line where some of the very best pecan pies are created. It was on a trip to Virginia that I found this excellent pecan pie served at the Inn at Colonial Williamsburg. My wife traded Chef Rolf Herion a persimmon pudding recipe for this.

Thomas Jefferson was fascinated with the pecan trees that grew along the Mississippi River and transplanted hundreds of them. He gave some to the first president who planted them at Mount Vernon, where at last report several are still growing along the banks of the Potomac River.

SUGGESTED CRUST	Half-and-Half, Whole Wheat or Hot Water (pages 72– 82).
INGREDIENTS	Pastry for a single shell, to be partially baked beforehand.
	Filling: ½ cup (1 stick) butter, melted 3 eggs ¼ teaspoon salt 1 teaspoon vanilla extract ¾ cup sugar 1 cup dark brown Karo syrup 1 tablespoon all-purpose flour 1½ cups pecan halves or pieces
PIE PAN	One pie pan of choice.
PREPARATION	*Crust:* Prepare and partially bake crust beforehand according to instructions, page 62.

10 min.   *Filling:*
Melt butter in small saucepan and set aside. In a medium bowl beat eggs and salt for about 3 minutes, or
until light and lemon-colored. Add vanilla. Beat in the
sugar, ¼ cup at a time. Pour the syrup into the warm
butter and stir well to blend. With a wire whisk fold
the butter-syrup mixture into the eggs. Stir or fold
slowly until all the ingredients are blended. Blend in
the tablespoon of flour.
          Preheat oven to 425° F.

Working note: Pecans placed on the crust beforehand
will float to the top and arrange themselves perfectly
when the filling is poured over them in the shell. Arrange pecans, in a layer, on the crust. Pour filling into
the shell.

BAKING   Place pie on the middle shelf of the hot oven. After 10
425° F.   minutes reduce heat to 350° F. Continue baking for 30
10 min.   minutes, or until a silver knife inserted near the center
350° F.   of the pie comes out clean. (The heat continues to
30 min.   cook the filling even after it is removed from the oven,
                    so don't leave overlong in the oven.)

FINAL STEP   Place pie on a rack to cool.

VARIATIONS

Chocolate Pecan Pie: Melt 2 squares unsweetened chocolate with the
butter. Proceed with the balance of ingredients.

Black Walnut or Hickory Nut Pie: Any nut can be substituted for pecans
in this recipe, although I like black walnuts or hickory nuts the best.

LIME CHIFFON PIE

[ONE 8- OR 9-INCH SINGLE-CRUST PIE]

"Light as air" and "tangy" describe this fine chiffon pie made with fresh
or frozen lime juice. The addition of Florida's Key limes, if you have a
supply, would not a Key lime pie make, but the juice would give this
even more tang.
     The gelatin in chiffon and cream pies deserves special attention
because it is the cause of many failures. It should be completely dis-

solved before it is added to the prepared mixture. Gelatin should be soaked for at least 5 minutes in cold water. Unflavored powdered gelatin is always used in chiffon and cream pies unless recipes specify otherwise.

Lift a spoonful of gelatin and drop it back into the mixing bowl to check for the correct consistency. If it forms a soft mound, about the consistency of an unbeaten egg white, it is ready for the addition of the other ingredients.

Chill the custard, lime juice and gelatin mixture in the refrigerator until thickened slightly to be certain all ingredients are evenly distributed. If not, they may separate.

Pie shells, baked to a light golden brown, must be completely cooled before filling with the chiffon filling.

SUGGESTED CRUST	Half-and-Half, Crumb or Hot Water (pages 78–87).
INGREDIENTS	Pastry for a single shell, to be baked beforehand

Filling:
1 teaspoon finely grated lime rind
½ cup lime juice, frozen or fresh (about 5 limes)
1 envelope unflavored gelatin
¼ cup cold water
3 eggs, separated
1 cup sugar, to be divided
⅛ teaspoon salt

Whipped cream, to garnish

PIE PAN	One pie pan of choice.
PREPARATION	*Crust:* Prepare and bake single crust beforehand according to instructions, page 62.

Filling:
Beforehand, grate limes and squeeze fruit for ½ cup juice. Set aside.

12 min.	Dissolve gelatin in water in a small bowl. Separate the eggs. Place the yolks in the top of a double boiler over hot water. Add ½ cup sugar and salt; cook, stirring constantly, until thickened, about 5 minutes. Add gelatin to hot custard and stir to blend. Add lime juice and grated rind. Blend.
CHILLING 1 hour	Chill the mixture until slightly thickened, about 1 hour in the refrigerator.

| 5 min. | Beat 3 egg whites until stiff and gradually add the remaining ½ cup sugar, a tablespoonful at a time. Blend well. |

Fold egg whites into the chilled custard. Turn mixture into the shell.

| REFRIGERATION 1 hour or longer | Chill. Garnish with sweetened whipped cream in any fanciful pattern that pleases the eye. I like to pipe the cream through a shell or star tube around the rim of the pie and top this with a thin sliver of lime in the center. Twist the slice so that it stands alone on the sea of chiffon. |

| FINAL STEP | Serve. Enjoy. |

VARIATIONS

Orange Chiffon Pie: Substitute orange juice for lime juice and water, and orange peel for lime peel.

Lemon Chiffon Pie: Substitute lemon for lime juice and lemon peel for lime peel.

GRASSHOPPER PIE

[ONE 8- OR 9-INCH SINGLE-CRUST PIE]

The cool green essence of a famous after-dinner cordial made with crème de menthe and crème de cacao was the inspiration for this excellent refrigerated pie that combines those liqueurs with whipped cream and melted marshmallows in a dark crust of chocolate crumbs. Its name: Grasshopper Pie.

Like other refrigerated or frozen pies, it has the special virtue of preparation well ahead of time, to be taken from the refrigerator just before serving or, if frozen, out of the freezer 15 to 20 minutes early so that the pie can soften.

| SUGGESTED CRUST | Crumb, Half-and-Half or The Basic (pages 69–87). |

| INGREDIENTS | Pastry for pie shell, to be baked beforehand |

Filling:
7 ounces (about 24 large) marshmallows
½ cup milk

¼ cup crème de menthe
3 tablespoons white crème de cacao
1 cup whipping cream
1 or 2 drops green food coloring, if needed

1 tablespoon grated chocolate, to garnish, optional

PIE PAN   One pie pan of choice.

PREPARATION   *Crust:*
Beforehand, prepare shell according to instructions, page 62. My preference for this pie is a crumb crust made with chocolate wafers, a great companion for this filling.

18 min.   *Filling:*
In the top of a double boiler melt marshmallows in the milk. Stir occasionally to be certain all are melting. When melted, remove from heat and cool to room temperature. Blend in crème de menthe and crème de cacao.

Whip cream until stiff and fold into marshmallow mixture. Fold in drops of food coloring, if desired. Pour the mixture into the crust. Give it a swirl with the spatula to give it peaks and valleys. Grate dark chocolate over the top to add an eye-appealing touch. Or sprinkle chocolate crumbs over the top.

FREEZING OR CHILLING 2 hours or longer   Freeze or chill several hours until set.

FINAL STEP   If the pie has been frozen, take it from the freezer ½ hour before serving to allow it to soften.

VARIATION

Alexander Pie: Inspired by another *pousse-café*—substitute ¼ cup dark crème de cacao for crème de menthe and 3 tablespoons brandy for white crème de cacao.

Cream Puff Paste—Pâte à Chou

Piped from a bag or dropped from a spoon, *pâte à chou*—cream puff paste—is one of the basic doughs of pastry making. It can become a puff to be filled with whipped cream, or an eclair, coated with chocolate, embracing a filling of *crème pâtissière*. Piped small it is a caramel-covered *profiterole* or an hors d'oeuvre filled with a blend of seafoods. It can be shaped into a swan or other fanciful shapes to decorate other desserts. The smallest become soup nuts, and those dropped into deep hot fat blossom into lovely brown *beignets*, fritters.

How does a puff with no leavening rise so grandly? The chemistry is simple. The flour and eggs that have been cooked together form an expanding network of dough that captures and holds the steam generated by the heat.

Pâte à chou is easy to make, and the results are predictably good when the several steps are taken in sequence.

First, use a hard wheat flour that can withstand a three- or fourfold expansion of the dough. For the best results use either bread or unbleached flour. All-purpose flour can be used, but the dough will not rise as spectacularly.

Second, the butter must be completely dispersed in the hot water which has been brought to a rolling boil. If the butter should remain as a film on the surface, the flour, water and fat will not mix properly and tend to separate. (For this reason, commercial bakers often use an oil rather than a hard fat.)

Third, the flour must be poured into the hot liquid all at once and beaten vigorously with a wooden spoon or spatula until it pulls away from the sides and forms a solid mass.

Fourth, the dough must be allowed to cool somewhat before the eggs are added. When taken from the heat the dough is about 160° F. If the eggs were added at that point they would bake. Allow the mass to cool to at least 140° F., or for about 15 minutes. Stir occasionally to help speed the cooling process.

Fifth, use large eggs (or their equivalent in volume) and add one at a time, beating carefully after each addition to blend completely and make a smooth batter.

Finally, depending on the moisture content of the flour, it may be necessary to vary the volume of eggs to produce the desired stiffness of dough. This is easy to determine when blending the flour and eggs.

To be certain the dough is of the proper consistency, lift a spoonful out of the saucepan. The edge of the paste will retain its form. The sharp points along the edge will not slump. If the dough is too thick, however, the points will be stiff and not soft; in that case add egg to the mixture.

To prevent the dough from spreading when it is piped or dropped from a spoon, line the pan with parchment paper or aluminum foil. Grease on the pan would allow the shells to spread and bake flat.

When the shells are on the pan, flatten the points and rough edges with a delicate pastry brush (I use one made of goose feathers) or a fingertip. Dip the brush or finger into egg or milk before smoothing the dough. This also gives the shells a luster.

The shells should be baked at 425° F. until crisp. A French baker wants his shells to feel "crackly" or almost brittle before they are removed from the oven. Shells removed too soon may shrink and flatten. Overbaking in an oven that is not hot enough will produce a shell that may crack and fall apart when it is filled.

Baked shells, if not used the same day, should be placed in a tightly covered container or wrapped in plastic and stored in the refrigerator. Exposed shells dry quickly and are difficult to fill. Empty shells may be frozen quite successfully.

The shells should not be filled with custard or cream while they are warm. This can cause curdling and invite a dangerously high bacteria count.

If, when you ice your first eclair, you feel it is not as smooth as you might wish it to be, turn it over and spread the icing on the flat bottom. When dry, the shells are cut in two and filled with cream. The smoothly iced bottoms are then replaced—on top! On cream puff shells, the icing should be thick to cover large cracks.

Ideally, all shells will have dried sufficiently in the oven, and the interiors are hollow and dry. If moist strands remain, fork out the filaments.

The most popular filling for puff shells is vanilla custard that has been cooked and chilled, or whipped cream. Fill the shells with enough custard or whipped cream that the filling will be tasted as soon as the shell is bitten into.

To preserve their crispness, do not fill eclairs and puffs until the day (or hour) they are needed. Then place them in the refrigerator to chill before serving.

Ice cream is a delicious filling. Slice the shells in half and fill with slightly softened ice cream. Replace the tops and place in the freezer, where they can be held for two to three months. The French call the tiny ones *profiteroles*. They mound them, frozen, in a compote dish or deep serving plate—and spoon a sauce over all! A bittersweet chocolate sauce is one of the best of all.

The small ones can also be filled with *crème pâtissière* (page 305) or whipped cream. Eclairs are often filled with vanilla custard and topped with chocolate frosting. The German taste is for coffee-flavored cream, frosted with coffee fondant or sugar icing.

One of the most spectacular desserts made with *pâte à chou* is *croquembouche*, a caramel-glazed pyramid of cream puffs filled with

chocolate pastry cream. The classic recipe calls for some thirty small puffs, each about 2½ inches in diameter, stacked one on top the other.

There are two other desserts whose reputations rest on *pâte à chou*: *gâteau Paris-Brest* and *gâteau Saint-Honoré*, the latter named for the patron saint of baking. The recipes for these follow the basic *pâte à chou* recipe.

Having once mastered the making and baking of *pâte à chou*, the door is open to a multitude of forms and fillings. The small ones, for example, can be filled with savory fillings and make excellent hors d'oeuvres. *Profiteroles aux crustacés*, small puffs filled with a blend of crab meat or shrimp in seasoned butter, are easy to make and a delight to serve.

The basic recipe for a fine cream puff shell is given here so that you will have the foundation on which to build a collection of fine puff paste desserts of your own choosing, ranging from a cream puff to an elaborate *gâteau Paris-Brest*. You can be imaginative, too, with the spicy savory fillings you choose to fill bite-size shells, to be served with drinks before dinner or at cocktail parties.

Pâte à chou is dropped by the spoonful into hot deep fat to become *beignets soufflés*. The *beignet* makes an excellent sweet for a brunch or dinner, but it can also become a delicious hors d'oeuvre by adding cheese or ham bits or onion to the batter. Paprika nuggets are ½-inch bits of dough into which finely chopped onions and paprika have been mixed.

CREAM PUFF PASTRY

(PÂTE À CHOU)

[1½ CUPS DOUGH FOR TWELVE TO EIGHTEEN MEDIUM CREAM PUFFS OR ECLAIRS, OR FOUR DOZEN PROFITEROLES]

This is the basic recipe for *pâte à chou* from which an impressive gallery of pastries can be prepared.

INGREDIENTS	¾ cup water
	¼ cup milk
	¼ teaspoon salt
	½ cup (1 stick) unsalted butter
	1¼ cups bread or unbleached flour, sifted before measuring
	4 large eggs (¾ cup plus 1 tablespoon)
	1 tablespoon milk ⎫ blended together, to brush
	1 egg ⎭
BAKING SHEET	One large baking sheet to fit oven, lined with parchment paper, foil or brown bag paper.
PREPARATION 30 min.	Pour water and milk into a medium saucepan, add salt and place over heat. Add butter and bring to a rolling

boil. The liquid must be boiling rapidly before the flour is added. Pour in flour all at once.

Stir the paste constantly until it pulls away from the sides in one mass. Mash the mixture down against the pan bottom and continue to cook for 1 or 2 minutes. Stir several times during cooking.

Remove from heat. The paste will be about 150° to 160° F. and must cool to 140° F., or less, to prevent the heat from cooking the eggs when they are added. The hot paste can be stirred and broken up with a spatula or in an electric mixer to hasten the cooling process.

In a small bowl beat each egg briefly and add to the warm paste. Stir until each is completely absorbed (and the paste smooth) before adding the next. Beat until the dough is shiny.

Working note: The paste must be soft yet retain its shape when piped or spooned onto the baking sheet.

A spoon lifted from the dough should leave standing peaks that do not slump back to the surface if the paste is the proper consistency. If it is too stiff, add a portion of an egg or a teaspoon or two of milk.

Preheat oven to 425° F.

The paste may be used immediately, or covered and refrigerated for later use, within two or three days.

SHAPING
12 min.

Fit a pastry bag or a parchment cone with a large, round ⅜-inch (no. 8) tube, and fill with paste. Press out a high mound of *pâte à chou* about 2 inches in diameter, equal to about a tablespoonful. Hold the end of the tube in place about ½ inch above the prepared baking sheet and press out the paste. Don't move the tip, but allow the paste to push up around it —and then withdraw. Repeat with the others. These will rise to three or four times their original size in the oven.

To make tiny puffs, use a plain round ³⁄₁₆-inch (no. 1) tube. Press out small rounds of *pâte à chou*, equal to a scant teaspoonful. Keep the little rounds as high as possible and spread apart on the baking sheet so that they will not touch as they expand.

The paste for puffs, both large and small, may be dropped from a tablespoon or teaspoon rather than piped from a tube if it is more convenient.

An eclair, however, is a more precise form and cannot successfully be made without the help of a pastry bag or parchment cone. The paste should be squeezed out of a large ¾-inch (no. 9) tube in a 5-inch length. When the paste has been pushed out, raise the tube and fold whatever thread of paste remains back and over the eclair shape.

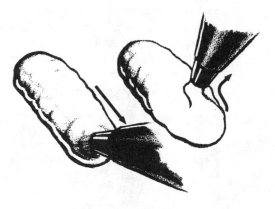

Before placing the pan in the oven, brush paste lightly with a flat pastry brush, goose-feather brush or a fingertip dipped in the milk-egg glaze. At the same time gently push down any untoward peaks that might destroy the symmetry of the shells.

BAKING
425° F.
15 min.

Place the baking sheet on the middle shelf of the oven. After 15 minutes reduce heat to 375° F. and bake until the paste is puffed and lightly browned. The smaller

375° F.
10 min.
or
5 min.
(if small)

puffs take less time to bake, perhaps only 5 minutes. The shells will be crisp when done. Tap gently to judge crispness. They should sound hollow. Prick each shell with the point of a knife or skewer to release any steam that might have been trapped in the center.

Turn off the heat. Partially open the oven door. Leave the shells in the oven for 15 to 30 minutes, depending on the size of the shells, to allow them to dry completely.

FINAL STEP

Remove from the oven. The freshly baked puffs or eclairs are best served within a matter of hours before they lose their attractive crispness.

Empty shells may be frozen quite successfully. While they are still warm, box and place them in the freezer. To restore crispness, place the frozen shells in a preheated 400° F. oven for about 8 minutes, or until they are crisp.

Working note: The filling for puffs and eclairs may be either piped into the shell through a hole pierced or cut in the bottom, or spooned into the lower half of the shell after it has been cut in half horizontally.

GÂTEAU PARIS-BREST

[ONE 9-INCH PASTRY, SERVES EIGHT]

The handsome *gâteau Paris-Brest* begins with a circle of *pâte à chou* shaped on a baking sheet, brushed with egg and sprinkled with almonds. In the oven it rises to become a craggy, golden shell, which is split and filled with flavored pastry cream or whipped cream. The top is replaced and dusted with confectioners' sugar just before it is served.

INGREDIENTS

2 recipes (3 cups) *pâte à chou* (page 124)
1 egg
1 tablespoon cream } beaten together, to brush
¾ cup sliced almonds
3 cups pastry cream (page 305) or whipped cream
2 tablespoons confectioners' sugar, to sprinkle

BAKING SHEET

Baking sheet lined with parchment or wax paper on which a 9-inch circle has been traced.

PREPARATION

Note: The dough can be either spooned in a wide 2-inch band around the circle or piped through a no. 9 (¾-inch) plain round tube fitted in a pastry bag.

If spooned, fashion a 2-inch ring of dough ¾ inch high inside the marked circle. Carefully mold with a spatula.

To pipe, make the first circle inside the marked line. Place the second circle inside and touching the first. Pipe the third circle on top of the lower two. Use a spatula to smooth the shape.

Preheat oven to 425° F.

Brush the paste with egg-cream wash and sprinkle generously with sliced almonds.

BAKING
425° F.
20 min.
375° F.
20 min.

Note: The oven door is to be left slightly ajar (½ inch at the top) to allow steam to escape so that only dry heat reaches the *gâteau*. I prop my door open with a wooden spoon handle.

Place the baking sheet on the middle shelf of the oven. Arrange the door prop.

Bake at 425° F. for 20 minutes. Reduce heat to 375° F. and continue baking for an additional 20 minutes.

CRISPING
30 min.

Turn off heat and leave the *gâteau* in the oven, with the door open several inches, for 30 minutes, allowing it to crisp further.

FINAL STEP

Remove *gâteau* to a rack to cool. When cool, slice the puff horizontally. Remove the top and fill the lower part with pastry or whipped cream.

Replace the top and sprinkle with confectioners' sugar. Refrigerate. Serve the same day.

GÂTEAU SAINT-HONORÉ

[ONE 9-INCH CREATION, SERVES EIGHT]

Gâteau Saint-Honoré is an elaborate dessert made with two doughs, *pâte à chou* and a rich tart dough. A round of tart dough, with an edge of *pâte à chou*, is baked, and this becomes the foundation on which the rest is built. *Crème Saint-Honoré* or pastry cream is piped into two dozen tiny puffs, which are then dipped in warm caramel syrup and placed around the edge of the baked pastry layer. The remaining cream is spooned in a swirl in the center of the pastry—and sprinkled with pieces of candied red cherries and chopped pistachios.

Elegant and rich.
Chill and serve.

INGREDIENTS ⅓ recipe Rich Tart Pastry (page 328), chilled
1 recipe (1¼ cups) *pâte à chou* (page 124)
1 egg
1 tablespoon cream } beaten together, to brush
2½ cups pastry cream (*crème pâtissière*) (page 305)
   (or 2½ cups *crème Saint-Honoré*, which requires
   adding the following to the pastry cream:
1 tablespoon gelatin
2 tablespoons cold water
6 egg whites
⅓ cup granulated sugar)

Glaze:
2 cups granulated sugar
¼ teaspoon cream of tartar
¾ cup water

4 or 5 candied cherries, quartered
½ cup pistachios, chopped } to garnish

BAKING SHEET Baking sheet lined with parchment paper or lightly
greased and dusted with flour.

PREPARATION *Tart Dough:*
On a lightly floured work surface, roll tart dough into
a circle or round somewhat larger than 9 inches and
no more than ⅛ inch thick. Using a pan lid or plate as
a pattern, cut from the dough round an exact 9-inch
circle. Prick all over with the tines of a fork and place
the round on the prepared baking sheet.
   Preheat oven to 425° F.

Pâte à chou:
Place the *pâte à chou* in a pastry bag fitted with a large
no. 9 (¾-inch) plain tube. Form a thick rim, 2 inches
wide, around the edge of the tart dough round. This
can also be done by carefully spooning a band of *pâte
à chou* around the edge of the round. The balance of
the *pâte à chou* will be used to make small puffs, described below.
   Brush the entire pastry with the egg-cream wash.

BAKING

Note: Leave the oven door slightly ajar (½ inch at the handle) while the base and the small puffs bake. Prop the door open with the handle of a wooden spoon.

425° F.
20 min.
375° F.
15 min.

Place the baking sheet on the middle shelf of the oven. Arrange the door prop.

Bake 20 minutes at 425° F.

Reduce heat to 375° F. and continue to bake for an additional 15 minutes, or until the border of *pâte à chou* is puffy and the tart pastry is brown.

While the base is baking, pipe or drop from a spoon eighteen to twenty-four small puffs *(profiteroles)* the size of small walnuts onto a prepared baking sheet. Use a no. 6 (½-inch) plain round tube in a pastry bag.

Brush with the egg-cream wash.

REPEAT BAKING
425° F.
15 min.
375° F.
5 min.

Place the base on a rack to cool.

Reset oven to 425° F., and when it has attained this level of heat (about 5 minutes for most ovens), put in the second sheet with the small puffs. After 15 minutes reduce heat to 375° F. and continue baking for an additional 5 minutes.

When the small puffs come from the oven, allow them to cool before proceeding.

Crème Saint-Honoré:
Prepare 2½ cups pastry cream *(crème pâtissière).* Soften gelatin in cold water and dissolve in hot pastry cream. Beat egg whites until they are stiff, and gradually beat in sugar. Fold the meringue into the pastry cream.

FILLING
15 min.

Place the pastry cream in a pastry bag fitted with a no. 4 (¼-inch) plain round tube. With the point of a small knife make a hole in the bottom of each puff into which the tube can be inserted. Fill each puff; then chill in the refrigerator.

Caramel Glaze:

10 min.

Put sugar, cream of tartar and water in a heavy saucepan over medium heat. Stir until the sugar dissolves. Stop stirring and allow the syrup to cook. When it reaches a medium caramel color, set the pan in a pan of cold water to prevent further cooking.

ASSEMBLY
15 min.

Take the puffs from the refrigerator. Place the baked round base at one side of the work surface. Spear the puffs, one by one, with a fork and dip each in warm syrup. Set them close together on the edge of the baked round base. Fill the center of the *gâteau* with the balance of the pastry cream.

FINAL STEP   Keep the *gâteau* in the refrigerator until it is to be served. Decorate with pieces of candied cherries and chopped pistachios. Cut into wedges and serve.

This should be served the same day.

FRITTERS

(BEIGNETS SOUFFLÉS)

[THREE DOZEN FRIED PUFFS]

Drop a dollop of *pâte à chou* from a tablespoon into deep hot fat, and out comes an absolutely delicious puff known as a *beignet soufflé* or fritter. It is deep-fried to a light golden color. The pocket on the inside can be filled with honey or jam, or whatever strikes your fancy.

Chef Wennberg, of the Hotel d'Angleterre in Copenhagen, makes his famous *beignets soufflés* the size of "plover eggs," sprinkles them with confectioners' sugar and serves them with strawberry jam.

Rather than making a full recipe of *beignets*, the next time you make puffs or eclairs put aside a dozen or so spoonfuls for the *beignets*. I find it worth sacrificing some of the puffs.

INGREDIENTS   1 recipe *pâte à chou* (page 124)
                ¼ cup confectioners' sugar, to sprinkle

DEEP FRYER   Deep skillet or small kettle to hold 2 or 3 cups oil.

PREPARATION   See detailed instructions for preparing *pâte à chou*, page 124.

FRYING   Heat oil in the skillet or kettle to 375° F.
375° F.   Drop rounded teaspoonfuls of batter into the hot
12 min.   fat. Cook until puffed and both sides are well browned, about 12 minutes.

FINAL STEP   Place the hot *beignets* on absorbent paper to drain.
                        While warm, arrange them on a serving dish and sprinkle with confectioners' sugar. Serve with honey

or jam to be spooned into the crisp halves when they are cut or broken open.

Café au lait is a fine accompaniment to be served at a special breakfast.

VARIATIONS

Cheese Beignet:
Add ½ cup grated Parmesan cheese to the batter and fry as indicated.

Ham Beignet: Add 1 cup chopped ham to the batter and fry as indicated.

Paprika Nuggets: Sauté in butter to a pale brown 1 cup finely chopped onions. Add to the batter with 1 teaspoon paprika. Make nuggets the size of a chickpea and fry a few at a time in hot fat (375° F.). Drain and sprinkle with salt.

Turnovers

A turnover is precisely what its name says it is—a round of pastry, filled, folded or turned over, and baked or sometimes fried. If fried, it may have the fancy name of *rissole* or the homey one of fried pie.

Nearly every culture has its own turnover (the Chinese have *won ton*, for instance), and generally each is filled with what is plentiful and well loved in that country or province.

Some turnovers, like large Cornish pasties, are complete meals in themselves; others, like the South American *empanada*, may be but one course in an elaborate dinner. When they are made in miniature—and all of them can be scaled down—they become delicious hors d'oeuvres.

This chapter is devoted to five classic turnovers. Four are entrée turnovers: Cornish pasties, Argentine *empanadas*, Russian *pirozhki/pirogi* and Italian *calzoni*. One is a dessert: apple. (Another apple turnover is found among puff pastries, page 211.)

CORNISH PASTIES

[FOUR 8-INCH PIECES OR TWO DOZEN SMALL ONES]

Along the wild Cornish coast of England, where copper miners and smugglers left a rich legacy of excitement and adventure, there is one dish that has come down through the years unchanged. Almost. Actually, it has gotten better. It is the Cornish pasty.

The original pasty was sturdy enough to be dropped to the bottom of a mine shaft without shattering. Surprisingly, there are county fairs in Cornwall today where the judges still hold to the old standards of durability of the crust rather than good taste, much to the annoyance of Cornish cooks.

My love affair with Cornish pasties began thirty years ago in Drake's Tavern in San Francisco but was restrained until I made a special pilgrimage to St. Mawes, Cornwall, almost three decades later. There I had two teachers. Margaret Blight, although born in Scotland, had lived in Cornwall for most of her life, so her credentials were impeccable. She was one of the cooks at Idle Rocks, a delightful small hotel built behind an impressive stone breakwater. Twenty minutes away at the Lugger, at Portloe, was my second pasty counselor, Betty Morse, whose mother was born in the building, now a hotel, when it was a rendezvous point for smugglers. Both hotels are owned by Colin I. Powell, who shares my love of pasties.

Here, from Margaret Blight and Betty Morse, is the authentic Cornish pasty—a deliciously moist meal wrapped in a crisp and flaky crust.

Some dos and don'ts:

A Cornish pasty is never eaten (at least in Cornwall) with a knife and fork—always out of hand.

Never use carrots, only potatoes, turnips, onions or leeks, salt, pepper and meat. The latter depends on the family's well-being at the moment—steak, fish, pork or just vegetables may be used. Beef is preferred.

A creation of the wives of Cornish miners, the pasty was a complete meal encased in an envelope of dough. The miner's initials were scratched into the dough so that the pasty could be retrieved by its rightful owner from among many laid on a mine timber. Today the initials are still used, but more often to identify whether the pasty is made with onions than to name to whom it belongs.

Each pasty has its "little corner," the last mouthful to be eaten. This is traditionally saved and eaten at bedtime or after an evening at the village pub.

One of my Cornish mentors places a tea towel over the hot pasties as they come from the oven to allow them to "steam" and to coax the juices back into the meat pieces. The other cook did not agree. No steaming for her.

Reenter Drake's Tavern: I like to do something to my pasty that I learned in San Francisco, which neither Cornish cook did. I pour a tablespoon of rich beef broth into one of the steam vents in the crust just before it is to be served. It also can be poured over the crust.

Cornish miners worked hard and were hungry men. The pasties

were as big as dinner plates. These are considerably smaller. Margaret Blight makes "cocktaily ones" with 3-inch rounds of dough.

Finally, the dough itself is best if it is left to relax and mature for a full day in the refrigerator, say my Cornish cooks.

INGREDIENTS

Dough:
3⅓ cups (1 pound) all-purpose flour, approximately
1 teaspoon salt
¼ pound (1 stick) butter or margarine, room temperature
¼ pound lard or vegetable shortening, room temperature
¾ cup ice water

Filling:
12 ounces (about 3) turnips, diced small (¼ inch)
12 ounces (about 4 medium) potatoes, diced small or sliced thin
1½ pounds round or flank steak, cut into ¼-inch cubes
1 large onion, chopped
Pinch salt
Pinch pepper
3 tablespoons butter
1 cup rich beef broth, optional

BAKING SHEET

Large baking sheet lined with parchment or brown sack paper, or greased lightly.

PREPARATION

Dough:
Note: Dough can be prepared by hand, electric mixer or food processor. Instructions for each are included in this first turnover recipe. For the balance of the turnover recipes, however, only the procedure for preparing the dough the traditional way, by hand, will be given explicitly, with cross-references to these pages for the electric mixer and food processor methods.

● BY HAND
8 min.

In a large bowl place 3 cups flour and stir in the salt. Cut the butter or margarine and the lard or other shortening into small pieces and drop into the flour. With a pastry blender or two knives work the fat into the flour until it has the even consistency of coarse meal.

Slowly dribble in the ice water. Work with the fingers or a fork to shape a mass of dough that is firm.

If too much water has been added the dough may be tacky. If so, add sprinkles of flour.

▲ ELECTRIC
MIXER
5 min.

Place flour and salt in the work bowl. Cut butter and lard into small pieces and drop into the bowl. Attach bowl and flat blade. At slow speed stir until the lumps of flour-covered fat are the consistency of small peas, about 1 minute. Add ice water, 1 tablespoon at a time, until all particles are moistened, about 10 to 15 seconds. Use only enough water to form a ball.

■ FOOD
PROCESSOR
3 min.

Attach the metal blade and add flour, salt, butter and lard to the work bowl. Process for 5 to 6 seconds, or until the mixture has the consistency of coarse meal. With the processor running, pour ice water through the feed tube in a steady stream. Stop the machine as soon as dough begins to form a ball.

REFRIGERATED
REST
1 hour or
24 hours

Press the dough into a ball, wrap in plastic wrap or foil and place in the refrigerator to chill and relax. Ideally, dough should be given a day's rest before using.

Filling:
Working note: The vegetables and meat, when diced and cut, are placed in prescribed layers—first the turnips, then the potatoes, meat and onions—and topped with a teaspoon of butter.

10 min.

Peel, dice and slice the vegetables, and cut the meat into small ¼-inch squares. To give the meat a richer appearance in the pasty, briefly sear the steak pieces in a small skillet before continuing.

When cut, place each vegetable and the meat separately, in the order in which they will be layered, on a piece of wax paper on the work surface before you. Unless you do this, the turnip may get mixed with the potato or forgotten altogether.

ASSEMBLY
20 min.

Remove the dough from the refrigerator and roll it into a piece ⅛ inch thick. With an 8-inch lid as a pattern, cut the circles with a pizza cutter or knife. Place these in the refrigerator to be taken out, one at a time, as needed to fill.

The dough will be folded over the filling, so position the vegetables and meat on one half of the circle of dough, with a ½-inch margin around the edge left

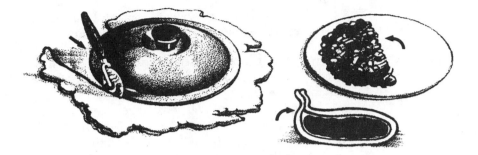

free to be pressed together. Add salt, pepper and butter. Moisten the margin with water.

Fold the top half of the circle over the filling. Gently lift the bottom edge to meet the top, and press together. Lifting the bottom in this manner helps shape a narrow turned-up strip to make the package more secure, with less chance of its leaking.

With a spatula, lift the pastry and place it on the baking sheet. Repeat filling and folding the others.

Preheat oven to 450° F.

With a knife or skewer, fashion an air vent in the center of each pasty to allow the steam to escape. Print or scratch guests' initials in one corner of the pasties. Initials may also be used to indicate the kind of filling or its variation, such as no onion.

BAKING
450° F.
0 min.

Place the pasties on the middle shelf of the hot oven and immediately reduce the heat to 400° F. Leave at this temperature until pasties begin to brown, or about

400° F.   20 minutes. Reduce the heat to 250° F. and continue
20 min.   to bake for an additional 40 minutes, or about 1 hour
250° F.   total.
40 min.   Midway through the baking process 1 tablespoon
beef stock may be poured into the pastry vent.

FINAL STEP   Serve hot with hot beef stock to accompany, if desired. Stock can also be poured into the crust before
serving.
    Baked pasties are delicious frozen and reheated,
but the Cornish cooks recommend freezing the unbaked pasties. Place frozen pasties directly in the hot
oven and allow an additional ½ hour to bake.

EMPANADAS DEL HORNO / ARGENTINE

[EIGHT 7-INCH ENTRÉE PIECES OR TWO DOZEN HORS D'OEUVRES]

Among *empanadas* it is necessary to say from where it came because
almost every Latin American country, state and province has its own
special one. The reputation of the hot Mexican *empanada* rests on a
blend of chili powders and peppers. The Argentine *empanada*, introduced to me by an Indiana University professor's wife born in Buenos
Aires, is relatively mild, with only a pinch of red pepper. In Spain the
empanada (which means "covered with bread") is filled with a mixture
of pork, ham, veal, sausage and saffron, as well as a salmon filling from
Madrid.
    This is the recipe for *empanada del horno*, or oven-baked. Other
empanadas may be *fritas*, or deep-fried.
    The large pastry is served as one of several dinner courses, usually
with a red wine; smaller ones are highly suitable as cocktail accompaniments.

INGREDIENTS   *Dough:*
2½ cups all-purpose flour, approximately
4 ounces (1 stick) butter, unsalted preferred
½ teaspoon salt
⅓ cup ice water

Filling:
1 large onion, chopped into small pieces
1 tablespoon olive or vegetable oil
1 pound lean ground beef

½ cup raisins, plumped and drained
2 teaspoons dark brown sugar
1 tablespoon paprika
½ teaspoon salt
¼ teaspoon *each* black pepper and oregano
1 teaspoon cumin
⅛ teaspoon cayenne
½ cup stuffed olives, chopped
2 hard-cooked eggs, chopped

1 egg
1 tablespoon milk } beaten together, to brush

BAKING SHEET   One large baking sheet to fit the oven, lined with parchment or brown sack paper, or greased lightly.

PREPARATION   *Dough:*
Note: Only the procedure for preparing dough by hand is detailed here. Please turn to page 136 for complete instructions for using the electric mixer or food processor to make dough for this turnover.

8 min.   Measure the flour into a medium bowl. With a knife cut the stick of butter into small pieces and drop into the flour. Add the salt. With a pastry blender or two knives, cut the flour into the butter until the particles resemble coarse meal. Dribble in the ice water, working it into the flour-butter mixture with a fork. When the flour has absorbed the liquid and becomes smooth and no longer sticky, pat dough into a ball.

REFRIGERATED   Cover the dough and refrigerate to allow it to relax
REST   while the filling is prepared. Don't knead the dough or
1 hour   it will become tough.

10 min.   *Filling:*
In a large skillet sauté the chopped onion in the oil over medium heat for about 5 minutes. Do not let the onion brown or burn. Break the lump of ground beef into the skillet and cook for about 5 minutes, or until it is lightly browned.

30 min.   While the meat is cooking, plump the raisins in hot water for 3 or 4 minutes. Drain and pat dry. Add to the meat. Measure the brown sugar, paprika, salt, black pepper, oregano, cumin and cayenne onto a piece of wax paper. Stir with a spoon to blend thor-

oughly before sprinkling the mixture over the meat. With a wooden spoon or fork, stir the meat, cover and allow to cook over medium heat for about 30 minutes. Stir frequently. (The chopped olives and eggs are added after the meat mixture is taken off the heat.)

SHAPING
8 min.

Take the dough from the refrigerator and roll into a sheet no more than ⅛ inch thick. Using a pan lid as a pattern, cut the desired number of 7-inch circles with a pizza cutter or sharp knife. Carefully move the pieces to one side without destroying the circular shape. Press and knead the scraps into a new piece from which to cut the remaining circles. Refrigerate all until needed.

When the meat is cooked, taste to check the seasoning and correct if necessary. Add the chopped olives and eggs. Allow the mixture to cool before placing it on the rounds of dough.

ASSEMBLY

Each *empanada* will need about 2 tablespoons of filling, perhaps a bit more. Make that judgment as you proceed.

20 min.

Place the filling in the center of each round, leaving a ½-inch margin around the edges.

Moisten this margin with a fingertip dipped in water. Fold and press the edges together.

Preheat oven to 400° F.

Working note: The seam of dough on the *empanada* may be left plain and unadorned, or it may be given the traditional design that looks like a cord or rope placed along the arc.

After the *empanada* is initially folded, curve the ends gently to form a crescent. The design is formed by turning one point, about ½ inch of the corner, toward the arc, forming a small triangle. Fold over another ½ inch of the edge to make another rough triangle, and continue to the end, making about a dozen small turns that together have the appearance of a piece of rope. Place on the baking sheet and repeat with the others.

Your first efforts may not produce a package as neat as later ones, but these early *empanadas* can be for the family.

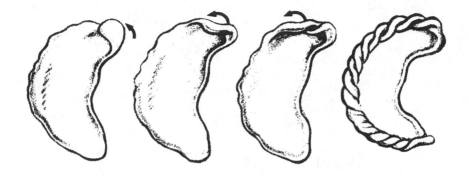

For a golden crust brush each *empanada* with the egg-milk mixture. The traditional wash is olive oil, but I prefer the egg. Also, prick each with a toothpick or skewer to allow steam to escape. If all pieces cannot go into the oven at one time, cover and refrigerate those that must be held.

BAKING
400° F.
20 min.

Place the baking sheet on the middle shelf of the hot oven and bake until lightly browned, about 20 minutes.

FINAL STEP

Serve hot. In Argentina *empanadas* are usually served as one course in a five-course meal, and always with a red Burgundy wine.

These may be wrapped and frozen for later use with great success. To serve, place frozen in the oven and reheat at 350° F. for 20 minutes.

CALZONI

[EIGHT MEDIUM ENTRÉE PASTRIES
OR TWO DOZEN SMALL HORS D'OEUVRES]

A blend of two cheeses and two meats is folded into rounds of leavened dough made with olive oil and speckled with freshly ground pepper.

The *prosciutto*, which is often difficult to find, may be replaced with boiled ham in thin strips. The mushrooms, optional in this dish, are used in other versions of *calzoni*. It is also customary in some Italian villages to serve *calzoni* with a tomato sauce and sprinkled with grated Romano cheese.

INGREDIENTS

Dough:
2 packages dry yeast
1 cup water
1 teaspoon salt
½ teaspoon freshly ground black pepper
2½ cups unbleached or all-purpose flour, approximately
1 tablespoon olive oil

Filling:
1 cup (5 ounces) diced *mozzarella* cheese
½ cup (2½ ounces) *prosciutto* or boiled ham
½ cup (2½ ounces) diced salami
⅓ cup grated Parmesan cheese
⅛ teaspoon *each* oregano, salt and basil
Pinch freshly ground black pepper
1 tablespoon finely chopped parsley
1 cup chopped mushrooms, optional
2 eggs

1 egg
1 tablespoon milk } beaten together, to brush

BAKING SHEET

One large baking sheet to fit the oven, lined with parchment or brown sack paper, or greased lightly.

PREPARATION

Dough:
Note: Only the procedure for preparing dough by hand is detailed here. Please turn to page 136 for complete instructions for using the electric mixer or food processor to make dough for this turnover.

8 min.

In a medium bowl dissolve the yeast in 1 cup water. Stir gently until the yeast particles have disappeared. Add salt and freshly ground pepper. Stir in 1 cup flour and, when blended, add olive oil. Add more flour, ½ cup at a time, and mix with a large wooden spoon until the mixture is a solid mass in the bowl. Scrape flour off the sides of the bowl and add to the ball of dough. Turn the dough onto the work surface. If it is sticky, add sprinkles of flour.

KNEADING
5 min.

Knead the dough with a forceful push-turn-fold movement, pressing down firmly with the heel of the hand. Occasionally lift the dough off the table and bring it down with a sharp whack. Do this three or four times before returning to the kneading rhythm. Don't be gentle. Be aggressive with the dough. Kneading builds its gluten framework and makes possible the lifting action of the carbon dioxide cast off by the growing yeast.

RISING
30–35 min.

Place the dough in a lightly greased bowl, cover with a length of plastic wrap and allow it to rise at room temperature while the *calzoni* filling is being prepared, about 30 to 35 minutes.

15 min.

Filling:
Dice the *mozzarella* cheese into small pieces no more than ¼ inch square. Cut the *prosciutto* or boiled ham into small ½-inch squares and place in a medium bowl with the salami and cheese. Measure the Parmesan cheese and add to the mixture. Add the oregano, salt, basil, freshly ground pepper, parsley and chopped mushrooms, if wanted. Beat 2 eggs in a small bowl, pour into the meat-cheese mixture. Stir to moisten thoroughly.

ASSEMBLY
15 min.

The circles of dough may be made in two ways. The dough can be rolled into a large piece, ⅛ inch thick, and cut into individual circles or rounds; or the mass can be divided into six or eight small balls. These are individually rolled into 5-inch circles or near-circles to be trimmed expertly with a pizza cutter around a pan lid or other convenient pattern. If a large sheet is rolled and circles cut from it, there will be scraps to press together for another but smaller sheet of dough.

Preheat oven to 400° F.

As each piece is rolled and cut, place to one side, taking care not to pull it out of shape.

Place approximately 1 tablespoon of the filling in the center of each piece of dough. Experiment with the precise amount, for it may take slightly more.

With a finger dipped in water, moisten the margin around the filling before folding and pressing the edges together. Pinch tightly with the tines of a fork. Repeat with the others.

Prick each *calzoni* with a toothpick or skewer to allow steam to escape during baking. For a bright golden crust brush each with an egg-milk wash. Arrange the pieces on the baking sheet.

BAKING 400° F. 20–30 min.	Place the baking sheet on the middle shelf of the hot oven. *Calzoni* are done when the dough is raised and golden, about 20 or 30 minutes.
FINAL STEP	Serve at lunch or dinner while hot. A cold *calzoni* for a picnic on a hot summer's day is very attractive. Either hot or cold, serve with crispy leaves of lettuce dipped in Italian dressing, followed by melon slices and grapes.

PIROGI / PIROZHKI

[ONE LARGE PIROGI OR TWO DOZEN SMALL PIROZHKI]

In Russia a *pirogi* is a meat or vegetable filling wrapped in puff pastry, large enough to be cut into dinner portions to serve. A *pirozhki*, or little pie, is small enough to be eaten out of hand at a picnic, a buffet or a cocktail party. The dough and filling may be the same—only the shape and size are different.

Often when I make a batch of dough and filling I make one *pirogi* for dinner that night and a dozen *pirozhki* to freeze and serve as hors d'oeuvres at a later date.

There are many fillings for this fine Russian pastry, including fish, vegetables, cream cheese, calf's liver, game, beef, pork, mushrooms and truffles. My favorite three are ground steak, cabbage and carrot. For an unusual *pirogi* (the large one) I have used all three fillings laid in sections, one after the other, wrapped in one crust to make a complete and delicious meal.

Pirogi and *pirozhki* are traditionally served at lunch with clear borscht or a meat broth. Tradition aside, they are delicious served almost anyplace and at any time.

One dough, made with a blend of butter and lard, is used for these pastries. (Other solid fats may be substituted for the lard, if desired.) The resulting pastry cases are short and crisp, with a subtle buttery flavor.

INGREDIENTS	*Dough:* 4 cups all-purpose flour 2 teaspoons salt 1 cup (2 sticks) butter 8 tablespoons (½ cup) lard (or other fat if preferred) ¾ cup ice water

Meat Filling:
3 tablespoons butter
2½ cups minced onions
1½ pounds lean ground beef
3 hard-cooked eggs, finely chopped
2 tablespoons finely chopped dried or fresh dill weed
¼ cup minced parsley (packed solidly in measure)
2 teaspoons salt
½ teaspoon black pepper
⅓ cup sour cream

1 egg
1 tablespoon milk } beaten together, to glaze

Cabbage Filling:
5 cups (1½ pounds) shredded cabbage
2 tablespoons salt
2 onions, minced
4 tablespoons (½ stick) butter
2 tablespoons finely chopped parsley
2 hard-cooked eggs, chopped
Pinch freshly ground black pepper

1 egg
1 tablespoon milk } beaten together, to glaze

Carrot Filling:
4 cups (1 pound) carrots, diced small or shredded
4 tablespoons (½ stick) butter
¼ cup sour cream
¼ teaspoon salt
⅛ teaspoon freshly ground black pepper
¼ cup minced parsley (packed solidly in measure)
3 hard-cooked eggs, finely chopped

1 egg
1 tablespoon milk } beaten together, to glaze

BAKING SHEET   One large baking sheet, Teflon or lined with parchment or brown sack paper. The *pirogi* will be assembled on one sheet or pan and transferred when it is finished to the sheet prepared for the oven.

PREPARATION   *Dough:*
Note: Only the procedure for preparing dough by hand is detailed here. Please turn to page 136 for com-

plete instructions for using the electric mixer or food processor to make dough for this turnover.

6 min.

In a large bowl stir together the flour and salt and drop small chunks of butter and lard into the flour. Cut the fat into the flour with a pastry blender or two knives until the mixture resembles coarse meal. Pour in the ice water, a tablespoonful at a time, and with a fork, gather the dough into a ball. If it is crumbly, add more water, a teaspoonful at a time.

REFRIGERATED
REST
1 hour
or longer

Wrap the dough in plastic wrap or wax paper and chill in the refrigerator while the filling is being prepared, or at least 1 hour.

Meat Filling:
Note: The meat and onion mixture is ground or processed fine *after* it is sautéed and *before* it is blended with the other ingredients.

20 min.

Place butter in a large skillet and, over medium heat, sauté onions for 8 minutes, or until they are transparent and soft but not brown. Stir in the ground beef. Mash the meat with a fork to break up lumps and cook until all of it is browned—no pink—about 5 minutes. Remove from heat. When the meat has cooled somewhat, either grind through the finest blade of a meat grinder, or chop the mixture finely with a knife. The smoothest result is obtained with a food processor, using the steel blade.

In a large bowl combine the meat, chopped eggs, dill weed, parsley, salt, pepper and sour cream. Taste and correct the seasoning as desired. Put aside while rolling the dough.

Cabbage Filling:

10 min.

Shred 5 cups or about 1½ pounds cabbage in a food processor or in a shredder (by hand or machine). In a large bowl mix the cabbage and salt together and let stand for 15 minutes (the aroma will be that of sauerkraut).

Put the shredded cabbage in a colander, pour boiling water over it and drain thoroughly. While the cabbage is draining, sauté the minced onion in the butter in a large skillet over medium heat until translucent and soft, about 10 minutes. Add the cabbage, cover tightly and braise over low heat for about 15 minutes. Don't burn or scorch. Stir frequently. Remove from heat. Stir in the parsley, chopped hard-cooked eggs and pepper.

Set aside to cool.

Carrot Filling:
In a large skillet over medium heat sauté the diced or shredded carrots in butter until they are tender but not mushy, about 8 minutes. Stir frequently. Remove from heat. Stir in sour cream, salt, pepper, parsley and chopped eggs. Refrigerate until needed.

Pirogi:

SHAPING

When preparing the dough for the *pirogi*, there will be scraps cut from around the edges. Put these aside to roll later into another flat sheet from which to cut a second *pirogi* or several small *pirozhki*.

18 min.

Roll the dough into a sheet ⅛ inch thick over which an 18 by 14-inch rectangle can be lightly traced on the surface of the dough.

Working note: The package will be turned upside down during baking so that the sealed edges are underneath.

Mark (but not cut) the 18 by 14-inch rectangle. Lay out the inner rectangle, where the filling will go, 4 inches from the outer markings.

Lay out a diamond from the midpoint or center of each of the sides. Cut along these four lines, reserving the large triangular scraps for making another *pirogi* or several *pirozhki* later.

(To understand this layout better, try experimenting one time with a paper pattern.)

Place the cut dough on a baking sheet or pan which can later be turned upside down over the sheet prepared for the oven.

Spoon the filling into the rectangle and mound as for a meat loaf. Bring the side and end pieces together over the filling. Moisten the edges and pinch together.

Place the prepared baking sheet over the *pirogi* and, with a quick movement, turn top and bottom sheets upside down. Remove the top sheet. With scissors cut two or three vents in the smooth top surface. I like to cut small 1-inch crosses which open during the baking period.

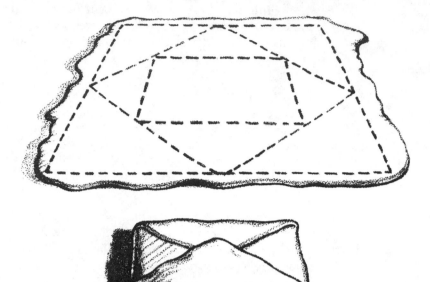

Brush with egg-milk glaze. Allow to rest for 20 minutes.

Preheat oven to 400° F.

BAKING
400° F.
15 min.
350° F.
15 min.

Place on the middle shelf of the hot oven and bake for 15 minutes, or until the dough begins to brown. Reduce heat to 350° F. and bake for an additional 15 minutes, or until golden brown.

FINAL STEP

Cut into ¾-inch slices and serve. Delicious.

Pirozhki:

SHAPING
10 min.

Remove the dough from the refrigerator. It may be quite stiff if it has been chilled overnight. Hit it several times with the rolling pin to make it malleable.

Roll the dough into a large piece ⅛ inch thick. Allow the dough to relax for 3 or 4 minutes before cutting a series of 3-inch rounds out of it. Place the rounds in the refrigerator to hold until all are cut, and then take only a few at a time to the work surface to fill.

ASSEMBLY

Working note: Think small when making *pirozhki* even though the rounds are 3 inches across. The dough is folded in half, which leaves room for little more than a heaping teaspoon of filling.

12 min.

Fill one. Fold the dough over. If you have used too much filling, reduce the volume. Don't try to pack the filling into a very small space.

The filled *pirozhki* may be sealed and presented in two ways.

One way is to moisten the margin around the filling with water, fold, pinch the edges together and lay it on its side on the prepared baking sheet. It will resemble a tiny pillow.

The other and more interesting way is to leave the seam upright across the *pirozhki*. The final touch, when the edges are sealed, is to press the dough between the thumb and index and middle fingers to leave a wavy ridge across the top of the pastry. The *pirozhki* is left upright.

Place each on the prepared baking sheet. When all are prepared, brush with the egg-milk glaze.

Pirozhki can be frozen or baked at this point.

If it is to be baked, allow to rest 20 minutes.

Preheat oven to 400° F.

BAKING
400° F.
15 min.
350° F.
10–15 min.

Place the baking sheet on the middle shelf of the hot oven and leave for 15 minutes, or until lightly browned. Reduce heat and continue baking for 10 to 15 minutes, or until the crust is a golden brown.

Frozen *pirozhki* must be baked an additional 15 minutes at 400° F.

FINAL STEP

Serve! Enjoy!

APPLE TURNOVERS

(CHAUSSONS AUX POMMES)

[ONE DOZEN 6-INCH OR TWO DOZEN 3-INCH PASTRIES]

While apple pie is wholly American, a close French cousin, *chausson aux pommes*, apple turnover, is a delicious in-hand dessert for a tailgate party, a stream-side picnic, an intimate buffet or a school lunch. This recipe is from Normandy, where cooks do wonderful things with apples.

A 3-inch turnover fits perfectly into most hands, the 6-inch one is large and attractive enough to be served at dinner, sprinkled with confectioners' sugar—not eaten out of hand, of course, but on a dessert plate.

The surprise is a small amount of apricot jam added to the apple filling.

INGREDIENTS

Dough:
2 cups all-purpose flour
1 teaspoon salt
½ cup (1 stick) butter
¼ cup (4 tablespoons) lard or other solid fat
⅓ cup ice water

Filling:
3 tablespoons butter
3½ pounds (about 12 medium) apples
  (*or* 3 to 4 cups prepared pie filling)
2 tablespoons confectioners' sugar
½ teaspoon cinnamon
1 teaspoon lemon zest or grated peel
¼ cup apricot jam

1 egg
1 tablespoon milk } beaten together, to brush

BAKING SHEET

One large baking sheet, Teflon or lined with parchment paper.

PREPARATION

Dough:
Note: Only the procedure for preparing the dough by hand is given here. Please turn to page 136 for instructions for using the electric mixer or food processor.

8 min.

In a large bowl place flour and salt. Cut the butter and lard into small chunks and drop into the flour. With a pastry blender or two knives cut the butter into the flour until the mixture resembles coarse meal. Pour in the ice water, a tablespoon at a time, and with a fork gather the dough into a ball. If the mixture is crumbly, add more water, a teaspoonful at a time. The dough should be moist but not wet. Do not overmix or the dough will be tough.

CHILLING
1 hour
or longer

Wrap the dough in plastic wrap or foil and chill in the refrigerator while the filling is being prepared, 1 hour or longer.

15 min.

Filling:
Melt butter in a large skillet or heavy pan. Drop in the apple slices. Stir in the sugar, cinnamon and lemon zest or peel. Cover and cook over medium heat, about 15 minutes. Stir frequently. The apple slices will be soft but not mushy and will retain their shape. Remove from heat. Stir in the apricot jam.

COOLING
30 min.

Set aside to cool, about 30 minutes.

SHAPING
15 min.

Remove the dough from the refrigerator. Roll it into a large piece no more than ⅛ inch thick. With a pan lid as a pattern, cut the desired number of rounds. Place the circles in the refrigerator as they are cut.

ASSEMBLY
15 min.

Remove circles from the refrigerator a few at a time. Spoon the apple filling into the center of each. The small 3-inch circles will need only 1 or 2 teaspoons of filling, whereas the large 6-inch ones will easily envelop 2 full tablespoons.

With a brush or fingertip, moisten the margin around the edge to secure the seal. Fold. Crimp the edge with the tines of a fork. Place on the prepared baking sheet. Repeat with the others.

Preheat oven to 425° F.

(For any to be frozen, place on a baking sheet and place in the freezer. Later, gather them in a plastic bag, label and store.)

BAKING
425° F.
15–18 min.

Brush each pastry with the egg-milk glaze. Place the baking sheet on the middle shelf of the hot oven. Bake until turnovers are a rich golden brown, about 15 to 18 minutes.

FINAL STEP

Place on a metal rack to cool. Serve warm. Delicious served with thick cream or ice cream.

Take frozen turnovers from the freezer and place them directly in a 425° F. oven for a total of about 30 minutes.

Kipfel and Cannoli

Whether judged by content or technique, *kipfel* and *cannoli* belong to no larger family of pastries, such as pie or Danish or dumplings, so I have placed them together here. They are unlikely companions, perhaps, but each is delicious in its own way—a good criterion for togetherness.

NUT CRESCENTS

(KIPFEL)

[ABOUT THREE DOZEN SMALL PIECES]

The history of this delicious pastry goes back to 1683, when a Polish king, John III Sobieski, arrived at the gates of Vienna to save the city from the Turks. To celebrate the lifting of the siege, the bakers used the last of the city's flour to bake this pastry in the shape of the fleeing enemy's insignia, the crescent.

    Kipfel is made with a triangle of lovely yeast-raised dough rolled into a crescent and filled with nuts and brown sugar. Also known as *rugelach*, it is a distant cousin of *gipfeltieg*, the Swiss crescent.

INGREDIENTS   *Dough:*
                ⅔ cup water
                1 package dry yeast

¼ cup non-fat dry milk
¼ teaspoon salt
½ cup (1 stick) unsalted butter
3 tablespoons sugar
3 egg yolks
3 cups all-purpose flour, approximately

Filling:
1 cup coarsely ground walnuts
1 cup dark brown sugar
2 tablespoons lemon juice

2 egg whites
¼ cup milk } beaten together, to glaze

BAKING PAN(S)	The four dozen pieces require two 12 by 18-inch pans lined with parchment paper.
PREPARATION	*Dough:* *Note:* Only the procedure for preparing dough by hand is detailed here. Please turn to page 136 for instructions for using the electric mixer or food processor.
2 min.	In a small bowl blend water, yeast, dry milk and salt. Set aside.
5 min.	In a medium bowl cream butter and sugar, and add egg yolks, one at a time, blending each until smooth. Add flour, ½ cup at a time, alternating with the yeast liquid, until a rough mass has been formed.
KNEADING 7 min.	Place the dough mass on a floured work surface. With the hands and a dough blade lift, turn and work the dough. If sticky, add liberal sprinkles of flour. Continue to knead the dough with the help of the blade until it is soft and velvety and is no longer sticky, about 7 minutes.
FIRST RISING 2 hours	Place the dough in a greased bowl, cover tightly with plastic wrap and leave at room temperature to double in bulk, about 2 hours. In the meantime, mix walnuts and brown sugar together in a small bowl. Add lemon juice. The mixture will be moist but not wet. Set aside.
SHAPING 12 min.	To prepare the dough to be cut into small triangles, roll it on a floured work surface into a 16 by 20-inch

rectangle, ⅛ inch thick. Allow the dough to relax as it is being rolled. Don't rush it or it will pull back. Several times during the rolling, turn the dough over. You can also help form the rectangle by patting and gently pulling the dough by hand. Allow the dough to relax for 5 minutes before cutting it into triangles.

With a yardstick as a guide, cut four strips of dough 4 inches wide. Mark these into 4-inch triangles and cut.

Lift the triangles off the work surface with a dough blade or spatula and place on a baking sheet.

REFRIGERATED REST 20 min.

Place in the refrigerator to chill and relax for 20 minutes.

Note: These are small pastries, so do not overload them with filling. Use slightly less than a level teaspoonful for each.

To start, place several of the chilled triangles on the floured work surface. Roll each lightly from its broad base to the apex. This will make each piece a little thinner and about an inch longer.

Place a teaspoonful of filling on the wide end of the triangle. Roll up dough from the broad base to the point. End with the point under the roll. Place on the prepared pan, shaping each into a crescent as it is

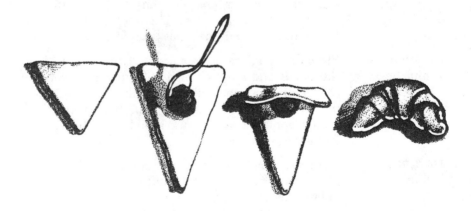

positioned on the pan. Complete the other pieces and place about 1 inch apart.

SECOND RISING
45 min.

When the pan is filled, cover with wax paper and leave crescents to rise until they are slightly puffed, about 45 minutes.
    Preheat oven to 350° F.

BAKING
350° F.
25 min.

Brush pieces with the egg-milk wash and place pan(s) on the middle shelf of the moderate oven. If the oven will not hold all the pastries, place the balance in the refrigerator. The pieces in the oven will be golden brown and baked in about 25 minutes.

FINAL STEP

Remove the pan(s) from the oven. Allow the pieces to cool for about 5 minutes before lifting the individual *kipfel* off the pan. Carefully loosen each so that the syrup does not stick.
    Serve warm, or freeze, if you wish.

CANNOLI

[TWELVE TO FOURTEEN PASTRIES]

Traditionally, crisp, crackly deep-fried *cannoli* shells are filled with creamy ricotta cheese and chocolate bits, then dipped in chopped pistachio nuts, but ingenious cooks have added an impressive list of other fillings—whipped cream, ice cream, fruit yogurt, pudding and custard cream.
    Cannoli dough, to which wine vinegar is added to keep it crisp after baking, is rolled as thin as your patience and the weight of the rolling pin will allow—no thicker than 1/16 inch.
    The recipe given here is for ricotta filling.

INGREDIENTS

Dough:
1¾ cups all-purpose flour, approximately
1 tablespoon sugar
¼ teaspoon salt
1 teaspoon cinnamon
3 tablespoons wine vinegar
3 tablespoons water
1 egg
2 tablespoons butter or margarine, room temperature

Filling:
2 cups (1 pound) ricotta cheese
½ cup confectioners' sugar, sifted
¼ teaspoon vanilla extract
2 tablespoons finely minced candied orange peel or citron
3 tablespoons grated semisweet chocolate
½ teaspoon cinnamon
2 tablespoons orange curaçao, optional

1 egg white, to brush
¼ cup chopped pistachio or other nuts, to garnish
1 tablespoon confectioners' sugar, to sprinkle

oil, for frying

CANNOLI TUBES
DEEP FRYER

Four *cannoli* tubes are usually sufficient since most deep fryers won't hold more. Each tube is used again almost immediately after the *cannoli* is slipped off. A deep fryer or deep saucepan is necessary, plus cooking oil sufficient to fill it to a 2-inch level.

PREPARATION
● BY HAND

Dough:
Measure 1 cup flour into a medium bowl and add sugar, salt and cinnamon. Make a well in the center of the flour and pour in vinegar and water. Stir to blend. Beat in the egg and add butter or margarine. Add more flour, ¼ cup at a time, to make a solid mass that can be lifted out of the bowl.

KNEADING
8–10 min.

Place dough on a lightly floured work surface and knead until it is soft and smooth. Add sprinkles of flour if the dough is sticky. Use a dough blade or metal spatula to help lift, turn and knead the dough. Knead for 8 to 10 minutes.

▲ ELECTRIC
MIXER
4 min.

In a mixing bowl measure 1 cup flour, sugar, salt and cinnamon. Attach bowl and dough hook. Turn to medium-slow speed and blend for approximately 45 seconds. With the mixer running, add vinegar, water, egg and butter or margarine. Mix to blend for 2 to 3 minutes. Add remaining flour, ¼ cup at a time, as needed to make a dough that clings to the hook.

KNEADING 5 min.	Knead for 5 minutes. If dough clings to the sides of the bowl, add sprinkles of flour. Dough will be smooth and elastic.
■ FOOD PROCESSOR 4 min.	Insert the steel blade in the bowl of the food processor. Measure 1 cup flour, sugar, salt and cinnamon into bowl. With the processor running, add vinegar and water and blend for 5 seconds. Remove the cover and add egg and butter or margarine. Process for 5 seconds. Add the balance of flour, ¼ cup at a time, through the feed tube, processing briefly after each addition. Add the final ¼ cup or portion as needed to make a dough that will come together in a mass around the blade.
KNEADING 45 seconds	Knead with the processor running for 45 seconds.
REFRIGERATED REST 1 hour or overnight	Wrap the soft dough in foil or plastic and refrigerate to relax and chill for at least 1 hour before shaping.
10 min.	*Filling:* Cream ricotta cheese in a bowl with a spatula or wooden spoon or with an electric mixer until smooth, about 5 minutes. Add confectioners' sugar, vanilla, minced candied fruit peel, grated chocolate, cinnamon and, if desired, orange curaçao. Continue beating for 4 to 5 minutes. Refrigerate until ready to fill shells.

ASSEMBLY
15 min.
	Heat vegetable oil to 375° F.
	    Place dough on a floured work surface and roll extremely thin—⅟₁₆ inch or less! Don't rush the rolling. When the dough pulls back, allow it to relax for 2 or 3 minutes. If it softens and sticks, return it to the refrigerator for 5 to 10 minutes.
	    Cut 4½-inch circles from the dough sheet using a pan lid or tart ring as a pattern. Roll the dough scraps into a new sheet from which to cut additional circles. A total of twelve to fourteen circles can be cut from the dough if it is rolled thin.
	    When the circles are cut, roll again just before they are placed on the *cannoli* tubes. This will give the piece of dough an oval shape, about 5 inches by 4½ inches.

The *cannoli* tube is 6 inches long (and 1 inch in diameter). Place the dough so that its longest dimension is the length of the metal tube. Brush the tip of the dough with egg white to seal. Roll dough on the tube.

DEEP FRYING
375° F.
2–6 min.

Note: The length of time needed to fry a shell depends on the thickness of the dough. A very thin shell will be golden brown and puffed in about 2 minutes. A thicker shell will take several minutes longer. Fry two or three *cannoli* shells at a time, depending on the size of the deep fryer or skillet. Turn over once during frying. Fry until a golden brown. Remove with tongs, slotted spatula or basket, and drain. Cool for a few minutes and then push the tubes free to use again and continue frying.

Cool shells completely before filling.

FINAL STEP

Use a small spoon or metal spatula to stuff the filling into the shells. Dip the ends in chopped nuts. Sift confectioners' sugar over the shells and serve.

Unfilled shells can be stored in a cool, dry place for three to four weeks, or frozen for three months.

Puff Pastry—Pâte Feuilletée

The creation of puff pastry is an experience that will mark a turning point in your pastry making. Nothing makes you feel more like a professional than to take from the oven a 3-inch-high golden pastry that has risen dramatically to twelve to sixteen times its original height, lifted on hundreds of layers of butter and dough. Nothing among the frozen products at the store has more warm appeal and delicious reward than this made-in-the-kitchen pastry.

In your kitchen, puff paste can become golden shells of infinite layers in which savory or sweet fillings are spooned, or it can be fashioned into *croissants de pâtissier, gâteau Pithiviers* or a Napoleon, with its thousand leaves *(mille-feuilles)* of flaky goodness. Or it may become the *croûte* for a Beef Wellington.

There are two ways to make puff paste.

The first, the *rapide* or 3-minute paste, is an excellent one for the home baker who is making this dough for the first time. It requires less time to prepare, since the particles of butter are simply mixed in with the dough.

The second method is the traditional or classical way to make puff paste—layers of butter between layers of dough resulting in tiers of flaky golden crusts.

159

The *classique* is the preferred dough for the recipes that follow, although *rapide* may be substituted, especially for the smaller pieces such as the *petites bouchées*. The true layered puff paste, the *classique*, will rise higher and do so with more layers of crust than the other. But unless the results are compared side by side, few will know the difference.

The Paste

Classic puff pastry is supposed to be the most difficult of all pastries to make. I believe that learning to make it is an exercise in confidence more than anything. Importantly, I also think I have found a way around one of the stumbling blocks to successful *pâte feuilletée classique:* determining the correct temperature of the butter and dough when they are layered together.

Until you have complete mastery of *pâte feuilletée* made in the classic way use *only* unbleached or bread flour (tempered with some pastry or cake flour) and butter. Butter and puff pastry are meant for each other, and it is only right that they remain together. Butter has the rich, satisfying taste expected of a fine pastry such as *pâte feuilletée*. Later you may wish to experiment with margarine and other flour combinations to obtain different textures and tastes. But not for now.

Puff paste (from which puff pastry is made) consists of two parts: the flour-and-water dough and the butter, which is "rolled in" (a *pâtissier's* term for the layering process).

The most critical two elements in making puff pastry, apart from the selection of quality ingredients, are the temperature of the butter and the temperature of the dough at the moment the process of building layer on layer begins. If the butter is too cold, it will break into pieces and large flakes and spread poorly when it is rolled. It may even break through the dough. If the butter is too warm, it will begin to enter the dough rather than retain its identity during the repeated layerings.

In a search through Europe and this country I could find no one who could tell me the precise temperature ideal for either the dough or the butter. *Pâtissiers* who make puff pastry day after day, month after month, could only warn: "Not too cold, not too warm, but just right!" It was no direction at all.

Then I made a breakthrough discovery—a small but accurate Taylor Bi-Therm thermometer (costing about $13) with which I could measure the interior temperature of the dough and butter. I stuck dozens of batches of dough and pounds of cold butter with its slender 5-inch stem in my own kitchen before I found the optimum temperature for each.

Dough Temperature

My refrigerator is at a constant 42° F., and prepared dough left there for 6 or more hours will also be at 42° F. Although this temperature is much too cold for the butter, it is ideal for the dough when it is rolled into a large square to receive the smaller slab of butter.

Butter Temperature

The best temperature for butter to begin the rolling-in process is 60° F. It will not flake or break, nor will it become oily or greasy.

Butter must first be worked into a square before it can be introduced to the dough. If the butter is very cold—just out of the refrigerator— beat it with a rolling pin to make it malleable. Push down the butter with the palm of the hand, lift and turn it with a metal pastry blade (a *coupe-pâte*) or a putty knife. While adding to the butter the small amount of stabilizing flour called for in the recipe, continue to work the butter for a minute or two until it can be shaped into a square. Do this on a large piece of wax paper, fold to cover and put aside in the refrigerator until an hour and a quarter before it is needed.

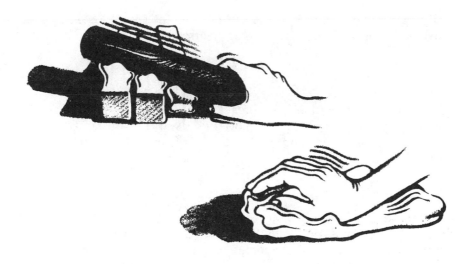

There is an easier way to shape butter. Several hours beforehand, allow the butter to come to room temperature. When it is soft, unwrap the butter. With a pastry blade, push, spread and turn the soft butter into the required shape, adding the flour as it is worked. Do this on a length of wax paper. When the flour has been absorbed, fold the paper over the butter and place in the refrigerator. Allow it to chill and solidify.

If the shaped butter (about ¾ inch thick and 6 inches square) has been left in the refrigerator for several hours or overnight, it will be at about 42° F. (in my refrigerator, at least) and should be taken out and left at room temperature for about 1¼ hours to reach 60° F.

To take a reading with the Bi-Therm thermometer, lay the slender stem across the face of the butter and push it under the surface.

If you have no thermometer, the temperature of the butter can be judged in several ways. It can be assumed that a cold slab of butter left at room temperature for about 1¼ hours will be about 60° F. Butter at 60° F. is solid but not hard. It is malleable. The square can be bent slightly without breaking. If pushed with a fingertip, the butter gives way slowly—not suddenly as if it were going to break into chunks. It is waxy. To test it, place a piece of wax paper over the top and roll with a rolling pin. If the butter moves smoothly, does not resist yet is not oily, it is ready to use. After this test, however, you may need to reshape the square of butter to fit into the square of dough.

MARGARINE

Although butter is the *pâtissier*'s first choice (and mine) for puff paste, margarine can be used for reasons of diet or economy. (See "Fat," page 29.)

FLOUR

The flours made with hard winter or spring wheat—bread and unbleached flours—have the gluten power necessary to withstand the punishment of being rolled and rerolled and yet contain the butter as layer is piled on layer.

CUTTING PUFF PASTE

A sharp instrument must be used to cut the rolled-out dough because the multilayers must not be mutilated when they are cut. The layers of butter and dough must not be forced together or pinched by a dull knife or pastry wheel.

A pastry wheel is good for thinly rolled doughs—⅟₁₆ or ⅛ inch thick—but thicker pieces (¼ inch) should be cut with a sharp knife.

When the cut is made, regardless of its keen edge, the wheel or knife will press the layers down somewhat. So to get the maximum lift or spring in the oven, turn the pieces upside down on the baking sheet *after* they have been cut. This will allow the bottom layers, which were least disturbed, to lift first and lift higher.

To Crisp

Often a thick piece of puff pastry, even though it is golden brown and flaky on the outside, carries a trace of moisture on the inside, especially those cut for Napoleons or rolled into *croissants de pâtissier*. It is easy to dry them out completely at the end of the normal baking period by opening the door to cool the oven to 325° F. Then, with the door closed, leave the pastry in the oven for 15 to 20 minutes to take out all the moisture. This additional period in the oven will help to ensure a crisp pastry and avoid soggy and underbaked pieces. Turn off the oven. The pieces may be left in the turned-off oven while it cools.

FEUILLETAGE CLASSIQUE

(CLASSIC PUFF PASTE)

[APPROXIMATELY 3 POUNDS, ENOUGH FOR TWO 8- OR 9-INCH
VOL-AU-VENT SHELLS OR THREE DOZEN CROISSANTS DE PÂTISSIER]

Most classic things are noted for simplicity of approach, form, line or body. So it is with *feuilletage classique*. Observe the basic techniques —allow the dough to mature under refrigeration, control the temperature of the butter and dough when layered—and the result will please you and delight guests. Remember that the chill of the refrigerator is a safe harbor if things should start to go wrong. If the butter softens or the dough gets sticky, chill them both.

INGREDIENTS
3 cups unbleached or bread flour
1 cup cake or pastry flour
1 teaspoon salt (omit if butter is salted)
2 teaspoons lemon juice, fresh or bottled
1½ cups water, approximately
2 tablespoons butter, room temperature

1 pound (4 sticks) unsalted butter, room temperature
¼ cup unbleached or bread flour

Note: The 2 tablespoons butter to mix into the dough can be taken from the 1 pound to be used in layering. The ounce will scarcely be missed in the process.

The recipe may be halved or doubled by decreasing or increasing the volume of all the ingredients alike. The small size of the work bowls for many food processors may dictate making only half the volume given here.

BAKING SHEETS   The need will vary, so refer to the individual pastry.

● PREPARATION BY HAND
4 min.

Blend the two flours and salt together in a large bowl. Form a well in the bottom and pour in lemon juice and 1 cup water. Pull in about half the flour from the sides of the bowl with a rubber spatula and stir to form a batter. Drop in the butter and blend into the mixture. Pull in the balance of the flour to make a shaggy mass that holds together and is moist but not wet. If more water is needed, add a tablespoonful at a time.

8 min.

Turn the ball of dough onto a lightly floured work surface. Knead with a strong push-turn-fold motion. If the dough is sticky, add light sprinkles of flour. Occasionally slam the mass of dough down onto the work surface. This aggressive action will hasten the formation of the gluten. Knead for 8 minutes. Dough will be smooth and elastic. It will not be sticky.

▲ ELECTRIC MIXER

Note: In a medium bowl combine the two flours and stir to blend.

8 min.

Place 2 of the 4 cups flour in the bowl of the electric mixer. Add salt and stir in lemon juice and water to make a smooth batter.

Attach bowl and dough hook to the mixer. Drop the butter into the mixture and start mixer at medium-low speed (no. 2 on my KitchenAid). Add remaining flour, ½ cup at a time, until dough clings to the hook and cleans the side of the bowl, about 2 minutes. Knead for 5 minutes, until the dough is smooth and elastic. If dough clings to the bowl, add sprinkles of flour and continue kneading. Stop the machine. Turn dough onto the lightly floured work surface and knead by hand for 15 seconds to be certain it is elastic and smooth.

**■ FOOD
PROCESSOR**

Note: The instruction booklet will indicate the maximum load for the work bowl. If less than 4 cups, use only half the ingredients listed in this recipe.

Note: Combine the two flours in a medium bowl and stir to blend. The sequence in which the ingredients are added is changed for the processor. Water comes last.

5 min.

With the blade in place, measure in 3 cups flour, salt and the butter cut into four or five small pieces. Process for 8 to 10 seconds, or until the flour and butter are fine particles. With blade running, pour lemon juice and water through the feed tube in a steady stream. Process briefly, about 10 seconds. Stop the machine and feel the mixture. If the dough is wet and sticky, add more flour, 1 tablespoon at a time, processing with a 3-second burst after each addition. When the particles come together in a ball to ride the top of the blade, process for 40 seconds to knead the dough thoroughly.

Turn dough onto a lightly floured work surface and knead several times to form a smooth ball.

**REFRIGERATED
REST
2 hours or
longer**

Wrap the ball of dough in plastic wrap, and place it in a plastic bag to chill in the coldest part of the refrigerator for at least 2 hours while the butter is being prepared. There is no deadline on this unleavened dough —it can be left to be completed the following day if that is more convenient.

Break down and knead and work the butter on the work surface. (See page 161 on butter temperature.) Knead into it the ¼ cup flour to give it stability in the hot oven. On a 12-inch length of wax paper, push and spread the butter into a 6-inch square, about ¾ inch thick. Fold the wax paper to cover the butter pad.

If the butter was cold when it was worked, it may be at or near the ideal 60° F. temperature. If it is, it can be introduced into the chilled dough. If not, fold the wax paper to cover it. If too warm (it will be soft and oily), place in the refrigerator. If too hard to be malleable and waxy, leave at room temperature but watch it closely. Place the thermometer in the butter if you have one.

Like the dough, the pad of butter may be left in

the refrigerator overnight or longer, but it must be taken out about 1¼ hours before needed, to warm to 60° F.

I often take this shortcut: Leave the butter overnight at room temperature and on the following morning mix the flour with the soft butter. Fashion into a 6 by ¾-inch block and place in the refrigerator for at least 2 hours, or until the butter is at 60° F.

TURNS

Note: The paste or dough is rolled and folded in a process known as "making a turn" for a total of five times. Each turn triples the previous number of layers of dough and butter.

Devote 2 hours to the first four turns, which will allow 30 minutes for the dough to rest in the refrigerator between turns. Slip the dough into a plastic bag each time it goes into the refrigerator.

Lightly touch the dough with a knife blade to mark the number of turns. It is easy to forget otherwise.

The first four turns should follow the timetable closely because the butter, which is still thick in the first turns, will break up if left too long in the cold. When the layering is near completion, however, the butter will have been spread so thin between the equally thin layers of dough that it can create no mischief even if left in the cold for several days.

ASSEMBLY
8 min.

With the rolling pin, roll the dough into a 12-inch square. Place the butter (still in the wax paper) diagonally on the dough. Fold over the corners of the dough to be certain the butter will be covered completely. If so, unwrap the butter and place it on the dough. Fold the four corners to the middle, covering the butter. Pat into a firm bundle, with all seams overlapping.

Note: Normally, "sprinkles of flour" are dusted on the work surface and the dough when it is being kneaded and rolled. Do this sparingly when rolling and turning puff paste. Use a wide 2-inch brush dipped in flour to dust evenly across the work surface and dough.

If you can see or feel the chilled butter breaking apart and not *spreading* evenly beneath the dough, leave it at room temperature for 15 or 20 minutes. Roll again. It should roll smoothly.

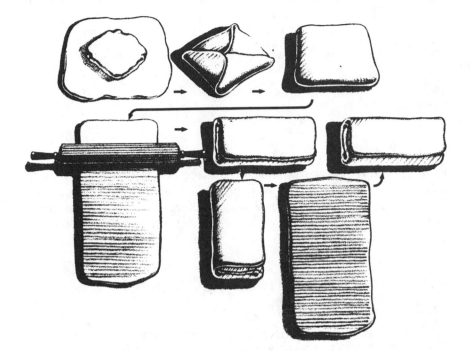

TURNS

Place the package of dough and butter on the work surface with the seams underneath. Roll it into a strip 24 inches long by 8 inches wide. (These dimensions are not critical.) Don't pound or squeeze the dough— let the rolling pin do the work. Do not roll over the ends. These will be folded in on the next turn. But do puncture the dough with the point of a knife if it should balloon with the air forced into the ends.

Fold the long strip into three, as if folding a letter.

Turn 1
20 min.

Place the folds of the dough at 6 and 12 o'clock. Roll into a long rectangular piece. Turn the strip over two or three times during the rolling process so that the side with the seams gets equal treatment. Fold into three, as for a letter. Slip into a plastic bag and refrigerate.

(Turns 1 and 2 may be done one following the other if the dough is sufficiently chilled and relaxed. But if there is any hint that it is softening, *refrigerate!*)

Turn 2 20–30 min.	Return the dough to the work surface and place the folded ends at 6 and 12 o'clock. Roll into a long strip, as above. Fold dough into three. Refrigerate.
Turn 3 20–30 min.	These are identical to the previous turns.
Turn 4 30–40 min.	
Turn 5 40 min. or overnight	
REFRIGERATED REST 3 hours or more	After the final turn, place dough in the plastic bag. The paste must be chilled in the refrigerator for a minimum of 3 hours before being cut and shaped. Often, overnight is the most convenient.

PÂTE FEUILLETÉE EN TROIS MINUTES

(THREE-MINUTE PUFF PASTE)

[APPROXIMATELY 3 POUNDS, ENOUGH FOR TWO 8-INCH VOL-AU-VENTS, ONE DOZEN BOUCHÉES OR FOUR DOZEN PETITES BOUCHÉES]

Pâtissiers call it *pâte feuilletée en trois minutes*—puff paste made in three minutes. My food processor takes considerably less time than this to whirl the loose flour, cubes of cold butter and ice water into particles of moist dough. When done by hand or under the flat blade of an electric mixer, the time is only a few additional minutes. Time aside, however, I especially like the uniformity of the fat particles the size of peas as they are processed by the steel blade.

The secret of this dough is that each piece of butter coated with flour takes upon itself the chore of releasing a burst of steam to expand the dough. There is no rolling in of the butter. It is all mixed together, but the mixing is stopped short so that the butter particles coated with flour remain intact. The dough is rolled into a rectangle and turned only three times before being chilled and then cut and shaped.

If your food processor has a bowl of limited size and cannot accept 4 cups of flour, cut the recipe in half.

For a richer dough, substitute a mixture of 1 cup sour cream and 2 egg yolks for the water.

INGREDIENTS	3 cups bread or unbleached flour 1 cup pastry or cake flour

1 teaspoon salt (omit if butter is salted)
1 pound (4 sticks) unsalted butter, cold
1 teaspoon lemon juice
1 cup ice water

BAKING PAN

Refer to individual recipe.

● BY HAND
4 min.

Place flour and salt, if needed, in a medium bowl. With a sharp knife cut chilled butter into several small cubes and drop into the flour. With a blender or two knives, cut the butter into particles about the size of large peas. Sprinkle with lemon juice and ice water (or the sour cream–egg yolk mix), and toss and stir until the liquid has been absorbed. The mass will be rough, but it will hold together if compressed gently by hand. Don't force it into a hard ball but leave it rough.

▲ ELECTRIC
MIXER
3 min.

Measure flour and salt, if needed, into the mixing bowl. Attach the flat blade. Cut the cold butter into small ½-inch cubes (cut each stick lengthwise into four pieces and crosswise into dice) and drop into the flour. Turn on the machine at low speed and stir briefly to coat butter pieces, about 10 seconds. Sprinkle in the liquid and stir only 5 to 10 seconds, until it has been absorbed by the flour. Butter pieces will remain large, but the moist mixture will hold together when pressed gently into a rough mass.

■ FOOD
PROCESSOR
40 seconds

Place the steel blade in the machine and pour in the flour, and salt if needed. Cut the butter with a knife into ½-inch pieces and drop into the flour. Process with two or three short bursts until the butter is reduced to particles about the size of large peas or beans. The material should be chunky rather than in tiny particles. Add lemon juice and water (or the sour cream mixture) and process with on/off pulses only until the dough begins to collect along one side of the bowl and *before* it becomes a solid mass. It will be loose but compressible by hand into a rough mass.

TURNING

Working note: Introducing the chilled butter and ice water into the flour lowers the temperature of the mixture in this recipe, so the dough does not need to be chilled before it is rolled into a rectangle to make the first of three turns. (In warm weather the flour may be chilled beforehand.) The work must be done quickly so that the butter does not soften. If the dough loses its chill because of a delay, refrigerate for 20 to 30 minutes and continue.

Turn 1   Place the dough on a lightly floured work surface. With the palms push it into a rough rectangle. Brush with flour. With a rolling pin roll into a 12-inch rectangle, ½ inch thick. Fold into three, as with a letter.

Turn 2   Turn lengthwise in front of you, with ends at 12 and 6 o'clock. Roll into a rectangle 12 inches long. Fold in three, as with a letter.

Turn 3   Again turn the folded dough lengthwise, with ends at 12 and 6 o'clock. Roll into a rectangle. Fold into three as for a letter.

REFRIGERATED REST 4 hours or overnight   Wrap the folded dough in foil or plastic wrap. Refrigerate to chill and relax the dough for at least 4 hours or until needed within two or three days.
     The dough is now ready to be rolled for any pastry recipe calling for a puff paste.

PETITES BOUCHÉES, BOUCHÉES, AND VOL-AU-VENT

Patty shells are airy cups of puff pastry in a range of sizes—tiny for a bite at the cocktail hour, or as large as a plate to hold an entrée to serve eight.

Carême, the great French cook and writer, wrote of the larger, the *vol-au-vent*, "It is always eaten with pleasure for its extreme delicacy and lightness, but to cook it perfectly demands the utmost care."

The same obtains, of course, for even the smallest puff paste creation. It is inviting on the hors d'oeuvre tray or the dinner plate, but, as Carême said, it *does* demand care.

These lovely brown shells progress in size from one-bite nuggets, called *petites bouchées*, to serve at the cocktail hour, to *bouchées* for individual entrée servings and finally a *vol-au-vent* ("wing of wind"), a large piece capped with a decorative lid to serve several.

An important instrument in creating a fine shell is a good pastry cutter. Don't buy a cheap, roughly made one. When buying one, place it on a flat surface to see if it touches all the way around. If it does not, it will leave a strand of dough that is exasperatingly difficult to break off. It must also have a sharp cutting edge or it will jam the layers of dough together and prevent the buttery creation from rising as it should.

The best are professional cutters—oval and round, fluted and plain.

They are crafted of heavily tinned steel, spot-welded to a strong supporting piece. The edges are honed and very sharp. They come in sets including round/plain, round/fluted and oval/fluted. The French cutters are sized in millimeters (stamped on the sides) and range from 20 mm to 100 mm, about ¾ inch to 4 inches. There are usually about nine cutters in a boxed set. The beauty of such matched sets is that there is always a smaller size, round or oval, to cut out the center of the piece that goes on top. My several *coupe-pâte* sets from the French firm Matfer are so exquisitely crafted that I show them as *objets d'art* in my studio kitchen.

It is not necessary to have the whole cutter set, of course. If, for instance, only one large cutter is available, cut out the basic piece or pieces. Then, with the point of a sharp knife, make a light incision through the top layers of dough, parallel to the edge all around. When the paste is baked and puffed, lift off the center. This leaves a well for the filling and makes a lid at the same time.

Patty shells sometimes bake "wild"—tip erratically to one side or the other as they rise in the oven. To steady them in an upright position, place *over them* an oiled sheet of heavy paper (parchment or brown sack). This will guide them upward—and not allow them to tip. When they have risen fully, remove the paper and continue to bake. (Also see "What Went Wrong?" page 375, for an explanation of why layers of puff paste sometimes slide apart—and what can be done about it.)

Circles cut from dough, no matter how thriftily laid out, leave many scrap pieces. Large scraps, of course, can be cut into smaller patty shells, but there are always odd-shaped pieces, long and skinny, that are too good (and too costly) not to utilize. During the baking session accumulate these in a plastic bag or wrap them in plastic and refrigerate so that they will not soften at room temperature. Or freeze them. Later, return to them and form them into new shapes.

All of these shells, both large and small, can be baked in advance and kept crisp in a warm (or warming) oven (100° F.) for use later today or tomorrow; tightly covered in a closed container for a fortnight; or securely wrapped and frozen for two to three months.

The preparation of the three basic shells—the *petites bouchées*, *bouchées* and the large *vol-au-vent*—is described here.

PETITES BOUCHÉES
(SMALL HORS D'OEUVRE SHELLS)
[APPROXIMATELY THREE DOZEN 1½-INCH PIECES]

Working note: These tiny cocktail shells are cut from a single layer of puff paste. The center is defined with a small cutter pressed through the upper layers of the paste. A typical pair of cutters for this would be 1½ inches (40 mm) for the round of dough, with a ¾-inch (20-mm) cutter to define the cup.

INGREDIENTS

½ recipe (approximately 1½ pounds) puff paste (page 163), chilled
1 cup water, to brush
1 egg
1 tablespoon milk or cream } beaten together, to brush

BAKING SHEET

One baking sheet, moistened with water or lined with parchment paper.

PREPARATION
15 min.

On the floured work surface roll the chilled paste to a thickness of about ⅜ inch, just over ¼ inch. Cut. As the pieces are cut, place them in groups of a half dozen in the refrigerator to keep chilled before making the center cut.

Preheat oven to 400° F.

Prepare a sheet of greased paper to lay on top of the shells as they bake in the oven to ensure that they remain upright during the baking process. Parchment or brown paper sacking may be used.

REFRIGERATED
REST
20 min.

When the first half dozen shells have been chilled for 20 minutes, remove them to the work surface. Press the small cutter about one-third of the way through the chilled dough—no more! Place on the prepared baking sheet.

After all are cut, place in the refrigerator for 15 minutes to allow the dough to lose tension.

BAKING
400° F.
15 min.

Remove the tray of shells from the refrigerator and cover it with the prepared paper. Put the tray in the hot oven. Watch the shells carefully. Inspect midway

350° F.
10 min.

through the baking period. Remove the sheet of paper when the shells are fully risen and allow them to continue to bake at reduced heat—and until a lovely golden brown.

FINAL STEP
10 min.

Remove the shells from the oven. With a sharp knife carefully cut through the top crust around the defined inner circle. Lift off the lid and put aside. With the knife scrape up the moist dough from the bottom of the shell. The dough can easily be picked out with a pair of small tweezers. Discard. The inner dough is easier to remove while the shell is still warm than when it is cold and set.

Use the shells the same day, or freeze and reheat them later with excellent results.

BOUCHÉES

(INDIVIDUAL ENTRÉE SHELLS)

[ONE DOZEN 3½-INCH PIECES]

Working note: These are assembled from two discs of dough of different thicknesses. The thinner of the two is for the base; the center of the other is removed. The piece with the hole is laid on top of the bottom disc and becomes the cup or well. The centers can be baked as lids or, later, can be rolled in granulated sugar and baked as delicious small pastries, "shoe soles."

A typical pair of cutters would be 3½ inches (90 mm) for the large round of dough and a 2-inch (50-mm) cutter to press completely through the center of the thicker piece. (A lovely *bouchée* can be made with the fluted oval cutters—115 mm and 75 mm.)

INGREDIENTS

½ recipe (approximately 1½ pounds) puff paste (page 163)
1 cup water, to brush
1 egg
1 tablespoon milk or cream } beaten together, to brush

BAKING SHEET

One baking sheet, moistened with water or lined with parchment paper.

PREPARATION
20 min.

Roll the chilled dough to ¼-inch thickness on a floured work surface or pastry cloth. Divide into two pieces. Return one to the refrigerator while rolling the second to a thickness of ⅛ inch. This provides the base pieces. Allow the dough to relax for several minutes before cutting the discs.

As the discs are cut, place them in the refrigerator to maintain the chill.

Remove the thicker ¼-inch piece from the refrigerator and cut out discs with the same cutter. When a half dozen or so are cut, return them to the refrigerator until all are done.

As it is best to keep the paste chilled so that it does not become soft and unworkable, put together only a few *bouchées* at a time. Remove a half dozen *thin* and an equal number of *thick* discs from the refrigerator. Place the thin bases upside down on the prepared baking sheet and brush each with water.

Select the small cutter for the centers of the thicker pieces. Cut out the center of each to create a ring of dough. Place this on the bottom disc, and turn the ring over (upside down) before it is positioned on the base. (Turning upside down enables the paste to rise higher.)

REFRIGERATED
REST
20 min.

When the *bouchées* are assembled, brush only the tops with egg wash and place them in the refrigerator for 20 minutes to chill and relax.

Prepare the sheet of heavy greased paper to place

over the *bouchées* in the oven to stabilize them as they rise.

Preheat oven to 425° F.

When they are removed from the refrigerator, prick the bottom of each with the tines of a sharp fork, the point of a larding needle or a skewer.

BAKING
425° F.
20 min.
375° F.
20 min.

Arrange the greased paper over the top of the *bouchées* and place the baking sheet on the middle shelf of the hot oven.

Inspect the shells midway through the baking period and remove the paper. Reduce heat and continue baking for an additional 20 minutes, or until the shells are crisp and a golden brown.

FINAL STEP

Remove from the oven. Some of the dough in the well may have puffed excessively, so scribe the inside with the point of a sharp knife—scrape and lift out the excess dough, exposing a solid, crusted bottom.

VOL-AU-VENT

(LARGE PATTY SHELL)

[ONE 8-INCH SHELL]

Working note: Two large 8-inch discs are cut from one sheet of puff paste using a cardboard circle or a pan or pot lid as a pattern to guide the knife. A small circle of dough is removed from one piece, which becomes the body. The circle that is removed becomes the cover —decorated with small circles, triangles and small circles, triangles and crescents.

A square *vol-au-vent* may be fashioned easily by substituting square objects as patterns and preparing them as described here. Also, rather than cutting the top square from a whole piece, the four sides can be made from strips of dough of equal width.

There is a 4-inch square *vol-au-vent* cutter ($15) that allows the cook to press down once (to make two cuts in the dough) and then to fold the cut pieces diagonally across each other to form the sides of a decorative shell. (It is easier to do than to describe!)

INGREDIENTS

1 recipe (approximately 3 pounds) puff paste (page 163)
1 cup water, to brush

1 egg
1 tablespoon milk or cream } beaten together, to brush

BAKING SHEET

One baking sheet or round pizza pan, moistened or lined with parchment paper.

PATTERNS

Select 8- and 5-inch pan lids, plates or cardboard circle as patterns. You will also need small cutters to cut *fleurons* in oval and crescent shapes to decorate the cover.

PREPARATION
22 min.

Roll the dough on a floured work surface into a rectangle about 18 inches by 9 inches and ⅜ inch thick. This is a thicker dough than is used for other shells, but it must be so to support more weight and to rise higher.

With a sharp knife cut two 8-inch discs out of the paste, spacing the circles away from the edges of the dough and each other.

With the aid of a rolling pin, lift one disc and place it *upside down* on the prepared baking sheet. Brush a margin 1½ inches wide around it with cold water to seal it to the upper layer, to come.

Center the 5-inch pattern on the second disc and cut the outside 1½-inch ring for the second layer of the pastry. To prevent the ring of dough from stretching unduly as it is being moved to the top of the first

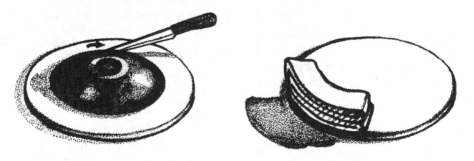

piece, dust it with flour and fold it into quarters. Place it on the disc and unfold. Position the two pieces together carefully and press with the tips of the fingers to get a good seal. In addition, use the back of a knife to press slanted lines into the sides of the two pieces at

1-inch intervals. This is both decorative and structural.

Reserve the small center disc in the refrigerator until needed later.

If the dough has warmed and is soft, place it in the refrigerator before continuing.

With the paste chilled and firm, cut just beneath

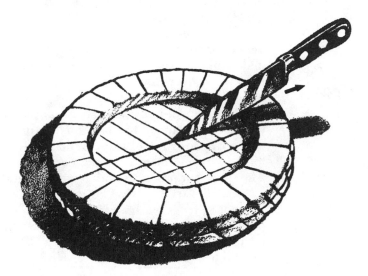

the surface of the dough around the inside edge of the bottom. When baked (and cut again) this can be lifted out to create more room for the filling.

Make other design marks—light spoke-like cuts across the top of the rim and cuts to make a checkerboard on the bottom (which may become the cover).

Brush the top of the rim and the bottom with egg wash. Do not allow the wash to run down the sides, or it may prevent the piece from rising to its fullest.

REFRIGERATED REST
30 min.

Cover the completed shell with a length of wax paper and refrigerate to relax before baking.

12 min.

Roll the 5½-inch disc to a larger dimension and use the 8-inch pattern to cut a cover that will completely top the *vol-au-vent*.

Lift the disc on the rolling pin and transfer it to the baking sheet to join the *vol-au-vent* if there is room for both. If not, use a separate small baking sheet. After moving it, check the size and shape of the disc with the pattern. Cut again if necessary.

Form a decorative trim around the edge of the cover by placing a slightly smaller lid or other round object on it and, with a sharp knife, pressing or cutting a scallop every inch or so.

Prick the disc at intervals with a rolling pastry piercer or the tines of a fork to prevent it from rising unduly in the oven. Do not prick the decorative edge, however. Cover and chill the dough for 25 minutes before decorating further.

Meanwhile, cut *fleurons* with a small pastry cutter, plain or fluted, to place on top of the lid in a decorative design. Cut a disc of dough. Move the cutter so that one edge is poised over the center. Cut. The single cut produces both a crescent and an oval!

Remove the pastry lid from the refrigerator. Brush it with egg wash and place the various shapes in position. Return it to the refrigerator while the oven heats.

Preheat oven to 425° F.

BAKING
425° F.
20 min.
375° F.
30–40 min.

Remove the *vol-au-vent* and lid from the refrigerator and brush again with the egg wash. Place the tray on the middle shelf of the hot oven.

Inspect the pastry in 20 minutes, when it should have risen to more than three times its original height. Reduce heat to 375° F. and continue baking until the paste is brown and crisp, 30 to 40 minutes. If the pastry is baking too fast (too brown), cover with foil or brown sack paper.

FINAL STEP

Immediately upon taking the *vol-au-vent* and lid from the oven, cut around the inside of the shell to free the bottom piece. With care, this can be lifted out to become a reserve lid. Try it. If not, you have the decorated cover to use.

Scrape and lift out the moist, uncooked dough down to the solid base. Do it gently with a fork or spoon.

DRYING
10 min.

Place the *vol-au-vent* in the turned-off oven for 10 minutes to dry out the exposed bottom area. But be certain the oven is not on!

Remove the shell from oven and place on a rack to cool before filling.

The shell will keep beautifully in a 100° F. warming oven for one or two days. If you need to store it longer, wrap it well in plastic wrap or freezer paper and freeze. To reheat a frozen or cold *vol-au-vent*, place in a 400° F. oven for 8 to 10 minutes, turn off heat and leave for a few minutes to get it completely crisp.

The Fillings

There are literally scores of delicious fillings, mostly savory, that can be presented in these golden and flaky cases.

Here is a selection of the best, chosen not only for their good taste but for their compatibility with the buttery goodness of the puff paste shells.

CRAB MEAT WITH MUSHROOMS

(VIANDE DE CRABE AUX CHAMPIGNONS)

[FOR ONE VOL-AU-VENT, SERVES FOUR,
OR TWO DOZEN PETITES BOUCHÉES]

This recipe for a fine seafood supper dish is from the kitchen of the Greenbrier Hotel in Hot Sulphur Springs, West Virginia. It is the creation of its famous chef, Hermann Rusch, and may also be served as an hors d'oeuvre in small puff paste shells.

INGREDIENTS

2 tablespoons butter
1 pound crab meat, fresh or frozen
¼ pound mushrooms, diced
2 tablespoons brandy
¼ teaspoon *each* salt and pepper
Juice of ½ lemon
1 cup white wine
1 cup fish stock or bottled clam juice

2 egg yolks, slightly beaten
½ cup cream
3 tablespoons grated sharp Cheddar cheese

PREPARATION
45 min.

Melt butter in a large saucepan and add crab meat, diced mushrooms, brandy, salt, pepper and lemon juice. Heat the wine and fish stock (or clam juice) in a small pan and add while warm to the crab and mushrooms. Simmer gently, uncovered, for 30 minutes. Combine egg yolks and cream, and add one-third of the mixture to the crab meat. Pour the crab meat mixture into shell(s). Top with the rest of the egg yolk mixture, sprinkle cheese over the top and place in a preheated broiler 3 inches from the heat until golden brown, about 3 to 4 minutes. Serve immediately.

CHEESE BOUCHÉES

(BOUCHÉES AU FROMAGE)

[FOR ONE DOZEN 1½-INCH BOUCHÉE SHELLS]

The surprise beneath the cheese meringue is a creamy cheese sauce, with a touch of cayenne.

INGREDIENTS

1 tablespoon butter
1 tablespoon all-purpose flour
½ cup scalded milk or cream
Pinch *each* salt and pepper
6 tablespoons coarsely grated Swiss cheese
Pinch cayenne
2 egg whites
Pinch salt
½ teaspoon curry powder
3 tablespoons finely grated Parmesan cheese
Paprika, to sprinkle

PREPARATION
20 min.

To make the cream sauce, place the butter in the top of a double boiler, over simmering water on low heat. Gradually add the flour, stirring constantly for 4 to 5 minutes. Pour in the scalded milk or cream gradually, stirring to blend well. Season to taste with salt and pepper.

Preheat oven to 325° F.

Stir grated Swiss cheese into the hot sauce until the mixture is smooth. Season with a pinch of cayenne. Set aside while preparing the meringue.

Add a pinch of salt to the egg whites and beat until stiff. Gradually add curry powder and finely grated Parmesan cheese.

Fill the shells with the cheese sauce and top with a swirl of meringue. Place the shells on a baking sheet or flat pan and heat in a 325° F. oven until the meringue is lightly browned. Sprinkle with paprika and serve.

VARIATIONS

A delicious version of *bouchées au fromage* is prepared with a tablespoon of diced cheese in each shell, over which is poured 2 eggs blended into 1 cup heavy cream. Add a few drops of Worcestershire sauce or a pinch of cayenne, plus salt and pepper to taste. Bake in a preheated 425° F. oven for about 15 minutes, or until the *bouchées* are puffed and brown.

This same mixture can be poured over other fillings such as diced cooked ham, chicken livers, shrimp, crab or lobster, flaked canned tuna or mushrooms.

CREAMED SWEETBREADS WITH MUSHROOMS
(RIS DE VEAU À LA CRÈME AUX CHAMPIGNONS)

[FOR ONE VOL-AU-VENT, SERVES SIX,
OR TWENTY-TWO PETITES BOUCHÉES]

One of the most delicate meats is sweetbreads, yet it is too little appreciated in this country. Abroad, certainly. This recipe, from the principality of Monaco, can be served to six in the large 9-inch shell, or individually in 3½-inch *bouchées*, or bite-size in twenty-two *petites bouchées*.

If served as an hors d'oeuvre to be eaten out of hand (and if over expensive rugs), be certain the cream sauce is sufficiently thick, not drippy.

The sweetbreads in this recipe are braised rather than blanched. I think they have more taste when prepared this way. They are also good served cold, in a salad.

INGREDIENTS

Meat:
3 tablespoons butter
¼ cup *each* finely chopped carrots, onions and celery
⅛ teaspoon *each* thyme, salt and pepper
2 bay leaves
1½ pounds sweetbreads
1 teaspoon butter, to grease baking dish
½ cup white wine
1 to 1½ cups chicken stock, approximately

Sauce:
2 tablespoons butter
3 tablespoons all-purpose flour
½ to 1 cup cream
⅛ teaspoon *each* salt and pepper
Few drops lemon juice
2 tablespoons minced parsley, to garnish

½ pound mushrooms, caps only—whole if small, or cut in half if medium-size

PREPARATION

Note: The sweetbreads can be braised one or two days beforehand and refrigerated.

20 min.

In a large skillet place butter and in it sauté the vegetables, uncovered, over medium heat until tender but not browned, about 12 minutes. Sprinkle on thyme, salt and pepper, and add bay leaves. Place sweetbreads in the skillet and cover with vegetables and juices. Cover and cook over medium to low heat for 5 minutes. Turn sweetbreads and cook for an additional 5 minutes.

Preheat oven to 325° F.

Butter a covered baking dish or casserole and transfer sweetbreads to it.

5 min.

Pour wine into the skillet and boil down rapidly to reduce liquid to half. Pour liquids and vegetables over sweetbreads in the baking dish. Add chicken stock to barely cover the sweetbreads.

SIMMERING
325° F.
45 min.

Place the baking dish over low heat and bring the liquid to a simmer. Cover the baking dish or casserole and place it in the oven on the lower shelf. Regulate heat so that the sweetbreads cook at a simmer for 45 minutes.

Remove the baking dish from the oven and allow the sweetbreads to cool in their liquid.

CREAMING
18 min.

If the sweetbreads are to be served in a *vol-au-vent* or individual shells, as an entrée, cut into slices ½ inch thick and set aside. If they are to be placed in small shells, dice.

Boil down and reduce the cooking stock to 1 cup. In a separate pan cook the butter and flour together into a *roux*, stirring the mixture as it cooks for about 2 minutes. Turn off heat. Strain the hot cooking stock into the *roux* and stir briskly to blend. Simmer for 1 minute.

Beat in ½ cup cream, then more by the spoonful until the sauce thins and coats the spoon. Season to taste with salt and pepper and a few drops of lemon juice.

SIMMERING
325° F.
45 min.

Place the baking dish over low heat and bring the liquid to a simmer. Cover the baking dish or casserole and place it in the oven on the lower shelf. Regulate heat so that the sweetbreads cook at a simmer for 45 minutes.

Remove the baking dish from the oven and allow the sweetbreads to cool in their liquid.

CREAMING
18 min.

If the sweetbreads are to be served in a *vol-au-vent* or individual shells, as an entrée, cut into slices ½ inch thick and set aside. If they are to be placed in small shells, dice.

Boil down and reduce the cooking stock to 1 cup. In a separate pan cook the butter and flour together into a *roux*, stirring the mixture as it cooks for about 2 minutes. Turn off heat. Strain the hot cooking stock into the *roux* and stir briskly to blend. Simmer for 1 minute.

Beat in ½ cup cream, then more by the spoonful until the sauce thins and coats the spoon. Season to taste with salt and pepper and a few drops of lemon juice.

Drop the mushrooms into the sauce and simmer, uncovered, for 10 minutes. Remove from heat and stir in the sweetbread pieces.

Spoon into the shell(s) and garnish with minced parsley.

A lovely dinner or supper dish to serve six is *vol-au-vent à la reine*, with the addition of 1 cup boiled chicken, cut into bite-size pieces and mixed with the sweetbreads.

BAY SCALLOPS IN VOL-AU-VENT

(VOL-AU-VENT DE PETONCLE)

[FOR ONE VOL-AU-VENT OR SIX BOUCHÉES]

The crisp and flaky puff paste shell(s) substitutes for the scallop shells on which this fine-tasting bivalve is usually served as *coquilles Saint-Jacques*.

INGREDIENTS

1 pound scallops (bay scallops preferred)
1 cup dry white wine
3 slices *each* onion and lemon
2 teaspoons chopped shallots
¼ teaspoon salt
4 whole peppercorns
3 sprigs fresh parsley
2 whole cloves
1 bay leaf
1 garlic clove

Sauce:
½ cup light cream
2 tablespoons butter
2½ tablespoons all-purpose flour
⅛ teaspoon salt
Pinch pepper

3 cups coarsely chopped mushrooms
1 tablespoon butter
1 tablespoon brandy, warmed

PREPARATION
20 min.

Wash scallops, slice in half and place in a saucepan with wine, onion and lemon slices, shallots, salt, peppercorns, parsley, cloves, bay leaf and garlic clove. Bring to a boil. Lower heat and poach gently for 3 minutes, or until the scallops are tender. Drain, reserving the broth. Keep both hot.

Strain broth and add enough cream to make 1½ cups liquid. Make a *roux* of butter and flour in a small saucepan over medium heat, stirring constantly for about 3 minutes. Pour in the broth and bring the sauce to a boil. Remove, and then return to heat to bring to a boil a second time. Strain through a fine sieve into another saucepan. Bring to a boil and taste for seasoning, add salt and pepper as needed.

In a small skillet sauté mushrooms in butter, about 4 minutes. Stir the scallops and mushrooms into the sauce.

When ready to serve, pour warmed brandy over the mixture and light with a match. When the flame dies, stir once lightly and fill *vol-au-vent* or hot *bouchée* shells.

CHIPPED BEEF IN SHELL

(BOUCHÉE AU BOEUF FUMÉ)

[FOR SIX INDIVIDUAL BOUCHÉES OR EIGHTEEN PETITES BOUCHÉES]

Chipped beef has always held a special place on my list of all-time good things to eat. My mother knew I loved it, and when I did anything especially well—mowing the yard or cleaning the cistern—I could expect chipped beef in puff paste or on toast. Imagine my surprise and delight after a day of bicycling against the wind through wheat fields near Tours to find my mother's reward in a small French café!

INGREDIENTS

8 ounces chipped beef
3 tablespoons butter
3 tablespoons *each* minced onion and green pepper
3 tablespoons flour
2 cups milk or light cream
1 tablespoon dry Sherry, optional
1 tablespoon chopped parsley

Note: My mother's recipe did not include either the green pepper or the Sherry.

PREPARATION
10 min.

Pull apart the chipped beef and shred with fingers or scissors. Sauté beef in butter in a skillet over medium heat (also mushrooms, if desired). Add onion and green pepper. Sauté for about 5 minutes. Sprinkle with flour and, stirring constantly, add 2 cups milk or cream. Simmer all until the mixture is thickened, about 5 minutes. Remove from heat and stir in dry Sherry, if desired. Serve in shell(s) garnished with chopped parsley.

VARIATION

Chipped beef and mushrooms are marvelous companions. Add ½ cup sliced fresh mushrooms to the mixture.

CHEESE AND HAM PUFF PASTRY

(FROMAGE ET JAMBON À LA CRÈME)

[ONE VOL-AU-VENT, SERVES FOUR, OR EIGHTEEN PETITES BOUCHÉES]

This delicious cheese and ham filling can be used in any puff paste case, whether round or rectangular, and served as an entrée or small hors d'oeuvres. I especially like it in a *vol-au-vent* or as a savory filling in the case made for the *gâteau Pithiviers* (page 209).

INGREDIENTS
2 tablespoons butter
6 ounces boiled ham, sliced thin
2 tablespoons minced shallots or scallions
2 egg yolks
¼ cup heavy cream
Several drops *each* Worcestershire sauce and Tabasco pepper sauce
Pinch freshly ground black pepper
6 tablespoons grated Parmesan, Swiss or Cheddar cheese
1 egg
1 teaspoon water } beaten together, to brush

PREPARATION
Note: The filling may be prepared one or two days beforehand and refrigerated until needed.
    While the butter is melting in a medium skillet, cut ham into small 1-inch squares. Sauté briefly in butter and add shallots or scallions. Warm them only. Remove from the heat. In a small bowl beat the egg yolks with the cream. Stir the mixture into the ham and add drops of Worcestershire and hot pepper sauces. Grind in black pepper to taste. (The mixture

may also need a bit of salt if the ham is not overly salty.) Warm over low heat, folding the ham into the sauce. Allow the sauce to thicken but not boil. Set aside to cool. It will thicken further. It should be cool when it goes into the shell(s).

SHAPING
8 min.

To shape an 8-inch case, roll out chilled puff paste on a floured work surface into a rectangle 20 by 9 inches and ¼ inch thick. With an 8-inch lid or pan as a pattern, use a pastry wheel or sharp knife to cut two circles of dough. Place one on the baking sheet; this is the bottom section.

Form a mound with the filling in the center of the circle, interspersing layers of ham with sprinklings of cheese. Leave a 1-inch margin clear.

With the point of a sharp knife or a pastry wheel, score the remaining circle with arcs radiating from the center. At the center make a ¼-inch hole through which steam can escape during baking. Brush the edges of the bottom piece with water. Place the second piece over the filling and firmly press together the wide edges of the two circular pieces. Carefully form the center in a mound over the filling. With a knife held vertically, make several indentations and scallops around the sealed edges to give it both an artistic trim and a better seal.

REFRIGERATED
REST
45 min.

Cover with wax paper and chill for 45 minutes to relax the dough and stabilize the pastry layers.

Preheat oven to 425° F. 15 minutes before baking.

BAKING
425° F.
45 min.
375° F.
15 min.

Remove the case from the refrigerator and brush with egg glaze. If some of the lines have become smeared or blurred, redefine with a knife point.

Place on the middle shelf of the hot oven. If midway through the bake period it seems to be browning too fast, cover with foil or brown paper. Reduce heat to 375° F. after 45 minutes and continue to bake for about 15 minutes, or 1 hour in all.

FINAL STEP

The pastry may be kept warm in the oven with the heat turned off for an hour or more. The sooner served, however, the more flaky and delicious it will be. To serve, cut into wedges with a serrated knife.

The unbaked case may be frozen, tightly wrapped in plastic, to be served another day. Place frozen in the oven without the wrapper and allow at least 20 additional minutes in baking time.

The Pastries

The versatile puff paste dough produces more than golden cups filled with savories and sweets. Turned and folded, sprinkled and filled with other good things, it becomes the pastry itself—from the lovely *croissant de pâtissier* and *sacristains* to *fromage et jambon* (cheese and ham) between crusts, to apple turnovers, and even the blanket for meats *en croûte* (Beef Wellington, for one).

Here is puff paste in its other varied and delicious roles.

ARCHES

(ARCS)

[ABOUT FOUR DOZEN PIECES]

Arcs are cut from a roll of puff paste embedded with sugar crystals for a sweet, or with grated cheese for a savory—and then, when laid flat, cut again. The second cut is to the middle of each piece so that it can open in the oven's heat to become an *arc*. An *Arc de Triomphe!*

INGREDIENTS	*Sweet:* ½ cup granulated sugar, approximately 1½ pounds puff paste (page 163), chilled *Savory:* ¾ cup grated Cheddar cheese or similar cheese of choice 1½ pounds puff paste (page 163), chilled
BAKING SHEET	Baking sheet lined with parchment paper.
PREPARATION 15 min.	On a work surface liberally sprinkled with granulated sugar or cheese, roll the chilled dough, on both sides, to a length that is 12 inches wide and ⅛ inch thick. Roll up like a jelly roll. Be certain both sides have been liberally coated. Wrap dough in wax paper and place in the refrigerator for half an hour to relax the dough and chill before cutting.

Brush sugar or cheese into a pile on the work surface to use later when the *arcs* are cut.

SHAPING

Remove dough from the refrigerator and return the pastry to the work surface.

With a sharp knife dipped frequently in cold water cut the roll into ¼-inch slices. Touch each *arc* to the sugar or cheese. Place on the prepared baking sheet. Allow room for the *arcs* to unfold to double in size.

With a sharp knife make one cut to the center of each piece. The *arc* will open at this cut and expand in the oven's heat.

REFRIGERATED REST
20 min.

Cover the *arcs* with wax paper and place in the refrigerator for 20 minutes.
Preheat oven to 400° F.

BAKING
400° F.
15 min.
350° F.
10 min.

Uncover the baking sheet and place it on the middle shelf of the hot oven. After 15 minutes turn each *arc* over so that it will brown nicely on both sides, and reduce the heat to 350° F. Continue to bake until golden brown and, if sugared, caramelized, about 10 minutes.

FINAL STEP

Place the *arcs* on a rack to cool. *Arcs* should be cooled before serving to allow them to reach their full crispness. They will keep well for a fortnight in a tight container. They freeze well for several months.

PUFF PASTRY CROISSANTS

(CROISSANTS DE PÂTISSIER)

[EIGHTEEN TO TWENTY-FOUR PIECES]

There is little difference to the eye between the *croissant* of the baker (*croissant de boulanger*) and that of the pastry chef (*croissant de pâtissier*). The *boulanger* makes his with a yeast-raised dough, the *pâtissier* with puff paste that rises because of the steam generated by the moisture in the butter and the dough.

The *croissant de boulanger* is perhaps slightly less delicate and is recognized by its faint yeasty taste and aroma. The *croissant de pâtissier* has perhaps less substance but is a miracle of scores of layers of tender flaky puff paste that shatter and scatter with each bite.

The *croissant de pâtissier* without further embellishment is a delight at breakfast or on a tea tray. Nevertheless, a delicious variation is the *croissant au confiture*—a *croissant* hiding a pocket of jam and, if you wish, sprinkled over the top with a shower of ground almonds or hazelnuts (my favorite).

But this versatile *croissant* can also become a savory—*croissant au jambon*, with ground ham hidden in the layers of flaky crust.

INGREDIENTS   *Plain:*
1 pound puff paste (page 163), chilled
1 egg
1 tablespoon milk } beaten together, to brush

Confiture:
1 pound puff paste (page 163), chilled
⅓ cup jam of choice
1 egg
1 tablespoon milk } beaten together, to brush
½ cup finely ground almonds or hazelnuts, optional

Jambon:
1 pound puff paste (page 163), chilled
1 egg
1 tablespoon milk } beaten together, to brush
6 ounces boiled ham
1 tablespoon *each* butter and chopped onion
½ teaspoon finely chopped garlic
2 tablespoons Marsala wine
Pinch *each* salt and cayenne powder

1 tablespoon all-purpose flour
½ teaspoon dry mustard
1 tablespoon Dijon mustard
¼ cup chicken stock
1 tablespoon heavy cream

BAKING SHEET   One or more baking sheets or trays. *Caution:* Do not use a flat baking sheet without sides or a lip, or one that is open at the corners, unless you form a liner of foil, with sides, so that the melted butter cannot drip into the oven. Line the sheet with parchment paper.

PREPARATION   If making the ham-filled *croissants*, prepare the filling before removing the puff paste from the refrigerator.

Jambon Filling:

15 min.   Grind ham coarsely and sauté in butter with onions, garlic, wine, salt and cayenne. Sprinkle with flour and mix in mustards and chicken stock. Stir over low heat until the mixture thickens. Add cream, blend and set aside to chill before filling *croissants*.

Croissants:

25 min.   Remove the puff paste from the refrigerator. Sprinkle the work surface with flour and roll dough until it is a little more than 10 inches wide and about 36 inches long and ¼ inch thick. If the work space is small, the length of dough can be cut in half. One piece can be refrigerated while you roll out the other.

Trim all around to make a strip 10 inches wide. Cut the strip in half lengthwise to make two 5-inch pieces. Keep the work surface dusted with flour to prevent stickiness if butter should be pressed out.

First, mark the strips in 5-inch triangles and then, using a yardstick as a guide, cut through the dough with a pastry or pizza wheel. Separate the triangles.

Anytime the butter softens and sticks, place the triangles in the refrigerator until they are chilled again.

Set the baking sheet near at hand.

Place the first triangle on the work surface, with the point away from you. Roll with a rolling pin from the broad side to the point to stretch and flatten the dough. The triangle will be longer, wider, and thinner.

Note: If you are preparing the jam-filled *croissant*, place 1 teaspoon jam on the wide end of the triangle.

For the ham-filled *croissant*, place a generous teaspoonful of the mixture on the wide end of the triangle.

The plain *croissant*, of course, has no filling.

With the fingers, roll the triangle from the bottom to the point, stretching the dough as it is rolled. Place the *croissant* on the baking sheet, with the point underneath. Bend into a crescent shape. Repeat until the sheet is filled.

GLAZING

Brush each *croissant* with the egg-milk wash.

CHILLING
1 hour

Place the tray of *croissants* in the refrigerator to chill and relax, about 1 hour.

Preheat oven to 425° F.

BAKING
425° F.
20 min.
375° F.
30–40 min.

Remove *croissants* from the refrigerator and brush again with the egg-milk wash. For the jam-filled *croissants*, sprinkle with ground nuts. Place on the middle shelf of the hot oven. After 20 minutes reduce heat to 375° F. and continue baking until *croissants* are puffy and golden brown, about 30 to 40 minutes. Midway through the baking period open the oven door and inspect the pastries. Turn the tray end for end so that the *croissants* bake evenly. If some are browning faster than others, move them around. If all are browning too fast, cover with foil or brown paper.

FINAL STEP

Remove the *croissants* from the oven and place on a rack to cool.

PALM LEAVES

(PALMIERS)

[THREE DOZEN PIECES]

Folds of puff paste, coated with granulated sugar and cut into slices, spread in the hot oven to become the rich brown caramelized Parisian specialty—*palmiers*, or palm leaves. (Some *pâtissiers* call them, with affection, little pig's ears.)

This recipe is for modestly small *palmiers*, the size that mix nicely with other delicate pastries on a tea tray. For larger ones, simply increase the size of the folds.

INGREDIENTS	1½ pounds puff paste (page 163), chilled ½ cup granulated or confectioners' sugar
BAKING SHEET	One or two baking sheets, as needed, lined with parchment or wax paper.
PREPARATION 12 min.	Spread the work surface with sugar. (This is a slightly sticky operation.) Roll the chilled dough over the sugar to make a strip about 10 inches wide and ⅛ inch thick. If the rectangle is not uniform, trim the dough with a pastry cutter or sharp knife to make it so. Mark the center of the strip and fold each long edge to meet at the center. Fold lengthwise again to make a four-layer compact strip which will be somewhat less than 2½ inches wide. Brush additional sugar over both sides of the dough to replace what might have fallen off.

REFRIGERATED
REST
1 hour
	Wrap in wax paper and chill for 1 hour.
	    Brush the sugar remaining on the table into a neat pile. Later, when the dough is cut, the *palmiers* will be dipped into it.
	    Fifteen minutes before baking, preheat the oven to 400° F.
	    Remove the dough from the refrigerator and place it on the work surface. Cut the long piece into ¼-inch slices.
	    As you pick up each *palmier* to place it on the baking sheet, touch the cut edges to the sugar remaining on the work surface.
	    Place *palmiers* well apart on the prepared baking sheet. Spread the cut pieces slightly so that they can spread during baking rather than push up the centers of each slice. Flatten slightly with your palm.

SECOND REFRIGERATED REST 20 min.	Return pastries to the refrigerator for 20 minutes.
BAKING 400° F. 25 min.	Place the baking sheet on the middle shelf of the hot oven. Midway through the baking period, remove the baking sheet and quickly turn over the *palmiers* with a

350° F.   spatula. This will allow them to caramelize equally on
20 min.   both sides.
                      Reduce heat to 350° F. and bake an additional 20
                 minutes, or until the *palmiers* are caramelized and
                 golden brown.

FINAL STEP   Place the *palmiers* on a rack to cool. These keep well
                 for one or two weeks in a tight container. They may
                 be frozen for two or three months and reheated in a
                 350° F. oven for 10 minutes.

VARIATION

Palmiers de fromage:
Grate 1 cup Parmesan cheese and ½ cup Gruyère or Swiss cheese and
mix together. Brush the rectangle of puff pastry with water. Sprinkle
generously with the cheeses (keeping 2 tablespoons in reserve) and a
few sprinkles of cayenne pepper. Roll both long sides to meet at the
middle. Press firmly together and wrap in foil. Chill for 1 or more hours.
Cut the roll into ½-inch slices and place on a parchment-lined baking
sheet. Chill 30 minutes. Bake in a 400° F. oven for 20 minutes. Turn
them over with spatula, brush with beaten egg and sprinkle with reserved cheese and cayenne. Bake for an additional 15 minutes, or until
puffed and golden. Makes thirty-six pieces.

DARTOIS

[EIGHT DINNER SERVINGS OR SIXTEEN SMALL PIECES]

Two thin layers of puff paste—together scarcely more than ¼ inch high
—form a golden block 2 to 3 inches high with a filling in the center.
      One of the easiest of all fine pastries to make, a *dartois* may be put
together in two ways.
      The first, and perhaps the most widely followed, is for the filling to
be spread on the inner section of the bottom layer and the second piece
placed on top. Nothing more.
      The other is to place narrow strips of dough around the bottom
piece, which will rise in the oven's heat to form flaky sides. The top is
made separately. Both are removed early from the oven. The bottom is
filled, the top laid in place and the assembled *dartois* returned to the
oven to finish baking. Of the two, it is probably the more spectacular.
      The *dartois* can also be a savory—with anchovy or sardine fillets
encased in the crusts; spinach cooked in butter, blended with *béchamel*

sauce to which grated cheese is added, or diced pieces of braised sweet-breads and diced carrots or celery (simmered to soften in butter in a covered pan) blended with a thick *velouté* sauce.

The filling for the classic *dartois* dessert is *frangipane* cream. A mixture of fresh apples and applesauce is very close in popularity.

INGREDIENTS

Dough:
1 pound puff paste (page 163), chilled
1 tablespoon water, to brush

Frangipane Filling:
1 cup *frangipane* filling (page 305)

Apple Filling:
1 cup (about 2) apples
1 cup applesauce
½ teaspoon vanilla extract
3 tablespoons granulated sugar

1 tablespoon confectioners' sugar, to sprinkle

BAKING SHEET

One baking sheet lined with parchment paper.

PREPARATION
12 min.

Dough:
The puff pastry should have been made earlier and rested at least 6 hours or overnight before it is finally rolled into a square or rectangle a scant ¼ inch thick. This is quite thin, so use a guide (perhaps the thickness of a yardstick) to help judge the dimension.

Although an 8-inch square is customary, the *dartois* can be made larger or into a rectangle to accommodate more guests, or smaller to fit precisely on a favorite cake stand.

Allow the rolled dough to relax for 2 or 3 minutes before cutting out two identical pieces of dough. Place on the prepared baking sheet.

If you wish the pastry to have sides, cut ½-inch strips from the remaining unused dough. The edges should be clean-cut. Avoid marking or turning at the edges, or the *dartois* may not rise freely and uniformly. Brush the margins of the bottom piece with water, position side strips and press together gently.

With the tines of a sharp kitchen fork or pastry piercer, prick the bottom and top at 1-inch intervals. Be certain the tines penetrate all the way through.

REFRIGERATED
REST
45 min.

Cover with wax paper and place in the refrigerator for at least 45 minutes while the preferred filling is made.

Frangipane Filling:
If the *frangipane* cream has been in the refrigerator, remove it and leave it at room temperature to soften so that it can be easily spread.

10 min.

Apple Filling:
Peel the apples, core, slice thin and dice small. In a small bowl mix with applesauce, vanilla extract and granulated sugar.

Remove the pastry pieces from the refrigerator.

FILLING
10 min.

If you are preparing the *dartois without* the sides, brush a ½-inch margin around the bottom piece with a brush dipped in water. This will be the seal, so don't cover it with filling.

With a small spatula or spoon mound the preferred filling on the center area—about 1 inch thick. Place the top carefully over the filling and fit it on the lower section. With the fingers press gently to seal the two layers.

SECOND
REFRIGERATED
REST
20 min.

Cover with wax paper and return to the refrigerator for 20 minutes to chill and relax.

Preheat the oven to 400° F.

BAKING
400° F.
20 min.
350° F.
45 min.

Remove the *dartois* from the refrigerator. With the point of a sharp knife lightly cut or trace a diamond, circle or other design on the top piece. This will stand out dramatically when the piece has puffed in the oven. You may wish to mark the top in the way you will later cut it to be served. This also is attractive.

Reduce heat to 350° F. and continue to bake the *dartois* until puffed and a dark golden brown, about 45 minutes.

Midway through the baking period, open the oven door and inspect the *dartois*. If it seems to be puffing too much or cracking along the knife marks, prick through with the point of a knife to release steam that may be building up inside. The holes made with the fork should have done this job, but sometimes they get clogged.

The *dartois* is done when it has risen grandly and is a deep golden brown.

(See "Glazing" below.)

PREPARATION
5 min.

To prepare the *dartois* with sides, remove the pieces from the refrigerator. Cut designs on the top piece. Do not cut through the dough, however. The most shallow cut or tracing will expand greatly in the oven.

Note: The two pieces are to be baked separately for most of the baking period, then removed from the oven, filled, assembled and returned to the oven.

BAKING
400° F.
20 min.
350° F.
35 min.
20 min.

Place the pan with the two pieces of *dartois* on the middle shelf of the hot oven.

After 20 minutes reduce heat to 350° F. and at the same time inspect the *dartois*. If the bottom is greatly puffed, prick with the point of a knife and push down with the fingers or a spatula. You may also cut the top surface of the bottom dough lightly around the inside edge. This will make it easier to push down the bottom.

When the two pieces are nicely browned, after about 35 minutes, remove from the oven. With a large spoon fill the cavity with the filling. Lift the top section and rest it on the filled lower part. Press down to make a tight fit. Return to the oven for about 20 minutes.

GLAZING
10 min.

For either *dartois* (with or without sides), remove from the oven and sprinkle the top with confectioners' sugar shaken through a fine sieve.

Move the rack to its highest position and return the *dartois* to the oven so that the sugar will melt and form an attractive shiny glaze.

FINAL STEP

Remove from the oven and place on a rack to cool. The *dartois* may be frozen, but it seems flakier served the same or the following day.

MATCH STICKS

(ALLUMETTES GLACÉES AND ALLUMETTES PARMESAN)

[APPROXIMATELY FOUR DOZEN PIECES]

An *allumette* is perhaps the most elemental piece of puff paste as well as one of the most versatile. This small rectangle of golden layers can carry, with equal distinction, a sweet topping or one of many cheeses and forcemeats.

According to French legend the *allumette* was created by a thrifty *pâtissier* who was left at the end of the day with unwanted icing. Rather than discard it, the frugal baker mixed it with a bit of flour (to give it body) and spread it on a narrow strip of puff paste. Apparently it reminded him of a match stick, for he so named it. V*oila, l'allumette!*

Allumettes and straws, in the following recipe, start out life together as rolled-out, flat pieces of puff paste. But here the similarity ends. The *allumettes* are either iced or covered with a cheese or meat topping and baked flat. Straws are twisted and thereby have a special charm of their own.

Unless the *allumettes* are restrained in some fashion as they are being baked, some will rise higher than others and one may tip one way while its mate tips another. If you wish uniformity, place an inverted cooling rack on 1-inch blocks over the pieces—and against this the rising *allumettes* will come to rest. I use three or four small dough cutters of equal height to hold the rack in position during the early part of the baking period, then remove it.

INGREDIENTS

For allumettes glacées:
1½ pounds puff paste (page 163), chilled
1 tablespoon flour
1 cup Royal Icing (page 310)

For allumettes Parmesan:
1½ pounds puff paste (page 163), chilled
1 egg, beaten, to brush
1 cup grated Parmesan or other hard cheese

BAKING PAN

One baking pan lined with parchment paper.

PREPARATION
20 min.

On a floured work surface or pastry cloth roll the chilled puff pastry into a rectangle about 30 by 8 inches and ⅛ inch thick. If the dough pulls back as it is being rolled, allow it to relax for a few moments before proceeding. If the dough and butter soften, place in the refrigerator for 4 or 5 minutes.

Working note: The long rectangle is to be cut into two pieces lengthwise. The icing or other topping is spread over them, and then they are cut into 1-inch *allumettes.*

With a yardstick and a pastry wheel or sharp knife, trim the large rectangle to a precise shape, which removes the folded edges to allow the dough to expand unhindered. Cut the piece lengthwise into two pieces.

3 min.

Glacées:
For *glacées*, mix 1 tablespoon flour into 1 cup Royal Icing to give it stability in the oven.
    With a small spatula spread the icing over one or both of the long pieces. Allow to dry for 5 minutes before cutting.

3 min.

Parmesan:
For *Parmesan*, brush one or both pieces with beaten egg. Sprinkle liberally with grated cheese.

CUTTING
5 min.

With a pastry wheel or knife, divide each long strip into 1-inch pieces. Lift these from the work surface with a spatula and place on the baking sheet, close together but not quite touching.

REFRIGERATED
REST
45 min.

Cover the pan with wax paper and place in the refrigerator for 45 minutes to allow the pieces to relax.
    Preheat oven to 400° F.
    If desired, select a cooling rack to cover the *allumettes* during baking, as well as the 1-inch blocks or spacers on which the rack will rest. Without the rack the *allumettes* will be just as good but not uniformly shaped.

BAKING
400° F.
10 min.
350° F.
15 min.

Remove the baking pan from the refrigerator and position the cooling rack over the *allumettes*. Place on the middle shelf of the hot oven.
    After 10 minutes reduce heat to 350° F. Fifteen minutes into the baking period, open the door and inspect the pastries. When they show a trace of brown, remove the cooling rack. Continue baking until they are a light golden brown on the sides and light and flaky throughout. If the cheese (or the Royal Icing) is done but the interior of the pastry remains moist (by inspection), cover with foil or brown paper. Heat may be reduced to 300° F.

FINAL STEP

Remove from the oven and place on a rack to cool. *Allumettes* keep well for several days in a tight container. Reheat *Parmesan* before serving. Both *glacées* and *Parmesan* freeze well. The *Parmesan* may also be frozen before being baked.

VARIATIONS

Any grated cheese may be substituted for Parmesan.

A delicious savory topping is chicken livers, seasoned, and blended or prepared in a food processor. Equally good is breast of chicken and mushrooms blended and mixed with a thick *velouté* sauce.

STRAWS

[APPROXIMATELY FOUR DOZEN PIECES]

Straws are long, thin, flaky, delicate and delicious. Straws are twisted. Straws are a sweet. Straws can also be a savory. Both kinds are presented here.

Although straws are similar to *allumettes* (see preceding recipe), they require different treatment and produce a different pastry. For a sweet the puff paste is rolled in sugar and cinnamon. For a savory it is rolled in grated cheese. Both are twisted.

INGREDIENTS	1½ pounds puff paste (page 163), chilled
	Sweet: ½ cup granulated sugar } 2 teaspoons ground cinnamon } mixed
	Savory: ½ cup grated Parmesan cheese 1 teaspoon paprika
BAKING SHEET	One ungreased baking sheet lined with parchment paper.
PREPARATION	For both pastries, the dough first is partially rolled out on a floured work surface, but then the chief ingredient, whether sugar or cheese, is substituted for flour and the final rolling is done to the desired thickness—less than ⅛ inch. The rectangle is folded in half, and the strips or straws are cut from this.
20 min.	*Sweet:* On a floured work surface roll dough into a rectangle ¼ inch thick. Brush away all the flour and replace with the sugar-cinnamon mixture. Continue rolling until the paste is ⅛ to ¹⁄₁₆ inch thick—very thin!

Trim the dough into a rectangle. (A piece 18 by 10 inches, for example, folds into a 9 by 10-inch piece.)

Savory:
Roll puff paste to ½-inch thickness on a floured work surface. Remove all dusting flour. Sprinkle the table generously with grated Parmesan cheese and continue rolling to reduce dough to ⅛ inch or less in thickness. Trim the dough into a rectangle.

Both:
Sprinkle the filling generously over half of the rectangle, whether sugar-cinnamon or cheese. (If cheese, also lightly sprinkle with the teaspoon of paprika.) Fold the dough and press gently with the rolling pin over the entire length of the piece. With a pastry cutter or sharp knife, cut ¾-inch strips from the double-layered rectangle. If the dough has lost its chill and is soft and rubbery, place in the refrigerator for about 10 minutes.

When all strips have been cut, twist each 4 or 5 times, or until the twist appears as a solid piece. Place the strip on the prepared baking sheet. It may resist and attempt to untwist! Fight back. Return later when all have been twisted and rework each piece.

REFRIGERATED REST
45 min.

Cover the twists with wax paper. Place in the refrigerator to chill and relax for 45 minutes. If the dough is not allowed to relax fully, the twists will attempt to unwind in the heat of the oven.

Preheat oven to 375° F.

BAKING
375° F.
20 min.

Remove the tray from the refrigerator and place on the middle shelf of the moderate oven. Check the straws midway through the baking period. If they are getting too brown, reduce the heat 25° and cover with foil. The straws will be done in about 20 minutes.

FINAL STEP

Place on a rack to cool. These may be kept in a tightly closed container for several days. They will always be crisper, however, if placed in a 300° F. oven for 5 minutes before serving.

CREAM HORNS AND ROLLS

(CORNETS ET ROULEAUX FEUILLETÉES À LA CRÈME)

[ONE DOZEN PIECES]

Nothing is more of a delight to the eye and as greatly anticipated among pastries than this sugar-encrusted cornucopia pouring forth its richness of cream. Known also as Lady Locks, the *cornets* are formed by winding strips of puff paste around metal horns. They have a tendency to push away the horns as the dough expands in the oven. To avoid this, the strips must be carefully overlapped as they are wound on. Less difficult is the roll, which is wound on an open cylinder of metal or a length of hardwood dowel.

Whipped cream is perhaps the most elegant choice of a filling because it is the least contrived. For a variation, use cocoa or a liqueur or instant coffee to flavor all or part of the filling, and dip the ends in ground almonds or chocolate sprinkles. These may also be folded into the filling itself.

Small horns and rolls become savory cornucopias when filled with finely ground meats and seafood, such as shrimp and lobster, bound with mayonnaise.

To make a small horn, wrap half the length of dough around the metal form. Use a dowel of a smaller dimension, and half the length of dough, to shape the smaller open-ended rolls, described below.

INGREDIENTS	1½ pounds puff paste (page 163), chilled 1 cup water, to brush 1 egg 1 tablespoon cream or milk } beaten together, to brush ½ cup granulated sugar
BAKING SHEET	One baking sheet, greased, or lined with parchment paper.
FORMS	An assortment of metal horns and tubes. Wooden dowels about ¾ inch in diameter and 4 inches long are fine to shape the rolls. Pieces of a broom handle can be used, for example.
PREPARATION	*Working note:* The long narrow strips, cut from the chilled dough, are brushed with water and carefully wound onto either the metal cone or the tube. The moist strip is overlapped by half its width (perhaps less

as you become more proficient), the moisture sealing the seam so that the dough expanding in the heat will not pull the shape apart.

The puff paste as it expands has a tendency to push out and eject the cone unless it is pinched securely at the tip. Also, the cone should *not* be greased. The tube, on the other hand, may be lightly greased so that the form can more easily be removed near the end of the baking period.

15 min.

Roll the puff paste on a floured work surface or pastry cloth into a rectangle about 24 inches long, 12 inches wide and less than ⅛ inch thick. It should be quite thin.

Allow the dough to relax a few minutes before cutting or it may draw back.

With a yardstick and a pastry cutter (one with a jagged wheel gives a decorative edge) or sharp knife, cut 1-inch strips from the long rectangle of chilled dough.

REFRIGERATED
REST
15–25 min.

After cutting the strips, place them on a baking sheet and place in the refrigerator for 15 minutes so that they are well chilled before attempting to wrap cones and tubes. Take only three or four at a time from the refrigerator as you begin the rolling process.

20 min.

Lay a strip flat on the work surface and brush it with water.

For the horn, start at the small pointed end, overlapping the first turn, and pinch together before starting to wind in a spiral. The moist side is up. The floured side is down.

Stop the spiral strip ½ to 1 inch from the top. Cut off the excess and tuck the cut end under the strip to seal, or press the loose end tightly against the dough. Place the seal under the form as you rest it on the prepared baking sheet. Repeat with the others.

For the tube, overlap the first circle of dough and continue to spiral to within ½ inch of the end. Tuck under the end or press to seal, as above. Repeat with the others.

Be careful not to cover the ends of either the horn or the tube because the metal forms must be removed

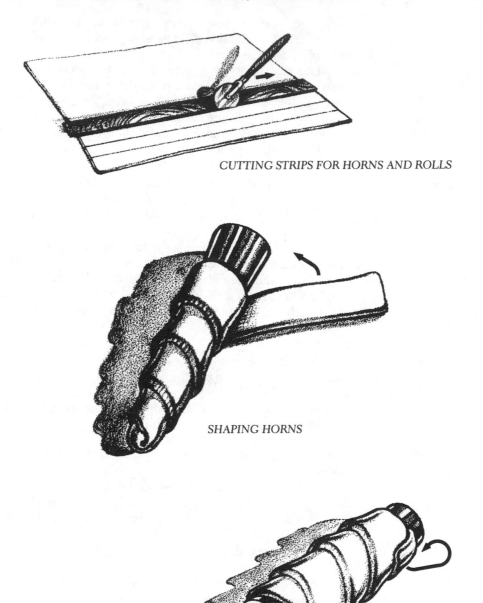

CUTTING STRIPS FOR HORNS AND ROLLS

SHAPING HORNS

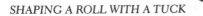

SHAPING A ROLL WITH A TUCK

during the later part of the baking period to allow the otherwise moist interior to bake through.

REFRIGERATED
REST
25 min.

Brush with egg wash and place in the refrigerator, uncovered, to chill and relax the dough. Do not brush the underpart of the piece.

Preheat oven to 425° F.

Remove the horns and rolls from the refrigerator and brush again with egg wash. Spread the ½ cup of granulated sugar in a shallow pan and in this dip each pastry carefully so that only the upper portion is sugar-coated.

Return each to the baking sheet.

BAKING
425° F.
15 min.
375° F.
45 min.

Place on the middle shelf of the hot oven. After 15 minutes reduce heat to 375° F. and continue baking.

Half an hour into the baking period, when the pieces are well shaped and lightly browned, take the sheet from the oven. Quickly and carefully free the metal or wooden forms. Put these aside and return the baking sheet to the oven to complete the baking, another 30 minutes.

FINAL STEP

Place pieces on a rack to cool. They are fragile while they are warm, so handle carefully.

When cool, pipe the desired filling into them.

PUFF PASTE TWISTS

(SACRISTAINS)

[APPROXIMATELY FOUR DOZEN PIECES]

A *sacristain* is simply a twist of puff paste coated richly with sugar and ground or slivered nuts—and one of the best pastries to serve.

You may vary the sugar used on the twists. I have used colored sugar crystals as well as coarse crystal sugar. Some *pâtissiers* suggest rock candy broken and crushed into tiny bits. It's your choice.

INGREDIENTS

1½ pounds puff paste (page 163), chilled
¾ cup granulated sugar (see above)
1 egg
1 teaspoon milk } beaten together, to glaze
½ cup medium-ground (not powdered) almonds or walnuts

BAKING SHEET One baking sheet lined with parchment paper.

PREPARATION
25 min.

With the sugar cast over the work surface instead of flour, roll the chilled dough into a rectangle at least 8 inches wide. Trim the four edges so that the dough will rise evenly in the oven. Cut the strip lengthwise into two pieces. Scatter more sugar if necessary. Turn the dough over and roll so that sugar will have been rolled into both surfaces.

Brush the egg-milk glaze over the pastry. Cover with half the nuts. Sprinkle with sugar. Roll the pin over the surface to press both the nuts and the sugar into place.

Turn the pieces over and repeat with nuts and sugar. Some sugar and nuts will fall off when the dough is turned, but that is of no great consequence.

With a yardstick and a pastry wheel or knife, cut the wide strips into 1-inch pieces (1 by 4 inches). As each piece is moved to the prepared baking sheet, twist twice to make a spiral. Press the ends down firmly so that they do not unwind.

REFRIGERATED
REST
1 hour

Cover the baking sheet with wax paper and chill thoroughly so that the small pieces will be relaxed and not untwist in the heat of the oven.

Preheat oven to 400° F. 15 minutes before the baking period.

BAKING
400° F.
15 min.
350° F.
15 min.

Remove the twists from the refrigerator and place on the middle shelf of the hot oven for 15 minutes. Reduce heat to 350° F. and continue to bake for 15 minutes, until golden brown and puffed. Midway in the baking period, check the pieces. If those along the outer rim of the sheet are browning more rapidly than those in the center, change their positions using a spatula.

FINAL STEP Place on a rack to cool. These freeze well and may be kept unfrozen in a tightly closed container for a fortnight or so.

BUTTERFLIES

(PAPILLONS)

[THREE DOZEN PIECES]

A *papillon* is a butterfly, and it quickly and lightly takes wing from any tea or dessert tray. Turned upside down it resembles a tiny Christmas tree, which does not slow its departure from the plate.

INGREDIENTS	1½ pounds puff paste (page 163), chilled ½ cup granulated sugar, to coat 1 egg white ½ teaspoon water } beaten together, to brush
BAKING SHEET	One baking sheet lined with parchment paper.
PREPARATION 15 min.	Roll chilled puff paste on a work surface sprinkled heavily with granulated sugar. Trim edges so that the fresh-cut sides will spread unhindered in the oven. *Working note:* Four strips are to be placed one on top of the other; they are folded and sliced into ¼-inch pieces. The bottom, second and third strips are to be brushed lightly lengthwise down the centers with egg white to hold them together. Cut four strips 4 inches wide and ⅛-inch thick. (The length, of course, determines how many can be cut.) Brush with the egg wash and stack one strip on top of the other. The top one is without the egg wash. With a narrow rolling pin or round dowel press down the center to secure the layers together. Fold in half down the indentation. Roll lightly over the top to compress the layers.
REFRIGERATED REST 30 min.	Wrap the dough in wax paper and chill in the refrigerator for 30 minutes before slicing. Brush the sugar into a pile to be used later when the pieces are cut.
SHAPING 15 min.	Unwrap the chilled dough and cut into ¼-inch slices with a sharp knife (rinsed frequently in cold running water). Dip each *papillon* lightly in the sugar.

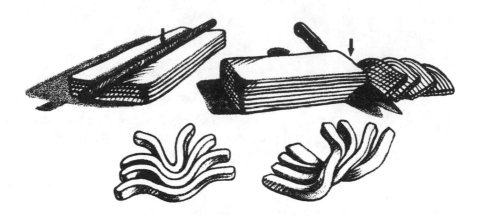

Working note: There are two ways to give final shape to the *papillon*. One is to open the folded layers after the pieces have been cut, *twist once*, and lay on the baking sheet, bringing the ends together but not touching. The other is to place the folded layers just as they are cut (after dipping in sugar) on the baking sheet.

REFRIGERATED REST
20 min.

Return the *papillons* to the refrigerator to allow the dough to grow accustomed to its new shape.

Preheat the oven to 400° F. shortly before the baking period.

BAKING
400° F.
20 min.
350° F.
15 min.

Place the baking sheet on the middle shelf of the hot oven.

Halfway through the baking period, turn over the *papillons* with a spatula so that they will brown evenly on both sides.

After 20 minutes reduce heat to 350° F. and continue to bake until the *papillons* are crisp and a lovely golden brown, about 15 minutes.

FINAL STEP

Remove the *papillons* from the oven and place on a rack to cool. They may be kept several days in a tightly closed container. They freeze very well.

PUFF PASTE CAKE

(GÂTEAU PITHIVIERS)

[ONE 8-INCH PASTRY]

Pithiviers, a small city seventy kilometers directly south of Paris, is the birthplace of this inspired and golden creation. The pastry rises several inches high from two modest layers of puff paste, between which is sandwiched a filling of *frangipane*.

INGREDIENTS

1½ pounds puff paste (page 163), chilled
½ recipe *frangipane* filling (page 305)
1 egg
1 teaspoon cream } beaten together, to brush
2 tablespoons confectioners' sugar, to sprinkle

BAKING SHEET

One baking sheet lined with parchment paper. A pizza pan is also good.

PREPARATION

Prepare *frangipane* filling (page 305) beforehand. Shape into a 4½-inch circular cake and chill. It must be hard before placing between layers of puff pastry.

25 min.

Dough:
Roll out chilled puff paste on a floured work surface or pastry cloth into a rectangle 20 by 9 inches and ¼ inch thick. With an 8-inch lid or pan as a pattern, use a pastry wheel (scalloped, if you have one) or sharp knife to cut two circles of dough. Place one on the baking sheet; this is the bottom section.

With the tines of a fork or a rolling pastry piercer, prick dough all over at ½-inch intervals—get completely through the dough.

Place chilled *frangipane* filling in the center of the bottom pieces, with a margin all around the edge where the two pieces will be joined.

With the point of a sharp knife or a pastry wheel, score the remaining circle with arcs radiating from the center. At the center make a small ¼-inch hole through which steam can escape during baking. Brush the edges of the bottom piece with water. Place the second piece over the filling and firmly press together the wide edges of the two circular pieces. Don't press

down on filling which is mounded in the center. With a knife held vertically, make several indentations and scallops around the sealed edges to give it both an artistic trim and a better seal.

REFRIGERATED
REST
45 min.

Cover with wax paper and chill for 45 minutes to relax the dough and stabilize the pastry layers.

Preheat oven to 425° F. 15 minutes before baking.

BAKING
425° F.
45 min.
375° F.
15 min.

Remove the *gâteau Pithiviers* from the refrigerator and brush with egg glaze. If some of the lines have become smeared or blurred, redefine them with a knife point.

Place on the middle shelf of the hot oven. If midway through the bake period the *gâteau* seems to be browning too fast, cover with foil or brown paper. Reduce heat to 375° F. after 45 minutes and continue to bake for 15 minutes, or about 1 hour in all.

FINAL STEP

The *gâteau* may be kept warm in the oven with the heat turned off for an hour or more. The sooner served, however, the more flaky and delicious it will be. To serve, dust with confectioners' sugar and cut into wedges with a serrated knife.

The unbaked *Pithiviers* may be frozen, tightly wrapped in plastic, to be served another day. Place frozen in the oven without the wrapper and allow at least 20 additional minutes in baking time.

APPLE TURNOVERS

(CHAUSSONS AUX POMMES)

[EIGHT PIECES]

Chaussons aux pommes are thin squares of puff paste folded into triangles, covering a delicious apple filling. Unlike many turnovers that are much the same coming out of the oven as they were going in, *chaussons aux pommes* undergo an almost magical transformation, pushed up by the hundreds of expanding butter layers.

Why so high on apples? They are one of my two favorite fruits. I planted eight trees several years ago, and now each fall I harvest bushels. I love apples!

If cherries are your dish, as they are also mine, then *chaussons aux cerises* it is. (My one cherry tree strives mightily to keep abreast of my family's appetite for its tart fruit.) Apricots and peaches also make a delicious filling.

INGREDIENTS	*Dough:*
	1½ pounds puff paste (page 163), chilled
	1 egg
	1 tablespoon milk or cream } beaten together, to brush
	½ cup sugar, to coat
	Filling:
	3 large apples (tart preferred) to make 3 cups, peeled and grated
	2 tablespoons butter
	¼ cup granulated sugar
	½ teaspoon salt
	½ teaspoon vanilla extract
	½ tablespoon rum or brandy, optional
	⅛ teaspoon freshly ground pepper
	1 tablespoon confectioners' sugar, to sprinkle
BAKING SHEET	One baking sheet lined with parchment paper.
PREPARATION 12 min.	*Dough:*
	On a floured work surface or pastry cloth, roll chilled dough into a rectangle about 10 inches wide and ⅛ inch thick. With a yardstick and a pastry wheel or sharp knife trim the dough into a 10 by 20-inch strip.

Be certain all the turned edges have been cut so that the dough will expand uniformly. Cut into two pieces lengthwise, and cut each length into four square pieces, eight in all.

No doubt there will be pieces remaining too good to be scraps. Cut into *sacristains* (page 205) or *allumettes* (page 197).

Place all the pieces of cut dough in the refrigerator covered with wax paper while the filling is being prepared.

15 min.

Filling:

Peel the apples and grate them coarsely. Sauté the apples in a medium skillet in butter until they are tender. Add the sugar, salt, vanilla extract, rum or brandy (if desired) and freshly ground pepper. Stir well and cook for 2 or 3 minutes. Remove from heat and cool before spreading on the cut pastry.

ASSEMBLY
25 min.

Prepare the egg glaze.

Take the chilled squares from the refrigerator. Brush each piece with egg wash, but don't touch the cut edges which must be free to rise grandly later.

In the middle of each square place a tablespoonful of apple filling. Don't force the small space to accept more than a level tablespoonful or the dough may balloon in the oven! Fold the dough into a triangle and press the edges with the tines of a fork to seal.

Place the completed turnover on the prepared baking sheet. Continue with the other pieces. Brush each with egg glaze.

REFRIGERATED
REST
30 min.

Cover with wax paper. Place in the refrigerator to chill for 30 minutes.

Preheat oven to 400° F.

Place granulated sugar in a pan or plate in which to dip the turnovers.

BAKING
400° F.
20 min.
350° F.
25 min.

Remove turnovers from the refrigerator. Pierce the top of each twice with the tines of a sharp kitchen fork. Brush again with egg wash. Dip the top in the sugar. If the holes have been closed by egg or sugar, open with a toothpick. When all turnovers have been sugar-dipped, place the baking sheet on the middle shelf of the hot oven.

Midway through the baking period reduce heat to

350° F. and turn the baking sheet end for end to distribute the heat evenly. Bake for a total of about 45 minutes.

FINAL STEP   Remove from the oven and place the turnovers on a rack to cool. When the turnovers are cool you may wish to sprinkle them lightly with confectioners' sugar before serving.

NAPOLEONS

(MILLE-FEUILLES)

[THREE DOZEN PIECES]

Whether in Paris, Budapest or San Francisco, one of the most exciting of all pieces on a pastry cart is a Napoleon, yet it is not difficult to make. The sheets of paste rise evenly in the oven, and then it is only a matter of choosing a filling to sandwich between the flaky pieces. A light-colored icing, with chocolate lines pulled into a design by a knife blade, is perhaps the favorite topping; but nothing more than a sprinkling of confectioners' sugar also makes a handsome presentation.

In France it would not be called a Napoleon but a *mille-feuille*. It would not be iced but only sprinkled with confectioners' sugar. This recipe presents it both ways.

Normally *mille-feuilles* and Napoleons are baked in large sheets, assembled and then cut into serving pieces. Equally attractive are small *mille-feuilles* cut from dough and made just the right size for one person.

There are several ways to build a Napoleon or *mille-feuille*. Some chefs assemble two layers of *crème* sandwiched between three of paste. The recipes that follow are more modest—one layer of *crème* between two of pastry.

INGREDIENTS   3 pounds puff paste (page 163)

Crème pâtissière:
2 cups milk
⅓ cup sugar
4 tablespoons cornstarch
3 egg yolks
1 teaspoon vanilla extract
½ cup heavy whipping cream, chilled

Glace royale:
1 egg white
½ cup confectioners' sugar
1 teaspoon lemon juice, strained

1 tablespoon water
2 ounces semisweet chocolate

BAKING PAN	One 18 by 12-inch baking pan lined with parchment paper. If this pan is too large for the oven, adjust the size of the pastry piece to a smaller baking sheet. Half the rolled paste can be held in the refrigerator while the other half is baking.
PREPARATION 15 min.	On a floured work surface, roll the chilled puff paste into a rectangle larger than the baking pan, ⅛ inch thick. Allow the dough to rest for a few moments to be certain it will not draw back. With a yardstick and a pastry wheel or knife, trim the dough to fit precisely into the baking pan. Drape the dough carefully over a rolling pin and place in the prepared pan. If it is too large, trim to fit with a sharp knife.

Pierce the dough *completely through* at ½-inch intervals with the tines of a large fork or a rolling pastry piercer.

REFRIGERATED REST 1 hour	Cover with wax paper. Place in the refrigerator to rest for 1 hour.

Preheat oven to 375° F.

Working note: To control the height of the pastry, invert a cooling rack over the top of the baking sheet, allowing it to rest on the sides of the pan, if they are about 1 inch high. If the sides are too high, rest the rack on blocks. I use four of a set of pastry cutters. Have these ready for baking.

BAKING 375° F. 40 min.	Remove the pan from the refrigerator and position the rack over the pastry. Place on the middle shelf of the oven. During the baking period, open the oven door to inspect the pastry several times and, if necessary, push down the rack if it has been lifted off the sides of the pan by the upward movement of the dough.

When it is puffed and golden brown, after about

40 minutes, remove the pastry from the oven and allow to cool on a rack.

Proceed with filling and icing.

PREPARATION
20 min.

Filling:

Place the milk, sugar, cornstarch, egg yolks and vanilla in a double boiler. Cook over medium heat until custard has thickened. Remove from heat. Whip the cream and fold into the custard. Set aside while preparing icing.

10 min.

Icing:

Place the egg white and ¼ cup confectioners' sugar in a deep bowl and beat with a whisk or electric beater until it begins to thicken. Add the remainder of the confectioners' sugar, beating constantly. Add lemon juice. Continue to beat the icing until it is thick and forms peaks when the whisk is lifted from the bowl.

10 min.

Chocolate:

Into the top section of a double boiler pour a tablespoon of water and broken pieces of chocolate. Place the double boiler over medium heat. When the chocolate softens, stir vigorously until smooth and creamy. Keep the chocolate warm over simmering water until the icing is spread.

Shape a paper cone (page 40) to pipe chocolate.

ASSEMBLY

With a long sharp knife (preferably one with a serrated blade) cut the cooled *mille-feuille* into two pieces lengthwise. Also lightly cut and trim away the outside crust around the other sides of each piece to reveal the inner layers and to make the sides uniform.

Split each piece horizontally. Do this carefully so that the layers do not crumble. Place to one side for a moment.

Working note: Because a Napoleon demands a flat surface to ice and decorate, the flat bottom becomes the top. The *mille-feuille*, on the other hand, is put back together, after it is filled, just as it was before it was cut, since it will be enhanced only with a heavy sprinkling of confectioners' sugar.

To assemble the Napoleon, place the *upper* half of the pastry on a large platter with the cut side *down*. Spread half the pastry cream smoothly over the pastry.

The lower half—now turned upside down to show the flat bottom—is placed on the top of the pastry cream —bottom up! Place a clean baking sheet over the pastry and firmly but carefully press down to join the two pieces and level the creation. If some cream is pushed out, carefully lift it away.

To ice, spread the *glace royale* evenly over the Napoleon with a small spatula. Decorate the icing with the melted chocolate piped through the very fine plain tip of a pastry tube or through a paper decorating cone with a tiny hole cut in the tip.

Pipe the chocolate in parallel lines about 1½ inches apart. For the traditional feathery chevron design, draw the dull side of a knife across the stripes at 2-inch intervals. Use care not to cut into the glaze. Complete the chevron by drawing the knife blade in the opposite direction.

When the chocolate has set, in 4 or 5 minutes, but before the icing has hardened, cut the large pieces crosswise into 2-inch-wide Napoleons, using a knife with a serrated blade and cutting with a sawing action.

If the second large piece is to be the traditional French *mille-feuille*, spread the remaining filling over the bottom section of the pastry. Reassemble as it was before it was cut and filled. Carefully press down the top piece to join the assemblage securely. Decorate with a heavy sprinkling of confectioners' sugar sifted through a fine-mesh sieve.

FINAL STEP

Chill Napoleons and *mille-feuille* for about an hour. Allow the Napoleons 20 minutes at room temperature so that the icing regains its glossy bloom before serving.

Although they are at their best served freshly made, both may be kept for several days in the refrigerator.

APPLE DUMPLINGS

(RABOTTES DE POMMES)

[APPROXIMATELY EIGHT PIECES]

The whole apple, peeled, cored and filled with sugar, cinnamon and raisins, is the heart of this fine dessert. A tart apple—Stayman, Winesap, Baldwin or Rome Beauty—is the best for cooking. Eating apples (Delicious, for example) tend to break apart or get mushy when cooked. Taste the apple to determine the amount of sugar to be used in the raisin mixture.

The dessert will grow in size in the oven's heat to become a golden ball, capped with a puffy topknot.

Apples vary in size, even those graded as small, so cut a paper square as a pattern for the piece of dough to be drawn up and over the prepared fruit. The dough may be stretched, but only a little or in the heat of the oven it may pull away from the apple.

INGREDIENTS
1½ pounds puff paste (page 163), chilled
8 apples, chosen as suggested above
1 cup raisins, plumped
½ cup granulated sugar, approximately, depending on sweetness desired
1 tablespoon cinnamon
¼ cup water, to brush
1 egg
1 tablespoon milk } beaten together, to brush

BAKING SHEET
One baking sheet with lip, lined with parchment paper.

PREPARATION
18 min.
With a sheet of paper determine the size of the square necessary to cover the apple, with the four points overlapping on top of the fruit.

Plump raisins in warm water while the dough is being rolled.

Roll the chilled dough on a floured work surface to less than ⅛-inch thickness. Allow the dough to relax a few moments before cutting the squares, or they will retract. If they do pull back, roll them into the appropriate-size square again.

REFRIGERATED
REST
15 min.

Place the squares on a piece of wax paper and put in the refrigerator to relax and chill while the apples are being prepared.

Apples:
Peel and core the apples. Drain the raisins and pat dry. In a small bowl mix the raisins, sugar and cinnamon.

Take the squares from the refrigerator and in the center of each place an apple. Fill the cored section with the prepared raisins. They can be packed fairly tightly.

Brush the edge of each square with water, overlap the points and pinch securely together. Gather up the dough between the points and work into small attractive folds. Press these against the apple so that it is completely covered with dough.

Cut a 1-inch circle of dough with a fluted cutter for each apple. Brush the top with water or egg wash and cap with the small circle.

Brush the entire apple with egg wash. Repeat with the remaining apples.

REFRIGERATED
REST
25 min.

Place apples in the refrigerator for 25 minutes while the oven heats and the dough relaxes.

Preheat oven to 425° F.

BAKING
425° F.
15 min.
375° F.
45 min.

Place the baking sheet with the apples on the middle shelf of the hot oven. After 15 minutes turn the heat down to 375° F. and continue baking for an additional 45 minutes. If the pastry browns too rapidly (before the apples are done), cover with foil or brown sack paper.

FINAL STEP

Ideally, serve warm. Delicious with thick or whipped cream.

ECCLES CAKES

[ABOUT TWO DOZEN SQUARES]

A layer of black currants pressed between two thin sheets of puff paste offers an exciting dark-light contrast that is enhanced even more when the paste becomes caramelized and golden. This delicious Canadian interpretation of the tea cakes of Eccles, a borough of Lancashire, England, is by a famous British Columbian chef, Bert J. Phillips.

INGREDIENTS 1½ pounds puff paste (page 163), chilled
½ cup granulated sugar
1 cup currants

BAKING SHEET Baking sheet with lip, lightly greased, or lined with parchment paper.

PREPARATION Plump currants in hot water 10 minutes, drain and set aside. Roll chilled paste on a floured work surface into a rectangle ³⁄₁₆ inch thick. Put aside for a moment while removing all dusting flour. Sprinkle the work surface generously with granulated sugar, and continue rolling dough to ⅛-inch thickness.
20 min.

Trim the large piece into a precise rectangle—a 24 by 10-inch piece or similar shape—out of which to cut a series of 2-inch squares.

Cover half the dough solidly with currants in a single layer. Sprinkle lightly with sugar. Fold the remaining half of the dough over the top of the currants.

Gently press a rolling pin over the entire surface until the black currants show through the sheet of thin dough. The result is a nice speckled appearance.

With a sharp knife or pastry wheel and a yardstick, cut the dough into 2-inch squares and place ½ inch apart on the prepared baking sheet.

REFRIGERATED Place in the refrigerator to relax the dough for 25 minutes while the oven heats.
REST Preheat oven to 375° F.
25 min.

BAKING Place the baking sheet on the middle shelf of the moderate oven. When the bottoms have caramelized and show light brown, carefully turn the cakes over and finish baking. At this point the layers may come apart if roughly moved.
375° F.
45 min.

FINAL STEP Place cakes on a rack to cool.

MEATS WRAPPED IN PUFF PASTE

(EN CROÛTE)

[TO COVER ONE ROAST]

Some critics say there are better things to do with a near-priceless *filet* of beef than to wrap it in a blanket of dough to become *filet de boeuf* Wellington or, simply, Beef Wellington. Nevertheless, it *is* one of the more spectacular meat entrées of the Western world, and its blanket of puff paste deserves a place here.

There are other meats, too, less expensive than filet of beef, that can be cloaked in puff paste and transformed into several other kinds of Wellingtons or dishes *en croûte*, including pork, lamb and other cuts of beef.

Puff paste can also wrap a salmon, sea bass or trout, with decorations made on the paste to resemble the creature itself—scales, tail, head and fins. Fish *en croûte* is an easy way to cook a whole fish, but it must be baked and served immediately; you do not have the luxury of being able to hold it for several hours or overnight as with meats.

To impress a party at a tailgate affair, try meat loaf *en croûte*. The guests will like the golden brick decorated with the school's insignia or the team's initials and record, and especially the taste of the *ground filet*.

The meats are accompanied with a *demi-glace*, *Bordelaise* or other sauce.

INGREDIENTS   *Dough:*
1½ pounds puff paste (page 163), chilled
1 egg
1 tablespoon milk or cream } beaten together, to brush

Meats:
Beef: 4 pounds *filet* of beef

or

Beef: 5 to 6 pounds standing rib roast, boned

or

Pork: 2½ to 3½ pounds boned and tied pork loin roast

or

Lamb: boned 4 to 5-pound leg of lamb, tied into a boneless roast, 5 inches in diameter

Fillings:
Mushroom (for beef or lamb):
4 tablespoons butter
1 pound mushrooms, chopped fine
½ cup chopped scallions
2 teaspoons Dijon mustard
1¼ cup Madeira wine or dry Sherry

Liver Pâté or Pâté de Foie Gras (for beef or lamb):
6 tablespoons butter, creamed
6 ounces liver *pâté* or *pâté de foie gras*
Pinch pepper
1 tablespoon brandy

Dried Fruit (for pork):
2 tablespoons butter
6 ounces mixed dried fruits (prunes or apricots), chopped
½ cup Port wine
2 teaspoons Dijon mustard

ROASTING PAN   One roasting pan and thermometer for meat.

BAKING SHEET
OR PAN   One baking sheet or pan, lined with parchment paper or greased.

PREPARATION
Times will vary   *Note:* The meat can be prepared one or two days before assembling the *en croûte* dish.

Place the thermometer in the thickest part of the meat for the following readings:

Filet and rib roast: 140° F. for rare, 160° F. for medium
Pork: 170° F.
Lamb: 150° F. for medium-rare

Allow the roast to cool to room temperature before trimming fat, covering and chilling overnight. Reserve any pan drippings for inclusion in the sauce.

Remove meat from the refrigerator 1 hour before wrapping in dough.

Filling:
Mushroom: Melt butter in a large skillet over medium heat. Add chopped mushrooms, onions, mustard and wine or Sherry. Stir occasionally and cook until soft.

Raise heat to evaporate all liquid. Cool to room temperature and refrigerate overnight.

Pâté: Cream butter in a food processor or blender. Add the *pâté*. Blend together with pepper and brandy.

Dried Fruit: Melt butter in a skillet over medium heat. Add chopped dried fruit, wine and mustard. Bring to a boil, then remove from heat. Cover and let stand until all liquid is absorbed, about 15 minutes. Cool. Refrigerate overnight.

SHAPING

Turn chilled dough onto a lightly floured work surface and roll into a ³⁄₁₆-inch-thick rectangle. Use a tape measure or piece of string to measure the circumference of the roast at its thickest point. Measure the length. With a sharp knife cut a rectangle out of the dough 2 inches longer than the circumference and 2 inches wider than the length. Save the trimmings for decorations.

Spread a thick 5-inch-wide strip of filling down the center of the dough and set the meat on it. Brush the edges of the dough with egg mixture and wrap around meat, pinching the edges together firmly. With care, place wrapped meat, seam side down, on the greased baking sheet. Brush all over with egg wash. Cut dough trimmings into decorative shapes (see *rognures*, page 223) and set them on top of the dough case. Do not brush decorations with egg. Make one or two small holes in the dough as part of the decoration to allow the steam to escape during baking.

REFRIGERATION
30 min. to 3
hours

Cover the dish with wax paper and refrigerate for at least 30 minutes.

Preheat oven 20 minutes before baking.

BAKING
400° F.
1–1¼ hours

Bake in the hot oven until richly browned. A meat thermometer inserted in the meat should read 135° F. If the crust browns before the meat is heated, cover with a piece of aluminum foil.

FINAL STEP

Prepare sauce. Remove the roast from the oven and let it stand for 10 minutes before cutting into ¾-inch slices with a serrated knife.

ROGNURES
(LEFTOVER PIECES AND SCRAPS)

In a commercial bake shop the volume of scraps of puff paste left in a day presents a costly problem for which the *pâtissier* has developed many solutions. But in the home kitchen the volume of *rognures* is seldom so overwhelming; indeed, it often presents a bonus.

The approach is simple. All pieces of scrap dough cut from the job at hand are covered and laid aside in the refrigerator. Later, when the major pieces are finished, I take this treasure and unfold it on the table. Then decisions are made.

Since our house can always use small hors d'oeuvres and tiny sweet things, I select a cutter, usually 1¼ inch (30 mm), fluted or plain, and punch out as many small discs as I can. These I turn upside down on a tray, brush with egg, sprinkle with freshly grated cheese (of which I keep a supply at hand) and place in the freezer. The next day these are gathered, packaged, labeled and returned to the cold to await their call.

While I have the small fluted cutter in hand I also cut out a dozen or so *fleurons* (crescents and ovals) against the day I may wish to decorate a Beef Wellington or a *gâteau Pithiviers*.

For a sweet, I sprinkle cinnamon sugar on some of the discs after they have been brushed with egg. These are frozen and stored as for the cheese ones.

Or, sensing that our supply of *allumettes* (page 197) has been sadly depleted during the recent visit of the grandchildren, I cut out small squares and rectangles—freehand, without the yardstick—brush with egg, sprinkle with cheese or cinnamon-sugar and freeze.

If, on the other hand, you need a sheet of puff paste for a special project that does not demand the best, here are two suggestions.

Press all the scraps into a ball, as do some *pâtissiers*. Chill, roll into a flat rectangle and cut from it small pieces for hors d'oeuvres, tartlets, *petites bouchées* or *fleurons*. It will rise but not very much, because the layering effect has been lost in the jumble of pieces.

A more rewarding technique is to assemble the pieces flat on the work surface to try to maintain the position of the layers in the dough. Arrange them into a rough square or rectangle. Brush the edges lightly with water (to help make a good seal) and then overlap them slightly. Press together with your fingers, dust the whole piece with flour and roll to join the seams. Chill before cutting.

For flakier scraps, spread 1 or 2 tablespoons butter on two-thirds of the rolled-out dough. Fold in three (to make two layers of butter), as if folding a letter. Wrap. Chill for 60 minutes and then roll, giving the dough two turns. Refrigerate overnight before using, or freeze for later use.

Strudel Dough and Phyllo Leaves

Tissue-thin strudel dough is the culinary achievement of Hungarian and Bavarian pastry makers, while the fragile and translucent *phyllo* leaf is a product of the Greek kitchen. Yet the unleavened doughs are identical. So are the techniques for stretching the doughs so thin that one could easily read this page of the book through them.

The delicate and crisp *phyllo* leaves are used in this chapter to make two different but equally delicious *baklavas* and the small cheese-filled *tiropetes*. The *phyllo* leaf is also used to make *spanakopita*, the entrée dish of spinach and *feta* cheese baked between layers of buttered leaves, the recipe for which is included among entrée pies (page 250).

The strudel dough is basic to the raisin–cream cheese strudel and Hungarian apple strudel, as well as the tall, multilayered strawberry-and-whipped-cream strudel, *hideg rétes epres*, a Budapest favorite.

There is a difference in how the dough is finally shaped. For both *phyllo* and strudel, the dough is stretched and pulled into a large sheet, perhaps 3 or 4 feet in diameter. But for strudel, the large piece of dough is covered with a filling and rolled into one pastry which is cut into lengths to fit a pan, then baked.

For *phyllo* leaves, the large piece of dough is allowed to dry and stiffen for 15 minutes before cutting with scissors into small squares or rectangles to make one of the Greek pastries. The leaves are stacked one on top of the other, folded and wrapped in plastic to store.

My preference is home-made strudel dough and store-bought *phyllo* leaves. I love the challenge of stretching the strudel dough as thin as possible, but I don't care to turn around and cut it into small *phyllo* leaves which I can buy at my supermarket. It is important to note that no large strudel sheet is made commercially so if you want to have the fun of putting together an old-fashioned strudel you must do it yourself. Commercial *phyllo* leaves can be used for making small strudel pieces.

Strudel Dough and Pastry

Apple strudel has received top billing among strudels in this country, but there are dozens more to intrigue you. The delicate fabric of dough is essentially the same for all; only the fillings differ.

The two chosen here—raisin–cream cheese and Hungarian apple —are perhaps the most popular both at home and abroad. A third recipe follows, a marvelous creation of a fine Hungarian cook—layered strawberry strudel, served chilled.

The stretching by hand of a small mass of soft dough into a large tissue-thin fabric to make a strudel is one of the miracles of pastry making. The challenge lies in the thinness of the outspread dough that will be rolled to form layer after layer of delicate crusts around a filling.

A worker of this small miracle in the Old World tradition is Iréne Jánosné, of the Grand Hotel Margitsziget in Budapest. She hustles around a huge work table stretching the dough to more than 8 feet in length and 4 feet wide. She moves constantly, counterclockwise around the table, lifting and pulling the dough. For her it is one of many strudels to be made each day before going on to the next chore in her big kitchen.

If your kitchen is small or only one card table is available for a work surface, divide the dough in half to make two strudels. Keep the second ball of dough covered under the pan or bowl until needed.

You will find speed not to be necessary. Be patient. Expect to work around the table for at least 15 to 20 minutes, stopping now and then to relax and inspect your handiwork.

Yes, you can do it. Perhaps not the first time, but very soon, you will master the stretching technique and will be able to read the printed words of this recipe through the almost-transparent film of dough. Surprisingly, the elastic dough is not fragile if it is handled in a special way.

If there is a secret to strudel dough it is the use of the *backs* of the hands—not the fingertips—to pull and stretch the dough. Initially, for the first few times around the table, the dough may be pulled gingerly between the thumbs and forefingers, but only for a short while. Invariably, fingertips will press into the dough and weaken it.

A further caution: sharp or rough fingernails and rings can tear the dough.

If you are working alone in this operation, the dough, in the beginning, will pull toward you. But if you can recruit a friend to work with you across the table, together you can move around the dough, gently pulling, one against the other. In a few moments, as the dough begins to stretch, it will hold its place in the center and not follow.

Lift the dough over the backs of your hands and gently stretch, pulling it toward you and at the same time spreading your hands—in effect, a two-way stretch. Pull gently. Allow the dough to move and stretch slowly between your hands before putting it down and moving on.

Resist the temptation to hurry the process by stretching the dough with your fingers. The thin skin of dough will certainly tear. Try also to get the backs of your hands under all parts of the dough, especially under the thicker areas, usually near the center.

If the dough tears, but only slightly, leave it alone; the hole will disappear when the strudel is rolled. If it is a large hole (the size of a dinner plate) and in a critical place toward the center, it can be covered with a larger piece cut from one of the ends. Even Iréne Jánosné's best efforts had some holes, which she blamed on the quality of the local flour. Some were small (left unpatched) and some large (covered with unwanted end pieces).

As the dough is stretched, a thick cord forms around the edge. When the stretching is finished and the skin is left exposed to the air for a few minutes to harden, the coarse edge is torn off or cut away with scissors and discarded. Surprisingly, about one-third of the total weight of the dough is in the discarded dough.

The work surface for making a 48-inch strudel would be at least 60 by 30 inches—a breakfast or dining table or two card tables pushed together. If space is a problem or if you wish to make a smaller strudel, make a 24-inch pastry on top of one card table.

The work surface is covered with an often-laundered damask tablecloth or folded sheet. I prefer the damask because it has a nap, a raised pattern woven into the cloth, that helps anchor the dough as it is pulled. For your first endeavors, tie or tack the cloth to the underside of the work surface so that the cloth does not slip.

The cloth serves two purposes. The dough can be stretched over it without sticking. When the dough is fully stretched, one long edge of the cloth can be lifted to gently roll the dough (and the filling) into the long cylindrical strudel shape.

In the two fine strudel recipes that follow—one from Budapest more than three-quarters of a century ago, and the other a recent Hungarian import—the recipes for making the dough and the technique for stretching it are the same. The fillings, however, are quite different.

One is apple, nuts and preserved cherries; the other, cream or cottage cheese and nuts.

RAISIN–CREAM CHEESE STRUDEL

(RÉTES)

[36- TO 48-INCH STRUDEL, FOR EIGHTEEN TO TWENTY-FOUR SERVINGS]

Iréne Jánosné was annoyed that her large sheet of strudel dough was broken in several places with small and large tears. It's the flour, she lamented, as she hurried around the big oak table covered with a floured cloth, gently pulling the film of dough toward her. The largest break was near the center, so she made two strudels: cream cheese and raisins rolled in one half of the piece; cherries, nuts and cinnamon in the other.

The table had been adjusted to her height so that when she reached to stretch the dough she did not have to stoop, an important comfort consideration for one who works daily at the task.

The same sheet of dough is the base for the deep-fried rounds with whipped cream and fresh strawberries sandwiched between them, *hideg rétes epres* (layered strawberry strudel, page 235).

Strudels and soups were her forte in the big kitchen of the Grand Hotel Margitsziget. She was a cook, and her tables, stoves, ovens and soup kettles reached to the edge of, but did not extend into, the domain of the pastry chef, Mosonyi Páe.

Lard is a favorite shortening of Hungarian cooks, and Jánosné was no exception. For a taste like the strudel served at the Grand Hotel Margitsziget, sprinkle and brush melted lard on the dough. If lard is not available or wanted, use butter and margarine.

The length of the strudel will depend on your ability to stretch the dough. If you're not an old strudel hand, your confidence and skill will grow as you practice, and so will the length and breadth of your strudel sheet.

(If my strudel dough stretches magically beyond my expectations —as it does on occasion—and I need more filling, I open a 1-pound can of dark sweet cherries, packed in heavy syrup, drain and use them to lay down a row of new filling, abutting the cream cheese and reaching to the end of the dough. Sprinkle the cherries in place, with ¼ cup granulated sugar and 2 teaspoons cinnamon. This was suggested by Jánosné, who often uses it for a delicious filling.)

INGREDIENTS   *Filling:*
          ¾ cups walnuts or almonds, ground medium to fine

¼ cup finely ground dry bread crumbs
¾ cup white raisins, plumped
2 8-ounce packages cream cheese, room temperature
1 egg, room temperature
3 tablespoons butter, room temperature
¾ cup granulated sugar
¼ teaspoon vanilla extract
½ teaspoon minced zest of lemon

Dough:
2¼ cups all-purpose flour
Pinch salt
1 egg
1 tablespoon butter, room temperature
¾ cup water, approximately

8 ounces lard or 4 ounces *each* butter and margarine,
    melted, to brush
½ cup confectioners' sugar, to dust

BAKING PAN — One 12 by 18-inch pan will hold the strudel after it is cut. Grease and flour, or cover the bottom of the pan with parchment paper.

WORK SURFACE — A kitchen table or two card tables covered with a cloth dusted with ¼ cup flour.

PREPARATION — *Note:* Prepare the work surface and filling before making dough.

15 min.

Filling:
Combine nuts and crumbs. Set aside.
    Plump raisins in warm water.
    In a medium bowl break up and stir the cream cheese. Mix in egg, soft butter, sugar, vanilla and lemon zest. Blend ingredients into cream cheese until smooth. Drain and dry raisins on paper towels and add to cheese mixture. Stir until raisins are uniformly distributed. Set aside.

● BY HAND
12 min.

Dough:
In a medium bowl measure flour and sprinkle with a pinch of salt. Form a well in the flour and break the egg into it. Add soft butter. Add ½ cup water. Stir all ingredients to make a soft but not wet dough. Add more water if necessary. The mass will be sticky. With a dough scraper in one hand, knead and toss the

dough for 10 minutes on a lightly floured work surface, adding sprinkles of flour if necessary to control stickiness.

▲ ELECTRIC MIXER
10 min.

Into the mixer bowl measure flour and sprinkle with a pinch of salt. Attach dough hook and bowl. Turn on low speed (no. 2 on my KitchenAid) and add egg and butter. Add ½ cup water and blend well before adding more liquid. The dough will be soft but not wet and will clean the sides of the bowl when there is a proper balance of flour and water. Knead at low speed for 8 minutes. Stop the machine and remove the mixing bowl. Feel dough to be certain it is soft, elastic and not sticky.

■ FOOD PROCESSOR
4 min.

Attach the metal blade in the work bowl and measure in the flour and salt. Drop in the egg and butter and process for 5 seconds until well mixed. With the machine running, pour water through the feed tube in a steady stream, but only as fast as the flour absorbs it. Remove the cover and scrape down the sides of the bowl if necessary. Let the processor run 45 to 60 seconds until dough is smooth and elastic.

RESTING
10 min.

Place dough under an inverted warm bowl or pan and allow to rest for 10 minutes.

SHAPING
5 min.

Flatten dough into a rectangle—about 18 inches in length and 8 inches wide. Brush lightly with shortening. Allow to rest 4 minutes.

STRETCHING
15–20 min.

Place dough on a floured cloth. Carefully pull and stretch the dough as described on page 226. Do not *pinch* dough between fingers. The dough must rest on the backs of the hands and be stretched slowly away from the center. As you finish at one position, give the dough a gentle wave so that the air lifts it off the hands and lets it drop to the table. Continue around the dough. Pay particular attention to thicker areas. Work away from the thinner spots until the dough is the same uniform thickness. If large holes appear, patch them with pieces taken from an end. Ignore small tears, which will not be noticed when the pastry is rolled.

DRYING
15 min.

Stop when you feel further effort will tear the dough. With scissors or a sharp knife trim the heavy edge off the dough. If some of the dough should hang over the side, remember that one edge will be lifted and folded over the filling while the trailing edge will come up and over the work surface as the cloth is pulled to roll the dough.

Allow dough to dry for 15 minutes on the cloth.

During the drying interval, melt lard or butter-margarine mixture and keep warm.

Preheat oven to 400° F.

FILLING
10 min.

Sprinkle dough with melted shortening. With care not to tear the fabric of the dough, you can brush the shortening on with a soft, wide pastry brush if you hold the brush at a 45° angle and *draw* it lightly over the dough—*do not stroke it back and forth*.

Sprinkle the surface of the dough with the nut-crumb mixture.

With a spoon, place the cream cheese filling along the length of the strudel, about 8 inches above the lower edge. The filling should be about 1½ to 2 inches thick.

Unfasten the cloth if it is tied or tacked to the table. Lift the edge near the filling and let the dough fall over and cover it. Brush this narrow width of dough with melted shortening.

Grasp the cloth with the hands 24 inches apart, lift and allow the dough to roll forward slowly. You will be surprised how easily this is done. Pull the cloth toward you so that the opposite edge is pulled to the top of the table. Continue to roll. The strudel will become a cylinder approximately 3 to 4 inches thick.

Brush the length of strudel with shortening.

Place the baking pan near the strudel and determine how long the lengths should be cut to accommodate the pan. With scissors or a sharp knife, cut strudel into desired lengths. Place each on the pan, and press ends together gently. The uncut length can also be laid on the pan in the shape of a horseshoe.

BAKING
400° F.
20 min.
350° F.
30 min.

Place the pan on the middle shelf of the oven. After 20 minutes reduce heat and turn the pan end for end to expose strudels to uniform heat.

Bake to a golden brown, another 30 minutes.

FINAL STEP   Remove from oven and allow to cool before cutting strudels diagonally into 3-inch pieces. Dust liberally with confectioners' sugar before serving.

Strudel may be frozen. Place the cut pieces in a plastic freezer carton to protect the fragile layers. When reheating, place frozen pastry in a 350° F. oven for 15 minutes.

VARIATION

Seafood Strudel:
Use chopped boiled lobster, cooked shrimp and flaked cooked fish sautéed in butter. Spoon cheese sauce over the seafood before it is rolled.

HUNGARIAN APPLE STRUDEL

(RÉTES)

[36- TO 48-INCH STRUDEL CUT INTO 2-INCH SERVINGS]

Regina Hollander, born in Hungary in the last century, made this apple strudel on April 17, 1921, to be served to members of her wedding party. Fifty-seven years later she made it for me in the kitchen of her Indianapolis home.

"Isn't this a miracle dough!" she exclaimed again and again as she walked around the table, stretching the dough over the floured cloth. It was a statement, not a question. It was abundantly clear she had not lost her fascination with the dough after making literally thousands of strudels in her kitchen over a long lifetime.

She was positive about one particular step in making the dough: after being kneaded, it must rest 15 to 20 minutes on a towel under a *warm* pot or bowl inverted over the dough. Also, during this interlude peel and grate the apples. If this is done beforehand, they will discolor.

The small ball of dough with which Mrs. Hollander started to work weighed 18 ounces, little more than a pound. After she had stretched and trimmed the dough, it measured 48 by 24 inches and weighed only 13 ounces; 5 ounces had been discarded in the trimming.

The final length of the strudel depends on the skill of the home baker. You will find this will increase with experience.

The walnuts in the filling complement the apples perfectly. Mrs. Hollander prefers a Jonathan apple, but other choices are Golden and Red Delicious.

INGREDIENTS

Dough:
2 cups all-purpose flour
½ teaspoon salt
1 tablespoon butter or margarine, room temperature
1 egg, room temperature
¾ cup water, approximately
½ cup flour, to sprinkle on cloth

Filling:
1 pound cherry preserves, drained
1 cup finely ground dry bread crumbs
1 cup granulated sugar
2 cups walnuts, ground medium to fine
½ teaspoon cinnamon
½ cup raisins, white or dark, plumped
1½ to 2 pounds (4 or 5) apples, peeled and grated
½ pound (2 sticks) unsalted butter or margarine, to
  brush

½ cup confectioners' sugar, to dust

BAKING PAN

One 18 by 12-inch baking pan, brushed with melted fat and sprinkled with flour. Parchment paper cut to fit can be used instead.

WORK SURFACE

At this point strudel may appear to be a major undertaking. It is. But be assured the result is worth it. Prepare the kitchen table or one or two card tables by covering with a length of cloth. An old damask tablecloth is very good. Secure the cloth with tacks or by tying, if it slips as you pull the dough.

PREPARATION
15 min.

Filling:
Drain cherries. Reserve the syrup for another use (breakfast pancakes perhaps), but reserve 2 tablespoons of it to dribble over the cherries after they have been placed on the dough.

Place at hand the bread crumbs, sugar, nuts and cinnamon. Plump raisins in hot water for 15 minutes, drain and pat dry on paper towels.

Clarify butter in a small pan. Set aside.

Select the apples to be peeled and grated later.

Dough:
Only the procedure for preparing dough by hand is detailed here. Please turn to page 230 for instructions

for using the electric mixer or food processor for this strudel dough.

5 min.

In a bowl mix flour, salt, butter or margarine and egg. Pour in about ½ cup water and blend. The dough must be soft and elastic—just beyond the sticky stage. Add more water if the dough is firm.

KNEADING
12 min.

Knead the dough with a dough knife or broad spatula, lifting the mass off the table surface and dropping and/ or throwing it down with considerable force. This is a long kneading period, so walk away from it occasionally if you tire.

RESTING
20 min.

Place the dough on a cloth and cover with a pot, pan or bowl that has been warmed in hot water. While the dough is resting, cover the work surface with a cloth and sprinkle with flour. Pat the ½ cup flour into the cloth.

Place the dough in the center of the work surface. Stretch and roll to a 15-inch round. Brush with shortening.

STRETCHING
15 min.

Caution: Remove rings and smooth rough fingernails.

Read the detailed description for stretching dough on page 230. Do not grasp between the fingers, which may weaken and pierce the dough at that point.

Stretching must be done with the backs of the hands. You may wish to have a second person pull (but gently) against you from across the table. Be patient. Don't hurry.

Stretch the dough uniformly, with special attention to the thicker parts. If a small hole appears, move away from it. Don't tease it. If a large tear suddenly confronts you in a critical place, patch with a piece taken from an end.

DRYING
10 min.

Stop when the dough has been stretched as thin as it can be without a serious tear. Trim off the heavy border with scissors or a sharp knife.

While the dough is drying, peel and grate the apples coarsely. Include some finely sliced pieces to give the filling more character.

Preheat oven to 375° F. Prepare the baking pan.

FILLING
10 min.

With a spoon, sprinkle melted shortening over the dough and follow with bread crumbs, sugar, nuts and cinnamon.

Before spreading the apples, place them in a sieve and press out the moisture with the side of a rubber scraper. Or squeeze out between the hands.

Scatter the raisins and apples evenly over the lower third of the dough (lengthwise). Place a row of drained cherries down the center of the raisins and apples.

Grasp the cloth with both hands nearest the filling and gently lift the dough to start it rolling, like a jelly roll. When the strudel is complete, shape it uniformly with the hands.

Cut into lengths to fit the baking pan, and place each on the pan with the edge underneath. Press open ends to close.

Brush strudel with melted butter or margarine.

BAKING
375° F.
35–45 min.

Place on the middle rack of the oven. Halfway through the baking period, turn the pan around to balance the heat distribution. Bake until golden brown, 35 to 45 minutes in all.

FINAL STEP

Place pan on a rack to cool. When cool, remove the strudels and place on a board to cut into 2-inch pieces. Dust liberally with confectioners' sugar before serving.

This freezes well. Rather than cut individual servings, freeze the length(s) of strudel. Be careful not to break the fragile crusts. When reheating, place frozen strudel in a 350° F. oven for 20 minutes.

LAYERED STRAWBERRY STRUDEL

(HIDEG RÉTES EPRES)

[AN 8-INCH CREATION, SERVES SIX]

It is fragile. It is spectacular. It is strawberry. It is whipped cream. It is sixteen or so layers of fried, wafer-thin dough. It is not difficult to make. It is delicious.

Cook Iréne Jánosné created *hideg rétes epres*, which is served in the dining room of the Grand Hotel Margitsziget to those fortunate enough to be in Hungary when fresh strawberries, big and succulent, are on the market. Other fruit could be used, fresh or frozen, but somehow in summertime, on Margaret Island in the Danube River, between Buda and Pest, the pastry calls for strawberries.

Its secret, apart from the freshness of the fruit and the richness of the whipped cream, is the deep-fried, delicate rounds of parchment-thin pieces of strudel dough.

With a plate or lid as a pattern, the thin rounds are cut with a pastry knife or wheel.

Because they are so thin, the rounds barely kiss the hot fat before they are lifted out and placed on paper toweling to drain.

The exact number of rounds is not critical, nor is their size. A dessert for four would call for 6-inch rounds; for a dozen guests, 9- or 10-inch rounds.

The rounds can also be cut from *phyllo* leaves purchased in the supermarket specialty food departments or Middle Eastern shops (see "Sources of Supply," page 47).

INGREDIENTS	*Filling* (for 9-inch rounds)
	1 quart fresh strawberries, stemmed
	(*or* 2 10-ounce packages frozen strawberries)
	1 cup granulated sugar
	2 cups water
	⅛ teaspoon salt
	1 cup (8 ounces) heavy whipping cream, chilled
	1 teaspoon vanilla extract

Dough:
One batch of dough prepared as for raisin–cream cheese strudel (page 228), which is stretched into a thin sheet from which approximately 18 9-inch rounds can be cut

24 ounces (3 cups) cooking oil, for frying
Confectioners' sugar, to sprinkle

FRYER   A heavy metal kettle large enough to deep-fry whichever size rounds are chosen.

PRIOR STEPS   Stem strawberries and slice each lengthwise. Bring sugar, water and salt to a boil in a large saucepan. Stir over low heat until sugar completely dissolves. Increase heat. Boil for 5 minutes without stirring. For fresh berries, remove the saucepan from the heat and drop in berries. Leave berries in the syrup until you are ready to assemble the strudel.
For frozen berries, unwrap and drop into the

syrup. Reduce heat and leave over low heat until the berries have thawed. Remove the saucepan from the heat and set aside until you are ready to assemble the strudel.

The cream to be whipped should be very cold. In hot weather also chill the bowl and beater. Whip cream to soft peaks. Place in the refrigerator until you are ready to spread it on the rounds.

PREPARATION

Prepare dough.

While the dough is drying, heat the oil to 375° F. The temperature can be tested by dropping a cube of bread into the oil. If it browns nicely in 60 seconds, the oil is ready. Do not allow it to get smoky hot!

Set aside long-handled tongs or two wooden spoons near the kettle to lift the rounds out of the fat. Also put several layers of paper toweling or brown sack paper alongside on which to stack the rounds.

CUTTING

Holding a pan lid or plate on the sheet of dough as a pattern, carefully cut the rounds with a pastry wheel or sharp knife.

FRYING
375° F.

The rounds will be fried one at a time and placed in a stack on the absorbent paper.

12 min.

When the oil is heated to 375° F., lift a cut round from the work table with both hands—gently—and drop it horizontally onto the surface of the oil. Don't attempt to slip the dough edgewise into the fat or it will buckle like an accordion. If there is a wrinkle or fold, immediately try to straighten the round. Don't attempt it after 5 seconds or it may break.

20 seconds

Stand by while the round fries—about 20 seconds, just time enough for it to harden into shape and take on a light tan coloration. Not dark *brown*, which means it is close to scorching!

With the wooden spoons or tongs lift the round, hold it over the kettle momentarily to drain and then stack. The fried rounds are brittle, so move them carefully.

ASSEMBLY
15 min.

The strudel is assembled on the serving plate in this order:
3 rounds
Whipped cream

2 rounds
Strawberries
3 rounds
Whipped cream
2 rounds
Strawberries
3 rounds
Whipped cream
3 rounds
Dust with confectioners' sugar

Lay down the layers as suggested above. If some rounds crack during assembly, no matter. They will not be seen.

Spread the whipped cream with a spatula. There are three whipped cream layers, so spread each not too thickly.

Place the strawberries by hand evenly over the surface.

If some fruit remains after two berry layers, spread the balance on the last layer of whipped cream. A few may be saved to decorate the top.

Finally, sprinkle with confectioners' sugar. Stand back and admire.

FINAL STEP Hold the strudel in the refrigerator until ready to serve. It will be a thing of considerable beauty, so present it to guests for a visual feast before cutting it into pie-shaped pieces. There will be some cracking and breaking of the delicate rounds when the knife is pressed through the strudel, but it will not affect the taste—or the delight.

Phyllo

Phyllo, the Greek word for "leaf," is the name of the leaf-like dough that is used for a wide variety of sweet and savory dishes. It is sometimes spelled *filo* or *fillo* and is pronounced *fee-low*. One of the most famous *phyllo* dishes, *baklava* (or *baclava*), made with layers of the tissue-thin dough, is presented here in two forms. There is also *tiropetes*, a puffy triangular cheese hors d'oeuvre, and *spanakopita*, a delicious spinach-cheese pie (see "Entrée Pies," page 250).

In the United States, it is possible to buy both *phyllo* leaves and *phyllo*/strudel leaves, which can be used interchangeably in pastry making. They can be purchased frozen in specialty food sections of big supermarkets or ordered fresh from Greek stores (See "Source of Supply," page 47.)

If you wish to make your own leaves, follow the strudel dough recipe and cut the large sheet into smaller pan-size sheets. (I find it not worth my time to do this, since I can buy the ready-made product at one of several stores in my small city.)

BAKLAVA

[APPROXIMATELY TWO DOZEN DIAMOND-SHAPED PIECES]

Baklava is one pastry that has the same name at home, in Greece, as it has abroad—*baklava!* Or *baclava*.

If there is a Greek national pastry it would have to be *baklava*, a delightful confection of fragile *phyllo* leaves, nuts, cinnamon and honey. Cut into golden brown diamonds, *baklava* has the delightful quality of disappearing from the dessert plate just one bite before it would have been too much.

The ground floor of Dionysos Zonar's, a block from Constitution Square in the heart of Athens, could have been the model for all those hundreds of fine Greek candy and soda shops that once upon a time were a part of American towns—mirrored walls, marble-topped tables, green leather chairs and delicious food. It smelled of sweets and chocolates and all sorts of other good things. On the floor below was the big modern bakery that supplied not only the café and restaurant upstairs but also a café perched spectacularly at the end of a funicular railway on Lycabettus Hill. It came as a surprise that even here, where one of the best pans of *baklava* in Greece is assembled, the delicate sheets of *phyllo* are purchased ready-made.

Zonar's *baklava* is made with ground almonds, with their skins, but an equally good *baklava* filling can be made with ground walnuts. The Zonar *baklava* is unusual in one respect: it is made with butter churned from goats' milk. It is an unforgettably good taste.

Baklava is an excellent after-dinner dessert, yet the Greeks favor *baklava* in the middle of the afternoon or as a late-night snack. Even if coffee and tea are served, *baklava* is also accompanied by a glass of ice water.

INGREDIENTS   *Pastry:*
1 pound (approximately 25) *phyllo*/strudel leaves

Filling:
¾ pound (3 sticks) butter, melted and clarified, to brush
3 cups (1 pound) finely chopped or coarsely ground walnuts or almonds
1 tablespoon cinnamon
1 cup water, to brush

Syrup (page 242)

BAKING DISH

Most commercial *phyllo* leaves are about 17 by 11 inches, hence a 13 by 9-inch pan is ideal and will produce about two dozen 2-inch diamonds. The pieces trimmed from the edges may be overlapped in the interior to make additional layers or saved to use in other *phyllo* pastries.

PREPARATION

Beforehand:

Overnight or
2 hours

Pastry: Remove the package of *phyllo* leaves from the freezer to allow thawing completely overnight in the refrigerator or 2 hours at room temperature. Don't remove the leaves from the sealed plastic package until completely thawed. When the package is opened and the leaves are unfolded, cover with a moistened cloth to prevent the leaves from drying out and breaking.

10 min.

Clarify butter in a saucepan by melting it slowly over low heat. Remove the pan from the heat; let it rest for 5 minutes, tilt pan, skim off foam and spoon butter into a small bowl or cup. Discard the milky solution that remains.

30 min.

Filling: Finely chop or coarsely grind nuts in a food processor, blender or nut grinder. Place in a bowl and mix with cinnamon.

Preheat oven to 350° F.

Unfold *phyllo* leaves into a neat stack on the work surface. Invert the baking pan over the stack, positioning it along one side and edge. With a knife or pastry wheel cut through the stack, to the shape of the pan.

Lay a slightly dampened paper towel or cloth over the stack of leaves to prevent them from drying out during preparation.

You may do one of two things with the unused portion of the leaves. You may reserve, refrigerate and use them at a later date for other *phyllo* pastries. Zonar's chef, during the layering of the *baklava*, several times crumpled small pieces of leaves and made a layer of these—to be covered with a whole leaf. He explained that the crumbled scraps give the *baklava* a lighter, less dense look. He also made flat layers by overlapping two or three narrow leaves.

With a pastry brush coat the pan bottom and sides with clarified butter.

PROCEDURE

There will be eight single leaves to form the bottom crust and then three alternating layers of nuts and cinnamon between *phyllo* leaves, topped with eight leaves. The number of leaves is not critical, nor is the number of layers of nuts and cinnamon. Make the number that pleases you and makes efficient use of the ingredients.

Carefully peel and lift the first leaf from the stack and place it on the bottom of the buttered pan. Brush the leaf with butter. Add seven more single leaves, brushing each with butter before proceeding. Sprinkle the eighth leaf evenly with about one-third of the nut-cinnamon mixture.

Cover the nuts and cinnamon with a leaf, brush with butter and add two more leaves, buttering each. These middle layers may be made with the crumpled scraps or pieced-together smaller leaves. Lay down a whole leaf before and after a nut-cinnamon layer, however.

Build three more nut layers and finish with a top crust of eight leaves, each buttered.

With the brush push the edges of the leaves down the side of the pan to make a neat, rounded trim.

Lay out a pattern on the top leaf with a ruler. The traditional shape is a diamond, but pastries may also be cut into squares and triangles. Use a sharp knife to cut through the pastry, including the bottom layer. This in-depth cut will allow the syrup to permeate all of the *baklava* when it is poured on after baking.

Preheat oven to 350° F.

An uncomplicated way to cut diamonds is to mark parallel lines, 1½ inches apart, lengthwise from one end of the pan to the other. Make a diagonal mark from one corner to the other, and lay out parallel lines

1½ inches apart. Make the deep cuts with a sharp knife.

BAKING
350° F.
1½ hours

Sprinkle the top leaf with water or spray with an atomizer to prevent *phyllo* from curling during baking. Zonar's chef explained that it was done "to give the *baklava* a good face."

Place the baking dish in the middle of the oven. Bake for 1½ hours, or until it has risen and has a rich golden color.

Syrup:
Although the syrup can be made several days before it is needed and held in the refrigerator, it may be more convenient to make the syrup while the *baklava* is in the oven.

Here is a choice of two syrups. One is from Zonar's in Athens and is made with four simple ingredients. The other, delicately flavored with spices, was brought from Pyolos to America in 1910 by Gust Nickas, who began a fine confectionery in Bloomington, Indiana. The choice is yours.

INGREDIENTS

Zonar's syrup:
2 cups granulated sugar
1 cup water
½ cup light Karo syrup
½ cup honey

PREPARATION
20 min.

Into a saucepan pour sugar, water and Karo syrup. Stir to dissolve the sugar. Bring to a boil and lower heat to simmer for 10 minutes. Remove from heat and stir in honey. The syrup must be warm (not hot) to pour over the pastry when it comes hot from the oven.

INGREDIENTS

Nickas's spiced syrup:
1½ cups water
2½ cups granulated sugar
6 whole cloves
2 sticks or 1 teaspoon ground cinnamon
⅛ teaspoon salt
Zest of 1 orange and 1 lemon
1 cup honey

PREPARATION
25 min.

Into a saucepan pour water, sugar, cloves, cinnamon, salt and zest of orange and lemon. Stir to dissolve sugar. Bring to a boil.

Lower heat and simmer for 8 to 10 minutes. Remove from heat and discard spices. Add honey. The syrup must be warm but not hot to pour over the pastry when it comes from the oven.

FINAL STEP
Overnight

Pour the syrup over the *baklava*. Allow it to mature overnight so that the syrup will permeate all the leaves and attain its peak flavor.

Baklava may be kept stored in a covered container at room temperature for four to five weeks.

Wrapped securely in foil or plastic, baked or unbaked, *baklava* can be frozen. Slip frozen and unbaked *baklava* directly into a 350° F. oven for 1½ hours, then reduce the heat to 325° F. and bake for an additional hour, or until the pastry is puffed and golden brown.

BECKY'S BAKLAVA

[THIRTY DIAMOND-SHAPED PIECES]

This moist *baklava* is made in a new and different way that not only does away with the tedious brushing, with butter, of each *phyllo* leaf as it is laid in the pan, but substitutes low-cholesterol vegetable oil for the butter. This innovative departure in making a thousand-year-old dessert in no way affects its delicious honey-sweet, nutty flavor.

It was created by Becky Hrisomalos, a neighbor of mine who thought of this, as she has so many other time-saving things, to help her keep abreast of a schedule in a busy household that includes a husband who is a doctor, four children and four dogs. Becky makes about ten "party-size" pans of *baklava* during the winter months, which are served on Greek holidays not only to the family but to a procession of Indiana University students of Greek ancestry who come to the Hrisomalos table.

Becky layers the entire *baklava dry*. There is no brushing of the leaves with butter. Not only is it easy to assemble; she can also press down on the growing pile of *phyllo* leaves and nuts to compress them into a tight formation without getting covered with the shortening.

When the layering has been completed, Becky cuts the *baklava* into diamonds and pours on the vegetable oil! It is allowed to permeate the half a hundred layers for 10 minutes before the pan is put into the oven.

When the sheets are laid down, Becky does not concern herself with torn pieces of *phyllo* leaves or with bumps and valleys across the surface of the completed *baklava*. No one will ever be able to judge the overall terrain by one diamond, she reasons.

Becky cuts small diamonds—1½ inches on a side—rather than large pieces which might be wasted. Better to serve two small diamonds than one too big, she says.

Tribute: Becky Hrisomalos deserves to have this *baklava* named for her because, unlike so many persons honored with the name on a recipe simply for having passed it along from one cook to another or from one generation to the next, she literally created a new way to make this pastry. *Efharisto*, Becky Hrisomalos; thank you!

INGREDIENTS

Pastry:
1 pound *phyllo*/strudel leaves
4 cups finely chopped walnuts
1 cup finely chopped almonds
1 cup granulated sugar
2 teaspoons ground cinnamon
1 cup polyunsaturated vegetable oil

Syrup:
2½ cups granulated sugar
2 cups water
8 whole cloves
5 cinnamon sticks
¾ cup honey
2 tablespoons lemon juice

BAKING PAN

One 8 by 11-inch pan with 2-inch sides, oiled.

PREPARATION
2 hours or
overnight

Beforehand, thaw frozen leaves, allowing 2 hours at room temperature or overnight in the refrigerator. Leave sealed in the package while thawing.

15 min.

Combine finely chopped walnuts and almonds in a large bowl. Add the sugar and ground cinnamon. Mix thoroughly. Set aside.

30 min.

Open the packet of *baklava* leaves or sheets and carefully unroll. If leaves are the usual size (17 by 11 inches), cut the packet in half with scissors to fit the 8 by 11-inch pan. There will be about fifty leaves when cut. Place a damp cloth over the leaves to prevent them from drying out and becoming brittle.

With a brush, spread oil over the pan so that the first layer of *phyllo* leaves will cling to the sides.

Working note: The first layer of *phyllo* leaves is draped up and over the sides so that later they can be folded over the almost-completed pile of leaves and nuts to form a tidy package. Successive layers are contained within the dimensions of the pan. If these leaves are somewhat larger than the pan, either fold over the sides and edges or cut with scissors to fit. Add the trimmed pieces to the layers.

Oil the pan liberally.

Lift about five leaves from the pile and lay them in the pan so that they cover one side and one end and extend above the side ½ inch or so. Continue around the pan with other leaves so that the sides are completely covered. If some of the *phyllo* leaves should slip, touch them with a dab of oil to make them stay in place along the sides. Allow the leaves to project above the sides while the layering continues.

Lay down about ten leaves at a time, an easy number to handle. Place them in the pan just as they are lifted from the packet. Do not separate them. The exact number in each layer is not critical.

When the first ten sheets have been laid down, spread about one-quarter of the nut mixture evenly over the surface.

Pick up another ten sheets and place them over the nuts. Press down firmly on the *phyllo* leaves with the hand and fingers to make a firm base.

Add a second layer of nuts.

Place ten more sheets and again press with the hand to firm.

Add a third sprinkling of the nut mixture.

Place ten more sheets and firm.

Spread the last portion of nuts.

Place six or eight leaves over the nuts, and fold down the leaves that were placed against the sides to make a solid package.

Fold under the edges of the last sheets to make a neat top covering, and press down to firm.

CUTTING
5 min.

The ideal knife to make the diamond-shaped pieces—and to make cuts to allow the oil to reach every layer of *baklava*—is a sharp one with a short serrated blade. The cutting strokes are short jabs through all layers, down to the bottom.

Cut six parallel rows, the length of the pan. Diagonal cuts will produce a diamond. The odd shapes at the ends are for family.

When making the cuts, hold the top layers of *phyllo* in place with the fingers so that they are not lifted off.

OILING
1 min.

Pour the vegetable oil over the *baklava*. Set aside.

Preheat oven to 325° F.

BAKING
325° F.
1 to 1¼ hours

Place the pan on the middle shelf of the medium oven and bake for 1 to 1¼ hours. If the *baklava* gets too dark, cover with foil for the final 15 or 20 minutes.

PREPARATION
15 min.

Syrup:

While the *baklava* is baking, prepare the syrup in a saucepan. Combine sugar, water, cloves and cinnamon sticks. Bring to a boil; turn down heat and allow syrup to simmer for 10 minutes or until it has thickened slightly. Remove from heat and stir in honey and lemon juice. Set aside until *baklava* comes from the oven.

FINAL STEP

Take *baklava* from the oven. Remove cloves and cinnamon sticks from the syrup and pour 2 cups of the warm syrup over the *baklava*. An hour later pour on 1 additional cup of syrup.

Place the pan in a cool place in the kitchen (not the refrigerator). Cover tightly when cool and leave for at least a day to develop flavor.

Baklava, stored in a covered container, can be kept at room temperature for several weeks.

CHEESE TRIANGLE PUFFS

(TIROPETES)

[ABOUT FIFTY HORS D'OEUVRES]

The layers of the delicate thin leaves surrounding the filling puff in the heat of the oven to make a crisp golden triangle that snaps and flakes when bitten into. Each small *tiropete* weighs only ½ ounce. They can be served at an elegant wintertime champagne party or at an informal summertime family gathering on the patio. They can be made as large as an apple turnover and served as the main dinner dish, but I like the tiny ones best—a fine appetizer to have on hand for unexpected, as well as expected, guests.

Feta cheese is the traditional filling, but a delicious variation is the spinach-cheese mixture in *spanakopita* (page 258).

Double the recipe and you will have about 100 pastries with which to build a frozen cache of goodness.

INGREDIENTS   1 pound (about 25) *phyllo*/strudel leaves, room temperature
8 ounces (½ pound) *feta* cheese
6 ounces pot cheese or pot-style cottage cheese
⅓ cup chopped fresh parsley
2 to 3 large eggs
¼ pound (1 stick) butter, melted, to brush

BAKING SHEET   One or more baking sheets, depending on oven size, ungreased or lined with parchment paper.

PREPARATION   Beforehand, remove frozen *phyllo* leaves from
24 hours   freezer; 24 hours beforehand if to be thawed in refrig-
or 2 hours   erator, or 2 hours if at room temperature.

15 min.   *Filling:*
Rinse *feta* cheese with cold water to wash off the milk-salt solution, if so stored. In a bowl crumble cheese by hand into small pieces, or use a food processor to cream the cheese lightly. Add the pot or cottage cheese and mix with *feta*. Stir or blend in parsley.

The eggs control the amount of moisture, so break one into the cheese to determine how much the mixture will absorb. It must be soft yet retain its shape. If dry, as some *feta* tends to be, it may need an additional egg. Blend well and set the bowl aside.

Over low heat melt butter in a small saucepan. Set aside.

15 min.   *Pastry:*
Unfold the *phyllo* leaves and cut in half lengthwise, with a pastry cutter, knife or scissors. Strips will be approximately 5½ by 16 inches. If the sheet is a different size (size varies among manufacturers), trim accordingly. Return one stack to the refrigerator in plastic wrap until needed. Drape a moist cloth or paper towel over the remaining half so that leaves will not dry out and become brittle.

Preheat oven to 450° F.

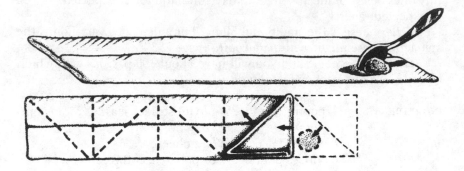

45 min.

Remove one sheet at a time from the stack and place on the work surface. Brush lightly with butter. Fold each long edge to the center. Brush again with butter.

Place a teaspoonful of filling near the bottom and to one side of the strip, 2 inches above the lower edge, so that it can be lifted and folded over the filling forming a triangle (as in folding a flag).

If some of the filling should be pressed out, no matter. It will be folded into and contained by the triangle as the folding proceeds. The filling must not be wet, however, or it will ooze out. If so, chill filling in the refrigerator or freezer for a few minutes.

Continue folding the strip into small triangles, about 10 folds for each *tiropete*. Although it takes about a minute to make one triangle, don't expect to make sixty in an hour. Allow a few minutes off to admire your handiwork.

Brush each *tiropete* with butter when folded, and place on a baking sheet. Triangles will puff, so space them out on the pan.

BAKING
450° F.
12–14 min.

Place on the middle shelf of the oven and bake until plump, crisp and lightly browned, about 12 to 14 minutes.

FINAL STEP

Tiropetes can be frozen after they have cooled. Freeze them separately on a baking sheet and then package in a plastic bag. Store for no longer than three or four months. To reheat, put baked frozen *tiropetes* into a 425° F. oven for 10 minutes.

Unbaked *tiropetes* can be frozen with great success. Brush each with butter and space on a baking sheet lined with wax paper or foil so that the triangles do not touch. Place in the freezer. When frozen (overnight), drop into a plastic bag and return to the freezer. Mark with name and date for reference.

To bake, place the frozen triangles on an ungreased baking sheet and set in a 400° F. oven for 30 minutes, or until they are puffed and golden. Test doneness by cutting open one *tiropete* to be certain it has been baked through. Cool 5 minutes before serving.

Entrée Pies

An entrée pie is a husky, handsome dish—large and tasteful enough to please robust appetites, especially those that respond enthusiastically to good food. It is the quality and the nature of the crust that elevate these four entrée pies to something above the ordinary and give them a special place at the table.

A delicious entrée pie can be made with a little or a lot of crust. In its simplest form, it is only one layer of dough spread over the dish. If you love the crust as much as you do what is inside, line the bottom and sides of the baking dish, and top the filling with dough to envelop the filling completely.

Two of these recipes are an ocean apart—beefsteak-and-kidney pie from England, and Plantation Chicken Pie from Louisiana. The third is from the ocean—seafood-and-mushroom pie. *Spanakopita*, spinach-and-cheese pie with Greek origins, is made with many layers of *phyllo* leaves. Although it is made with a different kind of dough and depends on moisture between the layers to make the pastry rise in the hot oven, this dish rightfully belongs here in the family of entrée pies.

These entrée pies are made with their own crusts; however, any pie, tart or puff dough in the book can be substituted.

BEEFSTEAK-AND-KIDNEY PIE

[SERVES SIX]

Beefsteak-and-kidney pie is a traditional English dish that deserves to be better known in the United States, at least in mid-America where I live. In this recipe there are two other major ingredients: oysters and mushrooms. A marvelous combination.

Ideally, the kidneys should be those of a calf or lamb, both delicate in taste and texture. If from older animals, the kidneys need a longer washing interval and perhaps more cooking time.

The "rough puff pastry" is so called by the British because bits of butter and lard remain intact throughout the mixing process and while the dough is folded and turned six times. It is a versatile dough that can be used for the pastries in the puff paste section (page 159). I especially like it for apple turnovers (*chaussons aux pommes*) and apple dumplings (*rabottes de pommes*), as well as for wrapping meats *en croûte*.

The deep dish is not fully lined with dough—only the sides, to which the top covering is crimped. This assures that there is no underneath layer of dough to get soggy.

The mistress of Burton Court, a lovely manor house near Leominster, Herefordshire, prepares this pie in a three-centuries-old kitchen. It is a family dinner dish for the four members of the Robert Simpson household, while crumpets and homemade jam is the fare for dozens of visitors who daily are guided through the stately rooms and over the grounds during spring and summer months.

In the Simpson recipe, the onion and meat pieces are sautéed in fresh bacon drippings rather than in butter or margarine.

INGREDIENTS
Dough:
3 cups all-purpose flour
1 teaspoon salt
¾ cup (1½ sticks) butter, or half butter and half lard
¼ teaspoon lemon juice
½ cup ice water

Filling:
1½ pounds sirloin or stew beef
½ pound kidneys, veal or lamb preferred
1 large onion, chopped
2 tablespoons fresh bacon drippings or butter
½ teaspoon salt
¼ teaspoon pepper

2 teaspoons Worcestershire sauce
1 teaspoon finely chopped parsley
1 bay leaf, crumbled
2 cups beef stock, undiluted if canned
5 tablespoons all-purpose flour
½ pound mushrooms, sliced, or whole if small
1 pint oysters
3 tablespoons Sherry, optional

1 egg
1 tablespoon milk } beaten together, to glaze

BAKING DISH   One 13 by 9 by 2-inch baking dish.

PREPARATION   *Dough:*
8 min.   In a large bowl place flour and salt. Blend. Add small pieces of butter (or butter and lard) and mix them lightly into the flour with a fork or the fingers. Add lemon juice, and a few drops of water at a time, a total of about ½ cup or enough to make a firm but not hard dough. The butter (and lard) will be seen as tiny yellow (and white) particles in the dough.

3 min.   If you are using a food processor, don't overprocess. Turn off the machine the instant the dough forms a mass and rides on the blade.

Working note: This is a puff paste; it will be rolled and folded six times before it is finally rolled to cover the pie.

40 min.   Wrap the dough in wax paper and refrigerate. When it has chilled, after about 20 minutes, roll it into a long rectangle about 6 inches wide and 24 inches long. Fold lengthwise into thirds, as if folding a letter. Turn so that the open end faces you. Roll a second time into a long rectangle. Fold as before and roll a third time. Fold into thirds.

Refrigerate for 15 minutes to allow the dough to relax.

Roll and turn the dough three more times—a total of six times.

Wrap and chill while the pie ingredients are being prepared.

Filling:
Beforehand, cut the beef into ½-inch cubes and set aside, or refrigerate.

30 min.

Place kidneys in a bowl under cold running water for 30 minutes. Remove from water, cut into large pieces and cut away the white fat, which is the core of the organ. Leave only red meat. Cut into small ½-inch pieces, and set aside.

12 min.

Sauté the chopped onion in bacon drippings in a large heavy pan or skillet over medium heat—until soft and translucent, about 8 minutes. Add the steak and kidney pieces. Sauté until the pieces are browned. Season with salt and pepper. Stir in Worcestershire sauce, parsley and bay leaf.

1¾ hours

Pour beef stock over the meat mixture to cover. Remove 1 cup liquid and blend it with the flour until all lumps disappear. (I sometimes press it through a fine sieve.) Return to the pot and mix in. Stir in the mushrooms. Simmer, covered, over low heat for 1¾ hours, stirring occasionally.

While the meats are cooking, remove the dough from the refrigerator. Roll the dough into a large sheet, a scant ⅛ inch thick. Using the inverted baking dish as a pattern, cut a rectangle of dough, allowing a margin of 1 inch. Carefully fold the cut dough, place on a length of wax paper and refrigerate until needed.

Cut 2½ inch strips from the remaining dough to be placed around just the interior sides of the pan. Moisten the interior sides with water, and arrange the dough strips in place, overlapping them slightly. Moisten at these joints. Allow the strips to extend ½ inch above the sides so that a crimped seal can be made between this dough and the top dough when it is placed.

When the dough has been stuck to the sides, place the dish in the refrigerator until needed.

Preheat oven to 450° F.

ASSEMBLY

When the meat mixture is cooked, remove from the heat and stir in the oysters and Sherry, if desired.

30 min.

It will be easier to assemble the pie if the meat mixture is allowed to cool somewhat, about 30 minutes.

10 min.

When cooled, spoon or pour the meat mixture into the baking dish, taking care that the pieces of dough along the sides remain in place.

Place the top piece and trim to allow a ½-inch margin. Moisten the edges of the top and side dough and crimp together with the fingers to seal. Cut a decorative circle or square in the center of the top to allow steam to escape.

Decorate with stars, crescents, triangles or other shapes. Brush all with the egg-milk glaze.

BAKING
450° F.
20 min.
350° F.
15 min.

Place on the middle shelf of the hot oven. After 20 minutes, when the pastry has risen and is slightly browned, reduce heat to 350° F. and continue to bake for an additional 15 minutes.

FINAL STEP

Serve piping hot!

SEAFOOD-AND-MUSHROOM PIE

[SERVES SIX]

The seafood can be flaked freshly cooked fish, scallops, shrimp, crab or a combination, made in a large 8-inch pie or six individual ones.

INGREDIENTS

Sauce:
2 tablespoons butter
2 tablespoons flour
1 cup milk or cream, scalded
1 egg yolk

Filling:
2½ cups cooked or canned seafood of choice
1 cup (4 ounces) sliced mushrooms
2 tablespoons butter
⅛ teaspoon salt
Pinch freshly ground pepper
1 tablespoon finely chopped chives

1 egg yolk
1 teaspoon milk } beaten together, to brush

2 tablespoons Sherry

PREPARATION
12 min.

Beforehand, prepare the white sauce: In the top of a double boiler, over low heat, melt butter and gradually add flour, stirring the *roux* for 3 to 5 minutes. Gradually add scalded milk or cream, stirring constantly. Add egg yolk. Stir. Season to taste. Cook sauce over hot water until thick. Set aside.

Cook seafood of choice. Have 2½ cups when cooked.

Sauté mushrooms in butter and drain well when cooked. Stir mushrooms into the cream sauce and add salt and pepper. Combine seafood and sauce. Add chives. Allow to cool. The filling is now ready to be spooned or poured into the prepared baking dish.

Cover and bake as directed in the recipe for beef-steak-and-kidney pie (page 251).

Note: During the final 10 minutes of the baking period, pour 2 tablespoons Sherry into the center hole.

FINAL STEP   Serve immediately.

PLANTATION CHICKEN PIE

[SERVES SIX]

Plantation Chicken Pie, from the deep South, Louisiana, is not your usual chicken dish with a rich white sauce. There is a strong touch of Creole in the pinkish red sauce (from tomatoes and peppers) in this recipe from a fine cookbook, *The Cotton Country Collection*, put together by the Junior Charity League of Monroe, Louisiana.

There is a hint of Sherry in the chicken as well as in the dough. Altogether it is an elegant dish. Mrs. S. A. Collins, whose recipe this is, says the dish can be prepared on Saturday and reheated on Sunday with no fear that it will become soggy. The secret, she says, is in the crust made with eggs, butter and lard or vegetable shortening.

This is an appropriate dish with which to introduce the family and guests to the pie bird, a small 4- or 5-inch-high bird that sits on the bottom of the pie pan and allows the steam to escape through its open bill. I have two of them. One is a rather ordinary ceramic blackbird; the other is an elegant piece of Royal Worcester flame-proof porcelain in which the bird is pushed up on its perch by the steam but then decorously settles back when the pie cools. Both are fun, and they are especially at home in meat pies. (See "Equipment to Make Fine Pastries," page 33.)

INGREDIENTS

Dough:

Working note: This is a large recipe. The ingredients may be halved for one dish, or the extra dough may be reserved for later use.

6 cups all-purpose flour, approximately
1 tablespoon *each* baking powder and salt
4 eggs
1 cup lard or shortening, room temperature
2 tablespoons Sherry
8 tablespoons (1 stick) butter, room temperature
⅓ cup water

Filling (makes 5 cups):
1 3-pound chicken
1 tablespoon butter
1 onion, chopped
½ green pepper, chopped
½ sweet red pepper, if available, chopped
1 garlic clove, chopped
2 tablespoons vinegar
½ cup Sherry
1 tablespoon sugar
2 cups tomato sauce
1 teaspoon salt
½ teaspoon freshly ground pepper
¼ teaspoon paprika
1 cup peas, small preferred
1 cup whole green olives, cut in half
2 hard-cooked eggs, sliced

1 egg
1 tablespoon milk ⎱ beaten together, to brush

BAKING DISH

One 12 by 18 by 2-inch baking dish.

PREPARATION
12 min.

Dough:
In a large bowl stir together 4 cups flour, baking powder and salt. Form a well. Drop in the eggs, shortening, Sherry, butter and water. Stir briskly to blend, pulling the flour in from the sides as you stir. Add 1 or 2 more cups flour, if necessary, to form a smooth, soft dough. Work together until the mass is well blended.

REFRIGERATED
REST
1 hour or
longer

Wrap the dough in wax paper or plastic wrap and re-frigerate until chilled and relaxed, at least 1 hour.

PREPARATION
1 hour

Chicken:

Beforehand, cook the chicken whole in salted boiling water until the meat is tender, about 1 hour. Allow the chicken to cool before removing the meat from the bones. Dice into small pieces.

35 min.

Make the sauce in a deep skillet or heavy pot by sauté-ing, in butter, the onion until soft and translucent, about 8 minutes. Stir in the peppers, garlic, vinegar, Sherry, sugar, tomato sauce, salt, pepper and paprika, and cook over medium heat for 20 minutes.

Remove the vessel from the heat. Add the chicken pieces and drained peas. (The olives and eggs will be added later.)

ASSEMBLY

Remove the dough from the refrigerator and, if using the full 6-cup recipe, divide into two pieces, reserving one for later use.

15 min.

The baking dish will be lined with dough rolled ⅛ inch thick. The dough may be placed in one piece, with the sides extending ½ inch above the dish. I find it easier to arrange wide strips of dough along the sides of the dish. These are moistened and the ends pressed to-gether where they meet. A rectangular piece of dough is cut for the bottom and dropped into place. It does not matter that the bottom piece is not joined to the sides. If less dough is desired, do not add the bottom piece.

Preheat oven to 425° F.

If you are using a pie bird, place it in the middle of the baking dish. Pour or spoon the chicken and sauce around it. The filling should come to within ½ inch of the edge of the dish. Arrange the olive pieces and egg slices over the top of the filling.

10 min.

Cut a rectangle of dough for the top, allowing a mar-gin of 1 inch. To assure a seal, moisten the margins before the top piece is positioned.

If you are using a pie bird, cut a small hole in the

center of the top crust to allow its bill to come through. The crust will rest on its wings. Otherwise, cut a pattern in the top with a sharp knife or razor blade to allow the steam to escape.

Trim the edges with scissors. With the fingers, crimp the dough into an attractive pattern. Brush the surface with the egg-milk glaze.

BAKING   Place the dish on the middle shelf of the hot oven.
425° F.   After 15 minutes reduce heat to 350° F. and continue
15 min.   baking until the pie is light brown and bubbling, about
350° F.   45 minutes.
45 min.

FINAL STEP   Serve immediately.

SPINACH-CHEESE PIE

(SPANAKOPITA)

[ONE DOZEN 3-INCH SQUARES]

It is difficult to keep *spanakopita*—a rich, colorful layer of spinach, eggs and *feta* cheese between delicate golden *phyllo* leaves—from stealing the accolades usually reserved for the main dish, whether skewered lamb or baked chicken pilaf. *Spanakopita* can also be made with a mixture of pot cheese or pot-style cottage cheese and Romano, substituting for the *feta*, which is made of goat's or sheep's milk; but it is not the same.

In specialty stores selling Greek foods in the United States, *feta* is cut from big pieces imported in a large barrel of salt solution. It can be kept indefinitely in the home refrigerator in a solution of 1 teaspoon salt in each cup of skim milk necessary to cover the cheese in a large-mouthed glass jar. Rinse the brine off the *feta* before using it. I have kept *feta* for almost a year with only a light crust forming on the milk, which I simply lifted off with a spoon. The cheese was fine.

Many supermarkets now carry a domestic *feta* packaged dry in plastic wrap. It is good, but the imported is better.

This delicious spinach filling may also be used for delightful little triangular tidbits of folded *phyllo* leaves, *tiropetes* (page 246), as well as mini *quiches* and puff paste hors d'oeuvres.

INGREDIENTS	18 sheets (about ¾ pound) *phyllo* leaves

18 sheets (about ¾ pound) *phyllo* leaves
3 10-ounce packages frozen spinach
   (*or* 2 pounds fresh spinach, chopped)
¼ cup olive oil
½ cup finely chopped onions
⅓ cup finely chopped scallions, including green tops
2 tablespoons dried dill or finely cut fresh dill
¼ cup finely cut fresh parsley
½ teaspoon salt
¼ teaspoon freshly ground pepper
⅓ cup milk
½ pound *feta* cheese, finely crumbled
4 eggs, room temperature
½ pound (2 sticks) butter, melted, to brush

BAKING DISH

One baking dish 12 by 7 by 2 inches, brushed with melted butter.

PREPARATION

Beforehand, remove *phyllo* package from the freezer and place in the refrigerator for 48 hours, or leave at room temperature for 2 hours before opening the package and unrolling the leaves.

Filling:
If the spinach is frozen, follow instructions on the package for initial preparation. If you are using fresh spinach, wash carefully, drain and chop it finely.

30 min.

In a large skillet heat olive oil over moderate heat and add onions and scallions. Cook for 5 minutes, stirring frequently, until they are transparent but not brown. If spinach is fresh, stir it into the onions, cover and cook 5 minutes. It's not necessary to cook the frozen spinach for these 5 minutes. Proceed with either kind of spinach. Stir in dill, parsley, salt and pepper, and cook for 10 minutes until most of the liquid has steamed away, or drain off liquid if necessary. Scrape the spinach into a large bowl and stir in the milk. When the spinach has cooled to room temperature, add the cheese. Beat in the eggs. Blend. Taste the mixture for seasoning.
    Preheat oven to 375° F.

20 min.

Pastry:
The stack of *phyllo* leaves may be cut to the exact size of the pan by inverting the pan over the leaves and

cutting with a sharp knife or pastry wheel. The surplus pieces can be kept refrigerated for other *phyllo* pastries. Or use the single sheets regardless of size, folding the edges over to make a snug fit. This small addition to the thickness of the baked *spanakopita* will hardly be noticed.

ASSEMBLY

Working note: There will be eight or nine sheets of buttered *phyllo* leaves laid down for the bottom crust. (The exact number is not critical.) The spinach-cheese filling will be spooned over this base. Eight buttered sheets will be laid down on top of the filling, one by one, to complete the dish.

15 min.

Line the buttered dish with a leaf of *phyllo*, pressing the edges into the corners and sides. Fold over excess. Butter each leaf as it is laid down and proceed with the next sheet.

Spread the filling over the last layer of *phyllo* and smooth it into the corners. Then continue to build the final layers of *phyllo*. With the tip of the brush gently push the edges of the *phyllo* leaves down the sides of the pan to give a neat, rounded trim. Butter the top leaf.

BAKING
375° F.
1–1¼ hours

Sprinkle on a few drops of water or spray lightly with an atomizer to keep the top leaf from curling.

Bake on the middle shelf of the oven for about 1 hour, or until crisp and lightly browned.

FINAL STEP

Cut into serving pieces and serve hot or at room temperature. There is no tastier spinach dish!

The unbaked pan of *spanakopita* may be placed in a plastic bag or wrapped with freezer paper and placed in the freezer for several weeks. When ready to bake, place pan directly in the oven and allow an additional hour, or a total of 2 to 2¼ hours. Lightly trace each serving piece on the frozen *spanakopita* with a knife point before it goes into the oven. This will provide an easy cutting guide when the pastry is baked.

Danish Pastry

Walk from Copenhagen's spacious Raadhuspladsen, the Town Hall Square, on the wide and bustling pedestrian way, Strøget, stretching eight shop-filled blocks across the city, and at its other terminus you will find one of the great hotels of Europe, the Hotel d'Angleterre, and its marvelous pastry shop, the Désiree. Marked only by a modest awning sign, and the traditional baking token of a regal crown atop a golden pretzel, the Désiree and the hotel's dining rooms are where Danes and visitors alike can get some of the finest pastries in the land.

These Danish pastries were created by d'Angleterre's late great chef G. L. Wennberg, who was one of Scandinavia's most famous *pâtissiers*. I was fortunate in being able to get his authentic recipes and, in the hotel's kitchen, to observe and assist the men who had worked with Chef Wennberg for decades.

Today these skilled *pâtissiers* continue to make superbly light and flaky *wienbrod*, the "bread from Vienna," known everywhere but in Denmark as Danish pastries. These pastries are far superior in flavor and texture to the often gummy and tasteless pastries sold and served as "danish" in many places in this country. They are a delicious cross between *croissants* and yeast rolls as a result of the perfect marriage of puff pastry and yeast-raised dough.

Two things are done to assure that this union is a happy one. First, a fine yeast-leavened dough is prepared. This alone would assure that the dough will rise lightly in the heat of the oven. But there is an important second step: rolling out the dough and layering it with butter, as with puff paste, to give it a golden flakiness.

261

Danish pastries, when baked, are crisp on the outside and soft and tender on the inside. They are not especially sweet but rely principally on butter for their good flavor.

Remonce, a delicious and widely used filling in Denmark, can be a mixture either of butter and granulated sugar, flavored with vanilla, or of butter and brown sugar, flavored with cinnamon. (See "Danish Fillings and Toppings," page 302.)

Danish pastry, a unique combination of ingredients and techniques, is not difficult to make if attention is paid to several steps, chiefly the chilling of the dough when the fat is layered in.

BUTTER TEMPERATURE

As in the preparation of puff pastry, the two most critical elements in making Danish doughs are the temperatures of the butter and the dough at the time they are brought together in layers. If the butter is too hard, the layering process will be uneven and lumpy. If the butter is too soft, it will be squeezed out of the layers or absorbed into the dough. In a series of tests in my kitchen I determined that 60° F. was the ideal temperature at which to layer butter into dough without its breaking apart or melting. The accurate way to determine the temperature is with a Taylor Bi-Therm thermometer, which has a slender 5-inch stem that is easily inserted into a block of cold butter. (See "Sources of Supply," page 47.)

Butter taken from my refrigerator at 42° F. quickly rises to 60° F. during the time it is being beaten with a rolling pin to break its form and prior to kneading in the flour with a spatula or dough blade. (The flour gives the butter greater stability during the baking process and makes it less likely to ooze from the pastries.) Normally, without the kneading process, it takes about 1¼ hours for butter taken from my refrigerator to reach 60° F., at which temperature it is waxy, flexible and easy to spread.

If you do not have a thermometer, do this test. After the flour and butter have been blended together and shaped into a rectangle, chill for 10 to 12 minutes. Now try to bend the rectangle of butter. If it is too cold, the butter will be brittle and threaten to break. At 60° F. it will accept the pressure by bending slightly. Press a finger on the butter. It will make a shallow impression. Place a piece of wax paper over the butter and roll with a rolling pin to be certain it will spread smoothly without flaking or breaking into pieces. If it should be soft and oily, refrigerate for 10 to 15 minutes.

The butter is now ready to be layered with the dough.

There are other authorities on Danish pastries in addition to the *pâtissiers* in the d'Angleterre's kitchen in Copenhagen, of course. In the big, rambling kitchen of the famous Budapest hotel, the Grand Hotel Margitsziget, Chef Mosonyi Páe introduced me to his creation which he smilingly defended as Hungarian, not Danish. Nevertheless, it is a yeast-raised dough enriched with egg yolks, with a combination of butter and margarine layered with the dough. I hope I have secured my friendship with Chef Páe by calling it Hungarian Pastry Dough (page 286).

In my studio kitchen I have tested and adapted scores of other recipes and put together many in an endeavor to find a rewarding way to make Danish dough easier and quicker. I believe I have found it. The result is Easy Flaky Danish Dough, a light and delicious creation (page 290).

Thus there are three collections of Danish pastries in the book made with three different doughs. The first is from the d'Angleterre's renowned pastry kitchen. The second one is breakfast pastry from Hungary. The third is made with Easy Flaky Danish Dough. The three doughs may be used interchangeably in the individual pastry recipes.

The fillings and frostings used in all of the pastries are in a section following the pastry recipes (page 302).

D'Angleterre Classic Danish Pastries

This is a baker's dozen of Danish pastries from the Hotel d'Angleterre's kitchen. I think you and your guests will be delighted with these authentic Danish delicacies. All are made with Chef Wennberg's basic pastry dough. Each pastry is different in the way the dough is cut and shaped, and in the selection of the filling.

There is great freedom of choice in the quantity of each pastry as well as in the filling to use. I often use half of the dough for one kind of pastry and the other half for another. Or I may make as many as four kinds.

Sometimes I make up a batch of dough in the traditional Danish size but, alas, three or four dozen of these d'Angleterre pastries don't last long when friends or students drop by for coffee. Or sometimes I make more than double the number in miniature form so that each is just a mouthful. We serve these mini Danish at more formal affairs, as is done in Denmark. Large or small, these pastries disappear so fast that I seldom expect to have any left to freeze for later use.

Danish pastries do freeze well, but cool them before wrapping and storing. To serve, heat frozen pastries until they are crisp. Glaze after removing from the oven.

D'ANGLETERRE CLASSIC DANISH PASTRY DOUGH

[APPROXIMATELY 3 POUNDS, FOR TWO MEDIUM BRAIDS OR TWISTS,
OR THREE DOZEN MEDIUM PASTRIES,
OR FOUR TO FIVE DOZEN MINIATURE PASTRIES]

INGREDIENTS

2 packages dry yeast
1½ cups water
½ cup non-fat dry milk
5½ cups all-purpose flour, approximately
⅓ cup granulated sugar
1 teaspoon salt
½ teaspoon ground cardamom, optional
1 teaspoon vanilla extract
2 eggs, room temperature
2 egg yolks, room temperature
2 ounces (½ stick) butter or margarine, room temperature.

¾ pound (3 sticks) unsalted butter, chilled, to layer
¼ cup all-purpose flour

PREPARATION
● BY HAND
5 min.

In a large bowl pour water over yeast. Stir to dissolve yeast. Add dry milk, 2 cups flour, sugar, salt, cardamom and vanilla and blend. Break in eggs and add egg yolks. Stir to blend. Drop in butter or margarine, beat 30 seconds and add flour, ½ cup at a time, to make a shaggy mass in the bowl.

KNEADING
5 min.

Lift the dough from the bowl and place on a floured work surface. The rich dough will be soft but should not stick to the hands. If it does, sprinkle lightly with flour.

Knead—push down forcefully with the heel of the hand, draw back, give the dough a quarter turn, fold it in half, push down, draw back, turn the dough again and fold—and so continue. If the dough becomes sticky, toss light sprinkles of flour on it and on the work surface. A dough scraper or putty knife is useful to turn and work the dough. Knead for 5 minutes, or until the dough is a soft, velvety ball—elastic to touch but not too solid.

▲ ELECTRIC
MIXER
5 min.

In a medium bowl mix yeast, water and dry milk. Stir to dissolve yeast. Place 3 cups flour, sugar, salt and cardamom in the mixer bowl. Attach bowl and flat beater blade. At slow speed blend dry ingredients.

Slowly pour in yeast liquid. Blend well. Add vanilla, eggs, egg yolks and butter or margarine. When all these ingredients are blended into a batter-like mixture, remove the flat blade and attach the dough hook. Turn to low speed (no. 2 on my KitchenAid) and add flour, ½ cup at a time, allowing each addition of flour to be worked into the dough. When dough clings to the hook and cleans the sides of the bowl, enough flour has been added.

KNEADING
3–4 min.

Knead for 3 to 4 minutes, or until the dough is soft, smooth and elastic. This is a shorter-than-usual kneading period for a yeast dough, but Danish calls for a weak gluten formation.

■ FOOD
PROCESSOR
4 min.

Dissolve yeast in water and add dry milk. Insert the steel blade in the bowl of the food processor. Measure in 3 cups flour and add liquid. Process for several seconds until well mixed. Add sugar, salt, cardamom and vanilla through the feed tube and process briefly. Drop in eggs and egg yolks. Process with one or two bursts until blended. Remove the cover and add butter or margarine. Process briefly. Add flour, ½ cup at a time, processing after each addition, until dough is soft but not sticky.

KNEADING
30 seconds

Knead for 30 seconds. Dough will form a ball on the blade and will push back when pushed with a finger.

REFRIGERATED
REST
1 hour

Wrap dough in plastic wrap or foil and place in the refrigerator. This begins the rising process and also cools the dough to accept the cold butter.

PREPARATION

Butter:
Note: The ¼ cup flour is blended into the ¾ pound butter to give it greater stability in the oven and to lessen the chance of its oozing from the dough.

10 min.

Place the three sticks of butter side by side on a length of wax paper on the work surface. Tap and beat the butter with a rolling pin until it is flat and softened. With a dough blade or spatula work ¼ cup flour into the butter. Shape the butter into a 10 by 12-inch rectangle. Cover with wax paper and set aside.

2 hours

There is an easier way to blend the flour into the butter and then shape it into the desired rectangle, but it must be done 2 or more hours before the fat is to be layered in. Allow the butter to soften at room temperature. With a metal spatula or dough scraper knead the butter into a soft mass and add the flour. Blend the butter and flour. Shape the mixture into a flat 10 by 12-inch rectangle on a length of wax paper. Place in the refrigerator to chill to 60° F.

LAYERING
4 min.

Take dough from the refrigerator and place on a floured work surface. Roll to a 12 by 20-inch rectangle. If the dough pulls back, allow it to rest for a moment or so before continuing. With the butter mixture still wrapped in paper, lay the piece on the dough to be certain it covers the lower two-thirds of the dough, with a 1-inch margin of dough projecting around the edges. Unwrap butter and place on dough.

Fold down the top unbuttered third, then over it fold the remaining third with its butter cover, so that the layers are dough/butter/dough/butter/dough.

FIRST TURN
3 min.

Turn the dough so that one open end is at 6 o'clock and the other at 12 o'clock. Gently roll the layered dough into a 10 by 18-inch rectangle. Sprinkle with

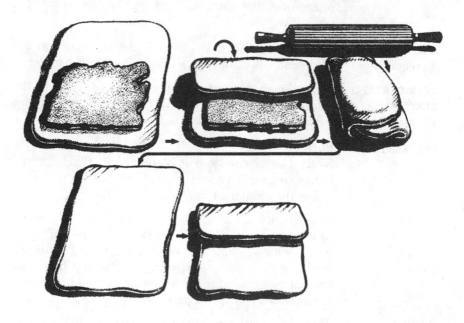

flour if butter breaks through. This will be unlikely if both dough and butter are properly chilled.

REFRIGERATED REST 10 min.	Fold the rectangle of dough into thirds, as for a letter, and slip into a plastic bag. Refrigerate for 10 minutes.
SECOND TURN 5 min.	Remove dough from the bag, lay on a floured work surface and roll to a 10 by 18-inch rectangle.
REFRIGERATED REST 10 min.	Fold into thirds and return to the plastic bag to refrigerate. Lightly touch dough with a knife blade to mark the number of turns. It is easy to forget otherwise.
THIRD TURN 3 min.	For the final turn remove the dough from the refrigerator and place on a floured work surface. Roll again into a 10 by 18-inch rectangle.
REFRIGERATED REST 30 min. or overnight	Place the folded rectangle in a plastic bag and put in the refrigerator. If to be left overnight, wrap the dough in a damp cloth so a crust will not form and then place it in an unrestrictive bag that will allow the dough to rise and expand without splitting and breaking through the plastic.
ROLLING OUT 8 min.	Place the chilled dough on a floured work surface and roll into a long rectangle, 10 by 18 inches.
FINAL STEP	Cut from the dough the amount called for in the recipe (a quarter, a third or half). Cut across the layers. Place reserved pieces flat in a plastic bag and return them to the refrigerator until needed.

DANISH BRIOCHES

[TWO DOZEN PIECES]

This *brioche* is a square of flaky pastry enveloping a small portion of *remonce*, the butter-and-sugar filling. A small topknot of dough crowns each ball to resemble, when baked, the classic *brioche à tête*. Although both are delicious, the resemblance goes no further.

INGREDIENTS	½ recipe d'Angleterre Classic Danish Pastry Dough (page 264), chilled *Remonce* No. 1 (page 303), room temperature 1 egg, beaten, to brush

BAKING PAN(S)   Baking pan(s) with a narrow lip, lined with parchment paper.

PREPARATION   *Note:* The dough is to be cut into 2½-inch squares, so roll a square or rectangle that can be cut most efficiently into a series of smaller squares—an 8 by 20-inch rectangle, for example.

SHAPING
25 min.

Place the chilled dough on a floured work surface. Roll to ¼-inch thickness. Allow the dough time to relax as it is rolled. Walk away from it occasionally if it draws back. With a yardstick and a pastry wheel or knife, cut a series of 2½-inch strips the length of the dough. Cut each strip into 2½-inch squares. Refrigerate for 15 minutes.

If the squares have shrunk, roll each to the full 2½-inch diameter.

Place a scant teaspoonful of *remonce* in the center of each square.

Close the square, gathering the edges at the center, and pinch to close. Gently roll into a ball. Place on a lined baking pan with the joint down. Press the ball to flatten slightly. Cut a small round of dough, ½ inch in diameter, moisten with egg glaze and place on the center of the brioche.

RISING
20 min.

Set aside in a cool part of the kitchen to rest and rise for 20 minutes.

Preheat oven to 425° F.

Brush topknot and ball with egg glaze before placing pastries in oven.

BAKING
425° F.
10 min.
375° F.
20 min.

Bake on the middle shelf of the 425° F. oven for 10 minutes. Reduce heat to 375° F. and bake until golden brown, or about 20 additional minutes.

FINAL STEP   Place pieces on a rack to cool. These may be frozen with admirable results. Place in a 350° F. oven while still frozen for about 25 minutes.

SPANDAUERS

[TWO DOZEN PIECES]

The square of dough blossoms in the oven heat to reveal dozens of layers of flaky pastry.

INGREDIENTS	½ recipe d'Angleterre Classic Danish Pastry Dough (page 264), chilled Remonce No. 1 or No. 2 (page 303), room temperature 1 egg, beaten, to brush Cake cream (page 305), chilled ½ cup ground almonds ½ cup orange or lemon icing (page 310)
BAKING PAN(S)	Baking pan(s) with a narrow lip, lined with parchment paper.
PREPARATION	*Working note:* The dough is to be cut into 3-inch squares, so roll it into a large square or rectangle that can be cut into a series of smaller squares with a minimum of scraps.

SHAPING
22 min.
	Place the chilled dough on a floured work surface. Roll to ¼-inch thickness. Allow the dough to relax. Place it in the refrigerator to chill if the butter softens.
	    With a yardstick and a pastry wheel or knife, cut the large piece into a series of 3-inch-wide strips. Cut each strip into 3-inch squares. If the squares pull back after cutting, roll each again to the full dimensions.
	    Place a scant teaspoonful of *remonce* in the center of each square and bend the four corners inward so that they touch at the center. Place on the lined baking pan and press the centers down slightly.

RISING 20 min.	Leave to rise for 20 minutes in a cool part of the kitchen (68° to 72° F.). When slightly risen, brush with egg glaze. Pipe, or place by spoon, a small amount (1 teaspoon) of cake cream in the center of each *spandauer*. Sprinkle with ground almonds. Preheat oven to 425° F.
BAKING 425° F. 10 min. 375° F. 20 min.	Place the pan on the middle shelf of the 425° F. oven for 10 minutes before reducing heat to 375° F. Bake until pastries have unfolded and are golden brown, approximately 20 additional minutes.

FINAL STEP   Place pieces on a rack to cool. They may be frozen with excellent results.

CRESCENTS

[TWO DOZEN PIECES]

Crescents resemble small golden *croissants* except that d'Angleterre *pâtissiers* do not shape them into crescents as the name suggests because they are too small and delicate to curve. Then, too, they have a double filling, which sets them apart from their French counterpart.

INGREDIENTS   ½ recipe d'Angleterre Classic Danish Pastry Dough (page 264), chilled
Remonce No. 1 or No. 2 (page 303), room temperature
Almond filling, paste or nut (page 304), room temperature
1 egg, beaten, to brush

BAKING PAN(S)   Baking pan(s) with a narrow lip, lined with parchment paper.

PREPARATION   *Working note:* The dough is to be cut into 5½-inch strips, and then into triangles, so roll it into a rectangle to accommodate these cuts with as few scraps as possible.

SHAPING
25 min.   Place the chilled dough on a floured work surface and roll to ¼-inch thickness. Allow the dough time to relax as it is rolled. With a yardstick and a pastry wheel or sharp knife, mark and cut the large piece into 5½-inch strips.

   Cut each strip into long, narrow triangles, 3 inches wide at the base. The most accurate way to do this is to mark with the knife the 3-inch cuts to be made along the bottom edge of the strip. Along the upper parallel edge, offset the yardstick 1½ inches and mark the apex of each triangle. Cut.

   If triangles pull back, roll to larger dimensions. Spread a thin layer of *remonce* and a thin layer of almond filling on the base of each triangle. Roll the triangles, beginning at the broad end, toward the point. Place on the lined baking pan with points under.

RISING
20 min.

Cover with wax paper. Place crescents in a cool part of the room to rest and rise for 20 minutes.
Preheat oven to 425° F.

BAKING
425° F.
10 min.
375° F.
20 min.

Brush crescents with beaten egg and place the pan on the middle shelf of the 425° F. oven for 10 minutes. Reduce heat to 375° F. and bake until golden brown, or about 20 more minutes.

FINAL STEP

Place pieces on a rack to cool.

DANISH NUT PRETZELS

(KRINGLER)

[THIRTY-TWO PIECES]

The pretzel shape is universal in bake shops in Denmark. Not only is it the sign of the baker's trade, but it is the model for many pastries, including this small and very tasty nut-covered piece.

INGREDIENTS

¼ recipe d'Angleterre Classic Danish Pastry Dough (page 264), chilled
1 egg, beaten, to brush
¼ cup finely ground almonds, to sprinkle
½ cup lemon or orange icing (page 310)

BAKING PAN(S)

Baking pan(s) with a narrow lip, lined with parchment paper.

PREPARATION
12 min.

Place the chilled dough on a floured work surface and roll out to a thickness of ¼ inch. The dough should be rolled slightly larger than the 8 by 8-inch square that is to be cut from it. Cut the square cleanly with a pastry wheel or sharp knife. With the help of a yardstick, cut into narrow strips ¼ inch wide.

Twist each strip several times and place on the work surface, pressing the ends against the surface so that they won't unwind. Allow each to relax while continuing with the others.

Return to the first strip. Shape into a pretzel, pressing the ends into the body to attach. Place on the lined baking sheet. Repeat with the others.

RISING
20 min.

Put pastries aside in a cool part of the kitchen to rise for 20 minutes. Cover with a sheet of wax paper.

Preheat oven to 475° F.

Brush pretzels with egg wash when risen. Sprinkle with ground almonds.

BAKING
475° F.
10 min.
375° F.
10 min.

Place pretzels on the middle shelf of the hot oven. These are tiny, so be watchful during the bake period. After 10 minutes reduce heat to 375° F. and bake until delicate brown, or about 10 minutes longer.

FINAL STEP

Remove pretzels from the oven. As each is lifted off the baking sheet, brush a light coat of confectioners' sugar icing over the top. Delicious served warm. If they are to be frozen, don't ice until after reheating.

SNAILS

[APPROXIMATELY TWO DOZEN PIECES]

These small, delicate pieces aren't much more than two bites—not for a lumberjack's breakfast, but great for normal appetites.

INGREDIENTS   ⅓ recipe d'Angleterre Classic Danish Pastry Dough (page 264), chilled

Remonce No. 1 or No. 2 (page 303), room temperature
Almond filling, nut or paste (page 304), room temperature
2 tablespoons finely chopped candied fruit peel
3 tablespoons currants or raisins, plumped
1 egg, beaten, to brush
¼ cup finely chopped almonds, to sprinkle
1 cup lemon or orange icing (page 310)

BAKING PAN(S)   Baking pan(s) with a narrow lip, lined with parchment paper.

PREPARATION   On a floured work surface roll the dough into a rectan-
11 min.   gle, about 14 by 9 inches. It should be ¼ inch thick.
               When the dough has relaxed and does not pull back,
               trim away irregular edges with a knife or pastry wheel.
               Spread on a thin layer of *remonce* followed by a thin
               layer of almond filling. Sprinkle the surface with can-
               died peel and currants or raisins that have been
               plumped for 10 minutes in hot water and patted dry.
                   Carefully roll lengthwise into a neat, tight roll.
               With a sharp knife cut the roll into ½-inch slices.
               Clean the knife frequently in cold running water. Lay
               each slice on its side on the baking pan, leaving about
               1 inch between.

RISING   Allow snails to rise for about 20 minutes.
20 min.   Preheat oven to 415° F.

BAKING   Brush each snail with egg wash and sprinkle with
415° F.   ground almonds. Place on the middle shelf of the hot
10 min.   oven. Bake for 10 minutes. Reduce heat to 375° F. and
375° F.   allow to bake for another 12 minutes, or until a light
12 min.   golden brown.

FINAL STEP   When the baking sheet is removed from the oven, lift
               off the snails with a spatula while still hot and before
               they stick to the paper. Over the snails pipe or drizzle
               by spoon a thin thread of confectioners' sugar icing
               while they are still warm. If they are to be frozen, ice
               after they are removed from the freezer and reheated.

CARNIVAL BUNS

(FASTELAVNSBOLLER)

[TWO DOZEN PIECES]

A favorite during Danish Shrovetide celebrations, the *fastelavnsboller* is a delicious ball of pastry surrounding a heart of *remonce*, currants and candied peel. Traditionally, thin icing is spread on the buns when they come out of the oven.

INGREDIENTS	½ recipe d'Angleterre Classic Danish Pastry Dough (page 264), chilled *Remonce* No. 1 or No. 2 (page 303), room temperature ½ cup currants, plumped and patted dry ¼ cup finely chopped, mixed candied fruit peel 1 egg, beaten, to brush ¼ cup ground almonds, to sprinkle ¼ cup vanilla sugar (page 309), to sprinkle ½ cup lemon or orange icing (page 310), optional
BAKING PAN(S)	Baking pan(s) with a narrow lip, lined with parchment paper.
PREPARATION 20 min.	Place the chilled dough on a floured work surface and roll to ¼-inch thickness. Allow the dough to relax as you proceed. With a yardstick and a pastry wheel or knife, cut the large piece into 3-inch squares. If the squares pull back when cut, roll again to the full dimensions. Place a scant teaspoonful each of *remonce* and currants in the center of each square. Sprinkle lightly with candied peel. Pull the corners and edges over the filling to form a ball. Pinch edges together gently to seal. Place on the lined baking sheet with seams underneath. Repeat with the other pieces.
RISING 20 min.	In a cool part of the kitchen allow buns to rise for 20 minutes. Preheat oven to 415° F. *Note:* Traditionally, carnival buns are iced with confectioners' sugar icing—piped or drizzled—when they come out of the oven. If they are not to be iced, brush each with egg wash and sprinkle with vanilla sugar and ground almonds *before* they go into the oven.

BAKING 415° F. 10 min. 375° F. 15 min.	Place on the middle shelf of the hot oven for 10 minutes. Reduce heat to 375° F. and bake for an additional 15 minutes.
FINAL STEP	While the buns are warm, ice if desired. Cool on a rack. These can be frozen, but do not ice until after they have been brought from the freezer and reheated.

SCRUBBING BRUSH AND COMB

(SKRUBBER OG KAMME)

[APPROXIMATELY TWO DOZEN PIECES]

The shaping of the pastry is the same for both the scrubbing brush and the comb. Only the manner in which they are cut differentiates one from the other. Both are delicious with an abundance of almonds.

INGREDIENTS	½ recipe d'Angleterre Classic Danish Pastry Dough (page 264), chilled *Remonce* No. 1 or No. 2 (page 303), room temperature Almond filling, nut or paste (page 304), room temperature 1 egg, beaten, to brush ½ cup ground almonds, to sprinkle ¼ cup vanilla sugar (page 309), to sprinkle
BAKING PAN(S)	Baking pan(s) with a narrow lip, lined with parchment paper.
PREPARATION	*Note:* The small 2½-inch *skrubbers* and *kammes* will be cut from a length of filled dough and not shaped separately.
SHAPING 12 min.	Place the chilled dough on a lightly floured work surface. Roll to ½-inch thickness. Allow the dough to relax at intervals while you work it. With a yardstick and a pastry wheel or knife, cut two 2½-inch strips, 25 inches long. After they are cut, roll lightly again so that they are thin and 3 inches wide. Down the center of each strip pipe or spoon a

narrow length of *remonce* and one of almond filling about the size of a lead pencil—not too much, or it will be difficult to fold the dough without some of the filling pushing out. Fold one-third of the dough lengthwise over the filling. Brush the exposed dough with egg wash. Fold the third side over the first, making a long, three-layered strip of filled dough. Roll lightly with a rolling pin to achieve a good union. Set aside and repeat with the second piece.

CUTTING
5 min.

Skrubber:

Turn dough over and cut diagonally into 2½-inch lengths. Place each piece on the lined baking sheet. Brush with egg and sprinkle with almonds and vanilla sugar.

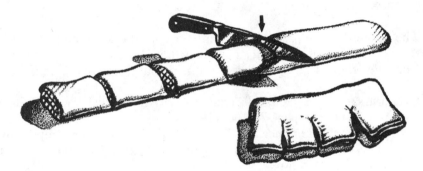

5 min.

Kamme:

Turn dough over and cut into 2½-inch lengths. With a sharp knife slash one side of each piece three or four times, cutting evenly but narrowly toward *but not into* the filling. No great harm will be done if cut, but some of the filling may ooze out as it bakes. Place on the baking pan and brush with egg. Sprinkle with ground almonds and vanilla sugar.

RISING
20 min.

In a cool place in the kitchen let pastries rest and rise for 20 minutes.
     Preheat oven to 415° F.

BAKING
415° F.
10 min.

Place the pan on the middle shelf of the hot oven for 10 minutes before reducing heat to 375° F. Bake until pastries are light golden brown, approximately 15

375° F. 15 min.	more minutes. Watch them carefully during the last 5 minutes so that they don't get too brown.
FINAL STEP	Place on a rack to cool. Delicious served warm. They may be frozen.

CRESTS/IMPERIAL CROWNS

[EIGHTEEN PIECES]

Although there is little difference between a crest and an imperial crown, each has its place on the Danish breakfast table. The crest is laid in a straight line on the baking pan, while the crown is given a slight curve to suggest a crescent. They are also known as cockscombs, and a young friend says they remind her of lions' paws.

INGREDIENTS	½ recipe d'Angleterre Classic Danish Pastry Dough (page 264), chilled Remonce No. 1 or No. 2 (page 303), room temperature Almond filling, paste or nut (page 304), room temperature 1 egg, beaten, to brush ½ cup almond slivers, to sprinkle 2 tablespoons vanilla sugar (page 309), to sprinkle
BAKING PAN(S)	Baking pan(s) with a narrow lip, lined with parchment paper.
PREPARATION 15 min.	Place the chilled dough on a floured work surface and roll out until it is no more than ¼ inch thick. If dough draws back, allow it time to relax, and roll again. The dough should be rolled into a rectangle 14 by 20 inches. Allow to rest for 3 minutes before cutting into 3-inch-wide strips. Lay strips lengthwise on the work surface. (If the dough and butter get warm, and the butter softens, chill!) With a knife or small spatula spread a thin layer of remonce and an equally thin layer of almond filling over the dough, leaving margins uncovered. Brush uncovered margins with egg to seal. Fold dough in half, in a long strip 1½ inches wide, pressing edges together and rolling lightly over the length of the dough with a rolling pin to flatten. Repeat for more strips. The se-

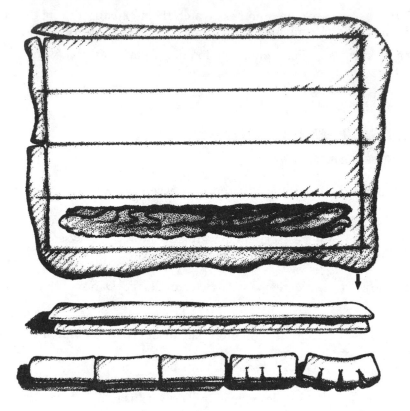

lection of *remonce* and almond filling may be varied from strip to strip.

When all strips are filled and rolled, cut into 4-inch lengths and make three cuts across half the width, completely through the dough. For crests, lay on the lined baking pan straight; for crowns, form into a crescent.

RISING
20 min.

Cover with wax paper. Place pastries in a cool part of the room to rise for 20 minutes.

Preheat oven to 415° F.

Brush each piece with egg glaze, decorate with almond slivers and sprinkle with vanilla sugar.

BAKING
415° F.
10 min.
375° F.
20 min.

Bake for 30 minutes on the middle shelf of the oven until golden brown, reducing heat after the first 10 minutes.

FINAL STEP   Place pastry pieces on a rack to cool. These are delicious eaten the same day or reheated later for 5 to 10 minutes in a 350° F. oven. If frozen, place directly into a 350° F. oven for about 25 minutes.

PASTRY STRIP

(WIENERBRODSSTANG)

[TWO 12-INCH STRIPS])

Each of these long, narrow strips of Danish is ideal for a breakfast for two. The filling can be as varied as one desires, as can the covering for the top surface.

INGREDIENTS   ¼ recipe d'Angleterre Classic Danish Pastry Dough (page 264), chilled
Remonce No. 1 or No. 2 (page 303), room temperature
Almond filling, nut or paste (page 304), room temperature
½ cup cake cream (page 305)
¼ cup chopped candied orange peel
½ cup raisins, plumped and patted dry
1 egg, beaten, to brush
¼ cup ground almonds, to sprinkle
¼ cup vanilla sugar (page 309), to sprinkle

BAKING PAN(S)   Baking pan(s) with a narrow lip, lined with parchment paper.

PREPARATION   *Working note:* The center of each strip will be spread lightly with the fillings. The edges will be folded to overlap ½ inch and sealed. The folded piece will be turned over on the baking pan with the seam underneath.

SHAPING
14 min.   Place the chilled dough on a floured work surface and roll into a rectangle 10 by 12 inches and ¼ inch thick. Cut the dough to those dimensions with a pastry wheel or knife. Divide the piece lengthwise into two 5-inch strips.

      Place one piece in front of you on the work surface. Down the center (leaving a margin for sealing at both ends) lightly spread the *remonce*, almond filling

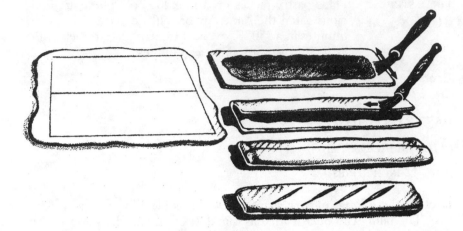

and cake cream. Sprinkle on half the peel and half the raisins. Pat the mixture to firm it on the dough.

With a brush spread egg wash along both ends. Lift one edge and fold to the center. Brush a narrow edge of egg wash down the length of this piece. Lift the other edge and overlap down the center by at least ½ inch.

Press all edges firmly to seal.

Place on the lined baking sheet, turned over with the seam under. With a razor blade or knife, make 5 or 6 diagonal cuts down the face of the pastry. Brush with egg wash. Repeat with the other piece.

RISING
20 min.

Cover with wax paper. Leave in a cool part of the kitchen to rise for 20 minutes.

Preheat oven to 415° F.

BAKING
415° F.
15 min.
375° F.
20 min.

Before placing in the oven, brush again with egg wash and sprinkle with almonds and vanilla sugar.

Place on the middle shelf of the oven and bake at 415° F. for 15 minutes. Reduce heat to 375° F. and continue baking for an additional 20 minutes, or until pastries are a golden brown.

FINAL STEP

When the pastries are removed from the oven, allow to cool for 10 minutes on the baking sheet before lifting to a cooling rack. Long pastries, hot from the oven, are fragile. These freeze well.

BURGOMASTER'S BRAIDED PASTRY

[TWO 12-INCH BRAIDS]

Each length of dough is filled with an almond filling before it is plaited into a braid.

INGREDIENTS	¼ recipe d'Angleterre Classic Danish Pastry Dough (page 264), chilled Almond filling, nut or paste (page 304), room temperature 1 egg, beaten, to brush ¼ cup sliced almonds, to sprinkle
BAKING PAN(S)	Baking pan(s) with a narrow lip, lined with parchment paper.
PREPARATION	*Note:* The best way to lay the almond filling down the length of a strip of dough is to pipe it on. It is neat and tidy, and it allows the piece to be folded and the seam closed without the filling pushing out. (See "Pastry Bag," page 40.)
SHAPING 18 min.	Place the chilled dough on a floured work surface and roll to ¼-inch thickness. Cut two rectangles 12 by 9 inches. From each cut three 3-inch strips, 12 inches long. Put the strips aside to relax while the filling is spooned into a pastry bag or paper cornucopia fashioned with parchment paper. Roll each strip again so that each is at least 3 inches wide, and thin. Brush flour off dough. Pipe a line of filling down one side of the strip. Moisten one long edge with water to enhance the seal. Fold dough over to cover the filling, then gently roll dough under the palms to fashion a tube-like length of dough. It will also become longer as it is rolled. Repeat for the other pieces. Plait three pieces together, starting at the middle and working toward one end. Pinch ends together securely to prevent their pulling apart during rising and baking. Turn piece and complete braid. Place on the lined baking sheet. Repeat with the other three pieces.

RISING 20 min.	Place the baking sheet in a cool part of the kitchen to allow braids to rest and rise for 20 minutes. Cover with waxed paper. Preheat oven to 425° F.
BAKING 425° F. 15 min. 375° F. 25 min.	Brush braids with egg wash and sprinkle with almonds. Place on the middle shelf of the oven and bake for 15 minutes at 425° F. Reduce heat to 375° F. and continue baking for an additional 25 minutes, or until a golden brown. During the last 10 minutes of the baking period open the door and check braids for color. If too brown, cover with foil or brown sack paper.
FINAL STEP	Remove from the oven and allow to cool for 10 minutes before attempting to lift (with the help of two spatulas) and place on a rack to cool.

CREAM BUNS

(CREMEBOLLER)

[APPROXIMATELY TWO DOZEN PIECES]

A *cremeboller* is deceptive. It looks like a small ball of golden pastry encrusted with sugar, but its secret is a heart of cake cream. I am not the greatest cake cream fancier, I confess, but the *cremeboller* won me over completely.

INGREDIENTS
½ recipe d'Angleterre Classic Danish Pastry Dough (page 264), chilled
1 cup cake cream (page 305)
3 tablespoons clarified butter, melted
¼ cup vanilla sugar (page 309)

BAKING PAN(S)
Baking pan(s) with a narrow lip, lined with parchment paper.

PREPARATION
20 min.
Place the piece of chilled dough on a floured work surface and roll to a scant ¼-inch thickness.

Mark the dough into 3-inch squares and cut with a pastry wheel or knife. Roll each lightly before filling. The piece must not be fat or chunky, as it cannot be formed into a ball around the soft cream center.

Place a dab of about 1 level teaspoon of cream in the center of the square. Gather the corners and pinch to form a ball. (If the first endeavors are overfilled with cream and can't be closed, fold the corners over the cream and leave upright to rise and bake as for a *spandauer*, page 269.)

Put the cream-filled bun on the lined baking sheet, seam down. Repeat with the others.

RISING
20 min.
Place the bun-filled baking sheet in a cool part of the kitchen and leave to rest and rise for 20 minutes. Cover with wax paper.

Preheat oven to 415° F. Melt and clarify butter.

BAKING
415° F.
10 min.
375° F.
15 min.
Place the baking sheet on the middle shelf of the hot oven. After 10 minutes reduce heat to 375° F. and continue to bake until buns are a medium brown, about 15 minutes.

FINAL STEP
Remove the baking sheet from the oven and brush the top of each bun with clarified butter. As each bun is lifted to a rack to cool, dip in vanilla sugar. Allow to cool before serving.

MACAROON BUNS

[APPROXIMATELY EIGHTEEN PIECES]

The icing of egg white mixed with almond paste and spread on the top of these small buns gives them the delightful flavor of macaroons.

INGREDIENTS   ¼ recipe d'Angleterre Classic Pastry Dough (page 264), chilled
Remonce No. 1 or No. 2 (page 303), room temperature
½ cup cake cream (page 305)
¼ cup vanilla sugar (page 309)
1 egg white
⅓ cup almond paste (page 304), room temperature

BAKING PAN(S)   Baking pan(s) with a narrow lip, lined with parchment paper.

PREPARATION   Place the chilled dough on a floured work surface. Roll
20 min.   to a scant ¼-inch thickness. (Err on the side of thin rather than thick!)

With a yardstick and a pastry wheel or knife, cut dough into strips 3 inches wide. Cut these into squares. In the center of each square spread a thin coating of *remonce*, cake cream and a sprinkling of vanilla sugar. Gather up the corners and close all seams carefully. With the seams down, place pastries on the lined baking sheet. Flatten slightly with the palm of the hand. Mix egg white with almond paste and spread on top of the buns.

RISING   Cover with wax paper and allow to rise for 20 minutes.
20 min.   Preheat oven to 400° F.

BAKING   Place on the middle shelf of the oven for 10 minutes.
400° F.   Reduce heat to 350° F. and continue baking for about
10 min.   15 minutes, or until pastries are brown.
350° F.
15 min.

FINAL STEP   Place on a rack to cool before serving or freezing.

DANISH BUTTER CAKE

[ONE 8-INCH PASTRY]

Slices of a roll of filled pastry dough are placed in a shell spread with *remonce* and cake cream. In the oven the slices rise and push together into a solid wheel of brown goodness.

INGREDIENTS   ⅓ recipe d'Angleterre Classic Danish Pastry Dough (page 264), chilled

Remonce No. 1 or No. 2 (page 303), room temperature
⅓ cup cake cream (page 305)
½ cup almond filling, paste or nut (page 304), room
    temperature
⅓ cup finely chopped mixed candied fruit peel
½ cup currants or raisins, plumped and patted dry
1 egg, beaten, to brush
¼ cup ground almonds, to sprinkle
¼ cup lemon or orange icing (page 310), optional

BAKING PAN

One round 8-inch pan with 1-inch sides. (I often use a tart pan with a loose bottom, because the sides are the right height. I place it in a larger pie pan to bake because the butter might run out.)

PREPARATION
22 min.

Line the shallow pan—bottom and sides—with an 11-inch circle of dough, rolled to a scant ¼ inch. Press the dough into the bottom. Allow the dough to drape up and over the sides. Roll with a rolling pin across the top to cut off excess dough. Cover and place in the refrigerator to chill and relax while the rest of the pastry is being prepared.

Roll out a square of dough 8 by 8 inches. Trim to make uniform. Spread the dough with a thin layer *each* of *remonce* and almond filling. Sprinkle with candied peel and currants or raisins.

Roll up tightly. Starting in the center of the roll, cut seven or eight ¾-inch slices.

Remove the pan from the refrigerator and again press dough into the sides to be certain of the fit. If a surplus pushes above the rim, trim it off. Spread a layer *each* of *remonce* and cake cream over the bottom.

Place the slices on their sides over the bottom pastry. Pieces should barely touch, since they will rise in the oven to fill the space completely. (If one or two slices remain, bake separately as snails!)

RISING
20 min.

Place the filled tin in a cool part of the kitchen to rise for 20 minutes. Cover with wax paper.

Preheat oven to 375° F.

BAKING
375° F.
1–1¼ hours

Uncover the pan, brush with egg and sprinkle with almonds. Place on the middle shelf of the moderate oven and bake for 1 to 1¼ hours. Watch carefully during the latter part of the baking period. If the pastry browns too quickly, cover with foil. Nevertheless, it should be a deep, crusty brown when completely baked.

FINAL STEP   Allow the tin to cool somewhat on a rack before removing the pastry. While still warm, ice with confectioners' sugar icing, either piped or spread with a spatula.
Delicious Danish!

Hungarian Pastry Dough and Blundel Tészto

It was not until I had returned from Budapest and prepared the dough from the Grand Hotel Margitsziget in my studio kitchen that I appreciated the close kinship it had with Danish pastry dough.

There are several differences, of course. Chef Páe blends his butter with margarine because even in that heavily agricultural economy, margarine is cheaper to use. Besides, he says, he finds little or no loss of taste. Also, margarine has a higher melting point than butter, so the combination has greater stability in the oven heat, lessening the chances that the fat will ooze out. Finally, the dough is rolled and "turned" only twice.

Although there is only one Hungarian pastry here—*blundel tészto*—this fine dough can be used for all the other Danish pastries.

This is a lovely dough to make because of its rich butter and egg content.

HUNGARIAN PASTRY DOUGH

[APPROXIMATELY 2 POUNDS FOR FOURTEEN 3-INCH PASTRIES
OR TWENTY-FOUR TO THIRTY SMALL HORS D'OEUVRES]

INGREDIENTS   4 ounces (1 stick) unsalted butter, room temperature
4 ounces (1 stick) margarine, room temperature
⅓ cup all-purpose flour
4 cups all-purpose flour, approximately
1 package dry yeast
1 teaspoon salt
¼ cup granulated sugar
½ cup non-fat dry milk

1¼ cups warm water (105° to 115° F.)
3 tablespoons butter or margarine, room temperature
3 egg yolks

PREPARATION

Cream together the butter and margarine. This is easy to do with a pastry or dough blade or putty knife, working on a flat surface such as a tabletop or counter. Blend in the flour.

On a piece of wax paper spread and form the butter-margarine mixture into a square, 6 by 6 inches. Cover with wax paper and refrigerate.

10 min.

In a large bowl stir together 1 cup flour and all the dry ingredients: yeast, salt, sugar and dry milk. Pour in warm water and stir until smooth. Add butter or margarine, in pieces, and 1 additional cup flour. Blend. Add egg yolks. Blend. Add flour, ½ cup at a time, sufficient to make a mass into which you can get your hands without undue stickiness. It should not be solid or dense. Lift from the bowl with the hands.

KNEADING
5 min.

Place the dough on a floured work surface and knead. The dough will be moist, soft (not sticky) and a pleasure to work. If it should stick to the hands, sprinkle with flour. It is not kneaded as long as other yeast-raised doughs, such as those for breads.

REFRIGERATED
REST
1 hour

Drop the ball of dough into a greased bowl, cover with plastic wrap and place in the refrigerator to chill for about 1 hour.

LAYERING
10 min.

Note: The butter-margarine square should be chilled to 60° F. at the time it is layered with the dough. The method for determining this with a thermometer or by pressing it with the fingers is described on page 262.

The dough will be chilled and firm. On a floured work surface roll the dough into a 10-inch square. Allow it to rest for several minutes to be certain it does not draw back to lesser dimensions.

Place the square of butter and margarine on the dough so that the four corners will meet in the center, forming a tight packet of dough encasing the butter and margarine. If the dough square is not large enough, remove the fat and roll the dough to increase its size.

When the dough fits over the fat, press the seams

together and roll the packet into a 10 by 18-inch rectangle, taking care to cover the fat.

FIRST AND
SECOND
TURNS

Note: This layered dough is given only two turns before it is refrigerated, rested and cut.

10 min.

Fold the lower third of the rectangle over the center third. Bring the upper third down on top of the center, as you would fold a letter. Turn so that the open ends are at 6 o'clock and 12 o'clock. Roll gently and firmly into a 12 by 36-inch rectangle. This is the first turn.

If the butter breaks through the dough, cover the tear with a sprinkle of flour. If the butter softens and oozes out between the folds, refrigerate 10 to 15 minutes.

For the second turn, fold the rectangle of dough in thirds as before. Turn. Roll into a rectangle. This is the second and final turn. After chilling, it will be rolled to whatever thickness is required for the individual recipe.

REFRIGERATED
REST
1 hour or
overnight

Fold the dough (separating the folds with wax paper) and wrap in a cloth soaked in water and wrung dry. Lay the wrapped dough on a baking sheet and place in the refrigerator for 1 hour or longer, up to 24 hours.

FINAL STEP

The dough is now ready to be made into pastries.

HUNGARIAN BREAKFAST PASTRY

(BLUNDEL TÉSZTO)

[EIGHTEEN 3-INCH SQUARES OR THREE DOZEN MINIATURE PASTRIES]

The delicious *blundel tészto* were piled high in a display to greet the breakfast guests coming into the big and old-fashioned dining room of the Grand Hotel Margitsziget on a lovely green and tree-shaded island between Buda and Pest in the Danube. The creation of tall, spare Chef Mosonyi Páe, *blundel tészto* is a square of pastry folded over a filling and capped with a tiny square of dough that locks the four corner points together. The Hungarian Pastry Cream is made with either cream cheese or Neufchâtel and is used for the breakfast pastry. *Blundel tészto* can also be made into a small and delicious savory pastry to be served at a brunch or at cocktails by substituting a filling such as anchovy paste or deviled ham.

INGREDIENTS

1 recipe Hungarian Pastry Dough (page 286), chilled
1 cup Hungarian Pastry Cream (page 306)
2 tablespoons jelly, optional
1 egg, beaten, to glaze

BAKING SHEET

One baking sheet lined with parchment paper.

PREPARATION

Note: The dough will be cut into 5-inch squares, so roll the dough into a rectangle that can be divided most efficiently into units of 5-inch squares. Small ½-inch squares of scrap dough are to be cut to make pieces that are placed over the four corners where the dough is drawn together.

12 min.

Remove the chilled dough from the refrigerator and place on a lightly floured work surface. Roll the dough to a scant ¼-inch thickness. If the dough resists and pulls back as it is rolled, allow it to relax for 2 or 3 minutes before proceeding.

With a yardstick lay out a series of 5-inch squares and cut with a pastry wheel or knife. Place the squares in the refrigerator as they are cut, and remove them singly as you form the pieces.

Place a square of dough on a floured work surface. Measure. It probably will have shrunk. Roll gently into a larger square. Place 1 scant tablespoon of filling in the center of the square. Push filling down slightly. Lift one corner and place in the center (over filling). Repeat with the other corners. Arrange neatly to enclose the filling completely and make a square packet.

Place on the baking sheet. Brush with egg yolk glaze. Roll out small ½-inch squares of dough into 1-inch squares. Place one in the center, over the points. Brush with glaze. Do not crowd pieces on the baking sheet.

REFRIGERATION
30 min.

When baking sheet is filled, place in the refrigerator to allow pieces to chill and rise slightly. If only one sheet is available, place other pieces on a pan to hold in the refrigerator until the first batch is baked.

Preheat oven to 380° F.

BAKING
380° F.
30 min.

Remove pieces from the refrigerator, brush with glaze again and put on the middle shelf of the preheated oven to bake for 30 minutes.

Twenty minutes into the baking period, check pastries to be certain they are not browning too fast.

Lift one pastry to check the underside. If too hot, cover pieces with foil or brown paper and reduce heat to 325° F.

FINAL STEP   Remove from the oven and place on a rack to cool.

Blundel tészto may be frozen *after* making and later put directly into the oven, as Chef Páe often does. They can also be frozen after baking and kept in the freezer for up to three months.

Easy Flaky Danish Dough and Pastries

Pastries made with Easy Flaky Danish Dough will pass any and all taste and texture tests with flying colors, yet they are not rich in butter or eggs. Sugar, too, has been held to the minimum, a plus, certainly, for those concerned with diet.

Hours in my Indiana studio kitchen studying, adapting and testing brought this flaky and easy-to-make Danish pastry dough to fruition. There is no butter or margarine in the dough as there is in d'Angleterre's classic recipe, and there is a third less butter layered between the sheets of dough. Clearly it is less rich than most other Danish pastry doughs but, I believe, with no sacrifice of quality.

Use this easy-to-make dough to prepare the six individual pastry recipes that follow. They, too, are from a wide range of recipes found here and abroad and are adapted for the American kitchen.

EASY FLAKY DANISH DOUGH

[APPROXIMATELY 2½ POUNDS, FOR TWO MEDIUM BRAIDS OR TWISTS, OR THIRTY-TWO MEDIUM PASTRIES, OR THREE TO FOUR DOZEN MINIATURE PIECES]

INGREDIENTS   1 cup water
3 packages dry yeast
⅓ cup non-fat dry milk
4½ cups all-purpose flour, approximately
1 teaspoon salt
¼ cup granulated sugar
1 teaspoon vanilla extract
1 teaspoon grated or finely chopped orange rind
¼ teaspoon ground cardamom
3 eggs

½ pound (2 sticks) unsweetened butter, to layer
3 tablespoons all-purpose flour

PREPARATION
5 min.

In a large bowl pour water over the yeast. Stir to dissolve. Add dry milk, 1 cup flour, salt, sugar, vanilla, orange rind and cardamom. Blend until the mixture is smooth. Add a second cup of flour. Stir. Add eggs. Blend. Stir in additional flour, ½ cup at a time, until the mixture is a shaggy mass in the bowl and too dense to stir.

KNEADING
5 min.

Lift the dough from the bowl and place on the work surface. With a putty knife or dough scraper in one hand, turn and knead the dough, adding sprinkles of flour if it is sticky. This dough should *not* be kneaded as vigorously as a bread dough, however. Knead it until it is smooth, soft and elastic—don't go beyond.

REFRIGERATED
REST
1 hour

Place the dough in a greased bowl, turn over to coat and cover the bowl with a length of plastic wrap. Place in the refrigerator to rest and chill while the butter is being prepared for layering.

Butter:
Note: As with the classic d'Angleterre Danish dough, one of the key considerations in the Easy Flaky recipe is the temperature of the butter and the dough when they are layered together. See "Butter Temperature," page 262, for the use of a thermometer to be certain butter is at 60° F. when it is spread in several large dabs over the chilled dough with a rubber or metal spatula.

5 min.

Place the two sticks of butter on a length of wax paper and hit several times with a rolling pin to break the butter's shape and make it flexible. With a dough blade or sturdy metal spatula, knead the dough into a mass. Spinkle over it 3 tablespoons flour and knead until the flour is absorbed.

The butter may be momentarily returned to the refrigerator to hold its 60° F. chill while the rectangle of dough is shaped.

LAYERING
15 min.

Place the chilled dough on a lightly floured work surface. Push and flatten the dough with the hands into a rough rectangle before rolling. Turn the dough over frequently as it is rolled, and keep the work surface

dusted with light sprinkles of flour. Roll and shape the dough into a rectangle 24 by 8 inches. If the dough has been sufficiently chilled, it will not pull back. If it does resist, allow it to rest for 2 or 3 minutes during the rolling process.

To spread the butter, visualize the rectangle of dough divided lengthwise into four equal parts—1, 2, 3 and 4. With a spatula, spread two-thirds of the 60° F. butter-flour mixture over sections 2 and 3, close to the top and bottom edges. Usually eight large dabs will do it. The butter dabs need not touch, for they will join when the dough is rolled. Fold the end sections (1 and 4) over the butter to meet in the center. Spread the remaining butter over one of the sides of folded dough. Fold in half, as a book, covering the butter.

There are now seven layers: dough/butter/dough/butter/dough/butter/dough.

REFRIGERATED
REST
30 min.

With the hands press the dough into a firm package. Slip it into a plastic bag and place on a refrigerator shelf to chill for 30 minutes.

FIRST TURN
5 min.

Remove the dough from the plastic bag and place it on a lightly floured work surface. Turn the dough so that the open ends are at 6 o'clock and 12 o'clock. Press down and spread the dough gently with both hands before starting to roll. Roll the layered dough into a rectangle three times longer than it is wide— about 24 by 8 inches. Fold in thirds like a letter.

REFRIGERATED
REST
20 min.

Slip the dough into the plastic bag and return to the refrigerator to chill.

SECOND TURN
5 min.

Repeat as with the first turn.

REFRIGERATED
REST
20 min.

Return the dough to the refrigerator as above. Each time lightly touch the dough with a knife blade to mark the number of turns. It is easy to forget otherwise.

THIRD TURN
5 min.

Repeat as for the first and second turns.

REFRIGERATED
REST
20 min.

Return the folded dough to the refrigerator as above.

FOURTH TURN
5 min.

This is the final turn. Repeat as for the other turns.

REFRIGERATED
REST
1 to 12 hours

Working note: Any of the four turns may be extended in time in the refrigerator from 20 minutes to several hours if it is more convenient than carrying out the schedule above. Keep in mind, however, that this is a yeast-raised dough and that it will continue to rise even in the refrigerator, though imperceptibly when cold.

The final refrigerated rest is to chill and relax the dough thoroughly before it is rolled and made into pastries. I have left dough in a cold refrigerator (42° F.) for one or two days before using it.

Wrap the dough in a damp tea towel (well wrung out) and place in the plastic bag so that air does not form a crust.

FINAL STEP   The dough is now ready to be made into whatever pastries you desire.

LARGE DANISH TWIST

[ONE 12-INCH RING]

This is a large, handsome piece that looks like a holiday wreath, thanks to its irregular surface coated with nuts and a sparkling glaze, and it deserves a special place on a holiday or anniversary table. This is sometimes called a ring, but I prefer *twist*, which best describes what it really is.

INGREDIENTS   ½ recipe Easy Flaky Danish Dough (page 290), chilled
1 cup poppy-seed, cheese, prune or *frangipane* filling (page 305)
1 egg, beaten, to brush
⅓ cup slivered almonds, to sprinkle
⅓ cup apricot or currant glaze (pages 308, 309), hot, to brush

BAKING PAN(S)   Baking pan(s) with a narrow lip, lined with parchment paper.

PREPARATION   Beforehand, prepare 1 cup of the preferred filling—poppy-seed, cheese, prune or *frangipane*—and have it at hand.

20 min.   On a floured work surface, press and roll the chilled dough into a rectangle 25 inches long, 6 inches wide and ¼ inch thick. If it pulls back when rolled, allow it to relax before proceeding.

With a spatula spread the filling in a thin layer over the dough. Fold lengthwise in three, one side over the other. The long strip of dough will now be about 2 inches wide. Roll it gently to press together and, at the same time, to lengthen.

Straighten the dough into a long piece. With a yardstick and a sharp knife make two cuts lengthwise, spaced equally, almost the full length of the strip, leaving about 1 inch uncut at the ends. The cut should be deep enough to slice through both the top and bottom layers of dough.

Holding an end in each hand, twist the length of dough to form a long twist. Stretch the dough slightly

as you work. Hold or weigh down the ends for a moment to allow the twist to relax, or it may unwind. Shape into a ring. Cross the uncut ends and press to join.

Hold the joined sections together firmly with one hand, and with the other hand flip the ring over so that the ends are hidden beneath. Place on the prepared baking sheet. Press the top of the ring to flatten it somewhat.

REFRIGERATED
REST
45 min.

Cover the twist with wax paper and place the baking sheet in the refrigerator to chill. The pastry will rise somewhat despite the cold.

Preheat oven to 425° F.

BAKING
425° F.
15 min.

Remove pastry from the refrigerator and brush with egg wash. Sprinkle with almonds.

Place on the middle shelf of the hot oven. Bake

375° F. 30–40 min.	for 15 minutes, then reduce heat to 375° F. and continue to bake for an additional 30 to 40 minutes, or until a golden brown. In the meantime heat the preferred glaze.
FINAL STEP	Remove twist from the oven and while still hot brush with glaze. Move to a rack to cool.

SMALL DANISH TWISTS

[TWENTY PIECES]

These are miniatures of large twists or rings, and they glory in a filling and topping that include currants or raisins, rum, pecans or almonds, cinnamon sugar and a currant glaze.

INGREDIENTS	½ recipe Easy Flaky Danish Dough (page 290), chilled 1 cup currants or raisins 3 tablespoons rum or hot water, to plump currants or raisins 1 egg, beaten, to brush ½ cup finely chopped pecans or almonds ⅔ cup cinnamon sugar (page 309) ⅓ cup slivered almonds, to sprinkle ½ cup apricot or currant glaze (pages 308, 309), hot, to brush
BAKING PAN(S)	Baking pan(s) with a narrow lip, lined with parchment paper. If the oven can accommodate only one pan, refrigerate remaining pastries.
PREPARATION 30 min.	Beforehand, soak currants or raisins for 30 minutes in rum or hot water.
20 min.	On a floured work surface roll chilled dough into a long strip 12 inches wide and ⅛ inch thick. Trim with a pastry wheel or knife to make the dough into a precise shape. (Save scraps for other pieces.) Brush dough with beaten egg. Drain and pat dry currants or raisins and spread evenly over the dough. Sprinkle with nuts and cinnamon sugar. Using a rolling pin, lightly roll the filling to press into the dough. Fold the dough in half lengthwise to make a strip 6 inches wide. Press together and roll lightly with a rolling pin. With a yardstick and a sharp knife, cut

dough crosswise into 1-inch-wide pieces, 6 inches long. Make an incision down the center of each strip almost to each end. With the fingers lightly press to firm the filling in place.

Twist each piece, stretching the dough slightly. If it attempts to unwind, press the ends hard against the work surface. Proceed with all pieces in this fashion before shaping into small rings. When the twisted lengths have relaxed, shape each into a ring, crossing the ends. Press ends together firmly to join. With one finger on the joint, flip the ring over and place on the prepared baking pan.

REFRIGERATED REST
20 min.

Cover with wax paper and place in the refrigerator to chill for 20 minutes.

Preheat oven to 425° F.

BAKING
425° F.
10 min.
375° F.
12 min.

Remove the tray from the refrigerator and brush pieces with egg wash. Sprinkle with almonds. Place on the middle shelf of the hot oven. After 10 minutes reduce heat to 375° F. and bake for an additional 12 minutes, or until golden brown.

Heat currant or apricot glaze to brush.

FINAL STEP

While the pastries are still hot from the oven, brush with the hot glaze and lift each twist to a rack to cool.

CUSTARD OR JELLY SNAILS

[APPROXIMATELY TWENTY PIECES]

These attractive pastries can be made either as custard snails or jellied ones—or as an assortment of both—at the moment they go into the hot oven.

INGREDIENTS

½ recipe Easy Flaky Danish Dough (page 290), chilled
¾ cup pastry cream (page 305)
    (or ½ cup jelly, of choice)
½ cup apricot or currant glaze (pages 308, 309), to brush custard snails only

BAKING PAN(S)

Baking pan(s) with a narrow lip, lined with parchment paper. If the oven can accommodate only one pan, refrigerate remaining pastries.

PREPARATION
On a floured work surface roll the dough into a thin rectangle, 18 inches wide and ⅛ inch thick.

With a yardstick and a pastry wheel or knife, cut dough into ¾-inch-wide strips, the length of the piece (18 inches). There should be about twenty pieces.

Hold the ends and twist. Pin one end on the work surface with a finger and wind the twisted dough into a coil. As you lift the snail to place it on the prepared baking pan, tuck the outside end under the body.

REFRIGERATED
REST
20 min.
Cover snails with wax paper and place in the refrigerator to chill for 20 minutes.

Preheat oven to 425° F.

Beforehand, have the pastry cream and/or jelly at hand.

Remove snails from the refrigerator. Press down the top of each snail slightly and drop a level teaspoonful of either pastry cream or jelly in the center.

BAKING
425° F.
10 min.
375° F.
10–12 min.
Place on the middle shelf of the hot oven. After 10 minutes reduce heat to 375° F. and continue to bake for an additional 10 to 12 minutes, or until a light golden brown, with a light brown bottom crust.

Heat glaze for custard snails.

FINAL STEP
Remove pastries from the oven. Brush custard snails with hot glaze. If desired, you may sprinkle the custard or jam centers with ground nuts or place a whole nut in the middle.

Place on a rack to cool.

CHEESE OR PRUNE ENVELOPES

[APPROXIMATELY TWO DOZEN PIECES]

You may wish to make half these envelopes with a cheese filling and the other half with prune. Both are very good.

INGREDIENTS
½ recipe Easy Flaky Danish Dough (page 290), chilled
¾ cup cheese or prune filling (pages 307, 308)
1 egg, beaten, to brush
⅓ cup slivered or sliced almonds, to sprinkle
½ cup apricot or currant glaze (pages 308, 309), to brush

BAKING PAN(S) Baking pan(s) with a narrow lip, lined with parchment paper. If the oven can accommodate only one pan, refrigerate remaining pastries.

PREPARATION On a floured work surface roll dough ⅛ inch thick.
20 min. When dough has relaxed and doesn't pull back, mark dough into a series of 3-inch squares, and cut with a pastry wheel or knife. If necessary, roll each piece individually with a rolling pin to a full 3 by 3-inch square.

Place a teaspoonful of cheese or prune filling in the center of each square. Lift two opposite corners and overlap in the center. Pinch together to secure, and place on the prepared baking pan.

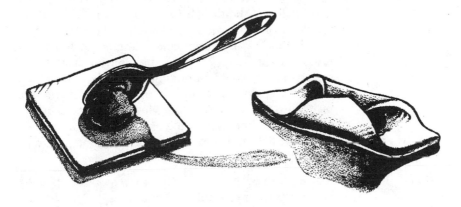

REFRIGERATED Cover with wax paper and place in the refrigerator to
REST chill.
30 min. Preheat oven to 425° F.

BAKING When envelopes are removed from the refrigerator,
425° F. brush with egg and sprinkle with nuts.
10 min. Place the baking sheet on the middle shelf of the
375° F. hot oven for 10 minutes, then reduce heat to 375° F.
10–12 min. for an additional 10 to 12 minutes.
Heat the glaze.

FINAL STEP When envelopes are removed from the oven, brush with hot glaze. Place on a rack to cool.

ALMOND COCKSCOMBS

[APPROXIMATELY TWENTY PIECES]

The cockscomb, one of the traditional Danish shapes, is crisp with a sugar glaze on the outside and rich with *frangipane* filling on the inside.

INGREDIENTS   ⅓ cup granulated sugar
½ recipe Easy Flaky Danish Dough (page 290), chilled
1 cup *frangipane* filling (page 305)

BAKING PAN(S)   Baking pan(s) with a narrow lip, lined with parchment paper. If the oven can accommodate only one pan, refrigerate remaining pastries.

PREPARATION   Spread the granulated sugar over the work surface,
18 min.   and on it roll the dough to a thin (⅛-inch-thick) rectangle, 10 inches wide by 24 inches long. Spread the dough thinly with *frangipane* filling. Fold lengthwise into thirds, making a strip 3 inches wide. Lightly roll the strip to make it thinner and somewhat longer.
      With a yardstick and a sharp knife, cut the large piece into slices 1 inch wide. Make four cuts along one side of each slice, extending about halfway across.
      Lift each pastry to the prepared baking pan, curving it slightly to spread the splits.

REFRIGERATED   Cover the cockscombs with wax paper and place in
REST   the refrigerator to chill for 20 minutes.
20 min.   Preheat oven to 425° F.

BAKING   Uncover pastries and place the baking pan on the mid-
425° F.   dle shelf of the hot oven. After 10 minutes reduce heat
10 min.   to 375° F. and bake for an additional 12 minutes, or
375° F.   until a light golden brown.
12 min.

FINAL STEP   There is no need to glaze the pastries because of the sugar coating. Place on a rack to cool.

CINNAMON BUNS

[APPROXIMATELY TWENTY PIECES]

Cinnamon buns get high marks among the many kinds of Danish pastries. Soaking the currants or raisins in rum is optional, but it adds a continental and delicious touch. Try it.

INGREDIENTS

1 cup currants or raisins, plumped and patted dry
3 tablespoons warm rum or warm water
½ recipe Easy Flaky Danish Dough (page 290), chilled
1 egg, beaten, to brush
¾ cup cinnamon sugar (page 309)
⅓ cup sliced almonds, to sprinkle
½ cup apricot glaze (page 308), to brush

BAKING PAN(S)

Baking pan(s) with a narrow lip, lined with parchment paper. If the oven cannot accommodate all of the pastries at one time, refrigerate the others.

PREPARATION
20 min.

Beforehand, soak currants or raisins in warm rum or, if preferred, in warm water for 20 minutes to soften and plump. Pat dry.

Roll dough on a floured work surface into a rectangle 16 inches wide and ⅛ inch thick. Brush with egg. Be certain to leave a 1-inch margin free of filling along one side to make a good seam. Sprinkle with cinnamon sugar. Drain currants or raisins and spread over the sugared dough. Roll the filling with a rolling pin to press into the dough.

With the hands form the dough into a tight roll, pressing the seam firmly into the dough. With a sharp knife—frequently wiped clean under cold running water—cut the long roll into ¾-inch slices. (If the several end pieces are uneven because of irregularities of the roll, cluster them into a small greased pan for a special pastry for family only.) Place slices 1 inch apart on the prepared baking pan. Press each down to flatten slightly.

REFRIGERATED
REST
20 min.

Cover the buns with wax paper and place in the refrigerator to chill for 20 minutes.

Preheat oven to 425° F.

BAKING
425° F.

Brush pieces with beaten egg and sprinkle with nuts. Place in the oven. After 10 minutes reduce heat to

10 min.	375° F. and continue to bake until golden brown, or
375° F.	about 15 minutes longer.
15 min.	Heat glaze.

FINAL STEP   Remove pastries from the oven and brush with hot glaze. Place on a rack to cool.

SCRAPS TO BE CHERISHED

There is a note in my workbook on Danish pastries that reads: "Cherish scraps!"

For most Danish pastries to look good they should be trimmed to a precise dimension so that small pieces are uniform and large pieces don't carry more dough on one end than on the other.

Danish trimmings, because they have been carefully layered, should not be thrown together and kneaded again as one might do with pieces of other doughs.

Have a creative spree!

After a day of baking several formal Danish pastries, I have accumulated a dozen or so trimmings under a dampened cloth on a tray in the refrigerator. No piece is beyond salvation. I sort out the largest trimmings first. If I have one piece that is roughly 18 inches long and 1 to 3 inches wide, I roll it again, spread whatever filling I have left over it, fold it together and make a spiral roll, with the seam up. When it is baked it is a delicious snail.

Small pieces I may simply brush with egg wash, sprinkle with nuts and sugar (and even raisins) and bake. Children love them.

Or three narrow strips—braid, brush with egg and sprinkle with sugar. Delicious.

Or put a small scrap on the baking sheet to see how high it will rise with nothing in or on it. Eat—very good.

Throw nothing away.

Danish Fillings and Toppings

Authentic Danish pastry, according to Copenhagen's Chef Wennberg, has three classic fillings: *remonce* (a blend of sugar and butter), almond or hazelnut mixtures and cake cream. There are two popular *remonces*. One is a mixture of butter and granulated sugar, flavored with vanilla; and the other is a blend of butter and brown sugar, with cinnamon. To these, on occasion, are added candied fruit peel and currants or raisins.

These are also put together in different combinations for various pastries. The snail recipe, for example, calls for *remonce*, almond paste, cake cream, candied peel and raisins.

Surface toppings and glazes, says Chef Wennberg, include beaten egg, chopped or ground almonds or hazelnuts, vanilla-flavored sugar and icings.

But there are many other fine fillings and frostings that have been developed in kitchens in this country which are not included in the Danish chef's repertoire. A poppy-seed filling and one with prunes are among those included here. None is especially sweet, certainly not cloyingly so. They can be made sweeter, of course, simply by adding more sugar or honey. A thick sweet frosting can be laid over the top of a pastry instead of the not-too-sweet fruit glaze.

The *remonce* and almond blends can be stored for three to four weeks in the refrigerator or held six to eight months in the freezer. The cake cream can be refrigerated for four to five days or frozen for three months.

REMONCE NO. 1

[3 CUPS]

INGREDIENTS | 1 pound (4 sticks) unsalted butter, room temperature
2 cups granulated sugar
¼ teaspoon vanilla extract

PREPARATION
5 min. | In a medium bowl cream butter, sugar and vanilla into a smooth mixture. A heavy mixer or food processor is helpful. Store in a plastic container in the refrigerator or freezer until needed, but bring to room temperature and stir to soften and smooth before using.

REMONCE NO. 2

[3 CUPS]

INGREDIENTS | 1 pound (4 sticks) unsalted butter, room temperature
2¾ cups dark brown sugar
½ teaspoon ground cinnamon

PREPARATION
5 min. | In a medium bowl cream butter, sugar and cinnamon into a smooth mixture. A heavy mixer or food proces-

sor may be used. Store in a plastic container in the refrigerator or freezer until needed, but bring to room temperature and stir to soften and smooth before using.

ALMOND OR HAZELNUT FILLING

[3 CUPS]

INGREDIENTS

1 pound almonds or hazelnuts, ground
2 cups granulated sugar
5 eggs, room temperature

PREPARATION
10 min.

The almonds or hazelnuts may be with or without skins. Grind in a food processor or grinder to the consistency of coarse meal. Place in a medium bowl and mix with sugar. Form a well in the center and drop in the eggs. Stir eggs lightly, then draw in the nut-sugar mixture to form a paste. If it is difficult to spread without pulling on the pastry, add another egg to moisten.

Store in the refrigerator or freeze until needed. Before using, however, bring to room temperature and stir to soften.

ALMOND PASTE FILLING

[3½ CUPS]

INGREDIENTS

1 pound almond paste or marzipan (see below)
1 pound (4 sticks) butter, room temperature
¼ teaspoon vanilla extract

PREPARATION
5 min.

If almond paste or marzipan is hard and solid in its container, break into small pieces before blending it with butter and vanilla. A food processor or blender is excellent for this chore. Store in a plastic container in the refrigerator or freeze until needed.

ALMOND PASTE

[1⅓ CUPS, ABOUT 1 POUND]

INGREDIENTS
1½ cups whole blanched almonds
1½ cups confectioners' sugar, sifted
1 egg white
1 teaspoon almond extract
¼ teaspoon salt

PREPARATION
5 min.
Grind the almonds, a portion at a time, in an electric blender or food chopper, using the fine blade. Combine with confectioners' sugar, egg white, almond extract and salt. Work to a stiff paste. Refrigerate or freeze in an airtight container or plastic bag.

FRANGIPANE FILLING

[2 CUPS]

INGREDIENTS
½ cup unsalted butter, room temperature
1 cup almond paste or marzipan (see above)
2 eggs, beaten
1 teaspoon lemon rind, grated or chopped fine
2 teaspoons flour

PREPARATION
15 min.
Cream butter. Stir in almond paste or marzipan, a small portion at a time. (The flat blade of a heavy-duty mixer can be used for this chore.)
Add beaten eggs. Blend until smooth. Stir in lemon rind and flour. When mixture is smooth, store in the refrigerator or freeze until needed.

CRÈME PATISSIÈRE (PASTRY OR CAKE CREAM)

[2½ CUPS]

INGREDIENTS
2 cups light cream (half-and-half)
⅛ teaspoon vanilla extract
¼ cup granulated sugar

2 tablespoons cornstarch
4 egg yolks
Pinch salt
1 teaspoon granulated sugar, to sprinkle

PREPARATION
15 min.

In a saucepan bring to a boil cream, vanilla and 2 tablespoons of the sugar. In a small bowl stir together the rest of the sugar, cornstarch, egg yolks and salt. Stir into this 2 tablespoons of the hot liquid. Pour egg mixture into the saucepan, stirring briskly. Return to the heat and cook to thicken. Continue to stir. Remove from heat and cool quickly by setting the saucepan in a pan of cold water, or place in the refrigerator. Sprinkle sugar over the top of the cream to prevent a skin from forming. Stir well before using. It may be refrigerated for four or five days or frozen for three months.

HUNGARIAN PASTRY CREAM

[1 CUP]

INGREDIENTS

8 ounces cream cheese or Neufchâtel, room temperature
1 teaspoon vanilla sugar (page 309)
3 tablespoons margarine, room temperature
1 tablespoon all-purpose flour
1 egg yolk
⅛ teaspoon vanilla extract
½ teaspoon lemon zest
Pinch salt

PREPARATION
15 min.

In a small bowl break up cream cheese or Neufchâtel with a fork, and add vanilla sugar, margarine, flour, egg yolk, vanilla, lemon zest and salt. Blend together until creamy. Cover with plastic wrap and refrigerate.

POPPY-SEED FILLING

[3 CUPS]

INGREDIENTS

½ pound poppy seeds
½ cup butter, room temperature

½ cup honey
2 tablespoons heavy cream
1 cup finely chopped walnuts
1½ cups raisins
1 teaspoon grated orange peel

PREPARATION
Overnight
20 min.

Beforehand, in a medium bowl cover poppy seeds with boiling water and let stand overnight.

Drain poppy seeds well and put through the finest blade of a grinder three times. (There is also a grinder made especially for poppy seeds.) Cream butter and honey in a bowl, add cream and stir in poppy seeds, nuts, raisins and grated peel. If the filling is too thick to spread thinly over the dough, stir in 1 or 2 additional tablespoons of cream or milk.

This keeps well in the refrigerator for several days and can be frozen.

CHEESE FILLING

[2 CUPS]

INGREDIENTS

2 tablespoons raisins, dark or golden
1 tablespoon brandy or water, to plump
1 cup cream cheese or cottage cheese, or a mixture of both
¼ cup granulated sugar
1 tablespoon all-purpose flour
1 egg yolk
1 teaspoon butter, melted
1 tablespoon sour cream or yogurt
½ teaspoon lemon rind, grated or chopped fine
½ teaspoon vanilla extract

PREPARATION
15 min.

In a small bowl soak raisins in brandy or hot water for 15 minutes while assembling other ingredients.

15 min.

In a large bowl cream together cheese, sugar and flour. Stir in egg yolk, melted butter, sour cream or yogurt, lemon rind and vanilla. Drain raisins and add to mixture. Store in a plastic container in the refrigerator until needed.

PRUNE FILLING

[2 CUPS]

INGREDIENTS	½ pound medium prunes, plumped and pitted ½ tablespoon lemon rind, grated or chopped fine 1 teaspoon orange rind, grated or chopped fine ⅛ teaspoon nutmeg 3 tablespoons butter, melted ½ cup finely chopped walnuts 2 tablespoons granulated sugar
PREPARATION Overnight	Beforehand, pour hot water over prunes and leave overnight to plump. The prunes can be easily pitted when soft. Grind or chop them fine to make a smooth paste.
25 min.	Place prune paste in a medium bowl and stir in and blend the other six ingredients. Prune filling may be stored for several weeks in the refrigerator or frozen for several months.

APRICOT GLAZE

[1 CUP]

This gives a delightful sparkle to a Danish pastry.

INGREDIENTS	1 cup apricot jam or preserves 2 to 4 tablespoons brandy, kirsch or other liqueur, optional
PREPARATION 20 min.	Force jam or preserves through a sieve. This is easier to do if the jam is first warmed in a saucepan. When it has been passed through the sieve, heat it in a saucepan until it boils. Stir in flavoring, if desired. Use while hot. This keeps well in a closed container in the refrigerator. Reheat to a boil each time it is to be used.

CURRANT GLAZE

[1 CUP]

INGREDIENTS	1 cup currant jelly 2 to 4 tablespoons brandy, kirsch or other liqueur, optional
PREPARATION 5 min.	Heat jam in a saucepan and bring to a boil. Remove from heat. Stir in flavoring, if desired. Use glaze while hot.

VANILLA SUGAR

[2¼ CUPS]

INGREDIENTS	3 or 4 vanilla beans 1 pound granulated or confectioners' sugar
PREPARATION	Bury vanilla beans in sugar stored in a canister. Within four to five days the sugar will be fragrant with vanilla. It can be kept stored indefinitely on the shelf.

CINNAMON SUGAR

[2 CUPS]

INGREDIENTS	2 cups granulated sugar 2 tablespoons cinnamon
PREPARATION 10 min.	Mix sugar and cinnamon and store in a covered jar. Keeps indefinitely.

ORANGE OR LEMON ICING

[SCANT 1 CUP]

INGREDIENTS

2 cups confectioners' sugar
1 teaspoon grated orange or lemon peel
1 tablespoon orange or lemon juice
4 teaspoons hot milk or water, approximately
Drops of orange or lemon coloring, optional

PREPARATION

Note: Hot milk gives icing a creamy, fondant-like texture.

5 min.

Sift the confectioners' sugar into a medium bowl and add peel and juice into a well formed in the center. With a spatula pull in the sugar to absorb the liquid. Add the hot milk or water by the teaspoonful until the mixture is thick and smooth. Add drops of orange or lemon coloring if desired.

ROYAL ICING

[¾ CUP]

INGREDIENTS

1 egg white
1½ cups confectioners' sugar, sifted
Pinch salt
1 teaspoon lemon juice
Food coloring

PREPARATION
8–10 min.

In the bowl of the electric mixer beat together egg white, sugar, salt and lemon juice until light and fluffy, about 8 to 10 minutes. The more this icing is beaten, the better it becomes. The icing is ready for piping if it stands up at a sharp point when the beater is removed. Coloring can be added after beating. Royal Icing will keep for a week tightly closed in the refrigerator, or for two to three months frozen.

Dessert Dumplings

The dessert dumpling can be baked, steamed or boiled. Dumplings, whether filled with apple, peach, plum, cheese, cherry or cranberry, are one of the plainest of all desserts. They are also the most welcome and satisfying when presented with a fine crust. Thick rich cream, sour cream or ice cream is delicious with them. Some dumplings are served hot with cinnamon, sugar and melted butter.

Three kinds of dumplings are presented here. Each has its own dough; however, almost all of the pie and many of the pastry doughs, including puff pastry, can be used for baked dumplings. (The apple dumpling made with puff paste is on page 217.) The only caution about using a substitute dough is its fragility. If, in the original recipe, it must be treated with extra care while getting it from the work surface into the pie pan or flan ring, it is probably too fragile to be wrapped around an apple.

It is not possible beforehand to determine just how much sugar will be needed with fruit, especially tart fruit. It must be tasted and a judgment made. An average portion is indicated in these recipes. After tasting the fruit, judge whether you wish more or less.

APPLE DUMPLINGS IN SYRUP

[SIX DUMPLINGS]

A golden apple dumpling, the crust drawn up around the fruit like a folded brown blossom and resting in thick syrup, spiced with cinnamon or nutmeg, or both, is among the first warm memories of farm kitchens and grandmothers and church suppers.

Rather than guess how large to cut the square of dough to cover the apple, make a paper pattern. For instance, an apple 3 inches in diameter needs a 7-inch square. Allow a small overlap of about ½ inch at the top where the four points join. Rather than have an unsightly bulge of dough when I draw up the four points, I cut away a triangle of dough in each side, about an inch deep and pointing to the center. This means less dough around the apple and makes a tidy package. This delicious apple dumpling is one of two in the book; the other is made with puff paste (page 217).

Peaches can be substituted for apples in this recipe.

INGREDIENTS	*Dough:* 4 cups all-purpose flour, sifted 4 teaspoons baking powder 2 teaspoons salt 8 tablespoons (1 stick) butter, room temperature 1½ cups milk, approximately *Syrup:* 1 cup *each* sugar and water ¼ teaspoon cinnamon Pinch nutmeg ¼ cup granulated sugar, to sprinkle *Apples:* 6 medium apples, tart preferred, peeled and cored 6 tablespoons brown sugar 3 teaspoons butter (½ teaspoon for each apple) Pinch of salt for each apple Pinch of nutmeg for each apple
BAKING PAN	One 13 by 8-inch buttered baking dish.
PREPARATION	*Dough:* *Note:* Dough can be prepared by hand, electric mixer or food processor. Instructions for each are included in this recipe. For the other two dumpling recipes,

however, only the procedure for preparing dough by hand will be given explicitly, with cross-references to these pages for the electric mixer and food processor methods.

● BY HAND
8 min.

In a mixing bowl blend flour, baking powder and salt. Cut butter into small pieces and drop into the flour. With pastry blender or two knives cut the butter into the flour until it resembles coarse meal. Make a well in the center of the flour and pour in half the milk.

With a fork pull the flour into the milk. Add more milk—but only as needed—to make a soft but not sticky dough.

Knead the dough briefly, about 15 seconds, to be certain all the ingredients are blended.

▲ ELECTRIC
MIXER
5 min.

Pour flour, baking powder and salt into the mixing bowl. Cut butter into six or eight pieces and drop into the flour. Attach bowl and flat beater. Turn to slow speed and stir until the lumps of flour-covered fat are the size of small peas, about 60 seconds. With the machine at slow speed, add milk, ¼ cup at a time, until all particles are moistened, about 10 to 15 seconds. Use only enough milk to form a ball, soft but not sticky.

■ FOOD
PROCESSOR
3 min.

Place the metal blade in the work bowl and pour in flour, baking powder and salt. Process briefly to blend. Remove the cover and drop in pieces of butter. Process for 8 to 10 seconds, or until the mixture has the consistency of coarse meal. With the processor running, slowly pour 1 cup milk through the feed tube. Stop processing as soon as dough begins to form a ball. If additional milk is needed, add 1 tablespoon at a time.

REFRIGERATION
30 min.
or longer

Cover the dough with plastic and put aside in the refrigerator to chill while the syrup and apples are being prepared.

PREPARATION
20 min.

Syrup:

Into a medium saucepan pour the sugar, water, cinnamon and nutmeg. Bring to a boil. Reduce heat and simmer while the dumplings are being prepared. The syrup will fall heavily from the spoon after about 10 minutes.

6 min.

Apples:

Peel and core six medium apples. (For a full-flavored syrup, the peelings can be dropped into the syrup and lifted out before it is poured over the dumplings.) Reserve the apples in a bowl of water to which 1 tablespoon lemon juice has been added to prevent discoloration.

ASSEMBLY
20 min.

Working note: Divide the dough into two pieces to prepare three apples at a time.

With paper, scissors and one apple, determine the size of the square necessary to wrap the fruit.

Roll a length of dough from which three squares can be cut (21 inches by 7 inches is an example).

When the dough has been rolled, allow it to relax for 3 or 4 minutes so that it will not pull back when cut into lengths. If it does withdraw, wait a moment and roll it again.

Preheat oven to 350° F.

Place the cored apple on a square of dough. Fill the cavity with brown sugar and top with ½ teaspoon butter and pinches of salt and nutmeg. If you wish to take a tuck in the dough, do so now—a triangle out of each side.

With a fingertip dipped in water, dampen all edges.

Lift two opposing points (1 and 3) and overlap. Lift the remaining points (2 and 4) and overlap.

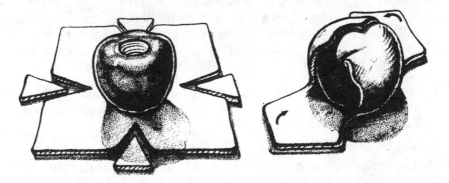

The dough should cover the apple in an attractive shield. Press down along the seams with the fingers to make a secure fit.

Place the apple in the buttered pan and repeat with the remaining five apples and pieces of dough.

If there is dough left over after covering the apples, wrap it securely and refrigerate or freeze it for a later occasion.

When all of the apples are wrapped, prick each four or five times with the tines of a sharp fork to allow steam to escape.

Pour the hot syrup over the dumplings.

BAKING
350° F.
50 min.

Place the baking pan on the middle shelf of the moderate oven and bake for 50 minutes. At 15-minute intervals baste the apples with syrup. (I use a meat baster.) Five minutes before the baking period ends, sprinkle granulated sugar over the dumplings.

FINAL STEP

Serve dumplings hot with pan syrup and cream or ice cream. Enjoy.

STEAMED PEACH DUMPLING

[ONE 7-INCH DUMPLING, SERVES FOUR]

Expect something very good to eat, especially with thick country cream poured over it, but do not expect it to be a crisp browned pastry. It will be puffy, moist and about the same color when boiled as when it went into the steamer: off-white. Not exciting in looks, but if you like steamed things, it's great.

It's made with suet dough, which marks the dessert as one of those marvelous products of the British kitchen.

A steamed dumpling should be prepared on a time schedule that will allow it to be cooked just in time to bring to the table and serve. The dough will be nicely raised and light.

INGREDIENTS

Dough:
2 cups all-purpose flour
2 teaspoons baking powder
1 teaspoon salt
¾ cup (3 ounces) grated or finely chopped suet, frozen
    preferred
¾ cup ice water, approximately

Peaches:
3 cups peeled and sliced peaches
⅓ cup granulated sugar
¼ teaspoon cinnamon
Pinch finely grated nutmeg

BAKING DISH   One 7-inch baking dish (oven-proof to withstand the heat) with 3-inch sides, 5-cup capacity. (I use a stoneware soufflé dish.)

PREPARATION   *Note:* The suet will be easy to grate if it is frozen hard. Otherwise it will be easier to chop fine with a chopper or sharp knife. Do not use a blender or food processor, which will smear the particles instead of leaving them intact.

Note: Only the procedure for preparing dough by hand is detailed here. Please turn to page 313 for complete instructions for using the electric mixer or food processor to make dough for this dumpling.

8 min.   Into a mixing bowl pour flour, baking powder and salt. Add the finely chopped or grated suet and mix it into the flour. Form a well in the center of the bowl and pour in half of the ice water. With a fork pull in the flour-suet mixture. Stir slowly to allow the flour to absorb the mixture. Add more water as needed to make a smooth but not sticky dough. When the dough is a solid mass, drop it onto a floured work surface and knead briefly for about 30 seconds.

Divide the dough—two-thirds to line the dish and one-third for the top.

8 min.   Roll the dough into a circle sufficiently large to line the entire dish and about ⅛ inch thick. Carefully line the dish, allowing the excess to drape over the sides. Do not trim until later. Roll the smaller piece of dough into a circle larger than the diameter of the dish. Place the dish on the dough and cut a precise circle to be used to top the dumpling.

REFRIGERATION   Place the lined dish and dough for the top in the re-
30 min.   frigerator while the peaches are being prepared, at least 30 minutes.

10 min.

Peaches:
Peel and slice enough peaches to make 3 cups. Place in a medium bowl and add sugar, cinnamon and nutmeg. Mix thoroughly. Taste for sweetness and add more sugar if desired.

ASSEMBLY
10 min.

Take the dish from the refrigerator and fill two-thirds full with peach slices. Add several tablespoons of the juice that has collected in the bowl.

Prick the top six or eight times with the tines of a fork. Place the top over the peaches, which are below the edge of the dish.

With a sharp knife, circle and cut the dough along the side, ½ inch above the top piece. Lift off the surplus dough. Moisten a ½-inch border of dough and fold the side dough over the top. With the fingertips press firmly against the seams to seal.

STEAMING

Working note: The dumpling dish must be placed in a steamer or in a large pan or pot in which the dumpling can be steamed. The dish should be on a platform 1 inch off the bottom. The pot must be large enough relative to the size of the dish to allow the free circulation of steam. I rest my dish on cookie cutters in a large 4½-quart saucepan (9½ inches in diameter and 5 inches deep). The lid fits tightly but is not locked.

2 hours

Assemble the equipment for the steamer and fill with water to the edge of the inch-high platform. Bring water to a rolling boil.

In the meantime, butter a square of parchment or wax paper and lay over the top of the dish. Tie in place with string. Place the dish on the platform.

Adjust the heat so that small puffs of steam constantly escape from under the pan lid. Boil gently rather than vigorously.

Check the water every 20 minutes and fill to the level of the platform. Don't let it boil dry. Steam is hot. Turn the lid away from you when you check the water. Don't direct it toward the face and hands.

FINAL STEP

Remove the dish from the steamer. Brush off water that may have accumulated on the paper covering the dumpling. Cut the string and carefully remove the paper.

Allow to cool for 10 or 15 minutes before serving.

BOILED PLUM DUMPLINGS

[TWELVE DUMPLINGS, SERVES SIX]

A boiled dumpling should be addressed by a hungry man, woman or child. It is plain but filling; good but not rich. It can be served with hot butter and sprinkled with sugar, or enlivened and enriched with cream or ice cream. The dumplings are a reflection of the season—dough wrapped around fruit that is fresh and delicious in the market. If not plums, then apricots or peaches.

If you have not tried boiled dumplings, do so; but do so before you serve them to guests. It is not the usual dessert. It is simple fare.

This is an adaptation of two fine recipes, one Czech and the other Austrian. One recipe is from a member of the Benes family—Czech diplomats, a president and several educators—and the other from the *familie* Moldan, the family that for many generations has operated the marvelous Hotel Brau in the high mountain village of Lofer, Austria.

This light yellow version of a boiled dumpling is unusual because the dough is yeast-raised. The nice touch of this recipe is the cube of sugar in the cavity recently occupied by the seed.

INGREDIENTS

Dough:
2 cups all-purpose flour, approximately
2 packages dry yeast
¼ cup *each* sugar and non-fat dry milk
3 egg yolks
½ cup water
½ teaspoon vanilla extract
¼ teaspoon grated lemon peel

Plums:
12 Damson or Italian-type plums or apricots, pitted
¼ cup granulated sugar, or more if needed
12 sugar cubes
1 tablespoon salt
½ cup (1 stick) butter, melted, to dribble
⅓ cup granulated sugar, to sprinkle
1 tablespoon cinnamon, to sprinkle

SAUCEPAN

One large 4½-quart saucepan, covered, to hold four dumplings while boiling.

PREPARATION

Dough:
Note: Only instructions for preparing dough by hand are given here. Please turn to page 313 for complete

procedures for using an electric mixer or food processor to make dough for this dumpling.

6 min.

Into a mixing bowl pour 1 cup flour, the yeast, sugar, non-fat dry milk, egg yolks and water. Stir to blend. Add the vanilla extract and grated lemon peel. Add ½ cup flour and stir well. Don't overpower the mixture with too much flour.

Gradually add the final amounts of flour and mix together with the fingers until the dough is a mass. Lift from the bowl and place on a floured work surface.

KNEADING
5 min.

Knead with the 1-2-3 motion of push-turn-fold, push-turn-fold, and so on. Break the rhythm occasionally by whacking the dough down against the work surface. This helps to develop the gluten necessary to yeast-raised dough. Add sprinkles of flour if the dough seems excessively moist or sticky.

FIRST RISING
45 min.

Place the dough in a greased bowl, cover with plastic wrap and leave at room temperature until it has doubled in bulk, about 45 minutes.

10 min.

Plums (or apricots):
While the dough is rising, split each fruit down one side and remove the seed. Leave the two halves attached, if possible. Place in a bowl, and when all of the fruit has been pitted sprinkle with sugar to your taste.

ASSEMBLY
8 min.

Lift the dough out of the bowl and place it on the work surface. Knead for 30 seconds. Roll into a large rectangle 12 by 16 inches and ¼ inch thick. Allow the dough to relax in this rolled-out position for 4 or 5 minutes so that it will not draw back when cut.

Note: With paper, scissors and one plum determine the size of a square of dough necessary to wrap the fruit. When the dough has relaxed and does not pull back, cut into appropriate-size squares. Allow a small overlap of about ½ inch at the top where the four points join. Cut away a triangle of dough in each side, about 1 inch deep and pointing to the center of the square. This means less dough around the fruit. Try it with a pattern first.

15 min.

Place a cube of sugar in the cavity of each plum and rest the fruit in the center of the square.

With a fingertip dipped in water, moisten all the edges. Lift two opposing points (1 and 3) and overlap. Lift the remaining points (2 and 4) and overlap.

Pinch the seams together securely so that the dumpling will not come apart in the water. Set the dumpling on a baking sheet and cover with a cloth. Repeat with other fruit and pastry squares.

SECOND RISING
15 min.

When all of the dumplings have been assembled, let rise under the cloth for 15 minutes while the salted water is heated.

COOKING
12 min.

Add 1 tablespoon salt to the water and bring to a boil. Lower four of the dumplings into the water. When the water returns to the boil, lower heat to simmer and cover. Cook for 6 minutes. Turn dumplings over with a spoon and continue cooking for an additional 6 minutes.

Lift the dumplings from the water with a slotted spoon and drain on paper towels, or on a metal rack with fine mesh. Cook the others. Drain.

FINAL STEP

When the dumplings are cooled, arrange on a serving platter and drizzle with melted butter. Sprinkle with sugar and cinnamon. Serve the fruit dumplings while they are warm.

Tarts and Quiches

A baked tart is a glory to behold. A bright red cherry tart, glazed with amber currant jelly, is a sensual sight. A golden *quiche* is a visual delight. And if a good tart dough is used, all will be delicious.

A French, German or English book on cookery would have a substantial chapter devoted to tarts, tartlets, flans and *quiches*, with perhaps only a passing mention of a peculiar New World culinary development, the dessert pie. In America the reverse is so—first the pie, and then the tart.

The tart is a marvelous creation that deserves more attention than it gets in this country's kitchens. More and more packaged doughs to line a tart tin or a *quiche* dish are appearing in frozen food displays, but why buy them when the dough is so easy to make? Not only can it be done at your leisure and refrigerated or frozen for later use, but it can be done at less cost—and more taste!

Tart crust is short, crisp and delicate, not unlike rich cookie dough. A filled tart remains crisp for days. It does not get soggy because it does not soak up juices. It has the strength to stand alone when prepared in a form that has no bottom, yet it is not tough. Tart pastry is similar to one of the basic pie doughs, the short-flake or mealy, except that it is richer. In both the fat is blended into and absorbed by the flour—unlike other doughs in which the fat pieces are left discrete to make a flaky crust.

Tarts may be made large or small (tartlets and *barquettes*). They may be made square, rectangular or round in forms without bottoms (sides only) or in tins with loose bottoms. Some tins are fluted; others are not. The classic French *quiche* pan is functional, handsome and expensive. But a pie pan can bake all of them just as well.

A word about flan: it is a tart made in a form without a bottom and baked directly on a baking sheet. It should not be confused with a French caramel pudding.

Preparing the Dough

Although *pâte brisée* is considered the *basic* tart dough, there are variations to which other ingredients are added to make them especially desirable for certain pastries.

The preparation of the *brisée* dough follows in its entirety. The other doughs are described, and their ingredients are listed. Their preparation, unless otherwise noted, is the same as for *brisée*.

All-purpose flour is used because high-gluten bread or unbleached flour would make a tough dough, and pastry flour would make a dough too fragile to be lifted into the pans and shaped.

Here is an easy way to figure how much dough is needed for the baking job at hand: each cup of flour in the recipe makes one 8-inch flan or tart shell or about four 4-inch tartlet shells, or fills at least twenty small *barquette* tins.

Recipes may be halved (for one tart) or multiplied as many times as you wish. (Dividing an egg, however, is a difficult feat unless it is first stirred and then measured by the spoonful.)

CHILLING

When it is prepared, tart dough demands the same tender care that is given to pie dough. It is richer than pie dough, and, like it, tart dough must be worked chilled.

Dough at room temperature can become a disaster. It may break or tear as it is being lifted off the work surface or when it is being fitted into a form. If this happens, you can start over by shaping the dough into a flat oval and returning it to the refrigerator to chill for an hour or so. You may also overlap the torn pieces and proceed to press the dough into shape with the fingers. The bottom and sides will be dimpled with finger marks where you pressed the dough into shape, but who's to know?

Perhaps do a rough patch job first, chill the dough and then refine your work. Small scraps can be pressed over thin spots. Push enough dough up the sides so that the edge can be fluted.

If, on the other hand, the ball of dough has been left for several hours or overnight in the refrigerator, it may be quite solid and firm.

Leave it at room temperature for about 30 minutes. Also, the dough may be tapped with a rolling pin to break the hard form before starting to roll it.

SHAPING

Note: Unless otherwise indicated, all tart doughs are to be rolled to a thickness of ⅛ inch.

The easiest way to prepare dough to be fitted into a pan or flan form is to flour the work surface lightly and roll the dough out in several stages. After each roll, move the dough and sprinkle it lightly with flour so that it does not stick to the work surface and rolling pin. If the dough splits along its edges as it is being rolled, press the cracks together.

Some of the excess dough protruding over the edge of the ring or form is folded back and over the inner edge to double the thickness of the side wall. First press the dough into the form. With scissors, roughly trim the dough, but leave an excess. Fold over. With the fingers, press the dough against the sides, allowing some to protrude above the rim. This may be decorated with fluting, or trimmed flush with the metal edge.

Rich doughs are fragile and sometimes cannot be rolled. They stick to the rolling pin, the work surface or the fingers—infuriating. Refrigerate for a short while to firm the dough and make it less sticky. Place the dough in the tin and proceed to shape it with floured fingers. If the dough begins to stick before the job is done—back into the refrigerator. Wash and dry the hands, and then finish the job.

To line small tartlet and *barquette* tins, cluster them together on the work surface. Roll the dough somewhat thicker than finally wanted because it must undergo some stretching in the tin. Place the dough over the cluster of tins. Roll with a floured pin. The cut pieces will be pressed into the tiny containers. The job is completed by pressing the dough down with the thumbs and shaping it to fit the forms.

Chill all dough in whatever form for at least 1 hour before baking, filled or blind.

Caution: Fluted pans have protruding and sharp edges. Some can cut like a knife. Be careful when lowering crust into a fluted pan. If the dough tears or rips, patch, pinch and proceed.

If your oven is large enough, bake tarts (and pies) on a baking sheet or pan to catch the filling if it should bubble over. Use one made of dark metal or Teflon to direct the heat toward the bottom crust, rather than reflect it away, as with shiny aluminum.

There is a marvelous selection of rings, forms, pans and tins in which to form these pastries (see "Equipment to Make Fine Pastries," page 33), but you can improvise one with heavy aluminum foil if you can't find one in your store. For a 9-inch ring, cut the foil 18 by 26 inches. Fold the foil lengthwise into a heavy 1-inch strip. Shape into a ring, overlapping the ends 1 inch. Staple or pin the ends together. Place the ring on a baking sheet, as with the store-bought ones, but cut off excess dough with a knife or scissors rather than rolling over the edge with a rolling pin. Any size and shape of flan ring may be improvised this way—square, rectangular, triangular and large or small.

A free-form shell can also be fashioned by turning up the edges of a dimension of dough—pleated and pinched in the corners, or fluted into a circle—and baked freestanding. (I consider it a major triumph when I am successful.)

A fine tart can also be made in an ordinary pie pan. It may not look like the classic tart, but it will be one, nevertheless.

BAKING

A filled but unbaked tart should be placed on the lower rack of a 425° F. oven. After 15 to 20 minutes reduce the heat to 375° F. and move the tart to the middle shelf. This directs the heat to the bottom of the tart and reaches the filling quickly. Bake until the filling bubbles near the center. For a *quiche*, insert a knife; if it comes out clean, the *quiche* is done. It will continue to bake for a few minutes after it is removed from the oven.

To bake a "blind" or unfilled tart either partially or fully, set the oven at 425° F. Prepare the dough, line the pan and fill it with dried beans, rice or aluminum pellets over a protective sheet of foil fitted around the inside of the crust.

To partially bake a tart shell, place in the oven for 10 to 12 minutes. Take the pan from the oven, remove the weights and return to the oven for an additional 3 to 4 minutes to dry out the bottom crust.

To bake a shell completely, bake for 18 to 20 minutes. Remove the pan from the oven, take out the weights and return to the oven for an additional 5 minutes to dry out the bottom crust, which then will be a light golden color.

GLAZES

A glaze gives a tart or tartlet that stylish continental look as well as a piquancy that sets off the filling and the crust. It's a smart touch.

Apricot and currant glazes are the two most used and certainly the easiest to prepare. They can be stored in the refrigerator for months, to be reheated when needed.

For an apricot glaze, press the contents of one 12-ounce jar of apricot jam through a sieve into a small saucepan. Bring the jam to a boil over medium heat and stir in 2 to 4 tablespoons of either brandy or a favorite liqueur. Use apricot glaze on light-colored fruits and other fillings such as peaches and apricots. Brush while hot.

The currant jelly need not be sieved, of course, so empty a 12-ounce jar directly into the saucepan. Bring to a boil and add brandy or a preferred liqueur. Use this darker glaze on darker fruits such as cherries and berries.

The glaze is spooned or brushed over the filling when both are hot. Brush carefully or pat, because the surface is fragile and can be torn by the brush if not spread delicately over the filling.

BASIC TART DOUGH

(PÂTE BRISÉE)

[ONE 9-INCH TART SHELL, OR TWO 8-INCH TART SHELLS, OR TWELVE 4½-INCH TARTLET SHELLS, OR TWO DOZEN BARQUETTE SHELLS]

Tart pastries call for a dough that is crisp but not flaky. It must be tender and not tough. *Pâte brisée* is made with butter, a little lard or vegetable shortening, some sugar, an egg and a touch of lemon juice. The tablespoon of sugar may be omitted if the dough is for a savory pastry. Although butter is the principal fat in this dough, a portion of it is lard or vegetable shortening, the latter added to enhance the shortness of the crust.

INGREDIENTS	2 cups all-purpose flour ½ teaspoon salt 1 tablespoon sugar, optional for a savory tart 4 ounces (1 stick) unsalted butter, chilled 1 ounce (2 tablespoons) lard or vegetable shortening, chilled 1 egg, lightly beaten 1 teaspoon lemon juice 2 tablespoons ice water
BAKING TINS	Refer to individual recipe.
PREPARATION ● BY HAND 8 min.	In a medium bowl place flour, salt and sugar. Cut the butter and lard or shortening into small pieces and drop into the flour. With the fingers, a pastry blender or two knives, cut and work the fat into the flour until the mixture resembles coarse meal. In a small bowl combine lightly beaten egg, lemon juice and 1 tablespoon ice water. Slowly pour the liquid into the flour-fat mixture while stirring with a fork. The mixture

should hold together in a rough mass—moist but not wet. If crumbly (dry), add water. It will stiffen considerably when chilled.

▲ ELECTRIC
MIXER
5 min.

Measure flour, salt and sugar into the mixing bowl. Attach the flat blade. Cut the butter and lard or vegetable shortening into small pieces and drop into the bowl. Start at low speed and stir until the pieces of flour-covered fat are cut into tiny particles, about 45 seconds. Stop the machine to check consistency. In a mixing cup blend egg, lemon juice and 1 tablespoon ice water. Turn speed to low. Add liquid a tablespoonful at a time until all particles are moistened and collect in a mass on the mixer blade, about 15 seconds. Use only enough liquid to make a ball. Don't overmix or the dough will toughen.

■ FOOD
PROCESSOR
3 min.

With the metal blade attached to the shaft, pour flour, salt and sugar into the work bowl. Cut the butter and lard or vegetable shortening into small ½-inch chunks and drop into the flour. Process with three or four short bursts until the mixture has the consistency of coarse meal. Stop the machine while blending egg, lemon juice and 1 tablespoon ice water in a small bowl. With the processor running, pour liquid through the feed tube in a steady stream. Add all or part of 1 tablespoon ice water if needed to moisten dough to form a ball. Stop as soon as the dough begins to form a ball and ride on top of the blade. Don't overprocess or the dough will be tough.

REFRIGERATED
REST
1 hour or
longer

Wrap the dough in foil or plastic wrap and refrigerate for 1 hour or longer.

NEUFCHÂTEL (CREAM CHEESE) PASTRY

[SAME VOLUME AS FOR PÂTE BRISÉE]

Neufchâtel is the name I have given to a longtime favorite dough made with Neufchâtel cheese, which is like cream cheese except it is smoother, mixes more easily and contains less fat (25 percent) but more protein and moisture.

The dough makes a rich, crisp pastry that is quick and easy to prepare and one that substitutes for other tart doughs, especially for savories and hors d'oeuvres. The dough is unsweetened.

Cream cheese may be substituted for Neufchâtel.

INGREDIENTS	2½ cups all-purpose flour
	1 teaspoon salt
	1 cup (2 sticks) unsalted butter
	1 cup Neufchâtel or cream cheese
	¼ cup light cream
PREPARATION	As for *pâte brisée*.

Note: Neufchâtel and cream cheese doughs should be rolled between sheets of wax paper. Loosen the upper and lower sheets several times while the dough is being rolled to keep it from sticking and to allow it to spread.

WHOLE WHEAT TART DOUGH

[SAME VOLUME AS FOR PÂTE BRISÉE]

Although white flour is most often used in pastry preparation, this recipe calls for whole wheat, which gives it a natural-foods goodness combined with the richness that comes from butter and egg. The crust is somewhat fragile to handle, and it bakes to a deep brown.

INGREDIENTS	2 cups whole wheat flour
	¼ teaspoon salt
	2 tablespoons sugar
	½ cup (1 stick) unsalted butter, chilled
	2 eggs, beaten
	2 tablespoons ice water
PREPARATION	As for *pâte brisée*.

SWEET TART DOUGH

(PÂTE SUCRÉE)

[SAME VOLUME AS FOR PÂTE BRISÉE]

This is a widely used tart dough, especially for tarts and flans with sweet fillings. Delicious.

INGREDIENTS	2 cups all-purpose flour
	¾ cups granulated sugar

Pinch salt
Rind of 1 lemon, grated or chopped fine
10 tablespoons (5 ounces) unsalted butter, chilled
2 eggs, beaten lightly
1 tablespoon ice water, or portion thereof, if needed

PREPARATION   As for *pâte brisée*.

RICH TART PASTRY

[SAME VOLUME AS FOR PÂTE BRISÉE]

Pastry shells made with this egg-rich dough have a lovely golden color.
To make a pastry less fragile but crisper in texture, 2 egg whites may be
substituted for the 2 raw egg yolks.

INGREDIENTS   2 cups all-purpose flour
3 tablespoons granulated sugar
½ teaspoon salt
¾ cup (1½ sticks) unsalted butter, chilled
2 teaspoons grated or finely chopped lemon rind
3 hard-cooked egg yolks, mashed (see note below)
2 raw egg yolks
   (*or* 2 egg whites)
½ teaspoon lemon juice

Note: In a small bowl mash the cooked egg yolks with
a fork. Stir this into the flour and butter. Use the same
bowl to lightly stir the egg yolk (or egg whites) and the
lemon juice.

PREPARATION   As for *pâte brisée*.

LINZER PASTRY

[SAME VOLUME AS FOR PÂTE BRISÉE]

While there are innumerable recipes for Linzer paste, some expensive
and others less so, all are derived from an original recipe created in 1823
by Johan Vogel in the town of Linz, Austria.

The traditional *Linzertorte* is not a torte but a tart filled with red
raspberry jam. It is distinguished, also, by two spices: cinnamon and

cloves. This pastry dough is for any flan or tart that calls for an almond-rich shell and, if for the *Linzertorte* or tart, the spices (see Linzer Tart, page 336).

INGREDIENTS

2 cups all-purpose flour
½ cup granulated sugar
Pinch salt
½ teaspoon cinnamon, if for Linzer Tart
Pinch cloves, if for Linzer Tart
1 cup finely ground almonds
2 teaspoons grated lemon rind
1 cup (2 sticks) unsalted butter, chilled
4 raw egg yolks
2 to 3 teaspoons ice water, if needed
    (*or* 1 tablespoon rum)

PREPARATION

As for *pâte brisée*.

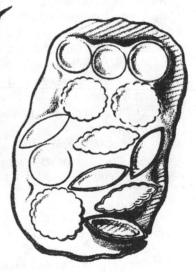

LINING A NUMBER OF
BARQUETTE AND TARTLET TINS
WITH LINZER PASTRY

Fillings

The tarts and *quiches* that follow are among the classic and traditional ones. There are literally hundreds of variations, but these are the ones about which poems have been written and songs sung.

Pie fillings may be used in these shells, too. All of those fillings in the pie section of this book will be at home here—even the venison-powered mincemeat (page 103), delicious and dainty in a *barquette*.

TARTS

PEACH TART BOURDALOUE

(TARTE AUX PÊCHES BOURDALOUE)

[ONE 8-INCH TART OR SIX TARTLETS]

Whether resting before you on a dessert tray in Vienna's Demel's or in Munich's Dallmayr's, or at home, there is nothing quite so pleasing to the eye—and the palate—as a *tarte aux pêches Bourdaloue* with the rounded halves of glazed peaches on a bed of almond cream. Or one peach half presented in a small tartlet shell.

Fresh peaches (*pêches*) or pears (*poires*) are the fruit chosen for the recipe. Eight halves will fill an 8-inch shell or eight tartlet shells.

The two fruits are beautifully proportioned to use in creating a series of glistening mounds in a large shell or a tiny spectacle in one small tartlet shell.

What sets *pêches Bourdaloue* apart from other fruit tarts is poaching the peaches (or pears) in a vanilla-flavored light syrup. Fruit canned in syrup can also be used, but there is little to be gained by poaching them.

SUGGESTED DOUGH	For an outstanding combination of shell and filling, use Linzer Pastry (page 328), or other choice.
INGREDIENTS	Baked shell(s) for one 8-inch tart or six tartlets 1½ cups water ¾ cup granulated sugar 1 teaspoon *each* grated lemon peel and vanilla extract 4 medium-sized fresh peaches (or pears) (*or* 1 large can peach or pear halves) 3 ounces cream or Neufchâtel cheese, room temperature

1 cup whipping cream
¼ cup confectioners' sugar
½ teaspoon grated lemon peel
1 teaspoon lemon juice
¼ teaspoon *each* almond extract and vanilla extract
2 tablespoons kirsch, optional
⅔ cup apricot glaze (page 308)
½ cup sliced almonds

BAKING PANS
AND TINS

One 8-inch tart pan or six tartlet tins.

PREPARATION

Dough:
Shape dough in tart rings, pans or tins of choice, and bake beforehand. (See "Shaping" and "Baking," pages 323–324.)

25 min.

Filling:
To poach the peaches (or pears), combine water, sugar, grated lemon peel and vanilla in a large pan. Bring to a boil. Stir until the sugar dissolves.

Let the syrup simmer while peeling the fruit (peaches may be dipped in boiling water for 3 seconds to loosen skins). Cut in half and remove stones. Place the halves in syrup, cover and simmer 8 to 10 minutes, or until fork-tender. Drain well and cool. The syrup may be saved to sweeten other fruit.

In the bowl of the electric mixer beat the cream or Neufchâtel cheese, slowly blending in the whipping cream. Add the confectioners' sugar, lemon peel and juice, almond extract, vanilla and kirsch, if used. Beat the mixture until it is as thick as stiffly beaten cream.

Spoon the filling into the pastry shell(s), spreading evenly.

If you are using a large shell, place one peach (or pear) half in the center, with the remaining fruit halves surrounding it; if you are using small tartlet shells, put one peach (or pear) half in each. Push the fruit gently into the surface of the cream.

(If pears are used, cut off the neck of the center pear to achieve symmetry.)

REFRIGERATION
1 hour

Cover and chill until firm, about 1 hour.

GLAZING 5 min.	Heat the apricot glaze and with a spoon lightly drizzle it over the peaches (or pears) and filling to form a glistening surface over all.
FINAL STEP	Cover with foil held off the glaze and refrigerate until serving time. Before serving, overlap almond slices around each fruit half.

APPLE TART NORMANDY

(TARTE AUX POMMES NORMANDIE)

[ONE 8-INCH TART OR SIX TARTLETS]

There are as many recipes for *tartes aux pommes* in Normandy's kitchens as there are for apple pies in this country. Normandy's orchards provide apples for some of the best cider in the world as well as Calvados, apple brandy. This recipe is from one of my favorite small French cities, Bayeux, *département* of Calvados, a half hour's drive from the World War II invasion coast.

If you have Calvados at hand, sprinkle 1 tablespoon over the apple slices before the tart goes into the oven. Other fine brandies, of course, will do almost as well.

In a round pastry-filled ring, a layer of overlapping apple slices is laid down and a rosette of slices fashioned in the center. Any of the green tart apples is a good choice. My Lodi tree has fruit ready for harvest about the middle of July—the start of the tart (and pie) season at our house.

The tart can be made in an open flan ring or in one with a loose bottom. It may also be shaped in a square or rectangular form in which the apples are arranged in decorative rows rather than in a circle.

It is not meant to be a thick pastry. Nevertheless, it will serve from eight to ten at a dinner party or tea. Admittedly, it might go around to only four Little Leaguers.

SUGGESTED DOUGHS	Basic *pâte brisée* or Whole Wheat (pages 325 and 327).
INGREDIENTS	Partially baked shell(s) of choice 2 pounds (about 6) apples, tart preferred Juice and grated rind of 1 lemon ⅓ cup granulated sugar ¼ cup (½ stick) butter ¼ cup raisins, light sultanas preferred

1 tablespoon Calvados or other brandy, optional
2 tablespoons apricot glaze (page 308)

BAKING PANS
AND TINS
One 8-inch tart pan or six tartlet tins.

PREPARATION

Dough:
Shape dough in tart rings, pans or tins of choice, and partially bake beforehand. (See "Shaping" and "Baking," pages 323–324.)

12 min.

Filling:
Peel, core and slice the apples in uniform ¼-inch slices—across the apple halves, not lengthwise. (Small end pieces can fill in under the rosette.) Drop into a bowl and sprinkle the lemon rind and juice over them. Add the sugar and mix thoroughly but gently.

8–10 min.

In a large skillet melt butter over medium to low heat. Place the apples in the skillet. Cook slowly for about 10 minutes. Turn slices over gently with a large spatula. Give it your constant attention, or those on the bottom may turn to mush if left too long. Remove the skillet from the heat. Add raisins and mix so that they are scattered among the slices.
    Preheat oven to 425° F.

5 min.

When the slices have cooled and can be picked up with the fingers, arrange close together in an overlapping pattern around the edge of the pan. In the center fashion an inner circle and build a rosette higher than the larger circle. The raisins should appear at random over and under the slices.

BAKING
425° F.
15 min.
375° F.
30 min.

Sprinkle Calvados or other brandy over the top of the apples and place on the lower shelf of the hot oven. After 15 minutes reduce heat to 375° F. and move the tart to the middle shelf.
    Heat apricot glaze in a small saucepan to have ready when the tart comes from the oven.
    The tart is done after 45 minutes, or when apple slices are tender when pricked with the tines of a sharp fork. Apples will be a light brown with occasional dark brown touches along the edges of the slices.

FINAL STEP

Remove the tart from the oven and place on a cooling rack. Carefully brush the hot glaze over the slices.

This may be more of a dabbing action than one of brushing so as not to destroy the surface of the tart. Do not unmold the tart until it has cooled.

GLAZED FRUIT TART

(TARTE AUX FRUITES)

[ONE 8-INCH TART, SIX TARTLETS OR TWO DOZEN BARQUETTES]

The *tarte aux fruites* is whatever you wish it to be. It might be lovely fresh peaches at the height of the season, or a late winter's dessert of canned but equally delicious pears. It might be fresh or canned Hawaiian pineapple. Seeded or seedless grapes. Sweet or tart cherries. The choice is almost limitless when one also considers the combinations that are possible—rhubarb and strawberries, to name but one of my favorites.

My version of this versatile dessert is made with tart red cherries, pitted. Although I prefer them fresh-picked from my own two trees, I have also used canned or frozen fruit. Red raspberries are high on my list of favorite fruits for this tart. The berries, especially the big red ones, make a handsome dessert piece, whether in a large tart or in individual shells.

For a touch of elegance in eating, place the cherries on a bed of pastry cream spread lightly over the bottom of the shell. If pastry cream is not readily at hand, spread toasted ground hazelnuts, pecans or walnuts, about ½ cup, over the bottom of the shell before adding the fruit.

SUGGESTED DOUGHS	Basic *pâte brisée* or Rich Tart Pastry (pages 325 and 328).
INGREDIENTS	Partially baked shell(s) of choice 4 cups fresh tart cherries, pitted (*or* 10 ounces frozen cherries) ½ cup granulated sugar ⅛ teaspoon cinnamon ¾ cup pastry cream (page 305), optional *or* ½ cup ground nuts ½ cup currant glaze (page 309), hot
BAKING PANS AND TINS	One 8-inch tart pan, or a selection of tartlet and/or *barquette* tins.

PREPARATION

Dough:

Shape dough in tart rings, pans or tins of choice, and partially bake beforehand. (See "Shaping" and "Baking," pages 323–324.)

8 min.

Filling:

Place the pitted fresh cherries in a large saucepan and stir in sugar and cinnamon. Over medium heat cook cherries *briefly* until juice begins to leave the fruit and gather in the bottom of the pan. This will be about 3 minutes after the pan is heated and the sugar begins to melt. Remove the pan from the heat and set cherries aside to cool.

If the cherries are frozen, thaw in a medium saucepan; add sugar and cinnamon. Bring to a boil and lower heat to allow the cherries to simmer for about 3 minutes. Put aside to cool.

Preheat oven to 425° F.

Spread a thin layer of almond cream or nuts, if either is desired, over the bottom(s) of the tart or tartlet shells. If using nuts, press gently into the crust to anchor.

Spoon the cherries over the bottom of the shell so that they are about two layers deep, or to the top. Add liquid from cooked fruit to cover the lower layer of fruit.

Turn cherries bottoms up so that the surface of the tart is one of dozens of tiny cardinal-red mounds.

BAKING
425° F.
15 min.
375° F.
40–50 min.

Place the tart or tartlets on the lower shelf of the hot oven so that the maximum heat gets to the bottom of the partially baked tart. Reduce heat to 375° F. after 15 minutes and move the shell(s) to the middle shelf. Small tartlets will take less time and will be baked 10 minutes before a large tart. The cherries near the centers of both large and small tarts will bubble when done—but don't prolong it! Remove from the oven, because they will continue to bake for several minutes longer.

Glaze:

Heat currant glaze until it is thin and can be brushed or spooned.

FINAL STEP

Ten minutes after tart(s) is taken from the oven, brush on the glaze (with care so as not to tear the surface of the tart) or pour from a spoon over the entire surface of the piece(s). Brush the top edge of the shell(s) so that it, too, glistens.

The tart may be served warmed or chilled—with equal acclaim.

LINZER TART

(LINZERTORTE)

[ONE 8-INCH TART, SIX TARTLETS OR TWO DOZEN BARQUETTES]

The many recipes for one of Austria's most famous pastries, *Linzertorte*, often call for a very thick red raspberry jam to be spread over buttery almond dough spiced richly with cinnamon and cloves. For some it is almost too rich.

A Paris recipe subtly lightens the texture and cuts the sweetness with applesauce, which blends unnoticed but perfectly with the heavy jam.

A touch that sets off the true *Linzertorte* (which *is* a tart and not a torte) is that the cross-hatching of the strips of dough over the top is not done at right angles (as with many pies) but diagonally, to produce diamonds rather than squares.

INGREDIENTS	1 partially baked Linzer Pastry shell (½ recipe) (page 328), or other choice (plus dough for strips to cover top) 1 cup (8 ounces) red raspberry jam ½ cup applesauce 1 egg, beaten
BAKING PANS AND TINS	One 8-inch tart pan, or a selection of tartlet and/or *barquette* tins.
PREPARATION	*Dough:* Shape dough in tart rings, pans or tins of choice, and partially bake beforehand. (See "Shaping" and "Baking," pages 323–324.) Preheat oven to 425° F.
15 min.	*Filling:* In a medium bowl mix the red raspberry jam and applesauce until thoroughly blended. Spoon the mixture into the shell(s)—about three-quarters full, whether

for the large flan or small tartlet. Smooth. Brush the sides of the shell(s) with beaten egg.

Roll out remaining dough into a rectangle long enough and wide enough that it can be cut with a jagger or pizza cutter into narrow strips to lay across the face of the pastry, whether large or small. For a large tart, ½-inch strips are fine. For small tartlets, cut them ¼ inch wide.

Place the strips diagonally across the face of the pastry to form diamonds (not squares). Press the strips to the edge of the shell and trim to fit.

When completed, brush the strips with egg to give a rich golden crust.

BAKING
425° F.
20 min.
375° F.
20 min.

Place the tart(s) on the lower shelf of the hot oven for 20 minutes, then transfer to the middle shelf. Reduce heat to 375° F.

Pastry is done when the filling bubbles near the center and the dough is a golden brown, about 20 minutes longer.

FINAL STEP

Place the pastries on a rack to cool, but remove them from the rings or pans while still warm, or at least loosen them. Many times it is best to store pastries in their baking tins for protection, but they should be loosened while warm before storing, or they may stick to the metal.

BAKEWELL TART

[ONE 9-INCH TART OR FIVE 4-INCH TARTLETS]

The Old Original Bakewell Pudding Shop in Bakewell, Derbyshire, England, insists its famous tart is actually a pudding. It all began in 1860, when the cook spread strawberry jam on the bottom crust rather than mixing it with the eggs, butter and almonds that were to follow. Pudding or tart, it has brought fame to Bakewell town. The English serve it hot with fresh cream. It is equally good cold, eaten out of hand on a walk across the moor.

The bread crumbs give it body without additional richness. Other jams may be substituted if you prefer.

SUGGESTED
DOUGH

Pâte brisée (page 325). Omit the egg from the recipe if you wish to make the authentic Bakewell dough.

INGREDIENTS	Partially baked shell(s) of choice 2 egg yolks (whites to be folded in later) ½ cup bread crumbs ¼ cup sugar ⅓ cup ground almonds ½ cup (1 stick) butter, melted 2 teaspoons lemon zest or grated peel 1 teaspoon lemon juice 2 egg whites Pinch salt ½ cup strawberry jam
BAKING PANS AND TINS	One 8-inch tart pan, or six tartlet or two dozen *barquette* tins.
PREPARATION 10 min.	*Dough:* During preparation, the chilled tart dough is rolled into a rectangle. Fold three times, as a letter. Roll. Fold a second time and roll. Fold again and roll.
CHILLING 20 min.	Fold and return dough to the refrigerator to relax and chill, about 20 minutes.
PREPARATION 10 min.	*Filling:* Beat eggs in a mixer bowl until frothy and yellow, about 3 minutes. Add bread crumbs, sugar and ground almonds. Pour in the melted butter and blend. Add lemon zest and juices. Blend. Scrape the egg mixture into a medium bowl. Wash beater and mixer bowl for egg whites. Add a pinch of salt to the whites in the mixer bowl and whip to hold a stiff peak. With a spatula fold egg whites into the egg mixture with several short, choppy strokes. Set aside. Place dough in pans. With a spoon spread a layer of strawberry or other jam over the bottom. Spoon the egg mixture over the jam. Fill to just below the level of the edge of the pan. Carefully push the egg mixture to the edges so that it touches all around. This seals the top so that the jam will not bubble out. Preheat oven to 425° F.
BAKING 425° F.	Place pan or tins on the middle shelf of the hot oven. After 15 minutes reduce heat to 350° F. and continue

15 min. 350° F. 15 min. or 20–25 min.	to bake until the tart is a deep golden brown and well puffed, about 15 minutes for small tartlets and 20 to 25 minutes for a large piece.
FINAL STEP	Served hot or cold—delicious! 　　　This freezes well, but I prefer it fresh from the oven or served within a day or so. It keeps well tightly wrapped in the refrigerator for several days.

BLUEBERRY TART

[ONE 8-INCH TART, SIX TARTLETS OR EIGHTEEN TO TWENTY-FOUR BARQUETTES]

The glistening blue-black of blueberries in this fine tart contrasts with the gold of the almond-rich pastry cream glimpsed here and there deep beneath the fruit.

　　In some parts of the country, blueberries (*Vaccinium*) are called huckleberries (*Gaylussacia*) and huckleberries are called blueberries. Either is delicious in this tart, although the true huckleberry (the one with a dozen seeds) is more difficult to find.

　　About one-third of the blueberries are cooked to form a thick jam-like liquid, which is mixed with the uncooked berries and flavored with an unexpected spice that will puzzle and delight guests: cinnamon!

　　The pastry is crisp, and a bite into the large succulent berries in blueberry dressing is a treat.

SUGGESTED DOUGHS	*Pâte brisée* (page 325) and *pâte sucrée* (page 327) are excellent for this filling.
INGREDIENTS	Baked shell(s) for one 8-inch tart, six tartlets or 18 to 24 *barquettes* 4 cups blueberries ⅓ cup granulated sugar 1 teaspoon *each* grated lemon rind and lemon juice ½ teaspoon cinnamon 1 cup pastry cream (page 305) 1 cup whipped cream, optional
BAKING PANS AND TINS	One 8-inch tart pan, or six tartlet or eighteen to twenty-four *barquette* tins.

PREPARATION   *Dough:*
Shape dough in tart rings, pans or tins of choice, and
bake beforehand. (See "Shaping" and "Baking," pages
323–324.)

Filling:
Working note: If blueberries are fresh-picked, inspect
them carefully to be certain all tiny green stems are
removed. They are easy to overlook.

12 min.   In a large saucepan combine 1½ cups blueberries,
sugar, lemon rind and juice and cinnamon. Cook over
low heat, stirring until sugar is dissolved. Raise heat
and boil rapidly until berries thicken to the consistency of jam, about 8 minutes.

COOLING   Set aside to cool, about 30 minutes, or longer if de-
30 min.   sired.

5 min.   When the jam has cooled, pour it over the 2½ cups
fresh blueberries and mix gently.
  Spread pastry cream over the bottom of the
shell(s). Carefully spoon the blueberry mixture into
the shell(s).

FINAL STEP   Refrigerate the tart or tartlets until serving time.
  A dollop of whipped cream placed in the center
of the deep blue filling just before serving makes a
striking addition.

ALMOND TART

(TARTE AU FRANGIPANE)

[ONE 8-INCH TART, SIX TARTLETS OR TWO DOZEN BARQUETTES]

This delicate, light brown almond-flavored pastry was the creation in
the early 1600's of an Italian named Frangipane who lived in Paris under
Louis XIII. It has been popular ever since. The Germans call it *Fran-
chipantortchen*, and it is served in coffeehouses everywhere there. In
England the same recipe is used for making Maids of Honour.

Some recipes call for almond paste (not always easy to find and
always expensive), but this adaptation is made with ground almonds
instead.

It is a delicate pastry, especially when made into *barquettes*, the
tiny 2-inch boat-shaped shells that grace any dessert tray.

| SUGGESTED DOUGHS | *Pâte sucrée* or *pâte brisée* (pages 327 and 325). |

| INGREDIENTS | Partially baked shell(s) of choice |

½ cup (1 stick) unsalted butter, room temperature
½ cup granulated sugar
2 eggs
¼ teaspoon almond extract
1 teaspoon grated lemon rind
1 cup finely ground almonds
¾ tablespoon flour
¼ cup apricot glaze (page 308)
¼ cup coarsely chopped hazelnuts or pistachio nuts

BAKING PANS AND TINS

One 8-inch tart pan, or six tartlet or two dozen *barquette* tins.

PREPARATION

Dough:
Shape dough in tart rings, pans or tins of choice, and bake *partially* beforehand. (See "Shaping" and "Baking," pages 323–324.)

10 min.

Filling:
In a medium bowl beat butter and sugar until blended and creamy. Add the eggs, one at a time, and mix well. Add almond extract, grated lemon peel, almonds and flour. Mix until well blended. (This can be done equally well in an electric mixer or food processor.)

The filling may be held in the refrigerator for several days or used immediately.

Preheat oven to 400° F.

If you are using an 8-inch flan or tart shell, fill almost to the top edge. The filling need only be spread roughly—the heat of the oven will soften and level it. Small *barquette* tins need about 1 scant teaspoon to fill. Don't smooth it out; the oven heat will do this nicely.

BAKING
400° F.
10–25 min.
or
25 min.

Small tartlets and the even smaller *barquettes* will be done in about 10 to 15 minutes. Watch them closely. A uniform pattern of tiny holes across the face of the pastry will indicate that it is done. Don't overbake.

The larger and deeper flan or tart will take about 25 minutes to bake. If you doubt the bubble pattern, pierce with a cake-testing pin or a toothpick. If it comes out dry, the tart is done.

FINAL STEP   Heat the apricot glaze and carefully brush the top of the tart(s) or *barquettes*. Sprinkle with pistachio nuts or hazelnuts.

CARROT-NUT TART

(RÜEBLI-TORTE)

[ONE 8-INCH TART, SIX TARTLETS OR TWO DOZEN BARQUETTES]

My favorite Swiss village for good things to eat is Wichtrach, in the shadows of the Alps, south of Berne, where Verena and Rolf Thomas bake fine pastries and bread. Rolf's reputation as a top-notch baker has reached far beyond the valley and mountain slope where the 120 families for whom he bakes live. At Christmastime his *haselnusslebkuchen*, holiday hazelnut cakes, are flown to customers in the United States.

Ruebli-torte, the Thomas tart, may not be as widely known, but it is a delicious blend of carrots and nuts that will go far, nevertheless. Verena, who makes the tart as one of her many shop chores, uses hazelnuts, although almonds can be substituted.

SUGGESTED DOUGHS   Basic *pâte brisée* (page 325) or Rich Tart Pastry (page 328).

INGREDIENTS   Partially baked shell(s) of choice
3 eggs, room temperature
⅓ cup granulated sugar
1 teaspoon *each* lemon juice and lemon zest
2 cups (6 ounces) finely shredded carrots
4 tablespoons (½ stick) butter or margarine, melted but not hot
½ teaspoon baking powder
⅔ cup all-purpose flour
½ cup finely ground hazelnuts or almonds
¼ cup apricot glaze (page 308)

BAKING PANS AND TINS   One 8-inch tart pan, or six tartlet or two dozen *barquette* tins.

PREPARATION   *Dough:*
Shape the dough in flan rings, tart pans or tins of choice, and *partially* bake beforehand. (See "Shaping" and "Baking," pages 323–324.)

12 min.   *Filling:*
                 In a medium bowl lightly beat eggs and add sugar,
                 lemon juice and zest, shredded carrots and butter or
                 margarine. In a second bowl stir together baking pow-
                 der, flour and nuts. Blend the dry ingredients into the
                 wet ingredients.
                     The filling may be held for several hours or over-
                 night in the refrigerator.
                     Preheat oven to 400° F.
                     Fill pan(s).

BAKING   Small pieces will be done in about 10 to 15 minutes.
400° F.   The larger and deeper flan or tart will take about 25
10–15 min.   minutes to bake. Test with a cake-testing pin or a
   or   knife. If it comes out dry, the tart is done.
25 min.

FINAL STEP   Heat the apricot glaze and brush the top of the pastry.

LEMON CURD TART

[ONE 8-INCH TART, SIX TARTLETS OR TWO DOZEN BARQUETTES]

The Danes call it lemon butter and spread it on toast and wafers. The
English ask for lemon cheese or lemon curd. Regardless, it is the filling
for a delicious tart or a cluster of tartlets and/or *barquettes.*

It may be topped with a dollop of Devonshire (clotted) or sour
cream—or a thin slice of lemon, cut to the center, twisted and placed
upright.

SUGGESTED   *Pâte sucrée* (page 327) or *pâte brisée* (page 325) are the
DOUGHS   favored choices for this filling.

INGREDIENTS   Baked shell(s) of choice
                 6 eggs, beaten
                 1½ cups sugar
                 Pinch salt
                 Juice of 3 lemons and grated peel of 1
                 ½ cup butter, room temperature
                 ½ cup sour cream, optional
                 6 lemon slices, optional

BAKING PANS   One 8-inch tart pan, or six tartlet or two dozen *bar-*
AND TINS   *quette* tins.

PREPARATION   *Dough:*
Shape dough in tart rings, pans or tins of choice, and bake beforehand. See "Shaping" and "Baking," pages 323–324.)

Filling:
Beforehand, prepare lemon juice and grated peel.

20 min.

In the top of a double boiler lightly beat eggs and add sugar and salt. Stir in lemon juice, grated peel and butter. Position bowl in the lower part of the double boiler in which there is an inch of water.

Bring water to a boil. Reduce heat to keep the water hot but not bubbling. With a whisk stir constantly until the mixture thickens, about 10 minutes.

Remove from the heat and set in cold water to cool quickly and completely.

Lemon curd may be used immediately or kept in the refrigerator for a week.

ASSEMBLY   Fill shell(s) and refrigerate until served.
5 min.

FINAL STEP   Add Devonshire or sour cream or decorative lemon slices before serving.

GOOSEBERRY TART

[ONE 8-INCH TART, SIX TARTLETS OR EIGHTEEN TO TWENTY-FOUR BARQUETTES]

Once upon a time gooseberry bushes, heavy with plump green fruit, were a part of almost every backyard garden in this country. In England they remain so today, while here the berries have yet to return to their former popularity.

"Piquant" or "tangy" describes the gooseberry's distinctive and unusually good taste.

This gooseberry tart may be made with fresh or canned fruit. The fresh ones must be washed and tailed (stems removed).

SUGGESTED   *Pâte sucrée* (page 327) and *pâte brisée* (page 325) are
DOUGHS   both delicious in this tart.

INGREDIENTS   Baked shell(s) of choice
1 16-ounce (1-pound) can gooseberries, in light syrup
(*or* 4 cups fresh gooseberries, washed and tailed)

½ cup water, for fresh berries only
¾ cup granulated sugar
2 tablespoons quick-cooking tapioca
Pinch salt
1 egg yolk, beaten
1 tablespoon butter
⅛ teaspoon vanilla extract

Meringue:
2 egg whites
Pinch salt
4 tablespoons granulated sugar

BAKING PANS AND TINS	One 8-inch tart pan, or six tartlet or eighteen to twenty-four *barquette* tins.
PREPARATION	*Dough* Shape dough in tart rings, pans or tins of choice, and bake beforehand. (See "Shaping" and "Baking," pages 323–324.)
15 min.	*Filling:* If the gooseberries are fresh-picked, mix water and sugar in a saucepan and bring to a boil. Add the fruit and cook until the berries are clear, about 10 minutes. Strain off and reserve the syrup. Place berries in a bowl to cool, and return syrup to saucepan. If the fruit is canned, open and pour ¼ cup of the light syrup in which the gooseberries are packed and ½ cup sugar into a saucepan.
20 min.	Add tapioca, salt, beaten egg yolk and butter to the saucepan. Let stand for 15 minutes to condition tapioca. Place the saucepan over medium heat and cook until thick, about 4 minutes. Remove from heat and add vanilla. Add gooseberries to thickened sauce. Preheat oven to 375° F. Spoon the cooled gooseberry filling into the baked shell(s). *Meringue:* Beat together in a mixer the egg whites and salt until soft peaks form under the beaters when they are lifted. Gradually add sugar to the whites and continue beating at high speed until firm, glossy peaks are formed. Pile meringue on top of the gooseberry filling. Spread meringue, touching the edge of the shell so that it will not draw back or shrink in the oven. Swirl

meringue with the back of a spoon to create decorative peaks.

BAKING
375° F.
10–12 min.

Place in the oven and bake 10 to 12 minutes, or until the meringue is delicately browned.

FINAL STEP

Place tart(s) on a cooling rack, and allow to cool for an hour or more.

SHREWSBURY TARTS

[ONE DOZEN 3-INCH TARTLETS]

Shrewsbury Tarts are known far beyond the boundaries of this small English county town of Shropshire, set on the Welsh border. More than a decade ago I piloted a canal boat across England into Wales. The big event each day was to tie up at a riverbank bake shop to buy pastries for afternoon tea (served by my wife while the vessel was traveling at three knots an hour). Shrewsbury Tarts were most prized of them all.

These are baked in deep tartlet tins. I have none, so I use fluted *brioche* tins or a muffin pan.

This recipe is from the kitchen at Burton Court, a lovely manor house near Eardisland, Herefordshire.

SUGGESTED
DOUGH

The basic tart dough, *pâte brisée* (page 325).

INGREDIENTS

12 partially baked tartlet shells of choice
8 ounces cream cheese
½ cup granulated sugar
¼ cup (½ stick) butter, room temperature
¼ teaspoon salt
Pinch nutmeg
2 egg yolks
1 tablespoon orange juice
½ teaspoon grated orange rind
¼ cup apricot glaze (page 308), heated

BAKING TINS

One dozen deep tartlet tins, approximately 3 inches in diameter. The exact size is not critical, but try to keep them on the small side. Bite-size in *barquette* tins is fine.

PREPARATION	*Dough:*
	Shape dough and bake *partially* beforehand. (See "Shaping" and "Baking," pages 323–324.)
10 min.	*Filling:*
	In the bowl of an electric mixer or food processor cream together the cream cheese, sugar, butter, salt, nutmeg, egg yolks, orange juice and grated orange rind.
	Cool shells before filling with approximately 1 tablespoon filling—to the edge of the tin.
	Preheat oven to 450° F.
BAKING 450° F. 10 min. 375° F. 25 min.	Place tartlet tins on the middle shelf of the hot oven. When they have baked for 10 minutes, reduce heat to 375° F. Tartlets are done when raised and golden brown, about 25 additional minutes.
FINAL STEP	Be forewarned that the tarts will fall when they cool. In my *brioche* tins they look like flower blossoms.
	Brush the hot pastries with hot apricot glaze. When tartlets have cooled, remove from the tins. Serve, or store in the refrigerator (for two or three days).

HAMANTASCHEN

[TWO DOZEN 3-INCH PASTRIES]

The merriest of Jewish holidays is Purim, and long a part of the festival has been a small tricornered pastry, the *hamantasch*, with its poppy-seed or prune filling. Haman was a villainous Persian prime minister who failed in his attempt to massacre the Jewish people and is remembered twenty-five centuries later by being symbolically eaten.

Two fillings are used in this *hamantaschen* recipe: poppy seed and prune-apricot. I use Sweet Tart Dough, with the addition of baking powder.

| INGREDIENTS | 1 recipe Sweet Tart Dough (page 327), chilled (When tart dough is being prepared for *hamantaschen*, add 2 teaspoons baking powder to the list of ingredients.) |
| | 1 cup prune filling (page 308) (Add 4 ounces dried apricots to the prunes to cook.) |

¾ cup poppy-seed filling (page 306)
1 egg
1 tablespoon water } beaten together, to brush
Confectioners' sugar, to sprinkle

ASSEMBLY
15 min.

Have the poppy-seed and prune-apricot fillings at room temperature.

For ease in putting the *hamantaschen* together, divide the dough into two pieces and return one to the refrigerator. Roll out the dough on a well-floured work surface. It should be thin—no more than ⅛ inch. Keep a light sprinkling of flour under the dough as it is being rolled or it may stick to the work surface.

Cut 3½-inch circles and put aside. Reassemble the scraps and roll for additional circles.

Don't overload a piece with filling or it will be difficult to seal the seams. Experiment with the amount needed. Begin with 1 full teaspoon for 3½-inch rounds.

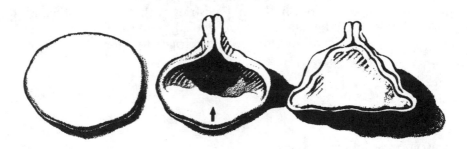

Brush margins with water. Place filling in the center of the circle. Lift up the three sides so that edges meet. Pinch raised edges together firmly. They will look like spokes radiating from the center and will be pronounced when baked. Place on the prepared sheet.

REFRIGERATED
REST
30 min.

Place the pastries in the refrigerator for 30 minutes. Preheat oven to 350° F.

BAKING
350° F.
25–30 min.

Brush the *hamantaschen* with egg wash and place on the middle shelf of the moderate oven. Bake until raised and a light golden color, about 25 to 30 minutes.

FINAL STEP   Place pieces on a rack to cool. Sprinkle lightly with confectioners' sugar before serving.

QUICHES

The reputation of the real *quiche*, that of Lorraine, rests as much on a delicious crisp, short crust as on its custard filling. It is the basic tart crust, *pâte brisée*.

Quiche is served as a first course at dinner, as a luncheon entrée or sliced thin in wedges or in miniature for hors d'oeuvres.

There are many delicious *quiches* made with a variety of cheeses, vegetables, meats and seafoods. Basic to each is the custard filling— rich, light golden brown, but never sweet.

Three fine *quiches* are presented here: the traditional *quiche Lorraine* from that part of France pressed against Germany, spinach *quiche*, and one made with shrimp (or crab or lobster, for that special and expensive entertainment).

Quiche deserves, and has, its own special pan, designed for both baking and serving. Usually white and opaque, the *quiche* pan is made of ceramic ware, often of porcelain, so that it will conduct the heat well and never scorch the bottom crust during the baking period. The sides are straight, 1 to 2 inches high.

Nevertheless, less glamorous loose-bottom tart and pie pans and the whole range of small tartlet tins bake equally good *quiches*. The difference is that the pastry is not presented as elegantly.

QUICHE LORRAINE

[ONE 8- OR 9-INCH TART, SIX TARTLETS OR TWO DOZEN BARQUETTES]

The ingredients of the Lorraine *quiche* are few and basic: bacon or strips of thin ham, eggs, cream and seasonings. Onion can be added, but it is not in the traditional Lorraine dish, which may also be spelled *kiche*.

Sometimes the filling is made with Swiss or Gruyère cheese, which I have made optional in this recipe. Thus it becomes *quiche Lorraine au fromage*.

In the past, *quiche* was made with bread dough. Modern practice has substituted a short crust, a *pâte brisée*, which is richer and better able to withstand the moisture. The shell is partially baked several hours ahead of time; the filling prepared and refrigerated in a mixing bowl. About 40 minutes before serving, the *quiche* is filled and set in a 375° F. oven for about 25 to 30 minutes. It will be puffed, and the top a golden brown. A knife plunged near the center should come out clean.

INGREDIENTS

Partially baked *pâte brisée* shell(s) (page 325)
¼ pound sliced bacon or thin ham slices
2 tablespoons butter
4 eggs
1 cup light cream (half-and-half)
Pinch salt
1 teaspoon freshly ground pepper
Pinch freshly grated nutmeg
¼ pound finely diced Gruyère or Swiss cheese, optional

BAKING PANS OR TINS

One 8- or 9-inch tart pan, or six tartlet or two dozen *barquette* tins.

PREPARATION

Dough:
Shape dough in *quiche* pans, tart rings or pans and tins of choice, and *partially* bake beforehand. (See "Shaping" and "Baking," pages 323–324.)

Preheat oven to 375° F.

5 min.

Filling:
Blanch bacon strips in simmering water for 5 minutes to remove smoky and salty taste. Drain. Brown ham lightly in butter in a skillet. Flatten bacon or ham against the bottom of the shell(s).

5 min.

In a small bowl beat the eggs until well blended. Pour in the cream, salt, pepper and nutmeg.

If cheese is to be used, cut into small dice about ¼ inch square. Sprinkle over the bacon or ham. Pour the egg-cream mixture to within ⅛ inch of the top. Often I only partially fill the form with the custard, move it to the oven shelf and then pour in the balance of the liquid—less chance of spills.

BAKING
375° F.
25–30 min.

Place the *quiche* in the center of the oven and allow to bake until puffy and lightly browned, about 25 to 30 minutes. A knife inserted in the center of the *quiche* will withdraw clean if it is done.

FINAL STEP

Serve while hot or warm. As it cools it will lose its puffiness. A *quiche* may be reheated, but it will not regain its earlier shape. Cold *quiche* makes a delightful picnic or tailgate snack.

Quiche may be frozen before baking. Bake at 450° F. for 10 minutes. Lower heat to 350° F. and bake for 50 additional minutes.

SPINACH QUICHE

(QUICHE AUX EPINARDS)

[ONE 8- OR 9-INCH TART, SIX TARTLETS OR TWO DOZEN BARQUETTES]

A spinach *quiche* is a handsome green round of custard that may be baked in tiny tins and served as hors d'oeuvres or prepared in a larger pan as an appetizing entrée.

Although the original recipe calls for fresh spinach (about 1½ pounds), I have used frozen chopped spinach with such good results that I now prefer it, not only for its ease in use but for its good taste as well.

For a buffet or brunch, bake in individual 4-inch pans an equal number of shellfish (page 352) and spinach *quiche*. Cut each in half and reassemble the halves—a spinach half and a seafood half—together as a whole.

INGREDIENTS	*Partially* baked *pâte brisée* shell(s) (page 325)
	2 10-ounce packages frozen spinach
	(*or* 3 cups fresh spinach, cooked and drained)
	2 tablespoons butter
	1 tablespoon finely minced scallions
	½ teaspoon salt
	Pinch freshly ground pepper
	Pinch nutmeg
	3 eggs
	1½ cups light cream (half-and-half)
	¼ cup grated Swiss cheese, to sprinkle
	1 tablespoon butter, to dot
BAKING PANS AND TINS	One 8- or 9-inch pan, or six tartlet or two dozen *barquette* tins.
PREPARATION	*Dough:*
	Shape dough in *quiche* pans, tart rings or pans and tins of choice, and *partially* bake beforehand. (See "Shaping" and "Baking," pages 323–324.)
	Filling:
	Beforehand, prepare spinach. Drain and set aside.
12 min.	Place butter in a skillet and cook scallions in it over medium heat for 2 or 3 minutes. Add the spinach and stir for several minutes to allow moisture to evaporate.

Stir in the salt, pepper and nutmeg. Taste for seasoning. Remove from heat.

Preheat oven to 375° F.

In a medium bowl beat eggs and cream to blend. Gradually stir in the spinach mixture. Pour or spoon the spinach mixture into the pastry shell(s).

BAKING
375° F.
25–30 min.

Sprinkle with grated cheese, dot with butter and place the *quiche* in the oven for 25 to 30 minutes, until puffed and brown.

FINAL STEP

Serve while warm and still puffed.

SHRIMP, CRAB OR LOBSTER QUICHE

(QUICHE AUX FRUITS DE MER)

[ONE 8- OR 9-INCH TART, SIX TARTLETS OR TWO DOZEN BARQUETTES]

This is a delicate dish that can be overpowered with too much onion or a strong hand with the seasonings. The *fruits de mer* will rise to the top of the cream-egg mixture and give form to the light golden surface of the *quiche*, whether it be a large one or several smaller individual servings.

INGREDIENTS

Partially baked *pâte brisée* shell(s) (page 325)
1 cup (¼ pound) crab, shrimp or lobster (cooked fresh, canned or frozen)
1 tablespoon thinly sliced scallions
3 tablespoons butter
¼ teaspoon salt
Pinch freshly ground black pepper
2 tablespoons dry white wine (dry vermouth preferred)
3 eggs
1 cup light cream (half-and-half)
Pinch salt
Pinch pepper
⅛ teaspoon freshly grated nutmeg
¼ cup freshly grated Parmesan cheese

BAKING PANS
AND TINS

One 8- or 9-inch tart pan, or six tartlet or two dozen *barquette* tins.

PREPARATION

Dough:
Shape dough in *quiche* pans, tart rings or pans and

tins of choice, and *partially* bake beforehand. (See "Shaping" and "Baking," pages 323–324.)

Filling:
Beforehand, prepare the shellfish, whether fresh, canned or frozen, and set aside.

Preheat oven to 375° F.

10 min.

Cook the scallions in the butter in a medium skillet for 2 to 3 minutes, over moderate heat. Scallions should be translucent but not browned. Add shellfish meat and gently stir for several minutes. Add salt, pepper and wine. Bring to a boil. Remove from heat and allow to cool while preparing the custard.

In a mixing bowl beat eggs and cream until well blended. Add salt, pepper and nutmeg.

Spread shellfish over the bottom of the shell(s). Pour cream mixture over the meat, and sprinkle with cheese.

BAKING
375° F.
25–30 min.

Place *quiche(s)* on the middle shelf of the moderate oven and bake for 25 to 30 minutes or until puffed and brown.

FINAL STEP

Serve warm.

Pizza and Pissaladière

There are two Italian pizzas in particular that are highly esteemed, not only in the country and island of their origin but in this country as well. One is the crisp, flat disc from Naples. The other is from Sicily, and for this one the dough is allowed to rise three times. It is then partially baked to rise, soft and bread-like, in the oven. It is taken out of the oven, dressed with a wide choice of garnishes and returned to the oven.

Both are delicious. The Sicilian pizza has only recently been introduced to the United States but it has fast overtaken the better-known Neapolitan pie.

Then there is *pissaladière*, a pizza from France that has cooked onions instead of tomato sauce as its principal topping. It is made with an egg-rich dough which is flavored and enriched by the olive oil in which the onions have been gently cooked.

I must confess that I had eaten few pizzas until I made them myself —and then, overnight, I became a believer. I found the sauces marvelous vehicles for dozens of different garnishes, ranging from seafood to cheeses, but I liked even better the good made-in-my-kitchen dough.

Other doughs can be used, of course—even ordinary white bread dough when you are caught short with nothing else to serve a famished band of young soccer players. Rye dough will puzzle and please pizza lovers.

A fine tomato sauce is essential to Italian pizzas. The recipe for one such is given here. Late summer, when red ripe tomatoes are burgeon-

354

ing in your garden, or your neighbor's, is the time to lay by a quantity of sauce for the winter months ahead.

Pizza and bread have been baked on the oven floor for several hundred years, but only recently has a baking stone been developed that produces the same results in the home oven. For pizza (and bread) this means a crisp and often hard bottom crust which many like. (See "Sources of Supply" for baking stones and tiles, page 47.)

Here are the three pizzas, the sauce recipe for the Italian versions, the onion topping for the *pissaladière*, plus several suggested garnishes.

All of the recipes for both doughs and toppings may be divided or multiplied to meet your needs.

FREEZING PIZZA

Partially bake the pizza shell, about 10 minutes. Allow the shell to cool, then spread with cheese and garnishes. Place in the freezer overnight and then wrap for freezer storage. No need to defrost before final baking —475° F. for about 25 minutes, or until crust is brown and crisp and sauce is bubbling.

PIZZA NEAPOLITAN

[FOUR 10-INCH PIZZAS OR SIX DOZEN 2-INCH HORS D'OEUVRES]

This famous Neapolitan pie is made circular, with a crust that is relatively crisp and thin. These can also be cut into bite-size hors d'oeuvres.

My food processor makes a lovely velvety dough in about 4 minutes overall. This recipe describes dough made by hand as well as with the electric mixer and food processor.

INGREDIENTS   *Dough:*
2 packages dry yeast
1½ cups water
4 cups all-purpose flour, approximately
2 teaspoons salt
¼ cup olive or vegetable oil, for dough

Sauce:
2 cups pizza tomato sauce (page 363)

Cheeses:
1 pound *mozzarella* cheese, grated or cut into small
   dice
½ cup freshly grated Parmesan cheese

Garnishes:
Choice of garnishes (page 364)

½ cup olive or vegetable oil, to sprinkle

BAKING SHEET   Large baking sheet to fit the oven, sprinkled with cornmeal or lined with parchment paper. Pizzas may have
to be baked in succession if oven space and baking
equipment are limited. Cover the baked pizzas with
foil to retain heat while baking the remaining ones.

PREPARATION   The food processor does the dough in a whisk. The
electric mixer takes a trifle longer. Both demand almost no work on the part of the home baker. An additional 3 or 4 minutes is needed if done by hand (but
it is more rewarding to the psyche). Here, in reverse
order, are the three.

● BY HAND   Dissolve the yeast in water in a large bowl. Stir in 2
5 min.   cups flour and the salt. Beat with a wooden spoon or
spatula until the flour has absorbed the water. It will
resemble a thick batter. Add olive oil and stir until the
oil disappears into the mixture. Add a cup of flour to
make a solid mass that can be gathered in the fingers
and lifted to a floured work surface. If the dough is
sticky, add liberal sprinkles of flour.

KNEADING   Knead under the hands for about 6 minutes, or until
6 min.   the dough is smooth, shiny and elastic. If sticky, add
sprinkles of flour.

▲ ELECTRIC   In a small bowl dissolve yeast in water.
MIXER   Fit the dough hook on the mixer shaft.
3 min.

4 min.   Measure 2 cups flour into the mixer bowl. Add salt.
Turn the mixer to low speed and pour in yeast. When

the flour has absorbed the liquid, add olive oil. Stir until blended. Add flour, ½ cup at a time. Don't rush the process. Allow the flour to be kneaded into the mass before adding more.

KNEADING
5 min.

When the dough cleans the sides of the bowl, knead for about 5 minutes under the hook. Stop the machine.

■ **FOOD**
PROCESSOR
4 min.

Dissolve yeast in water in a small bowl.

Place the metal blade on the shaft, and pour flour and salt into the work bowl. Turn on the machine briefly to mix flour and salt.

Pour olive oil into a measuring cup and have at hand. Turn on the machine and pour dissolved yeast down the tube. Turn the processor off/on twice. The flour will resemble coarse meal. Turn on the machine and pour in olive oil. Mix with four or five off/on turns. If the mixture is wet and will not form a ball, add 1 or 2 tablespoons flour. Process until dough forms a solid ball that travels on top of the spinning blade.

KNEADING
45 seconds

Allow the blade to knead the dough for 45 seconds.

FIRST RISING
1½ hours

Place dough in a bowl, cover with plastic wrap and put aside to rise until doubled in bulk, about 1½ hours.

While the dough is rising, assemble the pizza sauce and garnishes.

Preheat oven to 475° F.

ASSEMBLY
20 min.

Turn dough onto a floured work surface and knead a half dozen times to expel the yeast gases. Divide the dough into four pieces.

Note: Pizzas can also be made into rectangles or squares rather than rounds, which is especially useful if they are to be cut into small hors d'oeuvres.

With the hands flatten the first piece of dough and stretch it into a rough circle. Now roll the dough with a heavy rolling pin into a 6- or 8-inch disc. Lift the edge of the dough with the fingers and allow the weight of the dough to stretch it. But carefully. Don't let it tear. (If it does, however, it can be patched.) Work with the fingers around the entire circumference of the piece of dough. Not only will it stretch the dough but it will help form a thick rim.

If necessary, roll the dough again with the pin to make a 10-inch disc. With the fingers, pinch the edge all around to strengthen and enlarge the rim.

Place the finished shell on the baking pan.

Repeat with the remaining three pieces of dough.

Pour ½ cup tomato sauce on each disc, and spread with a spoon to the edge.

When the pizzas have been garnished as desired, dribble each with about 2 tablespoons olive oil.

BAKING
475° F.
25–30 min.

Place pan on the lowest shelf of the oven to get maximum heat on the bottom of the pizzas. The crust will be lightly browned and the filling bubbling hot in about 25 to 30 minutes.

FINAL STEP

Serve while hot.

The hot pizzas may also be cut into small squares and served, with great success, as small hors d'oeuvres.

PIZZA SICILIANA

[ONE 11 BY 16-INCH PIZZA, SERVES SIX, OR FOUR DOZEN 2-INCH HORS D'OEUVRES]

The three risings of the dough of this pizza take a while longer, but it is worth every extra minute. The third rising is in the pan when the dough is covered only with sauce and then partially baked. It is then taken from the oven, dressed with garnishes and returned to the oven.

The handsome rectangle (the shape is peculiarly Sicilian) can be served to six, or cut into small 2-inch squares to be served to several dozen at a buffet.

INGREDIENTS   *Dough:*
1 package dry yeast
1½ cups warm water (105° to 115° F.)
2 teaspoons salt
4½ cups all-purpose flour, approximately
2 tablespoons olive or vegetable oil, for dough

Cheeses:
1 pound *mozzarella* cheese, grated or cut into small
 dice
½ cup finely grated Parmesan cheese

Garnishes:
Choice of garnishes (page 364)

¼ cup olive or vegetable oil, to sprinkle

BAKING PAN   One 11 by 16-inch jelly-roll or similar pan with shallow sides, greased or lined with parchment paper.

PREPARATION   *Dough:*
Note: Only the procedure for preparing dough by hand is detailed here. Please turn to page 356 for instructions for using the electric mixer or food processor for making dough for this pizza.

5 min.   In a bowl dissolve yeast in water. Add salt and 2 cups flour to make a thick batter. Blend for 30 seconds. Add olive oil and continue beating for an additional half minute to blend in the oil. Gradually add the remaining flour to form a soft dough that pulls away from the sides of the bowl. If it does not (too sticky), add sprinkles of flour.

KNEADING   Turn the dough onto a lightly floured work surface—
10 min.   counter top or bread board—and knead with a strong push-turn-fold motion until smooth and elastic. Add sprinkles of flour if sticky. Knead about 10 minutes.

FIRST RISING   Place the dough in a greased bowl. Cover with plastic
1½ hours   wrap and set aside to rise for about 1½ hours.

SECOND RISING   Uncover bowl and punch down the risen dough.
45 min.   Knead briefly to flatten. Re-cover and leave for 45 minutes.

Meanwhile, during the periods when the dough is rising, assemble the pan, 2 cups prepared tomato sauce and your choice of garnishes.

SHAPING
5 min.

Grease the pan. Punch down the dough and place on a lightly floured work surface. With the hands flatten the dough and push into a rough rectangle. Let the dough rest for a few moments so that it will not draw back. Roll into a rectangle slightly larger than the pan. Allow the dough to relax before lifting and placing in the pan.

With the palms of hands press the dough uniformly across the pan and up the sides.

THIRD RISING
30–40 min.

Cover the dough-lined pan with a cloth or wax paper, and put aside to rise until doubled in depth. If the sides of the pan are only ½ inch high, this will mean the dough should rise even with the rim. If you are using a deeper pan, judge when the dough has doubled in depth, about 30 to 40 minutes.

Preheat oven to 475° F. about 15 minutes before the dough has risen and is ready to be covered with tomato paste.

ASSEMBLY

Working note: The dough will be covered with the tomato paste and baked for about 10 minutes. It will be removed from the oven and dressed with desired garnishes, then returned to the oven to finish baking for about 20 additional minutes.

5 min.

Uncover the pan and spread with tomato sauce.

BAKING
475° F.
10 min.

Place on the lower shelf of the hot oven and bake for 10 minutes. Remove from the oven and spread with cheese and your choice of other garnishes. Sprinkle with olive oil and return to the oven.

20–25 min.

Bake until the sauce is bubbling and the exposed edges of the dough are dark brown and well risen, about 25 minutes.

FINAL STEP

Serve! Enjoy!

FRENCH PIZZA

(PISSALADIÈRE)

[FOUR 7-INCH OR TWO 10-INCH PIZZAS, OR FIFTY HORS D'OEUVRES]

This inspired *pissaladière* comes from my sister's inspired kitchen in southern France, in the Alpes Maritimes, where she cooks overlooking shore and sea and, in the distance, the houses and palace of Monaco.

The onion topping of the *pissaladière* is subtly underscored by the onion flavor of the *brioche*-like dough made with the olive oil in which the onions were cooked. Butter or margarine can be substituted for all or part of the olive oil if the onion flavor in the dough is not wanted.

This excellent dough can be topped with tomato sauce and other garnishes as for the Italian pizzas. But try the onion topping first.

The onions are to be prepared first if the olive oil in which they are cooked is used in the dough; hence the ingredients for the topping are given first, below, following the order of preparation.

INGREDIENTS   *Topping:*
2 pounds onions, chopped
1 cup olive oil
1 cup shredded *mozzarella* cheese
16 anchovy fillets
24 black olives, halved
½ teaspoon *each* salt, oregano, cumin and fennel, optional
1 cup freshly grated Parmesan cheese

Dough:
2 packages dry yeast
¼ cup water
2¼ cups bread or unbleached flour, approximately
1 teaspoon salt, optional
6 tablespoons olive oil (in which onions were cooked)
   (*or* 6 tablespoons unsalted butter, room temperature)
2 large eggs

BAKING PANS

Selection of tart pans and flan rings. The dough can also be baked in a square or rectangular baking pan if it is to be cut into hors d'oeuvres.

PREPARATION
30 min.

Topping:
Chop onions and cook gently in olive oil in a covered heavy skillet or saucepan over low heat until translucent and soft, about 15 minutes. Uncover, turn up the heat slightly and cook, stirring frequently, until onions have turned a dark brown color (but are not burned), about 15 to 20 minutes. Set aside to drain, and save liquid if wanted for dough. Onions may be refrigerated until needed.

Dough:
Only the procedure for preparing dough by hand is detailed here. Please turn to page 356 for complete instructions for using the electric mixer or food processor.

5 min.

In a small bowl dissolve yeast in water. Measure 1 cup flour into a large bowl and add the salt. Stir in the 6 tablespoons olive oil drained from the cooked onions, *or* the butter. Beat with a wooden spoon or spatula, or mix. Add ½ cup flour. Stir in the eggs and blend well. When the dough is a rough mass, soft but not sticky, turn onto a floured work surface.

KNEADING
5 min.

This is a rich dough that is easy to knead. Use a dough scraper occasionally to lift it off the work surface and throw it down hard to help form the gluten in the dough. Add sprinkles of flour if dough should stick to hands or the work surface.

RISING
1½ hours

Place dough in a bowl, cover with plastic wrap and put aside to rise for 1½ hours.
Preheat oven to 425° F. with baking stone or tiles in place.

ASSEMBLY

When dough has risen, punch down, knead briefly and divide into the number of pieces needed. Roll dough into thin (³⁄₁₆-inch) rounds and place in pans. Push dough to the edges.

Distribute onions over the dough. Sprinkle with *mozzarella* cheese. Arrange anchovies in spokes radiating from the center. Decorate with olive halves, sprinkle with salt, herbs and Parmesan cheese.

BAKING
425° F.
20 min.

Place pans on baking stones or tiles. The pizzas will be done when bubbling and golden, about 20 minutes.

FINAL STEP

Serve hot!

A BASIC PIZZA SAUCE

[ABOUT 4 CUPS]

There are many sauces for pizza, but this one is a well-seasoned sauce of tomato, hinting of onion, garlic and olive oil, that can be spread over all pizzas, with confidence that it is one of the best—especially when it has been made with fresh-picked tomatoes and simmered on the stove to fill the kitchen with the enticing fragrance of good things to come.

INGREDIENTS

4 tablespoons olive oil
1 cup finely chopped onions
1 tablespoon chopped garlic
4 pounds fresh tomatoes
    (*or* 3 1-pound cans tomatoes)
1 tablespoon *each* basil leaves and oregano
½ teaspoon *each* sugar and black pepper
1½ teaspoons salt
1 6-ounce can tomato paste

SKILLET

One large, deep skillet or heavy saucepan in which to cook the sauce.

PREPARATION
5 min.

Beforehand, if tomatoes are fresh, drop them into boiling water for 30 seconds to loosen skins. Remove from water and slip off the skins. Seed, and chop into ½-inch pieces.

10 min.

In a heavy skillet or saucepan heat olive oil and drop in the chopped onions and garlic. Cook over moderate heat, stirring frequently, until the onions are soft and translucent, about 10 minutes.

Stir in the tomatoes, basil, oregano, sugar, pepper, salt and tomato paste. Bring to a boil over high heat, then lower heat and simmer, partially covered, until the sauce is thick, about 1 hour. (Fresh tomatoes should be cooked for an additional 30 minutes.) Taste for seasoning.

The sauce may be used immediately, or refrigerated or frozen for a later time.

The sauce may be beaten with a wooden spoon to make it smoother, but I prefer some coarseness to it.

CHEESES AND GARNISHES

Cheese spread over the tomato sauce or puree is the classic foundation for a myriad of garnishes. The amount of cheese here is for either of the two preceding pizzas.

CHEESE

1 pound *mozzarella* cheese, grated or cut into small dice
½ cup freshly grated Parmesan cheese

GARNISHES

Working note: These garnishes for atop the cheeses are for one of Italy's most popular pizzas. They can be changed or revised at the whim of the chef or his or her guests. Little is sacred in pizza making.

6 ounces fresh mushrooms, stemmed and thinly sliced
8 whole mushrooms, stemmed, to decorate
1 medium green pepper, seeded and thinly sliced
½ cup finely chopped onions
10 black olives, pitted and quartered

ALTERNATE
GARNISHES
Other garnishes for pizzas may include thinly sliced garlic cloves, sweet Italian sausage, pepperoni, ground beef, shrimp, anchovies, *prosciutto* slices, tiny meatballs, capers, diced hot peppers and so on.

These may be used alone or in combination and with or without one or both of the cheeses.

Miniature Pastries—Savory or Sweet

As Hors d'Oeuvres, Appetizers and Desserts

Your talents as a pastry cook will make a considerable impression when it comes to bite-size party fare—impressive to look at, intriguing to taste. Small pastries, whether served to a crowd or shared with a friend or two over a glass of wine or a cup of coffee or a glass of iced tea, tell your guests you really care about them. You have expended time and effort in preparing these delicious morsels, yet these miniatures never dominate the occasion but simply enhance it. Friends linger in conversation, appetites piqued, time suspended.

Small pastries have long been popular in every part of the globe— French hors d'oeuvres or *amuse-gueules*, Spanish *empanadas*, Greek *tiropetes*, Russian *pirozhki*, Indian *samosas*, Chinese *dim sum* and on and on. A good many of these little pastries, both sweet and savory, have found their way to our shores and into this book.

The dough, the filling and the shape of each of these tiny pastries are in the image of a larger pastry.

Scraps of dough and dabs of fillings from larger pieces can easily be tailored into an assortment of savory and dessert bits. The leftover pieces of tart dough from a large glazed fruit tart *(tarte aux fruites)*, page 334, can be dropped into tiny *barquette* or tartlet tins to be filled with the same fruit as prepared for the larger pastry. The pieces of puff paste dough left from a *gâteau Pithiviers*, page 209, can be cut into a half-dozen or so *petites bouchées*. These few may not be enough for a large party, but they can be frozen and held to augment a later bake session. Often I make a larger-than-needed amount of both pastry dough and filling for a Russian *pirogi*, page 144, for instance, so that I will have enough of everything left to make a dozen tiny, delicious *pirozhki*.

Following is a guide to the kinds of hors d'oeuvres or savories to be made with the variety of pastry doughs described in detail in this book. These range from puff paste and *pâte à chou* to tart doughs and *phyllo/* strudel leaves. Although complete instructions for preparing many fillings in the chart are given with individual recipes elsewhere in the book, some appear only in the chart to suggest the breadth of what is possible with pastries in miniature.

Miniature Pastries—Hors d'Oeuvres, Appetizers and Savories

PASTE OR PASTRY DOUGH	HORS D'OEUVRES SAVORIES APPETIZERS	FILLINGS AND GARNISHES	COMMENTS
PUFF PASTE of choice	Allumettes (match sticks)	Parmesan cheese or spread of ground chicken or ham and egg (page 197)	
	Palmiers	Parmesan cheese (page 192)	
	Gâteau Pithiviers	Ham and cheese (page 209)	The puff case is filled with ham and cheese, covered with a top and baked, sliced in narrow wedges and served.
	Croissants au jambon	Ground ham in light mustard sauce (page 190)	These tiny crescents are served hot.
	Viande de crabe aux champignons	Crab meat with mushrooms (page 179)	Served in tiny puff paste cups, *petites bouchées*.
TART of choice	Tartlets and barquettes	Thin layer of chicken puree or very thin slice of cooked breast of chicken. Alternate with thin slices of truffles. Glaze with half-set jelly of consommé.	Elegant. Serve cold.
		Diced shrimp and mushrooms, blended with gelatin-strengthened mayonnaise. Garnish with sieved hard-cooked egg and chervil. Coat with consommé jelly.	Serve cold. The consommé attracts the eye.

PASTE OR PASTRY DOUGH	HORS D'OEUVRES SAVORIES APPETIZERS	FILLINGS AND GARNISHES	COMMENTS
TART of choice		Garnish with fresh caviar	Very impressive.
		Shrimp, butter, crab or lobster. Herbed butters of choice.	Simple to make.
		One rolled anchovy, stuffed with a caper, or dab of tuna blended with mayonnaise. Surround with sieved hard-cooked egg and sprinkle with tarragon.	Serve cold.
	Quiche	Quiche Lorraine (page 349) Spinach quiche (page 351)	Can be made in small tins or cut into small servings from large quiche.
		Shrimp, crab or lobster quiche (page 352)	
PÂTE À CHOU (cream puff paste)	Profiteroles (tiny cream puffs)	Finely diced chicken or game, or shrimp, crab or other seafood blended and bound with seasoning and mayonnaise or thick rich cream sauce	To serve warm, use mayonnaise. To serve hot, use white sauce.
		Sweetbreads, diced, in thick rich white sauce	Serve warm.
		Cream cheese mixed with vegetable of choice such as asparagus tips, pureed green beans or spinach. Vegetables	Serve warm or cold.

PASTE OR PASTRY DOUGH	HORS D'OEUVRES SAVORIES APPETIZERS	FILLINGS AND GARNISHES	COMMENTS
		mixed with rich sauce. Combination of cheeses of choice.	
PÂTE À CHOU (cream puff paste)		Six ounces smoked salmon, 4 ounces cream cheese, ½ teaspoon each lemon juice and horseradish and 1 tablespoon finely chopped scallions, all blended smooth in a food processor. Add ½ cup mayonnaise or more for spreading or piping consistency.	Refrigerate when filled and serve cold. Held before party guests, they disappear like mayflies over a trout stream.
	Beignets soufflés (fritters)	Ham or cheese or onion and paprika mixed with batter before dropping into deep fryer (page 131)	Serve hot. Sprinkle paprika nuggets with salt before serving.
PHYLLO/STRUDEL	Tiropetes	Spanakopita filling (page 258) or feta, pot cheeses, parsley and eggs	Small triangles. Delicious and different.
	Seafood strudel	Seafood and white sauce rolled in strudel leaf	Cut in narrow slices to serve. Strudel is rolled only 1 inch in diameter.
TURNOVER of choice	Cornish pasties	Meat and vegetables (page 133)	Serve hot.
	Empanadas	Onion, beef, raisins, olives (page 138)	Serve hot.
	Calzoni	Cheese, ham and salami (page 141)	
	Pirozhki	Choice of meat or cabbage or carrot (page 144)	

PASTE OR PASTRY DOUGH	HORS D'OEUVRES SAVORIES APPETIZERS	FILLINGS AND GARNISHES	COMMENTS
PIZZA OR PISSALADIÈRE	Pizza	Tomato sauce, cheese, meats and garnishes	Hearty. Italian. Cut into 2-inch squares.
	Pissaladière	Onions, cheese, anchovy fillets (page 361)	Onion replaces tomato in this French version.

Freezing

Unbaked pastries, wrapped in plastic or freezer wrap, may be kept at 0° F. for three to four months. Allow large pieces to return to room temperature slowly before baking. Small hors d'oeuvres can be popped into the hot oven or microwave right from the freezer.

Ideally, baked pastries to be frozen should be baked only partially and not glazed or iced. Frozen pieces should be thawed first and then returned to a hot oven (400° F.) for about 4 minutes to improve color and restore flakiness.

Use plastic wrap, heavy-duty aluminum foil or polyethylene bags, all of which are moisture-proof and protect the pastry from the drying air of the freezer. Label and date the package.

I also keep a variety of new and used plastic cartons in which I freeze fragile pieces. Half-gallon plastic ice cream buckets are ideal to store at least a dozen or so Danish pastries in the freezer chest. Separate the layers of pastries with wax paper, replace the lid securely and mark the contents before freezing.

Large pieces, such as a Danish twist, place on a cardboard piece cut to fit and slip it into a heavy plastic bag. Tie it with a wire twist. Obviously I don't stack heavy things on top of it, but after it is frozen an accidental poke won't hurt it.

If there is room in the freezer, one of the most convenient storage devices for large pies and tarts is a round, heavy plastic box with a self-sealing lid called a "pie-taker." The pastry is placed inside with no prior preparation and frozen. The only drawback is its bulkiness.

Dough

Freezing pastry doughs presents no problem with one exception—leavened dough (for Danish) is less than satisfactory. Waiting for it to thaw and come to room temperature—and then rise—becomes tedious. I don't care to be bothered. Pie and flan dough can be rolled beforehand into circles and stacked with a layer of paper separating each circle. Circles will thaw in 10 to 15 minutes. Storage time at 0° F. is two to three months.

Pastry Shells

Unfilled shells may be frozen baked or unbaked. To defrost baked shells, thaw at room temperature about 15 minutes or in a 350° F. oven 6 to 10 minutes. Unbaked shells may be placed directly in a 450° F. oven for 10 to 12 minutes. Storage time for baked shells is about four to six months; unbaked, two to three months.

Pies in Particular

Pumpkin pie should be frozen *after* baking to prevent a soggy bottom crust and may be stored four to six months. Defrost as for a two-crust fruit pie (see below).

Chiffon pies should be frozen and then wrapped. They are defrosted 2 to 4 hours or overnight in the refrigerator. Storage time is about a month.

Bake covered fruit pies before freezing because the frozen unbaked pie will have a soggy bottom crust. Thickener must be increased in the filling to compensate for the extra juice that will develop during the freezing and thawing process (1 to 3 tablespoons more flour, tapioca or cornstarch per pie).

To defrost, let stand at room temperature 30 minutes. Remove the wrapping. Heat in a 350° F. oven for 40 minutes. Remove from the oven and let stand at least 15 minutes before serving. For unbaked fruit pie, remove from wrap, place on a baking sheet if using aluminum foil pans (to get a better crust) and bake as recipe directs, but increase time 10 to 20 minutes. Fruit pies should bubble at the center.

Baked pies may be stored four to six months; unbaked, two to three months.

Not Recommended

Cream and custard pies should not be frozen because they tend to weep and separate. Dumplings also are on the not-recommended-to-freeze list because they get soggy when defrosted.

YOUR FREEZER

It is important for you to know just how cold are the various levels in your freezer. The only way to determine this is with a freezer thermometer (see "Equipment to Make Fine Pastries," page 33). Just being frozen and hard to the touch is not good enough. A fruit pie held for a year at −10° F. will be of the same quality as one stored for five months at 5° F., for one month at 15° F. and for one week at 25° F.

What Went Wrong?

Although there is a margin for error in every recipe, even the most experienced pastry maker will sometimes have an unsatisfactory baking experience. Here are some of the things that can go wrong, and what can be done about them.

SOGGY BOTTOMS

First consider whether the oven is heating properly when the bottom of a pie or tart is raw or soggy. A reliable oven thermometer (a Taylor mercury oven thermometer is fine) will tell you if it is. The pastry may have been baked on an oven shelf placed too high. Bake on a lower shelf to allow more heat to be concentrated on the bottom crust.

A soft custard filling poured into an unbaked shell is often the culprit. Partially bake the empty crust before it is filled. The crust for a covered pie is not baked beforehand, but be certain it is placed on a lower oven shelf to bake. Brushing the inside of the bottom crust with egg white will help keep the bottom dry. So will cream cheese, thinned with a spoonful of the liquid filling, spread across the crust, as done for strawberry pie.

SHRINKAGE

Pieces of dough cut to a precise size or shape will draw back and shrink if the dough is not allowed to relax at various stages of preparation. Allow dough to rest on the work surface *after* it is rolled and *before* it is cut, about 5 or 10 minutes. If the room is warm, place in the refrigerator.

If the pieces shrink *after* cutting, let them relax and then roll again. A longer rest in the refrigerator will also minimize dough shrinkage in the oven. Let the shaped pastries rest for at least half an hour before putting them into the oven. A moderate to cool oven will encourage shrinkage. Bake at 400° F.

TOUGHNESS

If the shell is tough and not crisp, the dough was mixed too long. Be certain the dough is allowed to relax fully in the refrigerator before going into the oven.

"WILDNESS"

Wild is the baker's term for layers of puff paste slipping apart as the pastry rises in the hot oven. The dough may not have been given the required number of turns, in which case the layers of butter were too thick. You might try increasing the amount of flour mixed into the rolled-in fat from 2 tablespoons per pound of flour to 3 tablespoons.

TEARS AND BREAKS

If the dough tears or comes apart in your hands as you are lifting it from the work surface to fit into the pan, don't despair. Press torn edges together with the fingers. If the dough clings stubbornly to the fingers and/or the rolling pin and tears, or threatens to tear, dust with flour—or, better still, return the dough to the refrigerator to chill for 10 or 15 minutes. Thin dough will chill quickly.

Rolling dough on a piece of chilled marble will lessen the chances of its tearing or breaking apart.

Dough will sometimes tear when lifted off the work surface. Loosen it with the blade of a dough scraper or spatula. Move the blade all around it, pushing gently toward the center until it slides free.

Dough that is not fully relaxed will often roll into an irregular shape despite your best efforts to roll it into a circle or rectangle. Allow it to relax and try again. If the dough persists and fits poorly in the pan, patch the open area with a piece taken from another section of the dough. Moisten the edge to be joined with water and press to make a smooth, solid joint.

CRACKS IN SHELL

If a crack or break in an unfilled or "blind" shell develops in the oven, patch it with a scrap of dough and return it to the oven for 10 minutes. Patch it later if it is to be filled and returned for further baking.

Poor Seams

If seams on filled pastries, especially Danish, pull apart, reduce the amount of filling. Even though it may look like only a tiny dab of filling when placed on the square or triangle of dough, it may be too much when it expands in the oven.

Puff Not Puffed

Too many turns will leave puff paste thin and weak and unable to rise in the oven. Keep track of the turns as they are made by marking the number lightly on the dough with a knife blade, especially before it is returned to the refrigerator to chill. The mind forgets. An extra turn can triple the fifth turn of 729 layers into a total of 2,187!

Spills

If a pie is filled too full or the two crusts are not properly sealed, the filling may bubble out. The lack of vent holes in the crust may force the steam to escape through the sides rather than the top. Build a higher rim by folding the edge of the top crust under the bottom crust, thereby giving two thicknesses to be shaped into an attractive and protective edge.

Bake a juicy pie on a large baking sheet or over a piece of aluminum foil to catch drippings. To give small tartlets and *barquettes* a stable, level platform, place them on a large baking sheet before filling them and leave them there during baking.

Butter Out

In an oven that is too hot, fat from puff and Danish pastries will ooze into the pan and create a smoky haze that smells hot and scorched when the oven door is opened. It may also be that not enough flour was mixed into the rolled-in fat to give it stability in the heat. Next time increase the amount of flour mixed into the fat from 2 tablespoons per pound of flour to 3 tablespoons.

Collapsed Pastries

A too-hot oven will cause the steam in the dough to lift the layers and then drop them before the dough can stiffen sufficiently to hold the structure together. Check oven heat with a thermometer. If too hot, cool before placing the pastry in it to bake.

Not Flaky

Lack of flakiness in pastries is caused by the flour absorbing the fat. Chill both the flour and the fat before preparation, and keep the dough cold until it goes into the oven.

Blisters

Steam in pastries must be allowed to escape. A rolling pastry piercer is intriguing, but the tines of a kitchen fork will do almost as well. Don't hesitate to reach into an oven to puncture a ballooning pastry and press it flat.

Blisters (and shrinkage) in shells baked blind are easily controlled by lining the shells with foil or parchment paper and filling with weights such as dried beans, rice or aluminum pellets.

Stuck Shell

Many tart, tartlet and flan tins and forms are fluted, square or rectangular and with straight sides, which increases the difficulty of freeing a stuck shell. Before baking, be certain the dough is not pushed over the edge of the metal form, which will lock them together in the oven.

To loosen a baked shell, gently squeeze the sides of the pan. Either lift the shell out with a slender spatula or knife, or turn the pan upside down and drop the shell into the hand. The point of a sharp knife carefully slipped down the side of the pan where the tart is sticking will usually free it.

Occasionally dough will push out and bake around the bottom edge of a removable bottom. When the shell has cooled, gently force the point of a knife between the dough and the tin. The tin will pop off.

Too Brown

If you are fearful that a partially baked empty or blind shell has browned too much to be filled and returned to the oven to bake, fashion a strip of aluminum foil loosely around the edge to prevent scorching. Remember that the filling will absorb much of the heat and prevent the exposed crust from browning as rapidly as it did when unfilled.

Broken Shell

Next time don't be caught short because one or more of the fragile shells was broken. It happens in the best of kitchens, so make allowances for extras if a specific number of perfect shells is critical.

CRUMB CRUST TOO HARD

I once made a crumb crust as hard as sheet metal (or so it seemed) by pressing every last crumb into the pan without regard to the depth of the material along the bottom curve. More was *not* better, in this instance. It came out of the oven hard to cut and hard to bite. Spread crumbs across the bottom and sides no more than ⅛ inch thick at any point. Pat them into place. Discard the crumbs not needed, or use them to make another shell—but don't overload the crust at hand.

Home-Rendered Lard

Good lard is far better than some butter to make good eatable light pastry, and some sorts will make just as tall puff paste as butter will.—American Pastry Cook, 1894

There is a fine lard available to the home baker just for the making: leaf lard. This is from the finest quality of fat to be found on the animal—a firm, perfectly white substance surrounding the kidneys. Normally it would find its way into a blend of other lards, but it can usually be purchased in a piece in a pork store or dependable butcher shop or meat department just as it came from the carcass. Ask for a 1- or 2-pound piece.

It is easy to render. Cut the leaf lard into small pieces and place in a large flat pan. Place it in a 300° F. oven to cook down or render. A clear liquid will form, pour it into a bowl to cool and set. As it cools, the lard will become white and creamy. Continue rendering until only the light brown pieces of cracklings remain. (Reserve them and later stir them into a bread dough for a taste sensation!)

Keep the homemade lard covered in the refrigerator, where it can be stored for months and used to make superb crusts.

Pastry Nomogram

Nomograms have been used by engineers and scientists for some years to provide a simple and quick means of converting one set of values into other forms, sometimes using variable factors. The nomogram used here, which is the simplest type of all, gives a direct reading from U.S. cups through pounds/ounces (flour), pounds/ounces (sugar), fluid ounces, U.K. cups, kilos/grams (flour), kilos/grams (sugar) to liters/ centiliters (fluid measure).

To use this nomogram, place the straight edge of a ruler or the folded edge of a piece of paper on the number of U.S. cups called for in the recipe and on the center spot. Everything on that line is now an equivalent.

The example, shown by the dotted line, gives:

5 U.S. cups = 4 U.K. cups
               = 1 pound 4 ounces flour   = 580 grams
        or   2 pounds 8 ounces sugar = 1 kilogram
                                       170 grams
        or   40 fluid ounces   = 1 liter 170
                                       centiliters

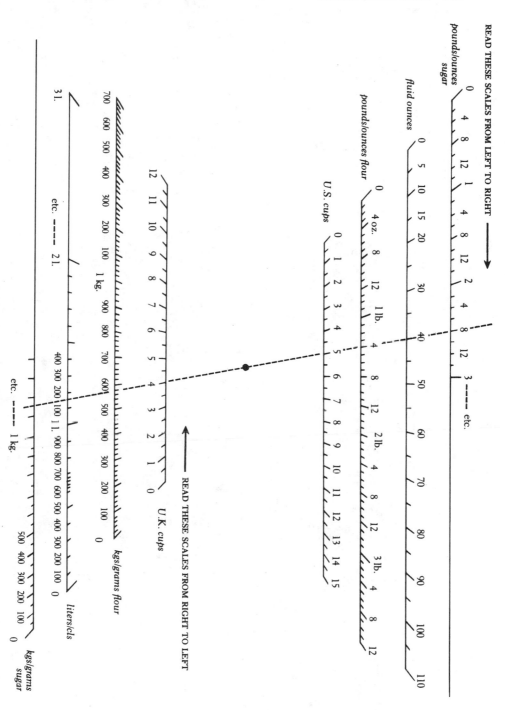

READ THESE SCALES FROM LEFT TO RIGHT →

pounds/ounces sugar

fluid ounces

pounds/ounces flour

U.S. cups

U.K. cups

← READ THESE SCALES FROM RIGHT TO LEFT

kgs/grams flour

liters/cls

kgs/grams sugar

Standard Weights and Measures

Make certain all measurements are level.

Dash	= 8 drops
1 tablespoon	= 3 teaspoons
4 tablespoons	= ¼ cup
5⅓ tablespoons	= ⅓ cup
8 tablespoons	= ½ cup
16 tablespoons	= 1 cup (dry)
1 fluid ounce	= 2 tablespoons
1 cup (liquid)	= ½ pint
2 cups (16 ounces)	= 1 pint
2 pints (4 cups)	= 1 quart
4 quarts	= 1 gallon
8 quarts	= 1 peck (dry)
4 pecks	= 1 bushel
16 ounces (dry measure)	= 1 pound

Comparative U.S., British and Metric Weights and Measures for Ingredients Important to Pastry Makers

INGREDIENT	UNITED STATES	BRITISH	METRIC
Almond paste	1¾ cups	16 ounces	450 grams
Apples, pared/sliced	1 cup	4 ounces	125 grams
Berries	1¾ cups	6 ounces	190 grams
Butter	1 tablespoon	½ ounce	15 grams
	½ cup	4 ounces	125 grams
	2 cups	1 pound (generous)	450 grams
Cheese	1 pound (generous)	1 pound (generous)	450 grams
Cheese, grated hard type	1 cup (scant)	4 ounces (scant)	100 grams
Cheese, cottage	1 cup	16 ounces	450 grams
Cheese, cream	6 tablespoons	3 ounces	80 grams
Cornstarch	1 tablespoon	⅓ ounce	10 grams
Flour (unsifted)	¼ cup	1¼ ounces	35 grams
	½ cup	2½ ounces	70 grams
	1 cup	4¾ ounces	142 grams
	3½ cups	1 pound	450 grams
Herbs, fresh/chopped	1 tablespoon	½ ounce	15 grams
Nuts, chopped	1 cup	5½ ounces	155 grams
Raisins (seedless)	1 tablespoon	⅓ ounce	10 grams
	1 cup	5⅓ ounces	160 grams
	3 cups	1 pound	450 grams
Spices, ground	1 teaspoon	¹⁄₁₂ ounce	2.5 grams
	2 tablespoons	½ ounce	15 grams
Sugar, granulated	1 teaspoon	⅙ ounce	5 grams
	1 tablespoon	½ ounce	15 grams
	¼ cup	2 ounces	60 grams
	1 cup	8 ounces	226 grams
Sugar, confectioners'	¼ cup	1 ounce (generous)	35 grams
	½ cup	2¼ ounces (scant)	70 grams
	1 cup	4½ ounces (scant)	140 grams
Sugar, brown	1 tablespoon	⅓ ounce	10 grams
	½ cup	2⅔ ounces	80 grams
	1 cup	5⅓ ounces	160 grams

Other Measurements

1 lemon	= 2–3 tablespoons juice and 2 teaspoons zest
1 orange	= 6–8 tablespoons juice and 2–3 tablespoons zest
1 cup heavy cream	= 2 cups whipped cream
2 cups water	= 1 pound
5 large whole eggs 6 medium 7 small	= 1 cup, approximately
8 large egg whites 10–11 medium 11–12 small	= 1 cup, approximately
12 large egg yolks 13–14 medium 15–16 small	= 1 cup, approximately

Fluid Measure Equivalents

METRIC	UNITED STATES	BRITISH
1 liter	4¼ cups or 1 quart 2 ounces	1¾ pints
1 demiliter (½ liter)	2 cups (generous) or 1 pint (generous)	¾ pint (generous)
1 deciliter (⅒ liter)	½ cup (scant) or ¼ pint (scant)	3–4 ounces

Weight Measure Equivalents

METRIC	UNITED STATES	BRITISH
1.00 grams	.035 ounce	.035 ounce
28.35 grams	1 ounce	1 ounce
100.00 grams	3.5 ounces	3.5 ounces
114.00 grams	4 ounces (approximately)	4 ounces (approximately)
226.78 grams	8 ounces	8 ounces
500.00 grams	1 pound 1.5 ounces	1 pound 1.5 ounces
1.00 kilogram	2.21 pounds	2.21 pounds

Glossary

BARQUETTES   Small boat-shaped pastries with either sweet or savory fillings.

BATTER   Ingredients beaten together into a moist or wet mixture that will pour.

BEIGNET   A pastry made with *pâte à chou* and deep-fried. A fritter.
[bān' yā]

BLEND   To fold or mix two or more ingredients or materials together to obtain equal distribution throughout the mixture.

Boil   Bubbles appear at the bottom, rise to the top and break. When all the liquid is in motion, it has come to a boil. Adjust heat to maintain the boiling point. Boiling harder won't cook faster, and it will destroy fragile food by its violent motion.

BOUCHÉE   A shell of puff paste for one entrée serving, usually 3 to 4 inches in diameter. A patty shell. A *petite bouchée* is a miniature of the larger, about 1½ inches in diameter, a single-bite hors d'oeuvre or sweet.
[boo shā']

BRUSH   To cover dough or shaped pastry lightly with a liquid or dry ingredient, such as flour or sugar, using a pastry brush.

CARAMELIZE   To heat sugar slowly until it melts and browns.

CHAUSSON   A turnover.
[shŏ sōn]

CLARIFY (butter)   Over low heat melt butter completely, allowing it to stand for a few moments until sediment settles to the bottom. Pour or spoon off butterfat into a container. Also known as drawn butter.

CORNET
[kôr nĕ]

A cone-shaped pastry.

COUPE-PÂTE
[küp pät]

A dough knife or scraper. A putty knife with a wide blade is an excellent substitute.

CUBE

To cut into small pieces, about ½ inch.

CUT IN

To mix fat and flour with a pastry blender, tips of fingers, crossed knives or machine so that fat particles are flour-covered but discrete.

DICE

To cut into small pieces (like tiny dice), about ¼ inch.

DOT

To place small bits of butter, fat or cheese over the top of a food.

DUST

To sprinkle lightly or brush with flour, sugar, etc.

FLAN
[flän]

A flan is a tart except it is baked in a metal form without a bottom and placed on a pan to bake.

FLEURONS
[flər' än]

Decorative shapes cut from puff paste.

FOLD

To gently incorporate or blend flour or other ingredients into a mixture with a rubber spatula or mixer at low speed so as not to destroy the texture of the mixture.

FROSTING

An icing applied to the top of pastries.

GLAZE

To create a glossy finish with a thin coating of sugar, icing, fruit syrups, jellies and other liquids.

GREASE

To rub lightly with butter, margarine, shortening or salad oil.

ICE

To apply a sugar preparation to the surface of the pastry.

MARZIPAN

A sweet confection of finely ground almonds and sugar used in pastry fillings and to sculpt decorative objects such as flowers and fruit.

MILLE FEUILLES
[mēl fû'y']

Thousand-leaf cake (Napoleon).

NEUFCHÂTEL
CHEESE

A form of cream cheese low in calories and fat. May be substituted for cream cheese.

PÂTE À CHOU
[pät' ä shōō]

Cream puff paste.

PÂTE
FEUILLETÉE
[pät fû' ė tĕ]

Puff pastry dough. Same as *feuilletage*.

PINCH

Approximately ⅛ teaspoon, or the amount of the ingredient that can be held between thumb and forefinger.

PIPE

To press cream puff paste, filling or icing out of a pastry bag. Commercial pastry makers also refer to it as "bagging out."

PISSALADIÈRE — A French flan, a first cousin to an Italian pizza, a specialty of the Nice region.

PREHEAT — Turn on and heat oven to desired temperature before putting in pastry, about 15 to 20 minutes.

PROFITEROLES [prə' fid ə rōl] — Little puffs made of *pâte à chou*, with sweet or savory fillings.

REMONCE — Fillings widely used in Denmark. Can be a mixture of butter and granulated sugar flavored with vanilla, or butter and brown sugar flavored with cinnamon.

ROGNURES [rȯ nyȗr'] — Scraps of leftover dough.

SIMMER — To cook just below the boiling point. There are no bubbles, but the surface moves slightly.

STIR — To blend with a circular motion, with a spoon, widening circles until all ingredients are well mixed.

VOL-AU-VENT [vo lo van'] — A large shell made of puff paste filled with meat, game, sweetbreads, lobster or fruit and cream.

WASH — To brush the surface of the pastry, before or after baking, with a mixture usually of whole egg lightly beaten and thinned with milk or cream. If a deeper golden crust is desired, use yolks instead of whole eggs.

WHIP — To beat rapidly, usually with an electric mixer or hand beater, to incorporate air and increase volume.

ZEST — Finely grated peel of orange, lemon or lime.

Index

Index

A Note About the Author

BERNARD CLAYTON, JR., a senior editor and writer for Indiana University News Bureau, is the author of *The Complete Book of Breads*, which is widely considered the most authoritative work on the subject, and the celebrated *Breads of France and How to Bake Them in Your Own Kitchen*.

Born in Indiana, the son of an Indiana country newspaper editor, Bernard Clayton worked on the *Indianapolis News* after Indiana University and then joined Time-Life magazines in New York City. He became Time-Life bureau chief in San Francisco and war correspondent for the magazines during World War II. Later he was vice-president and director of public relations for two major San Francisco–based firms. He has been with Indiana University since 1966.

Bernard Clayton has backpacked the length of the two-hundred-mile Muir Trail in the Sierra Nevada Mountains in California and has been oarsman on expeditions by raft and rowboat on the Colorado River, through the Grand Canyon and through Hell's Canyon, on the Snake River. He and his wife have crossed Europe by bicycle, England by canal boat and Ireland by a horse-drawn gypsy wagon in pursuit of pleasure and the perfect pastry.

(Pictured clockwise from left) Glazed Strawberry Pie; Danish Pastry Cheese Envelopes and Almond\Cockscombs; Cannoli; Gâteau Paris-Brest; Hungarian Apple Strudel; Apple Dumplings in Syrup; (in the middle) a plate of Danish Jelly Snails and Small Danish Twists